HUMANITY

HUMANITY

AN EMOTIONAL HISTORY

Stuart Walton

ATLANTIC BOOKS

LONDON

For KHL

Published in hardback in Great Britain in 2004 by Atlantic Books.
Atlantic Books is an imprint of Grove Atlantic Ltd.

ISBN 1 84354 104 1

Designed by Nicky Barneby
Typeset in 11.5/14.75pt Monotype Sabon
Printed in Great Britain by William Clowes Ltd, Beccles, Suffolk

Atlantic Books
An imprint of Grove Atlantic Ltd
Ormond House
26–27 Boswell Street
London
WC1N 3JZ

CONTENTS

ACKNOWLEDGEMENTS

I should like, first and foremost, to acknowledge the invaluable, never less than enlightening editorial attentions of my editor and publisher, Toby Mundy, in the writing of this book. He is, in a real sense, its co-progenitor, having encouraged me at the outset to broaden its scope so expansively and profoundly that I felt for a time like Caspar David Friedrich's Wanderer on the Sea of Clouds, peering into bottomless depths of inquiry. That the resulting production makes sense at all is largely owing to his formidable intellectual reach and capacity for unhurried speculative exchange. The debt is considerable.

I must also thank Dr Michael Palmer, formerly head of the Department of Religion and Philosophy at the Manchester Grammar School, for setting me on the right track with regard to the structure of my argument in chapter 1, and Tim Winter for his diligent scrutiny of my efforts on Beethoven in chapter 11. Margaret Stead has been an invaluable and sensitive copy-editor throughout. Antony Harwood, my literary agent, was once more the patient midwife, if I may so put it, in helping the work progress from an idea that entered my mind while I dallied over a sinkful of washing-up to one that might enthuse an imaginative publishing house, which Atlantic is.

Recoiling at the cliché, I forbear to say that without Ka Ho Lee it might not have been possible at all, but a wealth of further emotional education has come my way in the past four years that reached its peak on the rooftops of Hong Kong, with scarlet Liberation Day fireworks bursting all around us.

Stuart Walton
Brighton
May 2004

INTRODUCTION

In April 1732, in London, a bankrupt bookbinder named Richard Smith decided to end it all. His business had crashed to ruin amid a trail of unpaid invoices, leaving him with no prospect of relief. With a wife and child to support, his responsibility was not only to himself. After having apparently discussed the matter with Mrs Smith, they smothered their small daughter and hanged themselves, leaving behind a short letter to their landlord, containing an entreaty to make provision for the dog and cat whose lives they had spared, and money for a porter to make delivery of two further enclosed documents. One of these was to an associate, formally thanking him for his sustaining friendship, and expressing indignation at the opposite treatment Smith had received from another party. The second document had been signed jointly by husband and wife, and constituted the couple's suicide note.

The Smiths provided a painstaking explanation of the reasons for their actions, in terms wholly free of rancour or accusation. Tobias Smollett, in whose panoramic *History of England*, written in the 1750s, this story is retailed, comments that the suicide letter was 'altogether surprising for the calm resolution, the good humour, and the propriety, with which it was written'. In so ending their lives, the Smiths wrote, they were releasing themselves from a worse and otherwise unavoidable fate, that of 'poverty and rags'. They prayed in witness their immediate neighbours, who would be able to attest to the conscientious efforts they had made to earn an honest living. As to the ghastly business of taking the life of an infant, they argued that, cruel as the act may seem, it constituted a far less callous recourse than leaving her alone and unprovided for in a life of 'ignorance and misery'. And while they were aware, God-fearing as they were, that suicide was against the holy canon, they refused to believe that the Almighty God, in whom they still placed their utmost trust, would visit any needless suffering on his creatures. They expressed their confidence that they could entrust their souls to him for whatever arrangements he might make for them after their deaths. Smollett concludes by noting that, far from being a pair of reckless chancers, living on their criminal wits as so many in Georgian London did, the Smiths 'had always been industrious and frugal, invincibly honest, and remarkable for conjugal affection'.

What remains startling across the centuries about this case, as Smollett noted only twenty-five years after its occurrence, is the near-wholesomeness of the act, which apparently emerged after a measured, fastidious process of rational assessment as the wisest thing to do. We ask ourselves what the tone of their note might be today, and imagine the accusations, the dramatisation, the sense that such an extravagant act could only fittingly be prefaced by a communiqué that shrieked its defiance in the face of later judgement. For the Smiths, though, there was a necessity to put matters into some sort of order, to write the explanatory conclusion to their story, thus lightening the professional responsibilities of whoever might happen in upon their bedchamber and find their two bodies, hanging at the fitting marital proximity of a mere yard apart, perhaps still slightly swinging, while their baby daughter lay lifeless in her cradle in another room. Theirs was a courteous suicide, a discreet one, which would neither leave investigators puzzled, nor necessarily agitate the neighbours, but that nonetheless marked an end to a trio of lives that had become untenable. It was like the quick dispatch one might afford a lame dog or hobbled horse, merciful in its brief precision, and settled in its confrontation with the one gigantic and incalculable risk it incurred – that the Almighty, peering down in judgement, might not approve.

Smollett's airing of this tragedy caught the imagination of many foreign commentators, among them the French philosopher Denis Diderot, who saw in the clinical nature of the suicide a vivid emblem of the diseased emotional lives of the British. Only in their chilly, damp, phlegmatic habitat could such an extraordinary act take place. Suicide was indeed generally seen in this period as a particularly British preoccupation, so much so that 'in other countries it is objected to them as a national reproach'. Inasmuch as the reasons that lay behind self-extermination were understood at all, it was held to be the spasmodic action of the unbalanced, 'the effect of lunacy proceeding from natural causes operating on the human body'. And yet here was a case that began to challenge that assumption. Mindful of their manners during the first ascendancy of Georgian *politesse*, the Smiths had opted not for the public mess of flinging themselves off a bridge, but for a private act committed within their own four walls, screened off from society, and hedged about with the decorum of a letter of explanation and apology, as though they were the proprietors of an inn who had inadvertently overbooked their rooms, and were now having to disappoint an intended guest. Tempted though we may be to acquiesce in what the case seems to say about our national characteristics of reticence and politeness, the Smiths' avoidance of emotional display is less of a British idiom than an eighteenth-century one. The life of the emotions was simply not a public affair. There was a time and a place for despair, if it must impinge upon one's life, and that was outside business hours, indoors.

We err on the side of cultural relativity, however, if we read the Smith family suicide as the sad testament of an emotionally reserved era, whose people lacked any true faculty for emotional

articulacy. This is to overlook firstly the obvious status of all suicide as an emotional act, but also, more appositely to the purposes
of this book, the degree to which what was expressed through the
emotions was circumscribed within the duality of interior and
exterior by which the societies of early eighteenth-century Europe
lived. In other words, we should guard against drawing the wrong
conclusions about the period as a whole from the way the Smiths
chose to act. Nonetheless, there are certain continuities between
their era and ours that can assist our understanding of their case.
As Hannah Arendt argued in *The Human Condition* (1958), the
disjunction between the public and private realms is such that only
what is considered directly relevant to it can be aired within the former, thus consigning all other matters, including one's personal
financial difficulties, to the latter. The effect is not to make private
concerns irrelevant, but to suggest that there are certain aspects of
life that can only properly belong in the private realm. Here, they
are accorded the weight and the *gravitas* that public life denies
them, and the scrutiny to which they are subjected in private is in a
sense a version of the public attention they fail to receive. In the
Smiths' case, the private dispatch of their affairs was the only due
recognition their plight would receive. It wasn't that they were
unable to rage or despair at their circumstances, only that there was
no public forum in which to enact these emotions, and, what is
more, once confined with their tribulations within the walls of
their apartment, there was no final need to enact them. It wasn't
themselves they had to convince.

The present work takes as its starting point Charles Darwin's last
major contribution to genetic science, *The Expression of the Emotions in Man and Animals* (1872). *Expression*, as Darwin himself
referred to the book, represents one of those moments in scientific
history where a suggestive thesis arises in the mind of a researcher
who has neither the resources nor the full technical apparatus to

prove it, and which must await a later age to attain to its rightful validation as fact. It was to be virtually a century before Darwin's central postulates were subjected to anything like a rigorous, as distinct from strictly anecdotal, testing procedure. When they were, they were found to be accurate in all but the most minor particulars. The work for which he remains so important today – on evolution, natural selection, and the discovery that human beings were descended from higher primates – achieved readier acceptance during his lifetime than is sometimes imagined. Despite the fulminations of the Church, it passed into scientific orthodoxy with surprising ease. The work on emotion, though, remained very much hypothetical, although there is, throughout the book, a tone of insistent self-assurance. The theories being advanced were backed up as assiduously as possible by friends and academic colleagues living in parts of the globe that Darwin, when compiling a natural history of unfamiliar lands in his twenties, had not visited.

The principal contention of *Expression* is gloriously simple. It is that the emotions of human beings the world over are as innate and as constitutive and as regular as our bone structure, and that this is manifested in the universality of the ways in which we express them. By means of two sorts of muscular action, those that result in facial expression and those that control the movements of the body, we communicate what we are feeling to others, usually quite involuntarily, and as a result of animal instinct rather than learned behaviour. Not only is this communicative ability genetically determined, it enables us, while still in the crib, to recognise it also in the faces of adults, decoding their attitudes to us from what is written in their expressions. Furthermore, this intensely complex, non-verbal language shows strong continuity between different races today and – as far as one can make out – over time. Shown a photograph of a scowling Caucasian face, a member of a tribal culture in Papua New Guinea has no difficulty in recognising the feeling it depicts as anger, while the westerner contemplating the face of a Japanese, in which the inner ends of the eyebrows are slightly raised and the corners of the mouth turned down, sees it as the image of grieving sadness that it is. What this suggests is that while many details of our cultural lives, from the way we dress to what we eat to the kinds of marriage ceremony we perform and permit, may vary hugely across geographical distance, we are still all born with the same essential psychic structures, and are all subject at periodic moments in our lives to the uncontrolled flow of emotional activity.

Darwin posited that there were six basic, facially legible emotions – happiness, sadness, anger, fear, disgust and surprise – although he discusses many more than these in his text. Later researchers, led in 1966 by California psychologist Paul Ekman and others, elaborated this simple schema, adding other emotions as fancy dictated. The basic half-dozen have been supplemented by guilt or shame, embarrassment, jealousy and contempt, and – more speculatively – pride, sympathy, admiration, frustration, nostalgia, and even feelings that are more obviously states of mind rather than genuine emotions, such as defiance or puzzlement. Then there are those old bedfellows, love and hate, which seem to be complex alloys of several of the other emotions, all adding up to a compound state of feeling that outlives the initial impact of the emotions themselves. And it is very much the concept of an initial impact that must be decisive when we come to define what exactly an emotion is. One can experience a lifetime of unrequited love, a state that may be punctuated regularly by emotional peaks, and yet unrequited love is not in itself an emotion, more an attitude. An emotion must be a short-lived neurological reaction arising from what is often abrupt stimulation of the relevant nerve centres in the brain, so that the flood of tremulous panic one undergoes when the airliner hits a band of severe turbulence is readily identifiable as fear, while the red-hot detonation that inflames every corpuscle when the indignant partner in an argument slams down the phone on us is clearly anger. These are the flashpoints of our psychic lives, and while they may only last a few moments, they go on to inform our attitudes and strategies in the future, so that when faced with similar stimuli or provocations, we know how to react, or better still, to take evasive action. For it is a curious fact about the emotions that, with the saving exception of happiness, they are all negative feelings.

Mention of this leads one to pose a question familiar enough to us in the era of psychotherapy, counselling, self-help and anger management: whether it is possible, by strenuous exercise of the will, to sidestep the emotions, to survive them – not in the sense of getting over a bad attack of them, but rather arriving at some serene state of mental discipline in which we simply cease to be prey to them. The idea exercised some of the finest twentieth-century minds, including that of the writer Quentin Crisp, who firmly believed that the key to a successful life was to have no emotions. This was achieved, he argued, by *pretending* one didn't have any, to the extent that in the end, rather like the absence of wisdom teeth in certain genetically advanced individuals, they wither away through disuse. When an interviewer protested to him that such a course would result in one becoming quite cold, Crisp replied, 'That's right. Absolutely cold, and absolutely splendid.' Darwin doesn't explore the possibility of abolishing emotional reaction from our lives, and we may fairly assume that he would have considered such a postulate to be absurd. He does however note that, since giving the emotions free rein makes it harder to recover from having experienced them, so suppressing the degree to which they are expressed helps us to get over them more promptly. He cites the work of a French physiologist, Pierre Gratiolet, who in 1865 – a few years before the publication of Darwin's own work – had insisted on precisely this point. Even so, the effort at control can only ever be partially effective, at best, as Darwin says:

The free expression by outward signs of an emotion intensifies it. On the other hand, the repression, *as far as this is possible*, of all outward signs softens our emotions. He who gives way to violent gestures will increase his rage; he who does not control the signs of fear will experience fear in a greater degree; and he who remains passive when overwhelmed with grief loses his best chance of recovering elasticity of mind. [Emphasis mine.]

This tantalising set of suggestions hovers over the final page of Darwin's work, and yet it has not received quite the same degree of experimental attention that the central tenets of the thesis have been afforded. Is it possible, and indeed desirable, to have little or no emotional susceptibility? Would we be better off as a race attaining to the ice-pure rationality of Mr Spock in the 1960s' TV series *Star Trek*, who, despite having some human genetic material, was essentially Vulcan in his unruffled urbanity? The only flicker of emotion he appeared to experience was a frisson of contempt at the copious emoting of his fellow crew members on the *Enterprise*, and even though he possessed two hearts, the blood they pumped around his body was a cold green liquor that compared favourably to the hot red firewater with which humanity has been disastrously lumbered. This characterisation of Spock perhaps represented a certain strand of thinking, much in currency at the time within the behavioural sciences, as to the sources of human destructiveness. While Ekman was setting off for South America and Japan, armed with photo cards of furious, terrified and startled faces to show to the natives, the debate over whether the emotions were conquerable was gathering pace.

That notion rapidly lost ground to what would become the orthodoxy of post-Freudian psychoanalytic theory, that all psychological difficulties stem from repression, caused in particular by the socialised avoidance strategies to which western cultures had been subject since the eighteenth century. An emotion suppressed is not, as Gratiolet and Darwin had posited, thereby diminished, but only concentrated in potentially lethally toxic form, until its lack of egress poisons the whole psychic system, and the result is a neurotic patient. The 1960s were also the era of letting it all hang out, a studied emotional incontinence that was held – and still is in many quarters – to be the shining hope of a species so detached from its biological origins as to have become overwhelmed by alienation. This Freudian view has prevailed over the Darwinian, with the result that our emotional lives have become perhaps more intensely public than ever before. The evidences of public anger, public grieving, public revulsion are fed to us daily via the news channels, with the partial result that emotional response seems often just a little too conditioned, and hence potentially ersatz, when what is being striven for is exactly the opposite – living, breathing spontaneity. Enshrouded in semi-darkness at the cinema, we clench our fists at what happens to Tom Cruise in the military academy, or silently weep at the fate of Julianne Moore's ill-starred romance with her gardener, and perhaps map the contours of these emotional reactions on to our own less dramatic experiences.

Patrick West has argued recently that public displays of compassion and sadness have become endemic in western society, with the wearing of empathy ribbons and release of public tears in silent vigils for the dispossessed more like theatrical representations of emotion – 'recreational grief', he calls it – than evidence of genuine engagement with social problems. Whether this encourages a more general emotional facility in us, or whether these sympathetic displays replace emotions we are no longer able to feel spontaneously, owing to the alienated condition of modern life (which, in the title of Blur's second album, is famously 'rubbish'), is open to question. To the extent that each of the emotions considered in this book carries a freight of negative associations, so each demands the existence of a corresponding moral virtue that stands as its antithesis, and as the means by which an eruption of a particular emotion can be checked. There should, for example, be no fear without courage, no contempt without sympathy, no anger without forgiveness, and so forth.

In pondering the evolutionary development of the emotions, the universality of which he saw as further evidence that the human family shares one proto-human ancestor, Darwin establishes three principles about the way emotional expression works. These are: (a) that our emotional habits arise out of some functional process, serving the need to gratify a desire or relieve some sensation, and become normative through repetition; (b) that the effect of antithesis also applies, so that just as one set of expressions communicates a particular emotional state, a contrary set consequently articulates the opposite condition; and (c) that much emotional response derives from the constitution of the nervous system, which, through force of association, then governs those responses that derive neither from willed intent nor from habit, but are strictly involuntary.

The investigations of Ekman and others mount no serious challenge to these ideas, which hold as good today as when Darwin first proposed them. They are the founding truths of emotional expression, but the questions they bequeath to us belong as much to philosophical inquiry as to biogenetic research. Indeed, much recent work in this field, most notably the contributions of Antonio Damasio and William M Reddy, link the latest findings in the neurophysiology of the brain to considerations of the conditions of human life and the course of human history. This mirrors Darwin's own approach, with his frequent recourse to examples from literature, scripture and the performing arts, and the anecdotal evidence he provides from observations of his own children. What is new about later investigations in the field, including, I hope, the present study, is an awareness of the implications that these findings about the cross-cultural reach of the language of the emotions have for the future development – cultural, spiritual and political – of our species.

I have taken Darwin's basic six emotions, and added to them four others that seemed to me sufficiently distinct from them, while still being strictly definable as emotions. Under these ten thematic headings, I have explored both the psychological dynamics of the various states, and also looked at the influences these responses have had on different aspects of social and cultural history. It is not possible to make any kind of general judgement about when human beings started feeling in a particular way about certain issues. (When did anger first become a political force? When did disgust spread out from its purely physical origins and become a moral reaction?) That said, it is often instructive to reflect on the cultural codifications that these emotions have undergone in response to events in our history and to key works of art. Does not sexual jealousy take on a new cast after *Othello*, and yet another after *The Sorrows of Young Werther*?

To begin at the beginning, we can see primitive fear as the engine of all religious belief, which is not to say that spontaneous fear is felt every time one attends the Sunday morning service, but at the foundation of the structure that sustains it there is a sedimentary layer of ancient terror. In other words, the emotions are not just those spasmodic bursts of feeling that well up in response to external stimuli. They are the bedrocks on which much, if not all, of our social and cultural lives rest. It is that realisation that dispels the idea that, in some future utopia, we might evolve to a stage where we feel no emotion – that, and the fact that if we ever did manage to achieve such a state, we would arguably have ceased to be human at all.

I have studied each of the ten emotions concerned in what may be described as a declension form. For example, in the first chapter, which might be called the infinitive form of the emotion, 'to fear', I have examined it in its raw, intransitive state, expanding on its mental topology and also tracing its semantic history. The middle chapter of each section will explore the emotion in its active voice, 'I frighten you', in which I look at some of the ways in which it may be induced in others, by way of, say, social control. Finally, the concluding chapter of each section represents the passive voice of the emotion, 'I am afraid', and considers what happens in our psychic and cultural lives when we find ourselves subjected to an emotion, whether consciously instilled by others or because it arises pathologically.

I invite the reader to dwell on the active and passive forms our emotions may take, for it seems increasingly important that we be vigilant about the ways in which they are evoked – by whom and for what purposes. Once they have been misdirected in a particular context, it can prove extraordinarily difficult to reorientate them. During the Anglo-American intervention in Iraq in 2003, a truck containing an Iraqi family fleeing the chaos in Baghdad was held up at a US Army checkpoint just outside the city. Accounts differ as to what precisely happened, with the soldiers claiming that the truck ignored a warning to stop, while onlookers claimed it was already slowing down, but suddenly the vehicle was raked with machine-gun fire. Every one of its occupants, with the exception of a fifteen-year-old boy, was killed in the storm of bullets. The boy was pulled out of the cab at gunpoint, splattered from head to foot with his parents' blood. While their bodies and those of his sisters, his brother and an uncle were removed, laid out at the roadside and covered up, the boy remained in a strangely silent and tremulous state. His only action, until he was prevented from doing so, was nervously to keep lifting the blanket away from his dead father's face, as though in confirmation of what he could barely believe had happened. The story of this boy, whose name is Omar, was eclipsed within days by that of twelve-year-old Ali Abbas, who lost both arms and the whole of his family in a US rocket attack on his home near the Iraqi capital, and who soon found himself the international media's poster boy. Every step of his rehabilitation was meticulously covered, and in the week that I write this, he has appeared on the front page of one of the British tabloids, cheerily waving his newly fitted prostheses with a look that says, 'I forgive you all!' Our emotions are naturally engaged in both these cases, but the story of Ali has been used by news managers as a lightning conductor for the mass of angry dissent that the stories of Omar, and countless others like him, might otherwise provoke.

However capable of manipulation we may be as emotional beings, though, true hope lies in Darwin's proposals, and their subsequent verification. While postmodernism has taught us that we live in an age of irony, where there are no longer any overarching grand narratives, where an undiscriminating scepticism brushes matters such as morality and political ethics aside as so much anachronistic detritus, and where no one version of reality has any greater claim than any other on our attention, it is both bracing and deeply inspiring to reflect that, wherever we happen to come from, we have all been equipped with the same set of emotional aptitudes. While respecting each individual's right to cultural specificity, the fact that we all recognise and desire the happiness of others is more important than noting their peculiar dietary customs or attempting to understand their spiritual beliefs. A couple whose children got lost while walking on the Lancashire moors in lowering fog knew the same fear, momentarily, as those who hear, while at work, that a bomb has gone off near the school. There is a reservoir of unanswerable misery in the world, which some believe globalisation can alleviate – provided it isn't itself a major cause. We learn these continuities early, but find it too easy to forget them as we age. Infants of many different cultures have found the same resonance in works such as *Alice's Adventures in Wonderland*, the Harry Potter corpus, almost the entire output of Disney's golden age. There is in Dumbo's rage at the treatment of his mother, in the deferred justice of Snow White's case, in Pinocchio's mile-high face going cross-eyed with curiosity, and in the moment of elemental hurt in *Bambi* when the fatal shot rings out, the entire repertoire of adult emotion. We were not learning these feelings from Disney, though, when our eyes prickled and overflowed in the cavernous dark of the cinema. Instead, our already intact emotional receptors, tender and new as they were, were being marked out for future use.

There isn't only curiosity value in knowing that a Melanesian or a Maori makes the same face for sadness as we do. It is a profoundly sustaining piece of intelligence, since it provides us with the only knowledge we need with which to look at the world anew. If we are all capable of feeling the same way at certain times, whatever the specific causes of that feeling, then we should be able to help each other more, from the personal to the inter-governmental level. Sometimes this happens, but all too often it doesn't, and when it doesn't, it is because we forget our common humanity. That we do share that common humanity is handed down to us in two evidences in Darwin's work: first, that all races of humanity share one common ancestor, and secondly, that all have the same precisely evolved registers of emotional awareness. I hope it is clear from what follows which of the two discoveries I believe is of the greater magnitude, and I thus commend my work to Darwin's memory.

FEAR

The thing in the world of which I am most afraid is fear.
Michel de Montaigne

1. In Old English: A peril. 2. a. The emotion of pain or uneasiness caused by the sense of impending danger, or by the apprehension of evil. In early use applied to the more violent extremes of the emotion. Often *personified*. b. A state of alarm or dread. 3. The state of fearing (something); esp. a mingled feeling of dread and reverence towards God (or, formerly, any rightful authority). 4. Solicitude, anxiety for the safety of a person or thing. 5. In objective senses: a. Ground for alarm. b. Capability of inspiring fear. c. Something that is, or is to be, feared.

Darwin's physical indicators: opening wide of the eyes and mouth; raising of the eyebrows; motionlessness; breathlessness; crouching/cringing; increased heart rate; pallor; cold perspiration; erection of the hair; accelerated breathing; malfunction of the salivary glands, leading to dry mouth; tremor; failure of the voice; dilation of the pupils; contraction of the *platysma myoides* (neck muscles).

1

TO FEAR

Even before the emotion of fear, as the *Oxford English Dictionary* notes in its linguistic archaeology of the term, there is Fear, plain and simple. It exists objectively in the world, whether we like it or not, as a commodity, as a quality that certain phenomena are endowed with. A windswept precipice is a fear, as is a hungry predatory beast. It is the fact that the world is full of these fears that teaches us the feeling of dread with which we approach them. Fear is the appropriate response to these threats. Its name derives from an Old Saxon word that already sounds like an inarticulate cry, an ululation into which is compacted the meaning by which the term comes to denote not just something of which to be apprehensive, but something that is specifically lying in wait for us. In all fear lies a sense of ambush, of what might happen. Fears instruct us that our habitat is mined with disastrous potentialities, but precisely because fears represent the bad things that might happen but equally well might not, they also achieve victory over us by making us fear the non-existent and the unexplained.

Notwithstanding the mental armour that a good half-millennium of enlightened thinking has, in theory, bequeathed us, even today the most stubbornly rational people can find themselves succumbing to a flutter of panic at some inexplicable occurrence. A scratching sound in an otherwise empty room. The door that gently closes itself, having never done so before. The elusive bunch of keys that turns out to be sitting in the middle of the mantelpiece, where one had first, and many times since, gone looking for it. At such moments it often requires an almost physical effort to prevent the mind tugging off in a paranormal direction, momentarily saturated by fear.

However ready we may be to dismiss such events as insignificant, the lesson they teach is that, buried deep within the psyche of our species, is the instinct to turn reflexive fear into evidence that there is something out there to be feared. Everything that sustains the operations of systematic, and not so systematic, faith – from New Age occultism to the Vatican – was established in humanity's Palaeolithic infancy as a result of the inescapable sway of primal fear. The forms of faith thus created by fear are a product of the adrenaline produced by minatory external stimuli, which occurs within all species, alloyed with human consciousness and imagination. Not only that, but our very organisation into co-operative groups, and thus the beginnings of what may be recognised as societies, is attributable to the same pervasive fear, and there is one fear that, above all others, exercises something like the same corrosive influence in our souls as it did when we knew next to nothing of the world. We tread warily in the presence of death.

Around the time of the First World War, a series of excavations carried out by archaeologists near the village of La Ferrassie in the Dordogne region of France uncovered what appeared to be a family sepulchre in an unusually well-preserved state. It dated from a period known to palaeontologists as the Mousterian, which is to say, about 50,000 years ago. The site contained six skeletons – those of a man, an elderly woman, three children and a baby. Not only the number of the interred, but also the evidence of meticulous preparation that the burials showed, marked a new development in our understanding of the spiritual orientation of Palaeolithic peoples.

The adult male had been laid to rest with his right arm and leg drawn up close to his body, while the elderly female had been even more tightly flexed, with both legs folded into her body, and the right arm bent and pressed against her upper chest. One of the children, who had died aged between five and six years, had been buried in a similar position. To the initial bafflement of the excavators, this child's head was missing, but was later unearthed under a heavy limestone slab about three feet away from the body. The ritualistic nature of these prehistoric burials, and of others like them that have since come to light, indicates that the corpses were painstakingly bound into a position from which a living person could not escape. They were then committed to the earth under layers of stones, and sometimes of hot ash, buried together in all likelihood because they were of the same family. The inference to be drawn is that the dead were shackled as they were buried, so that they might not return to prey upon the survivors or – more disturbingly still – attempt to infect them with the pallid, rigid condition to which they had succumbed. In the case of the last child, perhaps for some reason peculiar to his or her life, the removal of the head and its secretion under a weighty rock slab seems to suggest a desire to ensure that the deceased could not spontaneously reconstitute itself and come back.

If it were possible, as some evolutionary psychologists maintain, to decide which of humanity's emotions is the oldest, then fear would surely enter the strongest claim. To our very early ancestor *Australopithecus*, shambling across the African grasslands in close-knit groups, the world was an intimidating, haunted place, in which violent storms, the threat of fire, unfathomable disease and suffering all held awesome power over him. So it was, in the beginning, that lack of understanding gave rise to primal terror.

With the development between two million and one-and-a-half million years ago of the more recognisably proto-human forms, *Homo habilis* and *H. erectus*, came the earliest attempt to make sense of this frightening world by anthropomorphising natural forces. The crashing of thunder now appeared as the rage of elemental powers that were displeased, but could be assuaged by rituals. An imagined cause-and-effect process came to be observed, whereby the making of offerings or some other symbolic behaviour would cure a sickness or abate a storm. Even if such practices were only sometimes successful, that was enough for them to become systematic.

By the time of the transition from the Middle to the Upper Palaeolithic Period, around 40,000 years ago, this symbolic behaviour had led to the founding of two great institutions of human history: art and religion. This was the time of the last major ice age, and what we think of as the very beginning of recorded history. If we see religion, at least in Europe and North Africa, as shifting from a belief in many and varied gods on the Egyptian and Graeco-Roman models, to the centralised unity of one in Judaism, Christianity and Islam, then we are starting in the wrong place. Although polytheistic belief systems certainly arose in prehistoric times, it is almost certain that, as palaeontologists such as Johannes Maringer came to assert in the post-war period, they were preceded by belief in – and fear of – one supreme being. Evidence of animal sacrifice and the burial of animal body parts, as well as the depiction of hunting scenes in the cave paintings of the Upper Palaeolithic, reveal a common unity of purpose: they were intended to solicit the favours of a divine dispenser of good fortune in the hunt. Within pitch-black caverns in the deepest recesses of the rock shelters in which these people dwelt, by guttering torchlight, the dismembered parts of cave bears were arrayed in propitiation of a god who might bestow success in the hunt, and therefore the survival of the tribe. In addition to the offerings, pictorial representations of the chase were painted on to the cave walls and ceilings in ochreous reds and clay blacks, images of fabulous richness like the late nineteenth-century finds at Altamira, or those made at Lascaux in south-west France in 1940. Numerous small figurines of the gravid female form – in limestone, soapstone, and ivory – have also come to light, betokening some magical invocation of fertility, so that, in a time of frozen scarcity, the hunted herds on which the tribe depended would reproduce sufficiently to ensure its own survival.

If it is fear, though, that motivates the turn towards a primitive theology, what exactly was our Palaeolithic ancestor frightened of, other than the unpredictable elements? We know from remains such as charred bones and ash deposits within the caves that fire was already being used for cooking, lighting and security. Violent encounters with rival tribes would have been few and far between, since the earth was sparsely populated and all the groups nomadic. And, unlike his earliest ancestors, the Palaeolithic hunter, peripatetic though he was, knew how to make reasonably secure dwelling places within the rock shelters and caves of his landscape. The primal terror he still felt, and that motivated all his devotional and cultural practices, is the same one that to a large extent motivates our own: the fear of his death and that of his family.

When early hominids learned how to control fire, not only could they now cook their meat, making it much more easily digestible, as well as keep themselves warm, but they could also protect themselves to some extent from the depredations of wild animals that roamed the open country – wolves, hyenas, panthers and the hideous sabre-toothed tiger with its massively developed upper canines. The domestication of fire must have had a profound impact on the consciousness of proto-humans. Fire was already a feature of human life by the Early Palaeolithic, 200,000 years ago. From being wholly at the mercy of their environment, they were now in at least partial mastery of it. In a footnote to one of his late works, *Civilisation and its Discontents* (1930), Sigmund Freud postulates that the means of taming fire must have arisen when men discovered that they could put it out by urinating on it, and that it was the individual who chose to forgo the erotic pleasure of this perhaps homosexual competitive behaviour, sparing the fire and finding a means of transporting it, who was the founding father of a great cultural leap. Whatever the explanation, the control of fire marks a milestone in the liberation from primal fear. Death, however, did not appear to Palaeolithic humanity to be susceptible to such ingenuity. It went its own way, consuming voraciously as it did so, and must therefore have been regarded as more powerful than living things.

What evidence we have in the form of cave burials (and in the era since the Second World War, it has become enormously more plentiful) suggests that the ice-age people who carried out these elaborate ritual interments did not necessarily believe that any change other than a physical one came over the dead. The cold rigor mortis and decay of the corpse could not help but be noticed, but it appears likely that the fellows of the deceased did not conceive him or her to have stopped living. On the other hand, it may have been felt that in this state of permanently suspended animation, the dead might well be able to affect the continued organic existence of those left behind. Perhaps this was how the death-state was spread? It certainly explains the repeated occurrence of burial postures in which the dead are committed to the ground in attitudes of restraint. Corpses discovered in the crouching position would originally have been tied up, the bonds having long since rotted away. Many are placed face down. On the Mediterranean coast, in what is now Italy, an old woman clasped tightly in the foetal position in the arms of a boy in his teens was uncovered. The boy's body seems to have been intended as a means of preventing the elderly woman from escaping. It could even be that the practice of burial itself is an attempt to lock up the dead, sealing whatever pernicious influence they might extend over the living securely in the ground with them.

For these early humans, death was just about the only thing in their world that was inevitable, for all that its precise moment of occurrence might appear random. Perhaps the god who dispensed luck during hunting also dispensed life and death as well, in the various forms of sickness, of predation by carnivorous beasts, and of starvation in the worst of conditions. Was it not this unseen force itself that was to be feared more than the thunderbolts of ill luck that it was wont to hurl down?

It was a commonplace of evolutionary psychology for at least eighty years after the publication of *The Origin of Species* (1859) that the formulation of systematic religious belief is what made natural forces apprehensible to early humans. In establishing the proprietor god (and then gods) of fire, of winter and so forth, the world to which they were subjected in the raw was made systematic – and, to a degree, comfortingly familiar. Only when two German philosophers of the Frankfurt School, Theodor Adorno and Max Horkheimer, wrote their *Dialectic of Enlightenment* (1944) was the idea postulated that, far from establishing a reassuring communicability with nature, as the humanist tradition had conceived it, what the development of religious belief actually created was the means for a far greater and more deeply imbued fear. Over and above the phenomena of the natural world, there was set some angry, vengeful, all-powerful super-being, in whose hands the unexpected lightning strike and devastating forest fire were mere tools, but whose own true nature could not by definition be known. All votive efforts must be directed to the appeasement of Him, or It, or Them.

The fear of death, and of the deity that dealt in it, was compounded by that fear with which we are all axiomatically familiar: fear of the unknown. Nature itself, including our own nature, remains opaque to us because it is the preserve of a god who can neither be seen nor understood, and the death that he visits on all living things appears the gateway to another, unknowable realm. What happens once we arrive at this murky destination becomes, with the establishment of the idea of a programmatic afterlife, a matter of consuming concern. The Orphic tradition in Greek cosmology, which arose hard on the heels of the Dionysian (around the late seventh or early sixth centuries BC), is one of the first to elaborate the notion of a continuation of spiritual existence beyond the grave, the sweetness of which will depend on how well we have acquitted ourselves in the physical life that precedes it. It represents an antithesis to the riotous forms of celebration that worship of the wine god Dionysus involved, reforming those rites in favour of a peaceful striving after purity, spiritualising the notion of divine possession away from present drunkenness and towards contemplation of the life to come. The Orphic afterlife is a home fit for heroes, but in Christian theology we find the concept of the afterlife presented as a simple matter of reward or punishment – eternally renewed at that – according to how we have behaved here on earth. 'Eye hath not seen, nor ear heard,' says the evangelist, 'neither hath it entered into the heart of man, the things that God hath prepared for them that love him.' While many thinkers, from the early nineteenth century onwards, have pointed out the under-current of blackmail in the church's efforts to get us to accept its nostrums, the fear of the eternal torture in Hell that awaits the heedless has probably been outweighed by the almost sensual comfort to be derived from the promise of Heaven that is never withdrawn.

Nonetheless, fear is what animates the eschatological vision of Christianity once humans have accepted that they are all immortal. Once one knows that one's sublunary actions are going to be a matter of infinitesimal reckoning in a final act of judgement, our lives cannot help but be shaped by a climate of ultimate dread. The concept of *Angst* – anxiety at the circumstances and sheer fact of one's existence – ushered in by Freudian psychology, and raised to the universal human condition by existentialism, has its roots in Christianity, in its insistence that all human conduct was subject to bottomless accountability. This is itself a modification of the vengefulness of Yahweh.

Before the fear of eternal punishment, however, strides a seemingly more intractable towering dread – the idea that there might, after all, be nothing. This is certainly the case argued by Arthur Schopenhauer in the 1810s, and again in the twentieth century by the German proto-existentialist Martin Heidegger. Jean-Paul Sartre devoted a number of years during the Second World War and the Nazi occupation of France to composing a gigantic text on the theme of *Being and Nothingness* (1943), arguing that what lies at the heart of all our naked terror at existence is the notion that things could just as easily not be. The feeling that there has to be some ultimate point to all the unhappiness in life is what impels us towards a belief in gods, or in other forms of the supernatural. One consequence of that anxiety is that there have been, throughout western theology, attempts to lay the foundations for the existence of God on a logical or rational footing – to prove, in other words, that he exists.

St Anselm, an eleventh-century Normandy abbot who would later become Archbishop of Canterbury, wrote a short treatise on the question of God that sought to establish, by force of argument, that there simply had to be such a being. His argument is an elementary one, contending that if it is possible to imagine the existence of a supreme entity, above which nothing else could be greater, then he must necessarily exist, on the grounds that to be able to imagine a greater one still would be impossible. The mere fact of our being able to imagine a greater being than whatever deity we initially thought of would render that first one decidedly suspect. Since a real entity is an immensely more compelling proposition than a purely imaginary one, there would come a point when the fact that no greater being can be conceived of must point to the real (and not imaginary) nature of such a being. It impresses itself upon us precisely because nothing greater is conceivable.

A little less than two hundred years later, St Thomas Aquinas would argue that God must exist not simply because the concept of

God was logically irresistible, as Anselm thought, but because the evidence of the world around us compels us to believe in him. If everything that happens in nature has a prior cause, there must, at the beginning of the whole chain of causation, be a first cause, a prime mover that does not in itself need anything else to cause it to be. If there weren't a first domino to initiate life's tumbling processes, then nothing would ever have caused anything, which would mean that nothing existed. There must therefore be a necessary first cause, and his name is God.

A refinement of this type of argument was offered at the outset of the nineteenth century by the theologian William Paley, in his book *Natural Theology* (1802). This asserts that, since the universe so obviously exhibits the intricate and harmonious workings of a designed artefact, it must therefore be the handiwork of a designing intelligence. The circumstances in which organic life can be conceived and sustained are so fantastically improbable that a single originating power is much more likely to explain it, as distinct from the operations of mere chance, the odds against which are astronomically high.

Others have argued that the occurrence of miracles is sufficient to attest to the existence of God, whether they be of the type that appear to contravene all known physical laws (such as the dead coming back to life), or simply fortuitous, improbable coincidences that result in a happy outcome, and that impress upon their witnesses some irresistible sense of the workings of God's grace. Still others point to the existence of the human awareness of moral law – the inner voice of conscience that persuades the mass of humanity that acts such as murder and rape and theft are wrong, and which Immanuel Kant in the eighteenth century called the 'categorical imperative' – as evidence for the existence of God. If God hadn't guided us to these beliefs, where would such an objective moral sense come from, given that it isn't evolutionarily necessary for the survival of the species?

The weakness of attempts to produce evidence for God's exist-ence is that such arguments are all equally capable of refutation. It remains the case that the best possible proof would be provided if God would only put in an appearance every now and then, instead of remaining hidden in some other world. Yet when all the eviden-tial arguments have been scotched, there remains the pragmatic view, famously put forward in the seventeenth century by the French mathematician Blaise Pascal, that one may as well gamble that God exists because even if he doesn't one has lost nothing, but if he does, the consequences of not believing in him are likely to be rather severe. The mercenary quality of this argument has been much commented on since its formulation, and we might think that any belief that has been postulated on the grounds of mathemati-cal probability (and Pascal is the great theorist of mathematical chance) has forfeited its right to be considered a matter of personal revelation. Anyway, it is Pascal himself who presents the best argument for rejecting the other evidence:

The metaphysical proofs for the existence of God are so remote from human reasoning and so involved that they make little impact, and, even if they did help some people, it would only be for the moment during which they watched the demonstration, because an hour later they would be afraid they had made a mistake.

And it is that 'afraid' which proves crucial. We can never quite buy into any one of these explanations, because the next might be just as persuasive of belief. For Pascal, blind faith – the mere trust that there is somebody out there – should be all we need, so that if St Anselm's ontological proof continues to elude our powers of com-prehension, best close the book and let it be. In any event, even if we do look for more objective evidence than the Pascalian wager allows for, it isn't simply the existence of God that is being estab-lished, but the correct attitude to him as well. In a classic statement of the argument from design made a generation before the birth of William Paley, Sir Isaac Newton muses on the fascinating intricacy of the structure of the eye, and how its improbable complexity is common to nearly all living creatures:

Did blind chance know that there was light, and what was its refraction, and fit the eyes of all creatures after the most curious manner to make use of it? These and suchlike considerations always have and ever will prevail with mankind to believe that there is a Being who made all things and has all things in his power, and who is therefore to be feared.

There is no possibility of merely noting his existence with an awestruck intake of breath and then moving on, rather as we might gasp at the view down the Grand Canyon before getting back on the bus. We have to prostrate ourselves in fear that this is how the world came to be. But is this what God wants? Is this state of 'fear and trembling' essential to faith, as Søren Kierkegaard suggested in the nineteenth century, so that we are asked to see that this is the way God likes us? Does that not make him no more than a monstrous tyrant, the heartless biblical persecutor of Abraham and Job?

However that may be decided, the removal of faith from the business of government and the state in western societies has marginalised this notional God, whose existence had been a matter of such anguished scholastic debate. What it has failed to do, however, is abolish irrational belief. That there is a spirit world, parallel to this one, seemingly more sentient of ours than we can ever be of it, is another enduring by-product of primal fear. It is to this world that we might hope eventually to travel when we die or, in the comforting argot of Victorian spiritualism, 'pass over', but it is also the world from which unwanted visitors return occasionally to disturb our equilibrium in this one. So hardy is the belief in spiritual presences, intangible forces, ghosts and revenants of all kinds, that it has survived the secular scepticism one might have expected to replace faith in a creator God. Similarly, a panoply of New Age beliefs, including various healing methods, the powers of crystals, the control of *chi*, tantric sex rituals and other such preoccupations, has moved into the space vacated by the orthodox western religions.

Thus it is that the paranormal industry in the west is booming as never before. In August 2002, the Roman city of York in the north of England was declared, by an organisation called the Ghost Research Foundation, to be officially the most haunted place in Europe. Manifestations have included the celebrated Roman legionary seen marching through the cellar of the Treasurer's House in the 1950s, and the Grey Lady who emerges from her confinement in the walls of the Theatre Royal from time to time in order to tickle the necks of patrons sitting in the dress circle. (With what aim seems difficult to determine. One might have thought that having been immured for centuries for an illicit love affair, she might be in the mood for something a little more vituperative than tickling on the rare occasions she is allowed out.) Organisers of haunted tours of the city report that school parties are increasingly common, because such tales have the power to captivate the pupils where real history fails.

In the case of ghosts, the relationship between fear and the supernatural has been reversed. Whereas we once posited the existence of a supreme being because of the terrors that the natural world held for us, we now persuade ourselves that we have been visited by messengers from the spirit world in order to feel the delicious thrill of terror. Psychical researchers report no shortage of volunteers willing to be enclosed in a 'haunted crypt' for the night, and even where they neither see nor hear anything untoward, they are happy to record mysterious sensations of being watched, of not being alone, of sensing the air turn strangely cold, or of feeling adventitious hands gently caressing or rudely shoving them. In a phenomenon with seemingly international reach, recorded in tribal communities in Africa as well as among aficionados of the bizarre in the United States and Europe, many people report being visited at night in their homes by a mysterious entity – to which paranormal investigators have actually given the uncomfortably cinematic name 'The Entity' – which attacks them physically while they are sleeping. A strange, transcultural feature of these reports is that, in many of them, the Entity takes the form of a ghastly old woman, a leering, evil hecatrix who climbs on to the prone bodies of her victims and crushes the breath out of them. A British man claims to have been anally raped by the Entity, so it can presumably change between genders at will. Perhaps there is a whole diabolical tribe of such beings, roaming the world in search of sleeping victims, permanently spoiled for choice as night chases night with the earth's rotation. The victims bring their own personal cosmologies to the investigations of these visitants, so that tribespeople in Africa recognise it as one of their own mischievous ancestral spirits, while scientific investigators in the USA, using ultrasound recorders in the company of a Catholic priest, found that a torrent of indignant static was unleashed on the monitors when the Entity was commanded to depart in the name of Jesus Christ. Presumably one can supply one's own green vomit.

We see all this on our television screens, read of it in magazines, and then climb into bed, douse the light and find ourselves incapable of sleep as we involuntarily turn it over in our minds. In the night-time we return to the infant condition of unreasoning terror, the same oceanic, resistless feeling we had when, left alone in the dark behind a closed door at the end of the day, we realised that there was a world beyond the safeguards of adults in which we would have to find a way to live. In that darkness, so unlike the uterine blackness in which utter contentment was the prevailing mood (according to those who claim to have clear memories of it), we helplessly invent fanciful demons, ogres who might turn out to be

holding their scabrous hands millimetres from our throats, or –
even more familiarly – those thin beings who skulked under the bed
ready to clutch at any unsuspecting ankle, and whose presence
made you leap across the last few feet of floor into bed.

When the lexicographers outline in the dictionary definitions
that 'mingled feeling of dread and reverence towards God', they
reflect the close link between the state of fear and the apprehension
of spiritual matters. Fear may be felt at the prospect of many other
phenomena than those of religion, but where religion is, there is
always, of necessity, fear. Which fact alone, if there were not
already many other reasons for scepticism, would bear witness
against it.

2

TO FRIGHTEN

To Niccolò Machiavelli, writing in the early sixteenth century, statecraft was both an art and a science. It required the exercise of precise judgement, subtlety and a gambler's ability to write off minor losses against future winnings. The addressee of his work, the absolute ruler of a territory probably taken by force, would benefit from reading the classical historians and philosophers, in particular their insights into military strategy, in case his power was challenged, but also their insights on human nature. Underpinning his advice to fledgling dictators, however, is a Renaissance faith in the well-ordered regularity of the world, a scientistic belief that, regardless of time and location, relentless application of the same policies will issue in the same results.

We learn that anybody who has assisted in establishing a prince in power through internal rebellion should be dispensed with, lest they consider the new prince to be in their debt. The remaining heirs and family of the old, usurped prince should be summarily wiped out, after which the new prince should take up residence in the occupied territory, to deter further rebellion and discourage an outside attack. On being conquered, a constitutional republic with ancient liberties and institutions should be demolished, because the memory of its former beneficence is likely to foment rebellion against a less permissive order. Driving people out of their houses in order to establish a new colony creates the right climate of fear to keep others in line. 'For it has to be said,' Machiavelli asserts, 'that men should be either caressed or crushed, for if the injuries are slight they can always gain revenge, but they cannot if they are heavy.'

The Italian city-states of the fifteenth and sixteenth centuries were, in the main, ruled by despots. Machiavelli's native Florence was controlled by the powerful Medici clan, first Lorenzo the Magnificent and later his son Piero, until the family were exiled in 1494. They were Dukes of Tuscany, although their influence eventually spread far wider, even into the Vatican, to which they supplied no fewer than four popes. Unsurprisingly, the machinations of Florentine politics bulked large in Machiavelli's life, ensuring that his success as a career diplomat was an episodic affair. In early 1504, and again in the summer of 1510, the then governor of Florence, Piero Soderini, sent him to France to attempt to form an alliance with Louis XII on behalf of the Pope. Florence's treaty with the Venetians of 1510 had particularly damaged relations with the French monarchy, with the eventual result that Louis convoked a cabal of dissident Florentine cardinals, incited to turn against Pope Julius II. For all Machiavelli's efforts, France was preparing to wage war against the Italian cities. In between these missions, Machiavelli was awarded a military commissioner's post in Florence under Soderini's governorship, having been responsible for organising an impressive civic militia to repel external hostilities. Nonetheless, an invasion was launched. But when, unable to consolidate their initial victories, the French withdrew in disarray from northern Italy in 1512, leaving Florence undefended, they left the way for Giuliano de Medici to overthrow Soderini, re-establishing his clan in power under the auspices of the Holy League, a papal alliance founded to counter the French. The following year, Machiavelli was implicated – wrongly – in a plot to unseat Giuliano. He was imprisoned and tortured, and was only released in a general amnesty declared when Giuliano's brother, Giovanni, was elected as Pope Leo X.

None of these events dimmed Machiavelli's belief in the science of political strategy. It is almost certain that his great text on the subject, *The Prince*, was composed in the very year that he had been subjected to the thumbscrews of the Holy League. On its publication in March 1516, he had intended to dedicate it to the victorious Giuliano, but the latter's death and succession by his twenty-four-year-old nephew Lorenzo forced him to make a substitution. Not content with inheriting the governorship of Florence, Lorenzo also conquered the Duchy of Urbino the same month. And so the author of Europe's most famous tract on political repression had before him the living image of the ruthless young practitioner of the art.

Perusing the stately progress of *The Prince* through the theory and practice of statesmanlike severity and artful deception, the young Lorenzo might have been struck in chapter 7 by the description of the conduct of a recent ruler of Urbino, Duke Valentino, better known to history as Cesare Borgia. The author recalls the kind of tactic for which Borgia's rule in Urbino became notorious. A particularly violent clampdown was blamed on the Duke's plenipotentiary, Remirro de Orco, so that when the iron grip was relaxed, the indignation of the populace could be swiftly cauterised by de Orco's removal. 'Removal' meant decapitating him in the dead of night and leaving his body in the main *piazza*, the blood-soaked knife by its side, for all to see. Accompanying an authorial shudder of horror is the smirk of a certain fondness too: '[H]e understood so clearly,' Machiavelli recalls of Borgia, 'that men must be either won over or destroyed.'

If its solemn counsels of wisdom on the correct moment to wipe out one's opponent's family, or on the need to be brutally rough with Fortune (because she is a woman and naturally respects that sort of treatment), have to modern ears more than a whiff of the Brothers Grimm about them, what remains as a political truism is the insistence in *The Prince* that all humanity is venal, selfish and corruptible. It is this notion that has been adduced to explain a lack of public faith in a broad spectrum of utopian initiatives, from the welfare state to charity pop records. Nor is it possible simply to wave such an assertion aside as reactionary cynicism. When Machiavelli assures his princely reader that 'you will find that men always prove evil unless a particular need forces them to be good', one might wish to call the whole of Renaissance humanism down on his head, were it not for the fact that many writers of the Renaissance agree with him. It is the evil that men do, as Shakespeare had his Mark Antony remind us less than a century later, that lives after them, while the good goes with them to the grave. Self-preservation is often the motive behind the disinclination to do good, and survival in an office seized opportunistically requires an exceptional facility for quashing one's better instincts. No maxim in *The Prince* must have resounded more tantalisingly in Lorenzo's head than Machiavelli's assurance to him that 'there is nothing more self-destructive than generosity'.

The biblical myth of the Fall of mankind is attributed to the first two humans becoming aware of knowledge that had been specifically forbidden to them. Leaving aside the question of why God pointed out the existence of the Tree of Knowledge to Adam and Eve in the first place, if he didn't want them to be curious about its effects, we may wonder exactly what knowledge it is that contributes so decisively and so early on to humanity's downfall. Peering through the veils of this mythology at the actual origins of humankind, we return once more to the notion of primeval fear, and the irresistible idea that the first major step in the spiritual imprisonment of human beings was the discovery that fear was not solely a sensation felt spontaneously, but that it could also be instilled deliberately in others. Our descent began not with access to dangerous knowledge, so much as the discovery of how to terrify. If the earliest conflicts in prehistory were between rival groups of nomadic hominids fighting over dwindling food resources or available shelter, then this is where it was learned that aggressive displays of menace could help to secure what was needed. Physical combat may have started from the belief that each party had an equal chance, but experience would come to show that certain individuals – by dint of superior physical prowess – always prevailed, and thus that the mere threat of violence from them was enough to win.

All political systems depend on the implied use of force. Although modern democracies reassure their citizens that nobody who observes the rule of law should have cause to fear the wrath of the state, nonetheless fear is as indispensably a component of them as it is of more totalitarian systems. It is in the nature and the extent of that fear that the difference between a dictatorship and a democracy may be marked. Yet states of fear are usually mutual. We seek to intimidate those of whom we are ourselves apprehensive, and legal systems are constructed gradually, as the state identifies internal threats to its stability. There is a gulf of difference between a civil polity that sends unpleasantly worded letters in red print to its citizens, and one that sends cadaverous officials to knock on the door in the morning because you had drunkenly called the President a shithead in a bar the night before. It is just that in the latter case (the now defunct German Democratic Republic of the early 1980s), the state would appear to have had a lot more to fear from its citizens than they had from it. Otherwise, why not let them say what they want?

Fear was the standard legal tender of Florentine politics of the sixteenth century. A leader could only govern if he had accumulated the right aura of *auctoritas* around himself, and it wasn't possible to achieve that without the exercise of fear. But as a political weapon, fear is a distinctly two-edged sword. It may slice through the defiance of citizens who have had their homes razed to the ground or seen their families killed, but as Damocles could have attested, to have it hanging constantly above your head hardly makes for a relaxed existence. As authoritarian states the world

HUMANITY: AN EMOTIONAL HISTORY

over have discovered to their economic cost, a frightened and resentful workforce is less productive than a relatively contented one. So it is that Machiavelli modulates his advice to the Prince by suggesting that if it is possible to rule benignly once his power has been established, he should allow himself to do so, while being permanently prepared to 'act badly when necessary'.

From the people's point of view, great advances in the social order can be achieved when fear is thrown off by a collective exercise of will. Then it is that 'The only thing we have to fear is fear itself.' When President Franklin D Roosevelt issued this celebrated rallying cry to the American people at his inaugural address in Washington on 4 March 1933, he was acknowledging the magnitude of the task of economic reconstruction that faced the United States, but beneath the exhortation not to despair, the words seem also to encapsulate the truth about the way order is maintained in civil society. This most famous of all morale-boosters is in fact deeply ambiguous. The words are generally taken to mean that fear should be discarded. If only we can cease to be afraid of fear itself, then we shan't be afraid of anything, and will therefore be correspondingly capable of achieving anything (such as bringing about an end to the Depression). What Roosevelt actually said, however, was that fear was the only thing that it was mandatory to fear. The fear of anything else could be overcome, but not that of fear itself. In other words, nothing in itself need be frightening, but the notion of fear must continue to be respected. Had its audience – or its speaker – but known it, in the subdued gloom of that least festive of all presidential inauguration days, they were hearing the most elegantly disguised manoeuvre that representative democracy has yet mounted in its defence of institutional fear.

If fear does indeed play an integral role in creating consensus within a democracy, then when that consensus is forfeited by a repressive regime, fear itself becomes the only social fixative. This has been seen in situations where power has been appropriated by the armed forces in support of a despotic ruler, as for example in Chile in 1973, when the elected government of Salvador Allende was overthrown by General Augusto Pinochet and a wave of massacres inaugurated what was to be a seventeen-year dictatorship. It has also been a feature of many post-revolutionary societies throughout history. An insurrection is frequently followed by a repressive phase, as a fledgling government seeks to consolidate the gains it has won. In so succumbing to authoritarianism, the legitimate authority by which a dynamic new government may have hoped to rule is sacrificed to the intimidation that will one day be its downfall. This was the case after the victory of Cromwell's forces in England in 1649, after the French Revolution declined into the Jacobin Terror from 1792, and catastrophically so after 1917 in the Soviet Union.

What motivates the recourse to violence is the certain knowledge that, however fervent the tide of popular support that swept the new regime to power, there will always be forces who are not satisfied with it and wish to restore the old dispensation, or at least improve on the new one. The English Commonwealth ushered in by the execution of Charles I – a nebulous and ill-defined political entity at best – suffered from chronic insecurity. Not only did it have on its doorstep unconquered Ireland and Presbyterian Scotland, which had immediately recognised Charles's son to be King Charles II following the removal of his father's head, but there were elements within the armed forces that clung stubbornly to their affiliation to the monarchy, and didn't give a sword's swish for the authority of Parliament. Constant skirmishes between rival factions were the order of the day in Cromwellian England, many disputes ending with drawn swords rather than recourse to the magistracy. Public disputation is often the common currency of popular revolutions. If the old order, and all the constitutional certitudes that went with it, have been swept away, then what replaces it is a kind of open debating society, in which each newly liberated citizen has the chance to have his or her say. In seventeenth-century England, it was the status and authority of the Christian religion around which these colloquies spun, with the Quaker and Puritan traditions insisting that faith was a matter of private revelation into which the would-be redeemed must willingly enter, while others still clung to a post-Catholic belief that the Church retained the monopoly of spiritual decision, and that its authority could not be usurped. These issues mattered, because it was in God's name that the Lord Protector and his successors presumed to govern. When Cromwell, in one of his most theatrical displays, dissolved the Rump Parliament of Commonwealth loyalists in 1653, the scene was set for a dictatorship of nominees to settle all such questions once and for all, brutally extinguishing dissent in the process.

In the post-revolutionary ferment of Paris, the equivalent turning point came in August 1792, when the first guillotine, on which criminals and other enemies of the state were to be executed, was set up in the vicinity of the Tuileries gardens. The blood from public executions flowed thick and fast from then on, peaking in the appalling prison massacres of the following month, when revolutionary mobs surged through the makeshift jails that had been created in abbeys and hospitals throughout the city, holding summary 'hearings' of the inmates that were followed swiftly by their murders. Some were renegade intellectuals, apologists for the *ancien régime*, others were Catholic priests who had spoken out against the abolition of the monarchy, but many were simply the same detainees who had been there when Louis XVI was still on the throne – petty thieves, muggers and beggars. At Bicêtre, the victims included forty-three boys below the age of eighteen. Many were literally hacked to shreds with axes, while members of the Legislative Assembly dilated on whether the massacres could be considered as understandable if regrettable revolutionary excesses, or whether indeed they were not perfectly legitimate expressions of popular retribution. 'By exercising vengeance,' ventured *Commissaire*

Guiraut, 'the people are also doing justice.' By the following year, such anarchic violence had been replaced by the organised public killing of those even half-suspected of harbouring secret distaste for the Jacobin regime.

The same paranoid fear of internal enemies polluted early hopes vested in the Union of Soviet Socialist Republics, proclaimed after the Bolshevik Revolution in St Petersburg in 1917. Using the example of the Jacobin Terror as historical precedent, and against the backdrop of civil war, the revolution's leaders summarily rounded up the leading figures of rival political parties and threw them into the dungeons of the Peter and Paul Fortress. In November 1917, the Cheka – the 'Commission for Struggle against Counter-Revolution and Sabotage', predecessor of the KGB – was established to facilitate, in the words of its first head, Felix Dzerzhinsky, 'a revolutionary settling of accounts with counter-revolutionaries'. Dzerzhinsky answered the job specification drawn up by Lenin, being 'a staunch proletarian Jacobin', and declared at the founding of the Cheka that it would be composed of 'determined, hard, dedicated comrades ready to do anything in defence of the Revolution. Do not think that I seek forms of revolutionary justice,' he assured his listeners. 'We are not now in need of justice. It is war now.' To emphasise the break with the past, new forms of torture and killing were invented specifically to deal with the prisoners. It is with the acquiescence in summary mob justice by the Bolshevik leaders, though, that the most striking similarity with the conduct of the French Revolution may be observed. A knowing smile was the only response to acts of hideous public brutality, whether they were directed against apologists of the old regime or everyday criminals. People's Courts, in which the proletariat, driven not by any form of judicial training but simply by the guiding light of their own 'revolutionary consciences', were empowered to visit vengeance upon the bourgeois classes, helped to create the right atmosphere of retribution. If the impulse of vengefulness could be unleashed among ordinary peasants, then in some perverse way the actions of an insanely repressive political order was legitimised. And even if state-sponsored terror appears to become its own justification the longer a demented regime clings to power, it issues first from the state's own mortal dread that it may not survive. 'Terror,' Friedrich Engels warned in the century before the Russian Revolution, 'is a matter of needless cruelties perpetrated by terrified men.'

George Orwell's crude but compulsive fable of political terror, *Nineteen Eighty-four* (1949), dramatises the mechanisms of repression with simple efficiency. Its most luminous insight into the operations of the totalitarian state is not to be found in the way in which resistance is dealt with, but in the degree to which the citizens of Airstrip One are trained to internalise the demands of the state, so that their very emotional lives are suspended. The novel's closing image, of Winston Smith choking back a childhood memory of a better existence by focusing through a film of dissident tears on the ubiquitous poster image of Big Brother, is his final act of capitulation. Theodor Adorno, in his late work *Negative Dialectics* (1966), argues that, viewed from one perspective, the progress of human history has been one of increasing domination. After learning to control the forces of external nature, we established the administrative means of controlling large concentrations of human beings through civic orders and political systems. The further development of the twentieth century, he posits, was to extend that administrative control into the psyches of modern citizens, so that the intellectual desires, cultural preferences and emotional demands of the contemporary individual are those that society prescribes for it. Indeed, its greatest victory has been to convince its clients that the desires it has implanted in them are their own, spontaneously arising, and selflessly satisfied by a system that has only their welfare at heart. (The slogan of a British chain of teenage clothes shops in 2003 read, simply but ominously, 'We are you.' 'Resistance', it might have added, 'is futile.') If one criticises the garbage broadcast by a digital TV channel, its chief executive points to the viewing figures. This is what people want. It is a need we are fulfilling. And from there it is a short step to the most threadbare argument of all to justify mass deception: 'But tens of millions of people can't be wrong!' Hans Christian Andersen's percipient small boy at the Emperor's parade had already dispensed with that objection in literature, and yet the citizens of Nazi Germany did so again in stark reality. 'And why ever not?'

As Orwell suggests, state control over humanity's inner nature cannot be absolute – at least not so far – otherwise one may be entitled to wonder how this Theodor Adorno character managed to escape its intrusions long enough to point it out. But it is Adorno's contention that we should be startled by the degree to which we are unconscious of the cultural programming we receive, and the extent to which fear keeps us from seeing that there is an alternative, radically dissatisfied way of looking at the world. Where dissatisfaction does exist, it is often deflected away from its true base in economic reality and towards some chimerical phenomenon, intended to strengthen our allegiance to the society we live in. An example of this is that streak of xenophobia that too often appears to be an essential ingredient in the patriotism or nationalism that is urged on us in various ways, when we are preparing to unleash another bombing campaign against a rogue regime perhaps, as well as when we are supporting our national team in the World Cup. Neither of these activities is necessarily xenophobic in itself, but the national mood that helps to spur them on does contain overt elements of racial prejudice. Resentment against the world of other people may begin innocently enough with distaste at the unfathomable habits of the next-door neighbours, but it is disquieting how easily it can turn into the ideology of a more sweeping bitterness against other ethnic groups, whether they arrive in our midst seeking refuge or send suicide bombers into the hearts of our cities. It may be, as some psychologists like to argue, that racial antipathies will never be eradicated from the human soul, but even if true, that realisation can't justify the active encouragement of xenophobia that runs through public discourse on matters such as the accommodation of political refugees.

The lamentable proposition that racism may not be curable returns us to Machiavelli's view of the corruptibility of human nature. If we are all potentially liars and cheats, easily controlled through the irrational fears instilled in us by those in positions of power, if nobody is truly altruistic and everybody has their price, then are we not doomed to live the embattled lives of beasts? A tenacious undercurrent in western philosophy takes much this view, from Thomas Hobbes' conception of human affairs as a 'war of all against all', to Arthur Schopenhauer's biologistic vision of the world in terms of the rapacity of ruthless nature, in which our own species is as inextricably implicated as the anaconda is. A crucial nuance that this bitterly pessimistic view seems to miss, however, is that it is possible – even if our spiritual corruption is ultimately inescapable – to behave as though it weren't. The most cynical exercise in manipulating public sympathies may result in substantial material relief being delivered to the malnourished. An encampment of economic migrants may suddenly appear less of a social hazard when we are told the story of one particular family's determination to risk everything to join our society. But above and beyond these almost accidental assuagements of our scepticism is the heroism of those who deliver groceries to the house-bound elderly, run helplines for the mentally ill, nurse the sick and decrepit, offer support to victims of harassment, intervene to protect those on the receiving end of domestic violence, make anonymous donations to the homeless, assist others to mount legal challenges against official persecution, forge documents to allow the hunted to escape from predatory regimes, lead campaigns against injustice that haven't a hope of changing the law, and many another act of unrewarded nobility. Machiavelli may have persuaded the Duke of Urbino that you can safely bet against humanity's better nature, much as Iago persuades Othello, or Mephistopheles persuades Faust, but precisely because it does seem such a plausible bet, the occasions on which humans behave in ways that may be described as good seem expressive of our innate potential. By the same token, when free elections are finally held after the fall of a repressive government, it is often the most idealistic politicians who find favour with the electorate.

What these exceptional occasions involve is the overcoming of fear – fear of the consequences of contravening the rules, but also fear of the ridicule that still attends those who try. To see that the social and cultural system under which we live has set out to make us afraid is to sense the first stirring of indignation that may one day enable us to laugh in its face. Much as fear prevented any real understanding of the gods we had invented, because we were too scared to see we had invented them, so at the social extremes it inhibits contact with the very people we should most urgently be squaring up to – our enemies, real or imagined.

3

I AM AFRAID

Little Prince Fritz of Prussia, born to King Friedrich Wilhelm and his Queen Sophia Dorothea in 1712, was introduced early to the requirements of royal duty. His father, architect of Prussia's first national army, was a firm believer in the military ethos. Friedrich Wilhelm did his best to live the hard, spare, unforgiving life of the model soldier, surviving on a frugal diet, dispensing with unneessary domestic staff, and remaining sexually continent to his second-choice wife (his favourite, Princess Caroline of Brandenburg-Ansbach had married his despised cousin, George II of England). Queen Sophia lived life at the opposite extreme, to the extent that her disapproving husband allowed, gossiping and gambling, permanently twittering in French as though it were the *dernier cri* of sophistication. She also enjoyed the kind of robust health that was to enable her to survive fourteen pregnancies, the twelfth of which, in 1723, caught everybody – including herself – unawares. One day she was feeling a little achy and flatulent, as if sickening for a chill or having overdone it at dinner once again, and the next she had delivered the Brunswicks yet another supernumerary heir.

Young Friedrich, known in his infancy and later to his devoted subjects as Fritz, was the first surviving male child. Virtually from the cradle, he was brought up at his father's insistence as a true son of what was perhaps – until the advent of Napoleon Bonaparte at least – Europe's most militaristic state. He was woken each morning with a reveille of cannon fire. Having attained his officer's majority at the age of six, he was given his first command, a platoon of kiddie cadets whom he was expected to drill and condition to the very same discipline to which he had been born. At seven, he was trained in the use of weaponry, and it was soon after this that the terrible punishments began. His father believed sincerely, as has many a sergeant major since, in the efficacy of public humiliation. Fritz was thrashed at regular intervals, for appearing surly during instruction, for being so unmanly as to allow himself to be thrown from a bolting horse, and for the lily-livered mannerisms that he may have picked up from his permissive mother. Mincing around lisping in French was bad enough, but when Friedrich Wilhelm came across his son actually wearing a pair of gloves on a bitingly cold day, the beating meted out was especially merciless. How could the destiny of the sovereign Prussian people be one day entrusted to such a milksop? However, the remedy lay at hand – quite literally – and if his father seemed to lay it on a bit thick, it was in the ultimate interests of a boy who would one day carry the eagle standard aloft into a radiant future.

It wasn't just the gloves and the French, though. There was a worrying feyness to the boy's manner, a soupçon of Gallic simper behind the pantomimed parade-ground belligerence. What we would now think of as homophobic taunts crept into the repertoire of belittlement visited on the still pre-pubescent Fritz. At the age of twelve he was subjected to a particularly violent and apparently unprovoked assault. The sarcastic pinching of his cheeks with which it began turned to ear-boxing, hair-wrenching and then punching. Perhaps it was the very stoicism under fire in which the boy had been trained that tipped the king towards apoplexy, but before the transfixed gaze of his chief minister, von Grumbkov, he resorted to smashing plates in his drooling fury. The hapless Grumbkov did his best to pretend that the ghastly scene was the result of high spirits occasioned by manly over-indulgence in brandy. Thinking to alleviate the king's subsequent embarrassment, he managed to fling the odd bit of eggshell china at the walls himself, as though to lend the occasion the air of an all-boys-together, barrack-room drinking bout. Fritz can't have been fooled for a moment.

The situation was given a particular piquancy by the fact that the king doted on one of Fritz's younger brothers, August Wilhelm, who was ten years his junior. Without appearing to have any intrinsic qualities to merit them, the boy rapidly became the object of his father's extravagant affections. Just as Fritz was having accusations of effeminacy heaped upon him (he had even taken up the flute now, as if there weren't other evidence enough), August was the dubious beneficiary of extraordinary displays of physical affection, in the form of showers of paternal kisses that might take fully fifteen minutes to subside. Meanwhile, the jealous Sophia, bored and resentful of the silly privations being visited on her in the name of a Spartan self-restraint, which included the indignity of having to wash up as there were now so few servants, took to amusing herself by egging the children on to annoy their father. Aware of just how rancorous his rages could be, she set up an arrangement of screens in the drawing room, behind which the children would hide once their whinging had brought on another explosion of plate-smashing rage.

The violence was occasionally interspersed with what modern psychology would call 'fugues' – periods of listless melancholy. While his children and attendants nursed broken noses and coughed out shattered teeth, Friedrich Wilhelm would descend into an almost cataleptic stupor, unable to speak to those around him, often sitting and quietly weeping for hour after hour. He seems to have been aware of the peculiar cruelty of his treatment of Fritz, yet his contempt for the boy only deepened at the fortitude with which his son bore the offences. Knocking the boy to the ground on a whim in polite company, the king observed that had he been treated so vilely by his own father, he would long since have killed himself. This was another indicator of his son's feebleness: no matter what degree of degradation he was subjected to, he lacked the basic courage to end it all.

Only when, at the age of eighteen, Fritz was severely roughed up by his father during a court visit to Sachsen, and then – having been dragged along the ground by his hair – sent off disarrayed and bleeding to an official engagement, did he finally plan his escape. He would leave the army and flee his dysfunctional family once and for all. Almost inevitably the scheme failed. The Palace got wind of it, and the king had his son imprisoned in the Küstrin fortress. His friend and supporter in the plot, a twenty-five-year-old lieutenant named Hans Hermann von Katte, was jailed with him. They were almost certainly lovers, and it must have been intolerable for Fritz to be forced to watch from the window of his prison cell when von Katte was decapitated. For a while, it seemed that the king would order his son's execution for desertion too, but in time he relented, and although he no doubt wished to find some way of signing over the inheritance of the throne to darling August, the threat was never carried out. The following year, at the age of nineteen, Fritz was married off to Elisabeth Christine von Brunswick-Bevern, a quiveringly plump, sixteen-year-old dimwit whose attempts to ingratiate herself with her unenthusiastic husband produced only an icy indifference.

Towards the end of his life, the king grew increasingly frail. Stricken with gout and horrendous intestinal pain, his weight increased relentlessly as he became less active. Despite his short stature, he weighed over 20 stone at the time of his death, and had to be wheeled about the palace in order to deliver his tireless fulminations against the useless brood he had somehow sired – always excepting the adored August. On 31 May 1740, he had himself wheeled into Sophia's bedchamber to announce that he was going to die that day and, ever the model of martial efficiency, did not let her down. Fritz succeeded to the throne, which he was to occupy for forty-six years, as Friedrich II, although he is better known to history as Frederick the Great.

In the world of contemporary clinical psychology it would be readily accepted that someone subjected to such a childhood could not help but be more or less seriously disturbed in later life. Yet the fascinating aspect of Frederick's biography is that his achievements as a monarch were so impressive. Although Prussia had been declared a kingdom as recently as 1701, and Frederick was only its third ruler, and still something of a parvenu among European royalty, it was under his reign that the country at last became a force to be reckoned with. He upheld the martial ethos that had been dinned into him as a boy, intervening profitably in the Austrian war of succession within months of acceding to the throne, and was the driving force behind the transformation of Prussia, from an agglomeration of largely agrarian lands expropriated from the monasteries after the Reformation, into the most formidable state in continental Europe. His image as the great unifier of the Teutonic peoples remained untarnished until German military adventurism in the late nineteenth century started to make the notion of a powerful Germany seem less desirable. Adolf Hitler took a portrait of Frederick the Great with him into the Berlin bunker in 1945, and it could be said that it was only in this last redoubt that the surging nationalism fomented by Frederick two hundred years earlier finally expired.

To grow up in a climate of relentless intimidation can have two seemingly contradictory effects. It can breed in mentally strong individuals a determination not to be cowed by it, and to that defiance can be attributed some of the statesmanlike glory with which Frederick was to cover himself. He also displayed considerable aesthetic sensibility. He and Voltaire maintained a famous correspondence, in which philosophical issues of the day were explored, for many years. As well as producing seminal tracts on military strategy, he wrote music throughout his life. A contemporary remarked that the king was as much at home composing an aria as he was directing a military campaign, and he was considered by those who heard him to have been a proficient, if not quite outstanding, flautist – although the expressiveness of his playing of slow movements was highly regarded, the liberty he took with the quicker passages was a little presumptuous.

Beneath the glory and the refinement of his public persona, though, darker forces held sway. Frederick grew increasingly prone, as he aged, to irrational fears and aversions. It is said that he had an unreasoning dislike for new items of clothing, particularly new uniforms, perhaps fearing that he became somehow less himself when he put them on. In this can be read the precarious foundations on which his adult identity had been forged. Even his marriage had a sense of the perfunctory about it, doubtless as a result of his uncertain sexuality. It is a feature of people who have had painstakingly to construct themselves in the face of a difficult upbringing that they tend to be consolidators, rather than risk-takers. As each success in life is attained, the temptation to rest on one's laurels for fear of falling back down again is very strong. Sudden radical change is experienced as too much of a shock to the psyche, and the conservative impulse may manifest itself in the most apparently insignificant aspects of one's life. To Frederick, the fear of losing his reputation, and thereby proving his tyrannical father right after all, was ever-present. And so to be attired in a new suit of clothes, to be aware of the unfamiliar contours, the lack of give, in a new uniform, was an episode of considerable torment. Could the strange new figure in the glass, bracing and relaxing the epauletted shoulders of a tunic, taking tentative steps in ominously creaking boots, be once more remade as himself? And how many more remakings might he be required to undergo?

More peculiarly still, he developed in later life a pathological fear of water. To have bowls of it slopping near him became an unendurable torment, the thought of bathing too appalling to contemplate. His servants devised a system for 'washing' him that involved sanding him down with dry towels impregnated with cologne or Spanish snuff. It may have been an imperfect recourse, and yet it was infinitely preferable to feeling that wetness trickling, without control, over his hypersensitive skin. A phobia about water is indeed a disabling species of irrational fear, and had he not been born to privilege, Frederick would have become an increasingly pathetic, pungently begrimed figure.

Psychologist Dr Isaac Marks, one of the world's leading theorists of fear and anxiety, believes that phobias are largely learned behaviour. There is a significant environmental factor at work, so that an overt fear suffered by a parent will often be passed on to at least one child. In addition to this, a childhood blighted by parental intimidation, for all that it may stop well short of actual violence, is a natural breeding ground for the kinds of unmanageable anxieties that will survive the passage to adulthood. Associations of ideas play a strong part, so that a child who had the backs of her legs soundly slapped in public may come to have a consuming fear, not of being slapped, but of the coat buttons that her face was mashed into while the chastisement was administered. She will choose garments with zips and press studs, perhaps without ever working out precisely why. Robert Graves had a fear of telephones because he happened to be taking a call when a bomb exploded in the neighbourhood during wartime. Some phobias are tactile rather than visual, so that the texture of cotton wool or the feel of soft jelly or aspic in the mouth might be harbingers of shuddering revulsion.

In chronic specific phobia, a condition that affects around 4.5 per cent of the population of the United States, we see fear reduced to its essence, a noxiously concentrated element that is doubly troubling because it is so irrational. At least when fear is directed towards a supreme being, or when it acts as the warden of our social habitat, we can see the point of it. A phobia is gratuitous, passive fear, one that feeds on itself and seems to have the power to grow far more readily than it can be subsumed. It is no use telling people who go into shock at the sight of a spider that the creature is more afraid of them than they are of it. This certain knowledge does nothing to soften the impact of unexpectedly seeing one scamper across the carpet.

Where do phobias come from? Dr Marks points out that, by and large, they are as much subject to the sedate rhythms of evolutionary development as our physical transformation from the lower primates has been. If certain phenomena appear to act as lightning conductors for phobic fear while others don't – so that one may have a phobia of snakes, but not one of, say, plastic bottles – then this is because these are the kinds of phenomena we had to learn to fear when we lived in hazardous natural environments. For all that there are instances of such phobias as enetophobia (pins) or pediophobia (dolls), most are based on organic stimuli. The paradox is that while we give in to irrational fears of snakes or sharks (where the statistical risk of meeting one in everyday life is minimal), we are nonetheless heedless of the threats that more realistically stalk us at every turn – when we drive too fast, have unsafe sex, eat the wrong foods, smoke twenty cigarettes a day. Even when we are concerned about such risks, they very rarely amount to full-blown phobia, with all its obsessiveness and disruptive power. 'We have been selected,' says Marks, 'to have nervous systems responding to dangers that were common in the past, not to evolutionarily new threats.' The point is a valid one, and yet it doesn't seem to take us very far.

This is perhaps because Marks lays insufficient stress on the complexity of our emotional state when under phobic assault. Phobia isn't simply about fear alone, not even the most heightened state of terror. It also involves a strong sensation of disgust, of revulsion, and the state of panic that arises from being reminded so forcibly that the external world is beyond our control. The good news is that much phobia appears to be treatable by exposure therapy, in which the patient is gradually introduced, in a controlled environment, to images and then real examples of the object of fear, until even its sudden appearance in normal circumstances loses the power to shock. But it doesn't always work. And does such treatment address the phenomenon that underlies all irrational fear, even the non-phobic kind – namely our capacity as sentient beings to find something to be frightened of, even where the need for fear is absent?

Marks's case histories include people who go to extraordinary lengths to construct evasion strategies so as not to have to handle food, touch their own hair or see pigeons in the course of their day-to-day lives, and we may justly acknowledge as a medical achievement every triumph over conditions as debilitating as these. He refers to the research that has established that 'the exposure approach works in most cases', leaving us with a residue of cases in which it fails. What constitutes success may itself be quite difficult to pin down. One woman's fear of dogs was cured after two sessions, whereas others may find that months of controlled exposure barely scratches the surface. For some subjects, the reduction of phobic fear to a state of mere tension, all muscles clenched but the gaze steady and the breathing even, may be landmark enough. It isn't clear whether the phobias that respond most readily to exposure were generally the mildest ones, but even if the most severe cases don't appear to be alleviated easily, that is presumably no reason not to persevere. The element of time is crucial, says Marks – both overall, and within each episode of exposure. It is incumbent on the sufferer who wishes to get better not just to confront the loathed object, but to contemplate it at length, to scrutinise and study it until the symptoms of fear are gradually deadened. In this way, 'the great majority of people who allow themselves to experience extreme panic eventually become unable to experience more than mild fear'.

There is an ambiguity in Marks's treatment and analysis of phobia and anxiety disorders. It is the question of whether fear is really being defeated, or rather constructively accommodated. And here we might think of President Roosevelt. Is it not the fear itself, the sensation of suddenly being pitched into panic at the un-expected appearance of a dog – and not the idea of the dog itself – that is being treated? The woman 'cured' after two sessions may not have discovered a willingness to have every passing spaniel leap up against her, panting its pet-foody breath all over her, licking her face and simulating sexual intercourse against her leg, but she may have come to realise that the continuing distaste she feels at such a prospect is something she can deal with, rather than dread. In other words, when considering whether negative emotions can be sur-mounted (that is, whether it is possible by mental discipline to arrive at a state in which fear or jealousy are banished from our lives), it is in the trade-off between the unconquerable nature of these emotions and the disposition that comes from accommodat-ing them, that there lies the best chance of the reconciled life that psychologists say we should seek. It may be good to conquer an irrational fear, but not so good to keep trying and failing, subject-ing oneself to serial panic attacks in the process. What if an evasion strategy works? The Dutch international footballer Dennis Bergkamp cannot conquer his morbid fear of air travel, and although his employers, Arsenal Football Club, might wish it otherwise, he has found that a life of rail and boat journeys makes for greater psychological health than repeatedly subjecting himself to torment in a fruitless attempt to face down the phobia. To a therapist like Dr Marks, this is the sad case of a man unable, despite his ample resources, to learn to master his emotions. Bergkamp's answer would no doubt be that he has mastered the fear – by cut-ting that which causes it out of his life.

Many of the traditional moral virtues may be conceived as existing in antithesis to the negative emotions, as a means of overcoming them. In the case of fear, it is courage that we are enjoined to. Fear may have a clear evolutionary utility, in the sense that it once taught us a proper respect for predatory animals, but when the feeling of fear expands cognitively from the self-preserving caution required on the hunt, to an unreasoning and intractable dread of such situations even when they are not immediately present, then a code of conduct for facing it down becomes useful. It is when that code of conduct itself becomes an ideological imperative that a sort of vicious circle closes around the mind. Acts of gratuitous bravery become a badge of honour, while the thing to be feared continues to strike the same old terror into one's heart. How does a boy whose father assaulted and humiliated him with no other motivation than to demonstrate his own authority come to lead troops into battle, slashing at the enemy with a sword, while being unable in the privacy of his toilette to bear the sensation of a saturated sponge against his skin? It is precisely by striving towards a virtue such as courage that some of our most deep-rooted and insoluble psychological problems come to prey upon us. Finding ourselves incapable of attaining the required virtue, we may become morbidly obsessed with what the failure to do so suggests. An inability, or unwillingness, to acknowledge fear may find its outlet in the pursuit of dangerous sports. Such activities may seem to be about demonstrating bravery, but these more containable versions of terror inevitably prevent us from bringing about our best chance of coping with (as opposed to vanquishing) fear – by seeking emotional solidarity, and thus avoiding any of the more traumatic recourses to which fear might drive us, in the form of excessive use of intoxicants, or violence towards others or against oneself. A good proportion of phobia sufferers who undergo therapy gain enormous relief simply from discovering that the world is full of people who can't bear the thought of dizzying heights or dental treatment. Comparing notes is therapy in itself.

There is a name – arachibutyrophobia – for the phobic fear of getting peanut butter stuck to the roof of one's mouth. And there is a concomitant choice between spending money on therapy to rid oneself of it, and saving on both mental anguish and cash by not buying peanut butter.

ANGER

Anger makes dull men witty, but it keeps them poor.
Elizabeth I

1. That which pains or afflicts, or the feeling which it produces; trouble, vexation, sorrow. 2. The active feeling provoked against the agent; passion, rage; wrath, ire. 3. Inflammatory state of any part of the body; physical pain.

Darwin's physical indicators: increased heart rate; facial flushing; contraction of the pupils; opening wide of the eyes; flashing of the eyes; accelerated breathing; flaring of the nostrils; compression of the lips; frowning; holding of the head erect; expansion of the chest; squaring of the elbows; clenching of the fists; vasculation in the forehead and neck; inclination forwards of the body towards the offender; clenching or grinding of the teeth; gesticulation of the arms; harsh vocalisation; aphasia; rapid, agitated speaking; frothing at the mouth; retraction of the lips, sometimes exposing the canine tooth on one side.

4

TO BE ANGRY

When fear and intimidation are felt persistently, they may turn to anger. This is revealed in the etymology of the word, where it is shown that initially an 'anger' was, much like a 'fear', perceived as a phenomenon in the external world that impacted on the hapless human subject. An anger grieved and troubled one, was the cause of vexatious sorrow and despair, until it roused one into a state of something like madness or demonic possession, at which point it becomes the emotion we recognise today, as the 'active feeling' provoked by that source of grievance. The Old Norse word *angr* is the root of both *anger* and *anguish*, in both of which a residue of its semantic origins in grief has precipitated. If we see fear as primarily a passive state, anger is very much a driving, compulsive force that encourages action of one sort or another. It is that access of passion into which sustained provocation impels one, and for which we have long since come to apply the metaphorical concepts of 'rage' and 'fury', referring as they do originally to the delirium of extreme mental states. Anger is also possessed of a dual psychosomatic value, so that, as the dictionary notes, it can also characterise a lesion on the skin. Goose-pimpled skin is not described as 'frightened', but a sore or scar can (perhaps a little archaically now) be referred to as 'angry'. This traffic runs in both directions: the descriptor for the precise colour of a bruise, that purplish-blue known technically as 'livid', is now also applicable to a state of intense rage, probably because the coloration of the face during high blood pressure suggests something of the mass of broken blood vessels that constitutes a bruise.

The moral status of anger as an emotion insists that to be angry is also somehow to be ill, to have sickened from an excess of vexation. The concept of anger management therapy confirms this. In one of the more astringently honest espousals of rage in the post-punk period, Howard Devoto opens a song by declaring, 'I am angry, I am ill, and I'm as ugly as sin.' There is perhaps ambiguity in our philosophical attitude to rage, a belief that to boil over with rage is a sign that indignation has been stifled for too long. But we also see anger as an indication that an individual has momentarily lost his grip on his emotions, which will surely prove capable of being checked just as promptly. Whatever the circumstances leading up to such a loss of control, however, it is generally felt that anger is an acute, brief, flaring emotion, whereas fear can, in the worst of its influence, persist morbidly for years.

A recent theorist of anger, the Los Angeles social psychologist Carol Tavris, makes a case for anger as having both mental and physical causes and effects. This, Tavris believes, is reflected in the fact that its genesis may arise in either the limbic or neocortical segments of the brain; the former is usually held to be the site of the emotions and the irrational impulses, while the latter houses the rationalising intellect. She suggests that anger can be as much the product of a period of logical cogitation, perhaps arising from mulling over the compelling evidence of our being passed over for preferment at work, as it can be a spontaneously erupting fury, requiring only the flagrant lack of compliance of some inanimate object with our will (the key that won't turn in the lock when our arms are laden down with shopping bags). Modern neurological findings support this contention, and provide belated verification of the theory already advanced in the fifth century BC by Plato, who argues in *The Republic* and the *Timaeus*, that the human soul is composed of three interconnecting elements – reason, the appetites and the passions. We know that the passions, which include anger, must be a discrete third category because they are capable of opposing themselves to either the intellect or the desires. In the dialogue of *The Republic*, Plato has Socrates remind his interlocutor Glaucon of the story of the warrior Leontion, who cannot resist taking a closer look at the corpses of some freshly executed malefactors, despite the fact that he knows the sight will appal him. His passions, in the form of indignation, reprove his prurient desire to see the dead bodies. By the same token, the rational faculties can come into conflict with the passions too, as is evidenced in classical literature when Homer has Odysseus strike himself on the chest at a moment of distress and call his heart to order. The heart, according to the Platonic scheme, is where the passions are located. We may now have transferred them to the brain, but not – as Tavris is at pains to establish – to any particular part of it, since both hemispheres turn out to be multi-functional in their influences on our feelings. (As though to provide further evidence of the separate actions of reason and emotion, Plato is said once to have handed over a disobedient slave to his associate Speucippus for physical chastisement, apologising the while that he could not undertake the matter himself, since he was too angry.)

There is a belief common to early and more recent literature, along with first Stoic and then Christian ethical thinkers, that anger demeans to the extent that it reduces the one who feels it to the level of bestiality – that is, that it causes a loss of control. Both Michel de Montaigne and Robert Burton, discussing anger around the turn of the seventeenth century, cite the same passage from Ovid, in which the countenance of the angered is compared to that of the petrifying power of the Medusa:

With anger faces swollen show,
The veins turn black with rush of blood,
The eyes with Gorgon fires aglow.

The angry are, as Burton has it, 'void of reason, inexorable, blind, like beasts & monsters for the time, say and do they know not what, curse, swear, rail, fight, and what not?' If reason is to have any purchase at all on rage, Burton tells us, it must await the ebbing of its first full spate, but in any case, those who give way to fits of wrath immoderate in their intensity or duration, or who yield to such tempers frequently, can only expect to decline into permanent mental perturbation, or that enduring melancholy of which he is the master anatomist. Burton differs greatly from Montaigne, who seems to anticipate Freud with his avowal that we endanger our mental health by suppressing our anger. 'I would rather make an exhibition of my passions,' he vouchsafes, 'than brood over them to my cost: express them, vent them, and they grow weaker.' Today's anger management counsellor, handing out foam rubber batons to her inwardly seething clients, can add little in the way of amplification to this proposal.

By the time of the Victorian era, it was possible to see the role of anger in human affairs as considerably more benign than Burton would allow. In the 1840s, Cardinal Henry Manning, Roman Catholic prelate, sometime Oxford don and Archbishop of Westminster, asserted that 'Anger is the executive power of justice', indicating that its role in the righting of wrongs was too constructive to be denied, a point that was starting to be intimated in the social arena as well as in the personal.

If fear may be held to be the principal social adhesive, then anger – when felt collectively – is more of a dissolvent. Its most concrete form is not the planned insurrection, but that more carnivalesque explosion of social disorder, the riot. When people gather to protest at a perceived injustice, and find the authorities immovable, or the police bent on keeping them away from any place where their cries of indignation may be heard, the mere fact of their numbers may have an incendiary effect. Numerical force can serve to release whatever inhibition each individual may feel, and the physical expression of rage is thereby not only facilitated, but sustained as well. Within the crowd, a citizen feels protected. Exactly who threw the first brick may never be known, but once a hail of them is flying, it will likely be impossible to identify the throwers from those who are only shouting. It is presumably for this reason that police forces often resort to making random arrests of anybody once a scene of protest becomes an affray. It is also why the Riot Act of 1715 makes it a criminal liability merely to be part of an unruly company once the order to be gone has been given.

The 1840s were a relatively pacific period in British history, notwithstanding continued metropolitan and rural poverty and the unruffled persistence of class privilege at a time when the average life expectancy of a male labourer in Manchester was fifteen. Despite these privations, the causes of such popular anger as was expressed are strange indeed. Changes to the Church of England liturgy introduced at a time when the attitudes of urban congregations had largely stripped it of its formality had not gone down well. The principal item of reform had been to place the sermon at an earlier stage in the order of service than the Intercession and the Communion. During his sermon, an officiating priest of the Church of England speaks to his flock as a private member of the faith (since the interpretation of scripture is a matter of individual conscience rather than ecclesiastical ruling), whereas during the dispensation of the bread and wine, and the prayers, he is acting as a minister of God. The outward symbol of this change of role is the surplice, the white covering that he wears over his vestments when acting in the latter capacity, and which he would remove in order to deliver the sermon.

The restructuring of the service necessitated not one costume change but two, with the priest now required to enter in white, disrobe to black for the pulpit, and then return to white for the Communion. An acolyte was on hand whose specific purpose was to help him on and off with his surplice, as the order of events demanded. To the congregation, schooled in that distrust of ceremonial that marked the Protestant liturgy from the Roman Catholic Mass, this successive removal and re-affectation of the surplice looked suspiciously like a partial return to high ritualism. For all they knew, it might prove to be the thin end of a reformist wedge that began with asking you amiably enough not to stick your wet umbrella in the font on arrival, but would then proceed, via ceremonial flummery such as this, to Mariolatry and the Vatican. Now metropolitan congregations let it be known that they didn't much care for this extraneous bit of nonsense with the surplice, but the Church stood firm. Sporadic outbreaks of civil unrest occurred, some of them of a ferocity to mandate the public reading of the Riot Act by the local magistrate. Demonstrations outside churches where the vicar had adopted the new dress code turned ugly. At St Barnabas's in Chelsea, the protesting crowds grew large enough to block the public highway. Horses bridled and whinnied among the shouting, jostling crowds as the magistrate's unheeded verbal orders to disperse were followed up by the use of batons.

At the root of expressions of collective anger such as these is always some form of hatred, which, when it issues in public disorder, is afforded a palpable sense of release. The release may only be temporary, however. If the corrupt president or the hated tax remains in place after the affray, as the protesters are taken into custody or retreat to nurse their wounds, a further accumulation of anger is the inevitable result. In Bucharest in 1989, shortly before the fall of the Ceauşescus, crowds that had been drilled to participate in another mass rally in support of their continuation in office found themselves suddenly rediscovering their real voices. A lifetime of loyally chanting the prescribed slogans was overturned in an instant, as jeers began to emerge from their throats, and the couple on the balcony was treated to the sight below of boots being stuffed through the images of their own faces. As Ceauşescus stammered in confusion at the microphone, his wife Elena was heard to hiss at him from the open windows behind, 'Quick! Offer them something. Promise them something.' It was much too late, of course, by then, but even though public disorder had hardly been common in Stalinist Romania, Elena Ceauşescus's instinct was sound enough. Once a crowd turns violent in its anger, there is only so much that state repression can do to bridle it. Either that, or sufficient violence and force must be applied, as in the British imperial massacre at Amritsar or the arrival of the tanks in Tiananmen Square, to dissuade any repeat expression of discontent. However symbolic or grudging the gesture, something must be done to assuage it. Much political change in western – and specifically British – history has been achieved by these means, and although the official line may be that the authorities don't give in to such blackmail, the reality is that, perhaps after some suitable interval, they very often do. Would women have waited longer for the franchise had it not been for the militancy of the suffragette movement? The official version is that it was women's efforts, and their passive suffering, during the Great War that swung the question, but the prelude of smashed windows, hunger strikes and burning rags dropped in pillar boxes established the urgency of the matter. The London poll tax riots of 1990 did not in themselves lead to the abolition of the community charge, but they acted as a decisive lightning conductor for dissent when the Prime Minister who had overseen its introduction was unseated. Each of the candidates nominated to replace her included in his personal manifesto a commitment to find a way of repealing it.

To a certain kind of social psychologist, expressions of public anger can only be healthy. Indeed, they don't even need to occur in the context of a crowd. Andrea Dworkin complains that women are still in a general way too nice to men, given the centuries of patriarchal oppression they have suffered, which is no less forgivable in the modern era for having become more insidious. Elizabeth Friar Williams argued in 1976 that if you don't let your anger out, it would be channelled into such symptomatic disorders as tension headaches, irritable skin, overeating or alcohol dependency. Reflecting on her own childhood misdemeanours, she tells us:

Although I was in many respects a normally nasty little girl, I always felt extremely guilty about my bad temper and 'selfish' behavior. Only recently have I been able to experience my average nasty self without feeling that I must produce, along with the awareness of my hostility, punishments such as headaches, rashes, and fatness.

This kind of therapy, self-legitimising in its assertion of the emotionally incontinent ego, may appear to have freed many women (and men) from the crippling delimitations of social restraint. But the cost of this emancipation might be a society of people so utterly unable to contain their fury at the world, and so possessed of a belief that nobody else had the right to make them contain it, that it becomes incapable of living with itself. It should be noted that the therapeutic practice of emotional catharsis fashionable in the 1970s (screaming, shouting and letting it all hang out) not only did little to reconcile its proponents to living in an unjust society, it also failed to diminish the incidence of headaches, rashes and fatness.

In some cultural contexts, the expression of anger is shameful, a public acknowledgement that one has surrendered to the animal passions raging within and lost control. Where survival itself is at stake, anger is a luxury that can be ill afforded. A nomadic group such as the !Kung bushmen of the Kalahari, dependent on hunting and foraging in a pitiless environment, know that their survival as a race relies crucially on co-operation at all levels, between the sexes and among the generations. Their social mores have evolved to the extent that when resentments flare up, they are quickly stifled by onlookers, and subsequently resolved through tribal discussion. To these people, anger is not some joyous release, a procedure by which the cowed individual asserts herself. It is a dismaying and nauseating calamity. Anger has not been abolished among the !Kung, although it is instructively rare, but it has become amalgamated into a powerful circuitry of self-restraint and social support, so that its destructive potential does not harm the collaborative cohesion of the group. The Inuit people resolve their disputes by resorting to singing duels, in which the two protagonists in an argument trade melodic insults in front of their companions, until the relative heartiness of the audience's laughter determines who has prevailed. On the way to this result, however, much merriment has been provoked, and the hostilities thereby abated. It is clear then that neither the !Kung nor the Inuit subscribe to the model of anger as a momentary flashpoint, feeling instead that if it is not drawn off in some way, it will continue to fester. There has to be some therapeutic or ritualistic practice to neutralise it, and framing it in this way diminishes the spontaneity and therefore the heat of it. In the Looking-Glass wood, Alice is fascinated to find herself helping the warring twins Tweedledum and Tweedledee to gird themselves for a ritual battle that each feels must be fought, for all that the absurdity of it progressively diminishes the impact of Tweedledum's first eruption at the broken rattle.

Japanese culture has been marked for many centuries by an etiquette of self-control. A samurai warrior might have been entitled to dispatch with one stroke of his sword any peasant who didn't bow humbly enough at his passing, but in civil society expressions of anger, however fleeting, had no place. In fact, many East Asian societies, including the Chinese, Vietnamese and Korean, are characterised by attitudes of forbearance in the face of extreme provocation or privations. The culture of quiescence in

Japanese society is older even than the medieval chivalric tradition in Europe. We find it expressed at eloquent length in the eleventh-century prose epic, *The Tale of Genji*, written by a court lady, Murasaki Shikibu. Early in the narrative, the youthful hero Genji, an emperor's favoured son, discusses with his cousin To no Chujo, what qualities are most seemly in a woman, and they agree without difficulty that a forgiving nature is best. 'She should be quiet and generous, and when something comes up that quite properly arouses her resentment she should make it known by delicate hints. The man will feel guilty and with tactful guidance he will mend his ways.' His cousin concurs, and in doing so, makes the point a matter of ethical moment.

It may be difficult when someone you are especially fond of, someone beautiful and charming, has been guilty of an indiscretion, but magnanimity produces wonders. They may not always work, but generosity and reasonableness and patience do on the whole seem best.

To this day in Japan, displeasure at a slight is often marked by smiling at the offender, as if to indicate the exercise of self-control that a hostile word or attitude properly calls forth. For the offended party to manifest anger, through facial expression or a raised voice, would denote that his self-discipline and manners had failed him.

If we turn back to the Britain of the early nineteenth century, and those crowds provoked by what the vicar was wearing, we are struck by an inevitable sense of dislocation between the disorderly public expression of rancour and the codes of social *politesse* that it disrupted. That cultivation of reserve that we often – wrongly – think of as the creation of the Victorian era had in fact already been embedded in Georgian society in the previous century. It was during the reign of George III that the British came to define themselves by their restraint in social manners, an attribute usefully at odds with the fiery, even hysterical temperaments of southern Europeans. Plain and honest dealing, the even vocal tone, an elaborate system of courtesies under which nobody wished to appear to be jostling for pre-eminence ('After you', 'No no, good sir, after you'), and most importantly, the withdrawal of emotional display into the private arena, all come to fruition in the later eighteenth century. By the time of Victoria's accession, these were the recognised modes of British – and especially English – public interaction, as Paul Langford has demonstrated:

Gentility was central to the character that emerged in the eighteenth and nineteenth centuries. Without the English gentleman and lady the idea of the Englishman and Englishwoman would not have been the same ... [I]ts peculiar appeal and function depended much on its social adaptability ... As that most self-consciously genteel of authors, Bulwer-Lytton, remarked, 'From the petty droppings of the well of manners, the fossilised incrustations of national character are formed.'

There was even a distinct conversational style that would sound quite alien to, and indeed be hopelessly beyond the capabilities of, the modern British. Drawing room or after-dinner talk proceeded not altogether differently from the way it is represented in the literature of the period. Exchanges between a country parson and his daughters sitting down to supper in the evening might well sound fascinatingly close to the dialogue of the Brontës. Acquaintances happening upon each other by chance in the street would strike up a formal colloquy that would proceed at stately length, completely at odds with the snatched updates we make do with today. G M Young, in his intricately detailed anatomy of Victorian society, *Portrait of an Age* (1936), dates the change in conversational habits to around the 1850s. After this time, conversation ceased to be a cultivable art and turned into something more sparely functional, the quickest means of imparting germane pieces of news, as the pace of living accelerated alongside developments in the modes of transport. If time was money, and progress, to quote Young's glittering aphorism, was now less an aspiration than a schedule, then pausing to chat came to seem something of a luxury. What then remained of the conversational art was finally and famously, according to one of the most enduring axioms of twentieth-century society, exterminated by television.

Many of Dickens's characters appear poised in the painful transition between the one mode and the other. In a society where entrepreneurial industrialists are dictating the rate of social change, and redesigning the urban landscape into the bargain, a figure like Mr Micawber can only imitate what appears to be the prevailing tone. There is the need to have some sort of plan in life, he realises, as well as some sort of audit of its success, expressible in the debit and credit terms of the accountant's ledger. But then there is his paralysed mystification at why other people's schemes work and his don't, from which the only refuge is a random providence ('Something will turn up'), mystifying in itself for its continual failure to provide. Micawber's philosophical dilatations belong to an age before the world speeded up, but the earnest appearance of business acumen he feels he must display is of the era of the careering freight train and the penny post. To the implicitly believing Mrs Micawber, by contrast, something really will – and does – turn up eventually, like spring sunshine after the frost.

The explanation for the feeling of disjunction we register on reading about riots in the streets over matters as parochial as the vicar's vestments, in an era when courtesy and restraint were something approaching a national duty, is to be found in the schism that economic progress wrought in a society fleeing *en masse* from rural ways of living into the big urban centres. It lies in the feeling that the forces that shaped one's destiny in this period were growing increasingly remote and opaque, and in the parlous mental and physical conditions that mass production in the factories bequeathed to those who worked in them. In short, Victorian anger stemmed from a growing intolerance of inequality. Public disorder tends to be a class phenomenon, and the working classes were not bound by the rules of social engagement that the ascendant bourgeoisie had taken upon themselves. They also had more to gain – certainly less to lose – from making their feelings so fractiously known. The suppression of anger in pursuit of the higher social graces was as much second nature to bourgeois Victorian manners as it was to the philosophical Genji, but by the industrialising nineteenth century, that need to keep the lid on it is more about maintaining equilibrium in a disastrously unfair society than it is about becoming a better human being.

Ultimately, we do the participants in spontaneous riots a disservice if we try to localise the cause of their anger to one specific point. On the evening of Friday, 13 August 1965, in a black neighbourhood in south central Los Angeles, a member of the then all-white LAPD flagged down a car that was being driven in an erratic fashion at around 15 mph above the speed limit. Its driver was a twenty-one-year-old black man called Marquette Frye, who was taking himself home from a friend's house. It became obvious that Frye was under the influence of the vodka he had drunk before getting behind the wheel. Under questioning at the roadside, he tried to make light of the situation by persuading the officer that it wasn't worth his time and effort arresting him, and the good-natured banter attracted a crowd of onlookers. When the officer, fearing a drunk black driver might become violent, called for back-up, the situation rapidly deteriorated. As Frye was put under arrest, he began to struggle, defiantly shouting that the police would have to kill him if they wanted to put him in jail. A gasp went through the crowd, and as he was pushed into the squad car, they began jeering and spitting at the police officers, calling them 'blue-eyed devils'. The police responded by making more arrests, all of which met with vigorous physical resistance. Once the police cars were full of arrestees, they pulled away through the baying crowd, and as they disappeared around the street corner somebody – Stephanie Griest's paper on the incident identifies him as a nineteen-year-old named Gabriel Pope – smashed a bottle on the ground. This single shatter lit the fuse. Within seconds, everybody had grabbed a weapon, and the neighbourhood was being reduced to splinters and ashes.

The Watts riot was, at least until the rioting following the Rodney King verdict in April 1992, the most spectacular exhibition of racially aggravated unrest that urban America had ever seen. It proceeded with cars being overturned and shop windows smashed, and escalated over the ensuing days to looting and arson. Apartments were broken into and ransacked, business premises were attacked and churches desecrated, all of them belonging to white people. Black property was left largely untouched. When it is said of the Watts riot in particular that inner-city rioting is self-defeating because it only destroys the perpetrators' own environment, a major point is being missed. The enforcement effort needed to contain the upheaval eventually amounted to a force of 16,000 – officers of the LAPD, backed up by the National Guard – who threw up roadblocks around the city. 'Turn right or get shot,' was the official written warning at one intersection. Nonetheless, it took six days to pacify Watts, by which time the hospitals were struggling with a thousand wounded, and thirty-four people, including a number of children, had been killed.

The Watts riot marked a turning point for the civil rights movement. The passive resistance of the 1950s, courageous enough in itself in those states where extra-judicial killing of black people for such infractions as being over-familiar with whites were a regular occurrence, was now superseded by a much fiercer militancy. Rioting broke out the following year in Chicago and in Cleveland, Ohio, and for much the same reasons. For a long time, there was much denial among white politicians about the true causes of Watts, although to a later day, they appear only too obvious – an incendiary cocktail of police harassment, bad housing, rundown schools and unemployment. To that amalgam of social discontent was added the fact that the Civil Rights Act, which had been passed only the year before, was being circumvented in many different ways by state legislatures unwilling to be bound by it. In California, the enactment of the notorious Proposition 14 – which made it possible for the state to ignore the fair housing provisions of the CRA – was a particularly myopic piece of incitement. Many black families lived in severely sub-standard housing, and the effect of Proposition 14 was to ensure that they stayed there. The prolonged experience of injustice, not some innate proclivity for lawlessness, is what sparked the Watts riot, and ensured that it continued for the better part of a week.

Within a couple of years, social dissent in the United States was acquiring its latest guise in the form of white middle-class dropouts turning on to the Summer of Love, a movement given much media attention after the film of the Woodstock festival of 1967 was released. Sitting in their mud bath blowing bubbles, or gyrating on LSD to the squalling guitar of Jimi Hendrix, the movement's only prominent black exponent, the Woodstock crowds, with their insistence on peace and love, rediscovered a quietude in the face of social oppression of which Genji and his cohorts would have been proud. The blacks had burned Watts. White hippies burned nothing more inflammatory than marijuana. Anger can seemingly be made to go away through the cultivation of passivity, but passivity leaves its causes intact all the way down to their foundations. Social justice is not advanced in this way.

5

I ENRAGE

While we can easily imagine the active uses of such emotions as fear and shame as social tools, a premeditated incitement to anger seems less useful. Our governing institutions may readily resort to making us afraid when they need to, but deliberately making us angry is not in their repertoire. Instead, this technique has been appropriated by dissident agencies in society, particularly within the field of the arts.

Rage as an aesthetic medium was a product of the recently departed, as yet unlamented twentieth century. It arose in cafés and nightclubs in Zürich and Berlin while the Great War was in progress, and spluttered its last on the streets of South Central Los Angeles, before the anger in which the black musical style known as gangsta rap was born turned to self-satisfied, monotonous bragging. The great political crises of the latter half of the century – the Vietnam War, the worldwide economic recession of the 1970s, the nuclear arms race – all spawned cultures of violent dissent in the visual arts and in music, and they all to some degree owed something to the first great wave of confrontational art in the second decade of the century. If there is a salient difference between the protests of Dada and those of British punk rock or American rap, it lies in what would, in 1916, have seemed the improbable migration of such modes from the *salon des refusés* into the cultural mainstream. Hugo Ball in his homemade cabaret outfit babbled incoherent poetry to an audience versed in Goethe and Schiller, but the Sex Pistols went to No. 1 in the pop charts.

This is not to deny that there are currents of anger in much earlier work. There is congealed rage in Goya's *Disasters of War*, a set of etchings he produced to make graphic the depravity of the seven-year Peninsular War, which France fought in Spain and Portugal between 1807 and 1814. 'Is this what you were born for?' asks the caption to one image of a wretched survivor puking over a heap of corpses. 'What more can be done?' wonders another, beneath the image of three imperial soldiers engaged in strenuously breaking the limbs and hacking away at the genitals of a semi-conscious captive. One of the most indelible of all the depictions, the lineaments of which were to recur in Salvador Dali's premonition of the Spanish Civil War, *Soft Construction with Boiled Beans* (1936), and in the work that Jake and Dinos Chapman showed at the *Sensation* exhibition that toured London, Berlin and New York between 1997 and 1999, shows three corpses that have been tied to a tree, one of which has been butchered, an arm torn off and nailed to a branch by its fingers, the head impaled rakishly on a twig. 'Wonderful heroism!' the caption exclaims. 'Against dead men!' Or in the Chapmans' version, *Great Deeds Against The Dead*. The sardonic vehemence of the captions leaves the viewer in no doubt that this is not some pseudo-classical exercise in pious lamentation. An accusing finger is being pointed at French generals who can converse genially while the wounded plead for help close by: 'Do they belong to another race?' Eventually, verbal access to these zones of despair deserts the artist, and he captions the final picture, 'Nothing. It speaks for itself.' The scandalous nature of the events Goya depicts is accentuated by the deliberately rough-and-ready draughtsmanship he brings to these late works. There is an almost childlike quality to many of the images, with their agonised figures sketched against an inert, scribbled background of stunted tree and blasted rock. This is the world of *King Lear*'s Act III brought starkly to present reality.

Although he did not work from direct experience, Goya's series is one of the earliest works of documentary art, the unblinking effort of a man determined to use aesthetic means to articulate spiritual desolation and personal outrage, just as later the photojournalist would come to use his camera. The works belong in that category of extreme art that makes no apology for offending mainstream sensibilities, because it feels that there is something radically wrong with a society that is not offended by the calamities it depicts. A group of exiled German artists working in Vienna in the 1960s and 1970s, under the name Wiener Aktionismus, was instrumental in founding a tenacious sub-current in contemporary art – now given the name of Body Art – through their ritualistic performances, in which they wallowed in industrial quantities of animal entrails, slashing their flesh and masturbating merrily to add to the bodily fluids. While other members of the group have fallen away over the years (Rudolf Schwarzkogler made the ultimate sacrifice, managing to kill himself through serial acts of self-mutilation at the age of twenty-eight), its founder, Hermann Nitsch, who lives in a castle in Prinzendorf, has persisted with what he calls these Orgy Mystery Theatre performances, still immersing himself in pig offal in his sixties. Another figure whose career ended in suicide, Sarah Kane, scandalised London theatregoers in 1995 when her play *Blasted*, about a moribund tabloid journalist who sexually abuses a retarded child in a hotel room, was staged at the Royal Court Theatre. Bret Easton Ellis's debut novel *Less Than Zero* (1987) once sparked a fizzle of indignation for its deadpan narrative of unthinking violence and mindless substance abuse among alienated, affluent LA youth. Social criticism was implicit in all these works, and is still often mistaken for the self-indulgence of a diseased intellect by audiences who may only have read about these outrages in the newspapers.

There are, however, qualitative differences between works of art that are motivated by the anger of an artist at a specific injustice, those in which anger appears in representational form, and those for which anger itself has become the means of expression. It is this latter phenomenon that appears to be unique to the twentieth century. Such rage can be detected in works of one of the lesser-known poets of the Great War, Arthur Graeme West. A captain in the Sixth Battalion of the Oxford and Buckinghamshire Light Infantry, he was killed in action by a sniper's bullet at Bapaume in 1917, at the age of twenty-five. West was a friend of Bertrand Russell, and came to loathe not just the war itself, but his own cowardice in finding himself unable to desert. His best-known poem, recovered posthumously with his war diary and published in 1919, is 'God! How I Hate You, You Young Cheerful Men', a coruscating attack on those who glorified the war, epitomised for West by a former Oxford contemporary, Rex Freston. The poem not only rejects the pusillanimous heroics of Freston's martial verse, but also the Christian faith that appears to sustain it. West's own faith rotted to nothing in the trenches of northern France, and in this poem – and the equally accomplished 'Night Patrol' – the coming century's bitterness at a *deus absconditus* who appeared to have left humanity to its own murderous devices is toxically distilled.

Although West's poems originate in a howl of outrage at the sentimental school of war poetry, and the Gehenna of the European war itself, that must be contained within the poetic art. The Dada movement of central Europe dispensed with such formal dictates. Its manoeuvres were designed, crudely and simply, to aggravate the sensibilities of a society sleepwalking through the inferno that the war had unleashed. Its tactics were calculated to cause maximum offence, and it used the apparatus of the fine arts in order to demonstrate to a complacent bourgeoisie that it didn't deserve to have fine art. Dada is often thought of as a momentary spasm, an infant's tantrum that woke a continent from its postprandial slumber and acted as a necessary prelude to the Surrealist movement. While Europe slept, it had a nightmare that a pointless war had consigned nine million combatants to death, but when it awoke, it found that everything still looked like a dream.

Dada never aspired to anything resembling a coherent aesthetic philosophy (there is no Dada*ism*, whatever the textbooks say), and neither did it aim to produce lasting works. It has survived today, if at all, in the form of the many replicas of Marcel Duchamp's 'readymade' sculptures – the urinal, the bicycle wheel, the bottle-rack – which have gone on dividing and reproducing themselves around the international galleries from the originals of the 1910s. To a modern audience, however, the provocation in which they were conceived has been lost. A very great proportion of contemporary work looks like this too. There was more than a breath of Dada in Joseph Beuys's arrangements of felt and fat, and a distinct murmur in Sarah Lucas's fried eggs and old mattresses. Every heap of land-fill garbage deposited in a gallery – and there has been no shortage of those in the last decade – seems to mock the viewer with the same taunt that Dada offered to its recipients: 'Expecting a finely crafted work of art, were you? Well, tough.'

What is irretrievable is the dimension of Dada that more than anything else defined it in its own era. First and foremost, it was a performance art, measuring the success of its own confrontation with the corrupt morality of the Great War in the provocative displays engineered in cafés and clubs in Zürich, Berlin and Paris. It conceived itself primarily as a kind of riotous anti-cabaret, replete with cacophonous music, pantomime costumes and gibbering poems bellowed through megaphones. And if Duchamp wasn't ever able to realise his idea of using a Rembrandt as an ironing board, he achieved the next best thing by defacing a poster of the *Mona Lisa* and adding a lascivious caption to it: 'L.H.O.O.Q.' (*elle a chaud au cul*, or something like 'She's got the hots', or 'She's up for it'). It looks so innocuous now, a faithful photographic reproduction of the original, the trim little upturned moustache sensitively applied, but its appearance in 1920 sparked a near-riot. It wasn't exhibited in a gallery, but at one of Dada's cabaret evenings. When the curtains parted, only an easel bearing this modified painting, the most famous in history, stood on stage. The alphabetic pun printed beneath it sank in only gradually, with the more eagle-eyed among the audience noticing the discreet growth of facial hair she had sprouted. As nothing else happened, and it seemed they were expected to react in some way, a crescendo of jeers and catcalls began to swell from the crowd. Some may have felt they were protecting the honour of *La Gioconda* or Leonardo. Others may have suspected they were being taken for idiots. Whichever it was, the bait had been swallowed, and it ensured that subsequent items on the programme would be received in the same dyspeptic manner. Fifty-seven years later, Johnny Rotten would begin a Sex Pistols performance by yelling into the microphone as the band cranked ineptly into action behind him, 'I 'ope you 'ate it!'

Dada coalesced from the ferment of artistic movements that characterised the second decade of the twentieth century. Launched amid a welter of manifestos, destined to be forgotten after the first and last exhibition of their works in some third-floor studio in Montparnasse, many of these spasmodic initiatives hardly ascended to the formal status of movements. What they had in common was a desire to supplant the lingering, mildewed vestiges of Impressionism that still dominated the European art scene.

Certain proponents of these pre-Dada groups remain important. Pre-eminent among them is the fascinating Arthur Cravan, a muscled-up thug with an unexplained yen for the aesthetic who described himself as a 'boxer-poet'. Born Fabien Avenarius Lloyd in Lausanne in 1887, he was the nephew of Oscar Wilde, and found something like his true *métier* in his twenties when he founded, edited and solely wrote five issues of a phlegmatic journal called *Maintenant*, which he filled with invective against the post-Impressionist lightweights to be found exhibiting their pallid landscapes at the Salon des Indépendants. Not just the works of these bourgeois artists, but their very existence, was cause for Cravan's deepest contempt. In issue 3 of *Maintenant*, he shudders at the thought of Victor Hugo spending decades living the life of the writer. 'I shall never understand how, over forty years, [he] could do the job. The whole of literature is nothing but ta ta ta ta ta ta. I couldn't give a fuck about it. God, it's shit.' In July 1914 he staged a one-man show in Paris during which, after some preliminary physical stuff (manic dancing, pistol-shooting and naturally some boxing), he delivered a ranting, inebriated lecture in which he told the attentive 'shitheads' who had gathered to hear him that artists were inferior beings compared to sportsmen. One might then have wondered what it was that kept drawing him back to art, but he insisted, in a statement that was perfectly in tune with the times, that 'every great artist has a feeling for provocation'. Furthermore, he added, admiring his own rippling deltoids, 'genius is an extravagant manifestation of the body'. In 1916, in an attempt to prove the point more forcefully, he put himself up for a real fight, against world heavyweight champion Jack Johnson, in Barcelona. When he stepped on to the canvas at the Monumental Bullring on 23 April, he was pissed out of his mind, and went down under a hail of blows in the very first round.

The one fight Cravan wasn't at all interested in joining was the Great War and, after darting around Europe to escape conscription, he eventually fled in 1917 to New York, where at a society salon he met the Anglo-Hungarian modernist poet Mina Loy, then in the throes of divorce from her first husband. Loy was utterly captivated by Cravan, and when the draft threatened to catch up with him even there, necessitating a further flight to Mexico City, she followed him and married him. They drifted around Mexico for several months, Cravan earning money by entering boxing bouts, until in the summer of 1918 Loy discovered she was pregnant. She sailed on a hospital ship to Buenos Aires for treatment, the plan being that Cravan would join her later. He never arrived, and indeed was never officially seen again. Some say he perished in a lost aircraft, in the manner of Amelia Earhart or Glenn Miller. American writer James Reich fancifully suggests that Cravan committed suicide in the Gulf of Mexico, opening his belly with a knife for the sharks to feed on him, slashing at them ferociously as they came for him in what would have been his last heroic bout. Others claimed to have spotted him back in New York or Paris in the 1930s and 1940s, but his fate remains obscure. He had vanished. Whatever happened to him, the traces of his influence were soon submerged in the international bedlam that was Dada; but he deserves to be remembered. By the time of her death in 1966, only Loy could recall the electricity of his presence. Her last poem, 'Letters of the Unliving', shows her obsession with him still enduring, nearly fifty years after an affair that had lasted barely twelve months. What Cravan demonstrated was that there is potentially limitless mileage to be had from upsetting an intelligentsia that considers itself ready for anything, and doesn't dare miss a revolutionary trick.

The opening of the Cabaret Voltaire in Zürich in early 1916 marked the formal inauguration of Dada. An informal assemblage of anarchist writers, disenchanted painters and moneyed *cognoscenti,* rebelling against their own backgrounds as much as the decadence of the art establishment, it filled its early statements and actions with contempt. 'Dada began not as an art form,' Tristan Tzara, one of its leading lights was to explain, 'but as a disgust.' Insulting the audience was a *sine qua non* of its operations, and an attitude that it maintained to the bitter end. A Paris exhibition in 1921 was preceded by a 'private view' for critics and society luminaries, at which the arriving invitees were subjected to a stream of abuse by a disembodied voice coming from a cupboard – the ghost of Arthur Cravan, perhaps. More than the redoubtable Tzara, more so even than Duchamp, Francis Picabia, who joined the inner circle on a visit to Switzerland in 1918, was the most prescient figure to emerge from the movement. Wealthy, ostentatious and nearly forty, he was an unlikely participant, and yet possessed the twin virtues a short fuse and a complete disdain for the artistic renown he had enjoyed since his first Paris exhibition of 1905. He sacked his dealer, forswore any attachment to the pastel vapidities of his earlier work, and plunged himself headlong into anti-art. He designed costumes and sets for Dada's theatrical antics, and it was he who, in one of the most celebrated of the gang's nihilistic gestures, sketched a drawing in chalk on a blackboard, which André Breton, biding his time with the anarchists while he waited for a more disciplined insurrection to happen along, then wiped briskly away.

Picabia was the moving spirit behind Dada's 'interventions', during which it disrupted lectures and shows by other artists, including the despised Jean Cocteau, one of whose agonising aesthetic dramas was undermined at its première by repeated shouts of 'Vive Dada!' from infiltrators in the audience. No mercy was offered even to Filippo Marinetti, godfather of Italian Futurism (which by now looked like nothing more revolutionary than last year's dance craze), who had turned up in Paris to launch a new movement called Tactilism, in which the works were intended to be handled and stroked. Members of the Dada group burst in on his talk with taunts and derisive laughter. It was Picabia, most of all, who knew when the game was up, though. As its momentum began to falter, he abandoned the movement. Tzara tried to keep the faith, continuing to stage mixed-media events in the name of Dada well into the 1920s, for which unimaginative, dogged tenacity even he became the object of Picabia's scorn. In a putdown worthy of Dorothy Parker at her most sulphurous, he declared à propos Tzara, 'The thing I find of least interest in other people is myself.'

There is a residue of Dada's desire to subvert in the early phases of Surrealism. Dali's work of the late 1920s and 1930s – the period from which works such as *Soft Construction with Boiled Beans*, *The Lugubrious Game* (1929), *The Great Masturbator*

(1929) and *Autumn Cannibalism* (1936–7) all date – mobilises Freudian motifs to produce some of Modernism's most truly unsettling icons. André Breton, the Surrealist movement's notional founder, and author of the line 'Beauty will be convulsive or not at all!' certainly could not have envisaged its eventual decline into whimsical transatlantic chic after the Second World War. For Breton, surrealism was a kind of wilful ultra-leftism, driven by anti-bourgeois politics and pungent anti-clericalism. Nonetheless, it gradually metamorphosed, like Dali's Narcissus, from a morose but passionate intellectual stance into something purely ornamental, an *objet* that invited aesthetic contemplation in the old way, a hand holding an egg with a flower coming out of it. By the time it arrived in New York in the 1940s, it had become merely a style craze, as fatuously capable of assimilation as the hula-hoop would be to the next generation. In its first flush, though, it gave form to the expostulations of Dada, without which it would never have been anything other than a slightly more febrile Art Deco. Dada provided Surrealism with its first chiefs of staff.

Much has been made, not least by myself in the feverish atmosphere of the high tide of British punk rock, the Summer of Hate of 1977, of the manifest links between that movement and Dada. The same desire to short-circuit the existing systems of dissemination – of art in Dada's case, of rock music in that of punk – was at work in both of them, and for a couple of years during the former, and about eight or nine months during the latter, the strategy seemed to work. The charged atmosphere of punk performances, which were always about so much more than merely listening to a band give a recital of some songs they had written, caught something of the calculated antagonisms of Dada. 'We're not into music,' claimed the Sex Pistols in February 1976, some months before they had a recording contract, 'we're into chaos.' Moreover, there was a sense – inaugurated by their notorious, expletive-laden appearance on teatime commercial TV – that what the Sex Pistols did mattered as much to the movement as the records they released. It was quite impossible to predict in 1916 what Dada was going to do next, except that it wouldn't involve regularly exhibiting new paintings and sculptures. It was also important, as Francis Picabia's attitude attested, to know when to abandon the sinking ship. This moment came cruelly early in the case of punk (by the late summer of 1977, there was already a scent of carrion about it), but sentimentality had never been the point. Once it lost touch with any sort of activist agenda, it became merely another fashion, another musical technique to take its place in the variegated tradition of such techniques ushered in by the skiffle bands of the 1950s. The movement had its Tzaras too, those who clung to the withered body long after the last breath of spontaneity had been squeezed out of it. 'Dada is the biggest confidence trick of the century,' announced one of the posters at Tzara's Salon Dada of June 1921. 'Ever had the feeling you've been cheated?' Rotten inquired of the audience on the final date of the Pistols' American tour in January 1978. It was to be his last official pronouncement as a Sex Pistol. Three days later, he had left the band, angrier at what punk had been reduced to (not least by the band's own manager) than at the rock establishment it was programmed to undermine.

From time to time, pop culture remembers that it contains within it the capacity for this kind of anger. There is rage to spare, allied to much acidic scorn, in the early lyrical output of Bob Dylan, and in the 1960s protest culture that it spawned. He is still able to sound angry on the opening track, 'Hurricane', of his 1975 album *Desire*, as he indicts a corrupt and racist judicial system in the celebrated case of the black boxer Rubin 'Hurricane' Carter. British rock bands have been somewhat readier than their American counterparts to abandon propriety when addressing the state apparatus. The anti-nuclear movement was handed a gift by the release in 1984 of the single and video 'Two Tribes' by Frankie Goes to Hollywood. A generation's anger at the bovine rush to destruction into which the power blocs seemed to be herding the world was brilliantly captured by the image of their then leaders, Ronald Reagan and Konstantin Chernenko, brawling in a sandpit. Racial grievance played its part in popular music once again in that furious brand of LA rap known as 'gangsta', most notoriously and best exemplified by a single track, 'Gangsta Gangsta', from the 1988 album *Straight Outta Compton* by NWA (Niggas With Attitude). When pop does anger well, the moment can feel liberating, and more incisive than party political oratory. It is precisely because the medium is normally so content with the cosmetic sheen of image alone, in which the banalities of the artists' foibles and eccentricities (this one a megalomaniac love-rat, that one a paedophile in denial) play an integral part, that its straying into alien territory can be so arresting. In these moments, which one might call the enraged sublime, pop breaks free of its commercial moorings for a time, at least until the moment of rage itself becomes a commercial success. British band Pulp's 1995 single, 'Common People', was just such a moment. The spoilt rich kid fresh out of art school, dabbling in poverty as a style statement (did somebody say 'Picabia'?), is pinned down with ruthless accuracy as the song builds to a frenzy of heartfelt indignation. You haven't the faintest idea what poverty is, the sentiment runs, triumphant in its ridicule of the class poseur.

What connects these disparate aesthetic strands is that their engagement with social and political themes of the day takes place alongside – or within the context of – an engagement with and ultimate struggle against an aesthetic establishment. Dada would have been nothing without its proliferation of fuming anti-journals, in which the work of the leading artists was repeatedly spat on. The jets of saliva in which punk performances seemed permanently bathed had originally been directed at the corpulent spectre of progressive rock (one of the movement's holy relics is a T-shirt celebrating 1960s psychedelicists turned 1970s technocrats Pink Floyd, above which Johnny Rotten had written in shivering green letters, 'I hate ...'). Arthur Graeme West, apoplectic in the trenches of France at the very moment that Dada was scandalising Switzerland, had a clear idea before him of the kind of poet he emphatically didn't want to be. Even 'Common People' announces its venomous loathing of the art-school dilettante by referring to her CV in its opening lines: she has been a sculpture student at St Martin's College of Art. And we shudder with contempt at the mere suggestion of it. Sculpture!

If contempt for the academies is what unites angry art, however, it is also what holes it below the waterline. It may start as alternative art, or anti-art, but it can't help – if it makes any sort of impact at all – becoming a part of art history. Which is why, compared to forms of real political activism, it never stands a chance of altering the *status quo*. When Pulp's Jarvis Cocker staged a spontaneous intervention during Michael Jackson's bombastic performance at the British music industry awards of 1996, the moment was pure punk, even Picabiesque in its subversion. Jackson's response, however, more caustic than he could possibly have known or intended, was to say that he had every respect for Pulp as artists. That is indeed, finally, all they are.

6

I AM ANGERED

Art turned angry in the twentieth century for sound socio-political reasons. During the last quarter of the century, however, that anger at the way things are, which confrontational artistic movements had articulated, began to turn inwards. If the punk and rap movements, and their attendant culture of provoking bourgeois society, represented the last gasp of that tradition, it wasn't long before that attitude of personal indignation with life found its way into the mainstream. The explosive growth, particularly in the United States, of psychotherapy and psychoanalysis appeared to be encouraging just such a critical stance towards the circumstances of one's own existence. Increasing numbers of people found themselves dissatisfied with their lives, and behind that dissatisfaction was the sense of being a passive victim, on whom the coldly mechanised workings of modern society inflicted their worst. The result of too much of this treatment was a bubbling quantum of repressed anger. How could that achieve release? And was the social cost of its expression so great that we would perhaps be better off availing ourselves of techniques for dispersing it through self-control.

The 'better-out-than-in' philosophy has been applied to anger in modern times more than to any other harmful emotion. Perhaps this is because anger is an emotion without an obvious behavioural etiquette attached to it. We may know how to express our fears, and look to others for solace or shelter in doing so, and we may know what is expected of us when the unhappiness of bereavement is upon us. Even if we fall short of these standards, there is nonetheless a socially acceptable code for its expression. Anger, however, knows no such protocol. The angry person wants to destroy, or at least injure, that which has harmed him and which he therefore hates, but fear of the consequences of lashing out may lead to a denial of that instinct, thereby creating the danger that it might be magnified by being repressed. The well-worn image of suppressed anger is that of the boiling pot with no air vent. As the contents continue to seethe, greater and greater pressure builds up within, until a spectacular explosion is the only outcome. Much contemporary psychotherapy has been predicated on the notion that giving expression to repressed anger is the healthiest strategy available, and represents the only hope of averting that terminal explosion that leads to electric shock treatment or a life on tranquillisers. Some practitioners organise group therapies, in which clients are encouraged to attack each other with toy baseball bats, tough enough to feel as though some sort of impact is being made, but not so tough that serious injury might arise. In a famous early episode of *The Simpsons*, Homer sells the TV in order to pay for family aggression therapy with a psychotherapist who advertises on TV. Strapped into electro-shock machines that are connected to each other, they are told that only in understanding the hurt they are causing each other will they come to feel sufficient guilt about it to control themselves. Within seconds, they are using the equipment so vindictively that the town electricity grid is beginning to buckle under the strain. Laughing off the whole charade, Homer gets the family's money back, and they go off and buy a brand new TV. The story makes a neat point about aggression therapy that had already been made in the 1980s by Carol Tavris, who argued that 'Letting off steam is a wonderful metaphor and seems to capture exactly how angry outbursts work, but people are not teapots.' (They aren't kettles or pressure cookers either, but one takes her point.)

Citing the findings of 1960s psychologist, Jack Hokanson, Tavris lays bare the mythical aspect of aggression, or catharsis, therapy. To strike out in retaliation in order to quench the raging physiological fire within is not instinctual behaviour, despite what had been posited by most psychoanalytic theorists since Freud. The notion that there is a reservoir of rage within us that must be regularly tapped has come to seem about as primitive as the medieval theory of the humours. Cathartic behaviour is not instinctual, Hokanson found, for the very reason that it doesn't work. It is learned behaviour, and very possibly gender-dependent. Hokanson established that women connected to mocked-up versions of the electro-shock machines seen on *The Simpsons* responded to shocks by sending their fellow-subjects a reward in an attempt to pacify them, whereas the men tended to respond in kind. In an extension of the experiment, in which the women were sent a reward for responding aggressively, while the men were instructed to respond to shock as the women had earlier done by sending a reward as a peace offering, both sexes were found to lose their anger (measured by vascular reduction in blood pressure) more quickly than before. In other words, it appeared to help the women to discover a capacity for aggressive response, while the men were helped by learning to placate the aggressor. A cathartic habit had been acquired in each case, but one that had different implications. Tavris rightly complicates the findings by pointing out that we can now acknowledge that these rules do not divide neatly across the gender boundary. There are naturally non-aggressive men, as well as women, for whom staged confrontation does not offer any sort of catharsis, but instead leads to increased anxiety.

Notwithstanding Hokanson's findings, there were still those who set much store by cathartic procedures in the decades that followed his research. For proponents of the school of bioenergetics that flourished in the 1980s under Alexander Lowen, all enactments and manifestations of anger were therapeutic releases of what could be seen as a kind of virus. Clients were expected to howl and stamp, bite and kick and threaten, until the anger was out of them and thus defeated. If it was the natural disposition of the angry man to fight, then finding ways of symbolically enacting that conflict could siphon off the rage that might otherwise spill forth unchecked. The cathartic approach even found its way in the 1970s as far as Japan – where learning stoical acceptance is an important rite of passage to adulthood – in the strategy by which effigies of members of the Board of Directors were provided in the car factories for the workers to belabour as the fury took them. It was at one time thought that introducing such a facility at the troubled British Leyland company might reduce the incidence of strikes there, but the experiment was never tried. If the fashion now is in the direction of mollification, that seems a less slapstick but potentially more hazardous recourse, since breathing deeply and holding hands with your workmate tends to leave the structures of exploitation as intact as beating up the dummies did.

What can happen to subjects coerced into undergoing catharsis therapy is itself highly inimical to emotional balance, and productive of further anxiety. Children experimentally encouraged into anarchic, destructive behaviour become not less aggressive in their normal lives, but more so, because they have learned another mode of emotional expression. Part of the reason that cathartic behaviour isn't instinctual and therefore universal is its lack of effect. If your retributive rage is directed against somebody for whom retributive rage is also an innate style, then the need to strike back is rekindled with each further provocation, until either sheer boredom or exhaustion sets in or real damage is done. This syndrome is beautifully depicted in the 1929 Laurel and Hardy short film, *Big Business*, in which the pair become embroiled in an argument with a man (James Finlayson) whom they have annoyed in their jobs as door-to-door Christmas tree salesmen. In the row that escalates between them, Finlayson tears lumps off their Model T Ford, while they do reciprocal damage to the exterior of his house. What makes the sequence so apt and painfully funny is that as each act of destruction is performed, its victims stand and witness it impassively before proceeding to respond. There is no air of destructive frenzy, but rather a solemn gentility, in which each is allowed the time and space to take his turn, the preposterous courtesy of it all accentuated by the bustling up and down the garden path from car to house and back again that dictates its rhythm.

Tales occasionally surface in the press of people who have been reduced to acts of extraordinary violence during feuds with their neighbours. It begins with the Dolly Parton being turned up too loud, and ends with the wringing of cats' necks. Clearly, for these people, no more than for Laurel and Hardy, catharsis is not cathartic. Why do they not see that each act of revenge calls forth another? The answer is that they do, but neither party can afford to be the first to blink. The whole point of releasing anger in acts of aggression is that you can't stop for fear of seeming to admit weakness and therefore defeat. The hope is merely that, by raising the stakes a little higher each time, you will have committed the decisive action that forestalls any further response and hands you the victory. When moralists observe that if neighbours cannot live tolerantly beside each other, then there can be no hope for people caught up in generations of sectarian enmity, such as the Protestants and Catholics of Northern Ireland or the Israelis and the Palestinians, they have a valid point about the mechanics of anger. There are issues here for impartial forces to help the belligerent parties to resolve, and that won't just be wished away by blandly enjoining them to learn to live together. There is, in short, history to overcome. But the moralists are right, at least, in insisting that they do have to stop rising to each other's provocations first. Interestingly, in both the cases mentioned, one resort of the dominant power has been to erect high walls to keep the two embattled communities apart, but we can be perfectly sure this recourse won't work either. All defensive walls (such as prison walls or the Berlin Wall) are asking to be breached, and even if barbed wire, electrified fences and lookout towers keep them impregnable in the short term, they nonetheless stand as monuments to the murderous animosity that constructed them. The nuclear arsenals of the Cold War may not have led to real war between the western powers and the Soviet bloc, but any suggestion that the paralysed, haunted state in which their client populations lived for forty years could be described as 'peace' was a mirthless joke.

What, then, is the answer to our anger? Another of the experiments Tavris cites involves children of both sexes. A control subject in the form of a little girl was instructed to provoke and antagonise a group of happily playing children. Once provoked, the children were allowed to respond in one of three ways: they could get angry at the girl, by yelling and firing toy guns at her; they could report their grievances to adults, who talked it over understandingly with them; or they were offered an explanation for the girl's behaviour (she had been upset by something, she wasn't feeling well, she was tired). The result of this rather tendentious experiment was that the only strategy that worked in defusing the tension and lowering the children's vascular rates was the last one. As we might well expect, the retaliation countenanced by option one only heightened the overall level of aggression. Perhaps surprisingly, however, talking it over with the adults had no effect either. That discovery led Tavris to establish this finding as the first of her five conditions for true catharsis: anger must be directed at its cause. Neutral third parties are ultimately of no help in assuaging it. The sympathetic ear – however well-intentioned – leaves the situation as it is, which perhaps is why all efforts to impose a settlement on warring parties are doomed to failure if the belligerents talk only to the interventionists, and not also to each other. Only when the children could see a reason for the behaviour of the fractious newcomer, which made some kind of logical sense, could they accept the situation. Seeing the reason for the behaviour is not the same as finding it forgivable, but the enlightenment that follows the explanation does much to defuse the indignation it creates. A judicial experiment now going on in parts of the UK, in which apprehended lawbreakers face the people who have suffered from their actions, appears so far to be largely successful, in spite of its being scorned by commentators who prefer not to believe in our capacity for betterment. The victim of the crime gets to put her anger and sense of violation behind her as she sees what caused the perpetrator to act, while the burglar is helped to see exactly how his ransacking of her house had such damaging consequences.

This crime liaison scheme acknowledges that directed anger is anger that is halfway to resolution. But what of that simmering mass of unacknowledged anger that, we may suspect, lurks beneath the surface of civil society? Much as everybody is now presumed to be depressed at least some of the time, so – perhaps not unconnectedly – it is also taken as axiomatic that people are often close to boiling point at the exasperations of modern life. This is a theme to which Hollywood has repeatedly returned in the last twenty-five years. In Sidney Lumet's 1976 film *Network*, Peter Finch plays Howard Beale, a grizzled American newscaster who is informed at the outset that poor ratings have led the television company to make him redundant. With alarming rapidity, he succumbs to a state of advanced mental disintegration, first announcing his intention to kill himself on air and then accepting instead the offer of a weekly slot, in which he will be at liberty to say whatever he wants about the state of the nation. The film fails on virtually every level, chiefly for the way in which the central character's repressed anger is portrayed. 'I just ran out of bullshit,' Beale confesses to his TV audience, and then proceeds to speak nothing else for the rest of the film. 'He's articulating a popular rage,' Faye Dunaway's ruthless programming director insists, sensing that the unscripted tirades could give the network's jaded schedules a much-needed ratings boost. When Beale does address his audience, the speeches have an uncomfortably familiar ring of Washington conservatism to them, which is not quite what the title for the segment – 'The Mao Zedong Hour' – and the involvement of a black woman on secondment from the Central Committee of the US Communist Party might lead us to expect. He enjoins middle America to go to its windows, fling them open and yell into the street, 'I'm mad as hell and I'm not going to take it any more!' But take what?

'The Arabs are simply buying us,' Beale screams in reference to OPEC's hiking of the oil price, but apart from the Arabs it seems hard to identify what it is that everybody is entreated to get so angry about. At one point Beale admits that even if the problem can be identified, it isn't necessary to know what should be done about it, only that a collective public voice should be raised in dissatisfaction. Vandalism and graffiti are alluded to, but it seems that the principal complaint is that the political process pays no heed to the wishes of the common man and woman. This is an old refrain of American disgruntlement, and an insult in which television, which speaks to the masses without hearing them, inevitably colludes. As if to emphasise the point, the studio audience listens to his sermons in respectful silence, only breaking into polite applause as each one climaxes with Beale crumpling unconscious to the floor. In a scene that excruciatingly betrays the real political colouring in the screenplay, Laureen Hobbs, once the doctrinaire communist, is now seen doughtily scrapping with the executives for her share of the advertising revenue. It has taken a matter of days for her to learn the predatory language of corporate capitalism, so we can be sure that whatever other prescription might answer the needs of the unacknowledged angry masses, it will have nothing to do with left-wing politics.

Howls of unfocused social anger were very much a cultural trope of the 1970s, and although their portrayal always involves much in the way of gibbering apoplexy, a keen sense of the ridiculous is never far from the surface. The hit BBC TV comedy series, *The Fall and Rise of Reginald Perrin* (1976–9), dealt with much the same territory, and passages of *Network* are played as unabashed farce. One uncomfortable lesson imparted by these narratives of incensed despair, however, is just what a reactionary, as well as reactive, emotion anger essentially is. A great deal of dissenting politics is founded on the notion that people ought to rise up angrily against their plight. If you don't get mad, you won't even get even, let alone have a chance of overcoming. The opposite of righteous anger, on this analysis, is held to be a sort of quasi-Buddhist passivity, in which you allow the impositions of a flawed world to wash over you. This was no more the truth about revolutionary politics than it was an accurate account of the way society impacts on its individual members. In any case, what is one supposed to do once the anger has subsided, as inevitably it must? When anger fails to achieve any proportionate degree of redress, what it becomes is despair, as Howard Beale's viewers will eventually realise. Michael Douglas's progressive unravelling in Joel Schumacher's *Falling Down* (1993) exemplifies the point.

The proliferation since the 1990s of a whole aetiology of social rage, from Road Rage and Air Rage to Queuing Rage and the rage felt by individuals who don't perform well in a TV quiz programme (pathologised in the United States as Post-Game Show Trauma), suggests that, despite rumours of widespread affluence, western citizens are suffering increasingly from a sense of alienation from modern life. What is misleading is the suggestion that these are new psychological conditions, which may in time appear in the schedules of the World Health Organisation. Pent-up fury at the way nothing works as it is intended to is hardly new, but the situations that give rise to it continue to proliferate: getting stuck in traffic; wasting money in a malfunctioning vending-machine; finding there are only two cashiers operating at the Post Office on a Friday lunchtime, when there is a queue to the door; being expected to sit quietly belted into a seat for twelve hours, denied the solace of a cigarette, and with the choice of either watching Jessica Tandy or listening to a Beatles tribute on the headphones. It is the sense of impotence occasioned by such grievances that contributes to that feeling of having had one's fur brushed the wrong way. A complaint to the rail company may be disregarded if it arrives in the form of a personal letter, as opposed to the official form on which the matter should now be reported, so that a catalogue of cancellations and delays that resulted in a long-distance journey taking half as long again as it was scheduled to must be briefly summarised in a space that will fit about thirty words. In due course the response comes, in which the company offers scant compensation, together with one of those hypothetical apologies: 'I am sorry if you found your experience with us less than satisfactory . . .' These strategies, drawn up by management consultants urging their clients to find ways of neutralising indignation and avoiding the admission of failure, only succeed in further inflaming the plaintiff, who discovers thereby that nothing about the way this state of affairs is arranged is in his favour. We return to another of Jack Hokanson's findings, which was that expressions of anger only work against one's peers or those in a subordinate position to oneself. Taking on an organisation or an authority is not cathartic. Furthermore, it conflicts with at least three of Carol Tavris's five noble truths about achieving catharsis: that it'must restore your sense of control over the situation', that it 'must change the behaviour of your target', and that 'you and your target must speak the same anger language'.

One thing at least is true about the identification of these various manifestations of what may be described as Rage Syndrome. They do appear to be intensifying, in the sense that the boundaries within which people feel confined, once enraged, seem to be loosening. A man who would once have blasted you on his horn and offered you his middle finger in your rear-view mirror for overtaking him is now quite likely to jump out of his van and challenge you to fisticuffs by the roadside. A lit cigarette in a no-smoking zone is as incendiary as a petrol bomb. All these reactions originate from profound constitutional impatience. It isn't that we are going from nought to sixty more quickly; it's more that we are starting from around twenty-five. We expect everything to work as quickly as our computers do, even while knowing that the world is slower than ever. The degree of impatience some people manifest while waiting for an internet search engine to produce its results, or while waiting for a website to open – operations that would, not so very long ago, have mandated a half-day at the local library in pursuit of the same information, and with rather lower odds of success – is deeply symptomatic of our current condition. Then again, information technology itself creates that climate of expectation. It promises the instant answers that it doesn't always give, and reminding us what a technical marvel it is seems pointless at the very moment that it is offering only a blank screen. It may also be true that waiting eleven months for a hospital test is better than the situation of a century ago, when no such test existed or was only available to those who could pay for it, but that knowledge doesn't make the present eleven months any easier to tolerate, especially when one knows that they could in theory be reduced to two weeks, given the resources and the administrative will.

Corporatism has resorted increasingly to bogus exercises in public consultation in recent years, in the hope that persuading people to fill in market research forms will make them less likely to complain when it does all go wrong. In return for being entered in a prize draw to win a holiday on Mauritius, we regress to the mentality of our school days, when compiling league tables of commodities, whether they were flavours of crisps or members of the opposite sex, felt like an intelligent way of appraising the world. Concomitantly, attributing the cause of our anger to localised situations, such as being an airline passenger or standing in a queue, occludes the real explanation for the perpetual red mist in which too many of us seem to live: that we resent the reification of human nature in which so much modern experience is couched. In its clumsy, reactionary way, this was the point that *Network* was trying to establish. The spirit tears at its chains, but is offered only complaint forms and tick-boxes. 'To what extent does your human potential appear to have been stifled by the brutally objectified society you inhabit? (a) Not stifled at all; (b) A little stifled; (c) Moderately stifled; (d) Very stifled; (e) Almost completely, disablingly, unbearably stifled.'

HUMANITY: AN EMOTIONAL HISTORY

DISGUST

Evermore in the world is this marvellous balance of
beauty and disgust, magnificence and rats.
Ralph Waldo Emerson

1. Strong distaste for food, drink, medicine, etc.; nausea, loathing. 2.
Strong repugnance excited by that which is loathsome or offensive; profound instinctive dissatisfaction. 3. An outbreak of mutual ill feeling; a
quarrel. 4. That which causes repugnance; an annoyance.

Darwin's physical indicators: opening wide of the mouth; spitting; blowing through protruded lips; throat-clearing sound ('ugh', 'ach'); shudder,
with arms pressed to the sides and shoulders raised; retraction of the
upper lip; eversion of the lower lip; wrinkling of the nose; dilation of the
nostrils; frowning; gestures of rejection of or self-protection against the
offensive object. In extreme cases: retching; vomiting.

7

TO DISGUST

The word 'disgust' only entered the English language in the early part of the seventeenth century, having been imported from the Italian (*disgustare*) via French (*dégouster*, later *dégoûter*). This isn't of course to suggest that the disgust response itself is a product of the era, only that the new coinage came to name everything that had previously been loathsome, repellent, abominable, revolting, abhorrent, right back to ancient times. Unlike fear or anger, disgust is a truly visceral, corporeal reaction to negative external stimuli. Extreme terror or fury have their physical effect upon the bodily system of their victim, but in turning the stomach and so preparing the oesophagus for an act of expulsion, the impulse of something disgusting – whichever of the five senses apprehends it – calls forth an intensely somatic reaction. It shares with fear the ability to make us recoil from the object that provokes it, as we perceive it to be too close for comfort (or for safety, with fear), but that act of physical rejection cuts deeper with disgust than with any other negative emotion. For this very reason, some may wonder whether disgust is properly an emotion at all, as opposed to a bodily reflex. Darwin had no doubt that it was one of the half-dozen primary emotions, although his brief but eloquent summation of disgust responses doesn't shed much light on the state of mind that accompanies it.

What he does focus on is the linguistic pointer that leads us to associate disgust pre-eminently with the sense of taste (the Latin word for which is *gustus*). In discussing the physical manifestations of disgust, Darwin orientates it securely in this field:

It is curious how readily this feeling is excited by anything unusual in the appearance, odour, or nature of our food ... A smear of soup on a man's beard looks disgusting, though there is of course nothing disgusting in the soup itself. I presume that this follows from the strong association in our minds between the sight of food, however circumstanced, and the idea of eating it. As the sensation of disgust primarily arises in connection with the act of eating or tasting it, it is natural that its expression should consist chiefly in movements round the mouth ... With respect to the face, moderate disgust is exhibited ... by the mouth being widely opened, as if to let an offensive morsel drop out ... Extreme disgust is expressed by movements round the mouth identical with those preparatory to the act of vomiting.

The very etymology of the word seems to announce its origin in a sense of dis-taste. The flared nostrils and wrinkled nose of the disgust response – as noted among the South Fore tribespeople of Papua New Guinea by Paul Ekman, when he asked them to imagine 'a dead pig that has been lying there a long time' – also mimics the facial contortions of a person who has put something repellent into his mouth. A recent anatomist of disgust, however, challenges this account as oversimplified, and is surely right to do so. There are, in William Ian Miller's estimation, quite as many disgusting sights and smells and things that are loathsome to the touch as there are offending tastes. (He suggests, less accurately perhaps, that the sense of hearing has notably lower significance in our capacity for disgust.) This etymological approach may work in English and the Romance languages, but it fails when it comes to German, where the relevant word, *Ekel*, retains no reference to any of the senses. It cannot escape our notice, however, that the provocation for disgust seems rooted in some physical example of noxious bodily secretions – spit, mucus, phlegm, earwax, urine, faeces, semen, blood (particularly menstrual blood) – or else the biological processes of decay and putrefaction. There are, however, nuances within this picture that complicate the issue. Anything that is thought to carry some defiling, toxic or polluting property may well sicken us too, even where the physical appearance or smell are not in themselves objectionable. Context plays a part, as Miller demonstrates by inviting us to compare the act of sucking blood from a cut finger with the prospect of drinking it, freshly exsanguinated, from a glass. Then, too, there are notions that only retain an ambiguous relation to biology, such as the near-universal perception of supernumerariness or multiplicity as disgusting. One spot of coffee on the café tablecloth can be calmly overlooked; a liberal spattering is disgusting enough to make us want to sit at another table or go elsewhere.

The idea of surfeit leads into the moral domain. A superfluity of food, alcohol, drugs or sex might leave us with a feeling of distaste at the self for having so indulged. Although these sensory pleasures are necessary to the feeling of living a full life, or at least one that features recreational interludes among the besetting spells of duty, there is a point beyond satiety, at which a state of moral indigestion sets in, augmenting the physical queasiness of having overdone it with a bilious self-accusation at finding ourselves so reduced to bundles of instinctual appetites. A due sense of proportion is what ought to separate us from the animals, we feel, and transgressing against it reminds us that disgust is not merely an emotion that responds to external influences, but can be inwardly directed as well. We can be disgusted at what we are, at what 'we might slide back into' (as Miller puts it), at the things we do and, as Hamlet painfully discovers, the things we don't do. When anger at a perceived injustice fails to lead to some form of remedial action, we often feel disgusted at ourselves for letting down the side, for falling short in our moral duty to our loved ones or to humanity at large.

The phenomenology of disgust changed soon after the introduction of the word into the English language. It achieved common currency just prior to the development of that alternative sense of the word 'taste', to refer to aesthetic judgement – a faculty for refinement, discernment and those discriminations by which art, literature, sartorial fashion and even nature itself could be evaluated in polite company. To lack 'good taste' in these matters was to run the risk of disgusting those more cultivated than oneself. Disgust became not just the retching reaction that the sight of pigs gobbling up excrement in the street induced; it was also provoked by exhibitions of the tasteless and the cloying, and at all kinds of shameless vulgarity. The physical facet of disgust was what in part led to the great philanthropic projects of the eighteenth and nineteenth century. At the same time, its moral status assisted with lethal efficiency in social demarcation. The sight of a gin-soaked mother suckling an emaciated infant in the streets of London was a disgusting social phenomenon requiring urgent address. But it was also disgusting that people were apparently content to live this way.

Miller breathes a sigh of parenthetical regret that this development of the concept of 'taste' post-dates the importation into English of 'disgust'. Had it been the other way around, a neat case could be constructed that 'taste', of which disgust marked the absence, was rather linked to lack of refinement than to unpalatable food. There is however another case to be predicated on an older sense of the word 'taste', one that pre-dates either aesthetic discernment or the arrival of 'disgust'. That is its usage to mean a predilection or preference, and for which the OED cites Jonathan Swift addressing '[w]hoever hath a taste for true humour'. If, hesitating between two examples of anything, whether it be port wine or human flesh, one is found to be preferable to the other, it is often a short step to feeling distaste, dis-gust, at having to make do with the one not favoured. 'The worst enemy of a good wine,' say the Portuguese, 'is a better one.'

Despite this metaphorical shift in the sense of disgust, it remains primarily a physiologically determined response, accompanied by that state of distress and mental disequilibrium that unequivocally qualifies it as an emotion. Disgust belongs first of all to the physical realm, to putrefaction, bad odours and the decomposition of waste matter. The advantage of this in evolutionary terms is that it once taught us to steer clear of rotting carcasses, faeces and so forth, because of the serious risk of infection they carry. Eventually, this recoil in the face of organic matter alienates us from our other, relatively innocuous bodily processes, and from the appetites and feeding habits of others. The New York poet and singer Patti Smith once announced in song that the transformation of waste was perhaps the oldest human preoccupation, and while the point itself is debatable, a key element in the socialising and civilising processes of prehistory must have been finding ways of dealing with the regularity of the bodily functions. Defecation, vomiting, involuntary emissions of all kinds, seem to remind us, sometimes painfully, that we are all still animals.

Queen Elizabeth I, it is said, was not much enamoured of the lavatory that her godson Sir John Harington devised for her. While it offered a sight more dignity than the normal recourse, which was to sit on a bowl or box that would then be carried away, slopping with its contents, by a lady of the bedchamber, there seemed more than a touch of the cabinet of curiosities about it. It was installed in Richmond Palace, and consisted of a tank of water with a leather valve, mounted above a base that opened and closed, so that Gloriana's waste could be sluiced efficiently away without the need to entrust it to a servant. It seemed an ingenious enough idea, and the Queen did occasionally resort to it, but the feeling of participating unwillingly in some piece of theatrical absurdity, allied to the fact that the valve was not entirely watertight, so that it dribbled constantly when not in use, meant that it never became part of the daily furniture. What was more, this contrivance and its inventor were the cause of a certain amount of suppressed derision at court, perhaps leading the defender of the realm to sit that little less comfortably on it. Despite the fact, therefore, that it was the prototype flushing cistern toilet, Harington never made another model, and the idea lay dormant until it was revived again in the London of Dr Johnson's day.

Alexander Cummings, a watchmaker of Bond Street, London, patented the first U-bend lavatory in 1775, reviving Harington's cistern, but building into the design a curl of pipe, bent back on itself and permanently filled with water, which emptied on flushing by means of a sliding valve. The design was perfected three years later by the multi-talented Yorkshire inventor, Joseph Bramah, deviser of the unpickable lock, who incorporated a double-hinged valve into the U-bend, so that the contraption was no longer prone to leaking, and was even more efficient than Cummings' device at protecting the user from the smell of the sluices into which it discharged. Prior to the development of the domestic lavatory, the removal of waste was effected either by connection of the privy pipe to the main drain, where legally permitted, or – more usually for the better-off household – by handing it to the night-soil men who carried it away for you to the town cesspit. Among the poor, much excretion went on in full public view, generally in the middle of the street so as to leave a strip of walkway on either side, where, however, there was always the risk of catching the worst of a bucketful being emptied out from an upper window. The accumulated mass, crawling with flies, would occasionally be cleared away by teams of labourers, but in the meantime, the best recourse was to let pigs loose in the streets, where they would hungrily devour whatever was freshest, and therefore smelled most rankly. Not for nothing were the earliest domestic privies known as 'necessaries'. It is often thought that eighteenth-century town-dwellers barely noticed the fetid squalor of the public thoroughfares, that they were somehow inured to the filth and the flies, but any glance at the literature of social improvement of the time, and indeed the comments of foreign visitors who published journals of their tours in Great Britain, will soon correct that impression. Giovanni Jacopo Casanova, passing through London in 1763, was appalled to note that Londoners who squatted to defecate in the alleyways didn't trouble to conceal their exposed posteriors from the public gaze. He was advised that to face the other way would run the risk of identifying oneself to passers-by, which is perhaps why men caught short on the journey home from the pub to this day still find a wall to urinate against. But what of those who crouched to crap in the middle of the road? The occupants of passing carriages could see who they were. In that case, Casanova's guide observed, it was implicitly incumbent on the people in the carriage – if they had any pretension at all to the social graces – not to look.

Outside the great urban concentrations, people went on defecating and urinating into rivers and streams, or else in the pigs' enclosure, just as they always had done. For the nobility, there was always a greater degree of amenity. By the fourteenth century, castles were being built with privies sited within the exterior walls, so that waste matter dropped directly through an iron grille and into the moat below. From time to time, the accumulation of excrement grew so great, especially in hot weather, as to dry up the moat completely, at which point a small fortune would be spent on a group of labourers known as 'gong-farmers', whose unenviable job it was to excavate it. As with all such conveniences, it was the rich and privileged that benefited first from domestic sanitation. Much of the ribaldry that surrounded the flush lavatory that Harington invented for his regal godmother devolved on the fact that it was hard not to imagine the seat of excretion as a kind of scatological throne, so sealing for ever in the popular mind one of the lavatory's many ironic soubriquets. It wasn't long after it had become a feature of standard domestic furniture, initially confined to an outhouse at the rear of a dwelling before being brought indoors (sometimes as a corner extension to the building above ground-floor level), that toilet design began to take on a more rococo aspect. A throne designed for Louis XIII actually doubled as a lavatory, so that the royal bowel could be evacuated during prolonged state business. By the Victorian era, the ornate domestic lavatories of the nobility demonstrated that, whatever reputation for shamelessness in public hygiene the British had acquired in the previous century, they now need defer to nobody in the splendour of the settings in which excretion occurred. This was the era not only of the great public conveniences, underground municipal temples to Ajax, god of cleanliness, but of the elaborately decorated porcelain magnificence of the home convenience, with its capacious bowl, polished wooden seat, and cistern mounted majestically above head height, from which depended a weighty chain with a porcelain grip at the end, inscribed in flourishing letters with the courteous entreaty, 'Please pull'.

Thanks to the ministrations of Daniel Bostel of Bostel Bros, sanitation engineers of London and Brighton, there had been, in 1889, a final refinement in the flushing operation, which was now effected by means of a ballcock, so that the lavatory could theoretically be flushed again even if the cistern was only half-full. Bostel's lavatory is truly the one we have been availing ourselves of ever since (even though, by retroactive attribution, the name of Thomas Crapper, manufacturer of lavatories by royal appointment, bulks rather larger in the history of Victorian sanitation). From Harington to Bostel, the British have prided themselves, not entirely without cause, as being the pioneers of all things salutary with regard to domestic plumbing. The British 'loo' (an abridged corruption of the old French warning cried from the window as a bucket was about to slopped into the street below – '*Gardez l'eau!*') is still a superior being compared with the standard French article, which only relies on a weight to seal the top of the outflow pipe, leading to the famous constant dribble and its attendant limescale accretion in the bowl. Notwithstanding that, we know that the latrines in the houses of the Roman nobility ran into the main drainage systems by means of running water, effectively a sort of flush. Rome's Cloaca Maxima, the most ancient city sewer still in operation anywhere in the world, dates from the eighth century BC. As so often, however, European developments turn out to have been comprehensively anticipated in antiquity further east. Archaeologists working on a site in Shangqiu county in the Henan province of central China in 2000 discovered the tomb of a king of the Western Han dynasty, dating from around 200 BC. It contains not merely a latrine, but a toilet complete with stone seat, flushing mechanism, and what appears to be an armrest upon which the occupant could drowse away the weary *longueur* while waiting for his bowel to stir. Even earlier than that is the evidence of a kind of water closet with a small tank and wooden seat, unearthed in the latrines of the Palace of Knossos, constructed during the Minoan civilisation on Crete and dated at around 1700 BC.

It was, as I have noted, the need to keep disease at bay that led our ancestors to try to separate the procedures and products of excretion from the spaces in which they lived, a lesson that would appear to have been comprehensively forgotten by the eighteenth century. In the fourth century BC, we find Aristotle instructing his pupil, Alexander the Great, to ensure that dung from humans and horses is deposited as far away as practicable from his army's encampments, a stricture by which he echoes the advice of the author of Deuteronomy, some three thousand years before him:

Thou shalt have a place also without the camp, whither thou shalt go forth abroad: And thou shalt have a paddle upon thy weapon; and it shall be, when thou wilt ease thyself abroad, thou shalt dig therewith, and shalt turn back and cover that which cometh from thee … (23:12–13)

The reason given in the succeeding verse is that the Lord thy God will walk in the camp when he comes to deliver victory over thine enemies to thee, and quite frankly won't want to be offended by the sight of soldiers shitting, but the understanding of hygienic precaution that underpins the advice is impeccable. Typhoid, the chief health risk of faecal material, carried off Prince Albert – probably as a result of waste matter contaminating the drinking water supply – as late as 1861.

To enter the lavatory of a smart modern hotel or restaurant today is to step into a minutely designed environment of clinical aesthetics, in which any suggestion of bodily functions is pushed to the margins. A kaleidoscopic pattern of coloured lights plays behind the glass urinal at one central London venue, while water softly gushes over the panel. There are flushes activated by means of a light sensor, over which one passes the shadow of one's hand, to obviate the vulgarity of pushing or pulling. Music plays, there are magazines strewn on a table, as though one might choose to tarry awhile, while a young man in a pristine white jacket is retained by the management to brush the facings of your jacket while you dry your hands, and proffer from a spotless tray an array of perfumes for you to trifle with, before you discreetly deposit a gratuity in the dish. Not some bit of vulgar physical necessity, but a voluntary commercial transaction has taken place. In such circumstances, it seems, we have moved about as far away from acknowledging the reality of excretion as we can without actually abolishing it.

For all that this effete pretension is preferable to shit-spattered roadways and typhoid, nonetheless it is also plangent with cognitive ambiguity. In so sublimating our instinctual disgust at our own bodily functions – and even more so, those of others – we further ratify the disastrous schism wrought in us when we started believing that our mental and spiritual natures were superior to our physical beings.

Anthropologists of disgust such as Andras Angyal in 1941 and Paul Rozin in the 1980s often stressed the alien nature of what disgusted, particularly in the gastronomic field, as though otherness itself could make the gorge rise. Let us test ourselves.

The cuisine of Tibet relies centrally on rancid butter. Derived from the milk of the *dri*, the female yak, it is an indispensable staple of the national culture. Used medicinally for stiff joints and as an unguent to prevent the skin from drying out at the rarefied altitudes where these mountain communities live, and as fuel for lamps, it is also an important component in the national drink, *po cha*. The tea from which *po cha* is made comes in dried black bricks, from which a lump must be crumbled off and boiled in water for many hours. When a batch is made – and the Tibetans drink it throughout the day to ward off the cold – some of this infusion is added to freshly boiled water. After a further brief boiling, the tea is poured into a churn, to which is added yak milk, a quantity of the rancid yak butter and a generous sprinkling of salt. It is then churned at length to amalgamate these other ingredients, and is often drunk with a final slick of yak butter floating on the surface.

Tsampa is another fortifying staple of the diet. It consists of barley, which is roasted in the husk and then milled into fine flour, before being mixed with crumbled tea into little dry dumplings that are eaten with the fingers. As they are, these are considered fairly plain, but they can be made more sumptuous by adding rancid butter, the soft, sour curds of churned yak milk, and perhaps a pinch of sugar. Meat is eaten too, principally beef and mutton, and no part of the slaughtered animal is wasted. All the offal is used, while the meat is hacked roughly into huge chuck joints, which are then boiled over a fire. When a piece is ready, it is fished out and carved off the bone with the all-purpose knife each person carries. An honoured guest, such as a western tourist, will likely be presented with the tail, which is the *bonne bouche*, and a young Tibetan man offered a mutton tail in the house of his intended will thereby understand that her parents approve of him. The blood is used to make sausages, rather like English black pudding, while any leftover meat is dried through the winter in bins lined with bricks of impacted yak dung, to be eaten raw the following spring.

Visitors to Lhasa eating at a modern restaurant will probably proceed in six stages. First comes a cup of butter tea, after which one chooses a cold dish (perhaps dried yak stomach or cold blood sausage), a hot dish (ox-foot stew, stir-fried sheep or goat lung with the trachea still attached, or steamed duck with insect-plant, with a few boiled mushrooms on the side), and a staple starch (either buttered *tsampa*, buttered and curded raw flour, or rice with butter). These items are accompanied by *chang*, Tibetan barley beer, traditionally yeasted with eagle droppings, or its distillate, *arag*, and then as a closing libation, a final cup of steaming yak-buttered tea.

It would be difficult to conceive of a cuisine more likely to arouse intense revulsion in westerners. There are one or two Tibetan restaurants in New York and London, but they don't serve yak meat and they can't obtain real yak butter, and so anybody who had nervously sampled the bill of fare at these venues will not have been remotely prepared for what's on offer in Lhasa. So prevalent in the diet is rancid butter that everybody smells of it. When in medieval times Mediterranean people raised on olive oil first ventured into the dairy fat cultures of northern Europe, the first thing they noticed was the lingering odour of rancid butter fat that clung to the locals. It seeped from their skin and hovered about their hair like a sickly miasma, forcing strangers to clasp a hand to their faces when caught in the jostle of bodies at a market. To Japanese encountering the earliest western visitors in their midst, the phenomenon was all but intolerable. *Bata-kusai*, they called these greasily off-putting newcomers, or 'butter-stinkers'. The daily washing and deodorising of the modern era largely neutralises its rankness, but in the Tibetan villages, butter itself is the cleansing medium. Washing with water is not much indulged in, as it is too cold for most of the year to disrobe, but greasing the skin with butter, which is then left on to blacken and dry, is the next best recourse. Although hair may be washed with water once a month, butter is also used to ensure a sleek sheen between times. The use of rancid butter by the Tibetans has sound medical reasons. This fact was once acknowledged in European physic – in the sixteenth century, it was recognised that drinking melted butter that had sat in the sun for several days was a specific against joint pain such as arthritis. It is now thought that the concentration of vitamin D means that it could also have been of benefit against rickets, as well as assisting in opening the bowel, rancid butter being a fine laxative.

If these culinary and medicinal customs arouse disgust in us, however, it is less because they are different to what we are used to, and more because they turn on the ingestion and application of a substance that our sanitary regulations have now accustomed us to see as dangerous, namely spoiled dairy products. And yet without lactic spoilage, we would have no cheese or yoghurt or *crème fraîche*.

In the founding principle of Platonic philosophy, the human organism is divided into a tripartite construction. Reason, its loftiest achievement, is located in the head, from which all the great contemplative glories proceed; the will, which is required for such heroic attributes as courage and fortitude, sits squarely in the chest, which may be seen to inflate in direct proportion to its exercise; and the appetites swill around somewhere in the abdominal region, threatening to disrupt the other two constituents by distracting the senses with the prospect of feasting, drinking and carnal pleasure. Although Plato recommends that the correct approach to life is to achieve a harmonious balance among the three, what this means in practice is that the appetites, the physical life, must be held in check – precisely because the chance of an evening of wine and sex is invariably a more appealing one than the opportunity to display one's bravery in the face of adversity. In the Christian faith, the strong anti-materialist leaning of Plato became central to the life of the devout. The body is swarming with those temptations that might undermine the health of the soul. It was not only that sexual temptation and a preoccupation with the pleasures of the table and of the wine jug were to be abjured; the entire leaking, rickety edifice of the physical body came to be seen as a prison. If the urge to pleasure oneself is as needling as St Augustine confesses it to be, how much more intolerable were those evidences of corporeality that involved no such enjoyment – all the bleeding, diarrhoea and purulence, the emunctuations, evacuations and disgorgements? Illness itself, when the body seems to sicken of its own organic functioning, is invested with special piquancy. As one groans and sweats on one's helpless bed, the chains of physical mortality come to weigh their heaviest. Puking and coughing and stinking, the sick grow to loathe the entire realm of the physical, and imagine the spirit within yearning to break free of its entombment.

The disaster this attitude was to wreak in humanity reached its apogee in the genocides of the twentieth century, in which we are plainly made to see that the physical body is as expendable as Plato held it to be. There could have been no Nazi persecution of whole ethnic, social and sexual groups without a driving sense of disgust. The modern paintings that didn't meet Goering's approval were displayed in a public exhibition entitled 'Degenerate Art', at which viewers were encouraged to view the barbaric daubs of Cubism as evidences of mental sickness. An index of internationally known Jewish stars of the entertainment industry that erroneously included Charlie Chaplin lists him as 'a disgusting Jewish acrobat'. Erich Fromm, in a sociological study of human destructiveness, which includes a long case history of Hitler, points out the peculiar look of offended distaste that appears to have been the Führer's default facial expression, the upper lip retracted, the nostrils flared, the eyes blinking rapidly, so that even when acknowledging the salutes of his officers, he appears to be trying and just failing to maintain an impassive look in the presence of some wretched smell.

The feeling could, of course, be mutual. Gitta Sereny, in her 1995 biography of Albert Speer, recounts how, after the Nazi architect saw the slave labour camps, and possibly became aware of the Final Solution, he suddenly found Hitler, whom he had previously idolised, physically repellent, to the point where he couldn't bear to look at him. To be regularly disgusted by others in this way is the prerequisite for wanting to obliterate them, and even though most of us are not much given to founding political parties with precisely that aim, the impulse is one that we must learn to resist. It is the same impulse that drives all xenophobia and, in the present day, much of the anxiety about immigration.

Only with the masterwork of Arthur Schopenhauer, *The World as Will and Representation* (1819), with its detailed acknowledgement of the physical realm we are all bound to inhabit, and which begins within the margins of our own vulnerable bodies, does the great enterprise of western philosophy start to take notice once more of the corporeal being. Even the eastern theology to which Schopenhauer felt drawn, however, provides little reconciliation with our physical state, offering only the same renunciation and mortification on which the western tradition is founded. Buddhism itself was born out of the prolonged bodily privation of its founder. There is no joy other than the abjuration of joy. In the extremes of physical suffering, enlightenment awaits, piercing the mundane veil of transitory pain to reveal the flash of bliss that lies behind it. The elevation of the spiritual at the expense of the corporeal is the closest thing to blasphemy of which the secular world can conceive. It, not sensual desire, is the root of all evil – and the root, one might add, of all culture. There is no such thing as a purely metaphysical life, as Bertolt Brecht brutally reminds us in pointing out that 'culture's mansion is built of dogshit'. It hates itself for smelling so bad. And so do we, when we find it hard to reconcile ourselves to the physical side of our humanity, feeling ourselves tethered by what the saint calls 'the clanking chains of my mortality', or – like him – suspecting that some celestial observer finds our self-indulgences repulsive. 'I stank in your eyes,' Augustine confesses to his creator, recalling the indiscretions of his adolescence, 'but I was pleasing to myself and I desired to be pleasing to the eyes of men.' Glancing back in pity across the centuries, we try to console him that the latter part of this statement, correctly construed, can represent our noblest aspiration.

8

I DISGUST

As with all the emotions, perhaps with the exception of happiness, the disgust response can be intentionally provoked in the interests of cultural investigation or entertainment. If facing down phobic fear (which often contains a pronounced element of disgust) by means of controlled exposure to its catalyst can illuminate the path to its abolition, could not a drawing near to that from which one naturally recoiled offer the chance of mastering revulsion? This impulse to demystify the horrible, to render it harmless by means of greater acquaintance, is what has driven many of the encounters that ordinary individuals have had in history with the processes of the organic self – either in its time of trauma, or after its physical expiration. What could be more disgusting than death, or more needful of reconciliation?

Our fascination with the workings of the body, as well as its disorders, is an ancient one. The western medical tradition and the earliest ideas about anatomy derive from the Greeks, who – among other investigative practices – are known to have carried out vivisection experiments on criminals. Even earlier, the quasi-surgical procedures involved in mummification as practised by the Egyptians shed much light on the biology of the human organism. When the dissection of corpses became a matter of public spectacle in the anatomical schools of Europe in the mid-eighteenth century, however, that fascination was made manifest. Although statutes existed in the United Kingdom, in France and in Austria that permitted a limited number of the corpses of convicted felons – generally hanged murderers – to be supplied to medical schools for the purposes of autopsy, the numbers were insufficient to meet their expressed needs. The provision of four bodies a year had been the English statutory arrangement since the time of Henry VIII. The shortfall was supplied by grave robbery, and by a brisk trade in the corpses of the executed (and of others of the recently deceased), which was transacted in an atmosphere of legal impunity, ecclesiastical disapproval and public revulsion. When common criminals were hanged at Tyburn in the mid-eighteenth century, it was not unusual for the group at the foot of the scaffold to be comprised of surgeons' assistants or their agents and relatives of the condemned, contending over the remains. Even prompt burial was no guarantee that the corpse would not be purloined, and if the body was to be dumped in one of the mass graves designated as the final resting place for paupers, it was even more vulnerable to procurement – not least because it was quite likely to be left in a heap with other bodies awaiting collective interment in several days' time.

The advances in medicine of this era commonly derive, despite their great variety, from anatomical pathology. When the body could be opened up, and its now defunct internal machinery laid bare and considered alongside the physical evidence and symptomatology of whatever had led to its death, medicine took several important steps forwards. Where once the medic could only observe the suffering organism from afar, noting its symptoms in the language of metaphorical allusion, he could now inspect it at the closest quarters, opening it up and peering into it, removing and analysing its constituent parts. As a result, the human body was subjected to the same types of formal classification that had been applied to the rest of the natural world. The understanding of common diseases that resulted from these researches added hugely to the medical, and then surgical, armoury against them, so that, as

Michel Foucault formulates it, the question asked of the patient by his or her doctor gradually changed from the 'What is the matter with you?' of the pre-anatomical era, to the 'Where does it hurt?' of the late eighteenth century. In the former enquiry, the medic relies upon the patient to announce the sickness. With the latter, he had arrived at the position of being able to inform the patient what the disorder was on the strength of a description of its attributes. Knowledge had passed to the medical authority, had become properly scientific, a state of affairs that persists today in the homily that still informs most diagnostic practice. 'Listen to the patient,' the medical student is taught. 'He is telling you the diagnosis.'

Notwithstanding the popular outrage that attached to what was seen as the defilement of the body by clinical dissection, public anatomical displays did not lack for interested parties. Although eventually confined to medical students and other clinicians, they were for a time, within the precincts of certain private anatomical schools, open to all whose natural curiosity, as well as a certain moral quiescence, fitted them to attend. Among the spectators at a series of dissections that Erasmus Darwin (grandfather of the theorist of evolution, and leading light in the group of so-called Lunar Men whose dedication to scientific enquiry led to the establishment of the Royal Society) gave in London in the 1760s were two Anglican clergymen of his acquaintance, who later wrote to tell him how much they had appreciated his enlightening demonstration, and how much they hoped there might be another before long. At the other extremity of tolerance, William Hogarth – alert as ever to manifestations of moral entropy in the Georgian cultural milieu – includes a scene of dissection in his series of engravings, *The Stages of Cruelty* (1751). Within the institutional splendour of the Company of Surgeons, before the scholarly gaze of an enthroned professor, and the ranks of mortar-boarded academics and the jostling *demi-monde*, a corpse is being dis membered by three doctors. One is pulling apart a deep abdominal incision to expose the viscera, another is penetrating the head by drilling through the anterior plates of the skull and inserting a probe through a vacant eye-socket, and a third preparing to make another incision in the ankle, while an assistant receives the extruded large intestine in a bucket of offal. A dog in the foreground sniffs hungrily at what appears to be the discarded heart. The skulls and long bones of other subjects, meanwhile, are rendering away in a bubbling pan set over a blazing fire. This last detail furnishes the scene with its diabolic Shakespearean resonance. When shall these three meet again?

The perception of investigative anatomy was helped by the judicial recourse made available in Britain from 1752 of prescribing dissection of his corpse to a murderer sentenced to be hanged. Exposure on the gibbet, so that the unburied body could be seen to decompose and putrefy in full public view, had been the juridical intensifier in crimes thought particularly heinous, but now the delivery of the body of the condemned to the surgical schools was provided for as a further torment. The tradition of a 'decent Christian burial' was to be denied in furtherance both of chastisement and of deterrence. Thus, while the schools and teaching hospitals received a readier supply of raw material, the idea that medical science was a scandalous blasphemy, a gratuitous invasion of the body intended to reinforce the point that not even in death could the felon escape the admonitory attentions of the law, was fixed in the minds of ordinary people. In the present day, the same excruciated indignation is aroused by vivisection and other experiments on animals, often erroneously seen by its protestors as the sanctioned indulgence of sadism in a minority of clearly disturbed professional individuals. A latter-day manifestation of horror at medical invasion was occasioned in Britain in 1999 by the revelation that the authorities at Alder Hey hospital in Liverpool had been permitting the removal and retention of patient organs and tissue for research, following *post mortem* examination, without consent being sought.

In 2002, an exhibition of the work of Dr Gunther von Hagens, which toured Europe under the title *Body Worlds*, seemed to arouse equal measures of disgust and fascination. A spume of affronted outrage in the tabloid press when it arrived in London focused on the exhibition's legality, rather missing the mark, but those who did venture to see it, myself included, found themselves having to resolve unexpected moral dilemmas. All of von Hagens's subjects had given him consent for his plastination studies of human anatomy, but did they realise their bodies would be as whimsically displayed as they are? The figure of a man holds his expertly flayed, translucent skin over one arm like a raincoat. An athlete is literally running out of his skin, leaving his partly detached muscles flying out in streamers behind him. One room is devoted merely to specimens of defective foetuses, presented in the old-fashioned way, as though von Hagens is waiting for public discomfiture to relax enough to be able to add a humorous tableau of an anencephalic baby. The unease provoked by the show seemed to lie in the uncertain status of the exhibits. Were they artworks, aids to scientific understanding, or even – as the torso split open to reveal the tar-blackened lungs of a smoker seemed to indicate – items of medical propaganda?

The same kinds of ethical questions, intensified by the greater receptivity to religion of an earlier age, informed the outcry over dissection in the eighteenth century. Neither science nor the law ought to have been surprised, however, by the degree of public revulsion aroused by *post-mortem* dissection. It was held to be both theft and desecration, as cheerfully oblivious to cultural taboos as whistling in cemeteries. Then again, it wasn't so much its cheeriness that was objectionable as the cultivation of that air of professional coldness, with which investigative science has largely been lumbered ever since, that inspired popular disgust. A sense of what we would now call clinical detachment might be forgiven in a surgeon overcoming his sympathy with a patient's screaming agony on the slab in order to open her body and remove a gallstone; but the opening of a dead body merely to see what was inside it spoke of a far more sinister motivation. The highest stage of such detachment was apparently reached by William Harvey, the English anatomist responsible for discovering the circulation of the blood in 1628, who dissected the corpses of both his father and his sister. Harvey studied at the pre-eminent European anatomical school at Padua. Long before the hue and cry over public dissection and the so-called resurrection men (grave robbers) in Georgian Britain, Italy had led the field in anatomical research, the subjects for which, as in Britain, were the bodies of hanged felons. All endeavours in the field, at least until the late eighteenth century, were in a sense merely footnotes to Leonardo da Vinci, whose work in Florence in the early 1500s was suppressed by the Catholic Church for being close to diabolism. His work on anatomy remained under ecclesiastical lock and key for over 250 years. When it was finally allowed to see the light of day, it was found to have anticipated many of the discoveries made by succeeding generations. Andreas Vesalius, who founded a celebrated anatomical school in Brussels in the mid-sixteenth century, was his first and most important successor. Dr von Hagens, performing an autopsy live on British television in 2002, is only his most recent.

By the Victorian era, the public had become considerably more reconciled to the notion of anatomical display, once it was live, consenting bodies that were being opened before audiences. The sizeable group that witnessed Dr John Collins Warren's operation on a patient at the Massachusetts General Hospital in Boston on 16 October 1846 had fewer of the qualms of viewers of the previous century. It was to be the first public demonstration of surgery using ether as an anaesthetic. Warren, then nearing retirement, had been impressed by a contraption invented by a dental surgeon, W T G Morton, which consisted of a glass globe containing an etherised sponge, the calming fumes of which were delivered via a pipe to a patient wearing a breathing mask. Gilbert Abbott had been admitted to the hospital for the removal of a benign congenital vascular tumour on the left side of his neck, and consented to have his scheduled operation delayed by three days in order that the new experimental procedure might be tested. Despite the fact that there could be no question of pre-medication in the 1840s, the patient appeared to be relaxed and trusting before the operation. In keeping with the professional solicitude that continues to this day in the anaesthetist's art, Morton was present to comfort the patient. He was heard to ask Abbott, 'Are you afraid?', and received an unwavering 'No' in response. The mask was then applied to Abbott's face, he was instructed to breathe deeply, and after about four or five minutes, he appeared to drift off into a deep sleep. As Warren made the incision, he fully expected the patient to be rudely roused, but he neither flinched nor emitted a sound. It then took him precisely ten minutes to excise the defective tissue, create a ligature in the vein and suture the wound. The patient didn't remain entirely unresponsive, as Warren records in his subsequent paper on the anaesthetic:

[D]uring the insulation of the veins he began to move his limbs and utter extraordinary expressions, and these movements seemed to indicate the existence of pain; but after he had recovered his faculties, he said he had experienced none, but only a sensation like that of scraping the part with a blunt instrument, and he ever after continued to say he had not felt any pain.

At the close of the procedure, Warren was heard to remark to colleagues, 'Gentlemen, this is no humbug.' Abbott was discharged, fully recovered, in the first week of December, having participated in ushering in a new and merciful era in the history of surgery. That it was watched by journalists and members of the public is in itself an important part of the story, since it marked a transformation in the act of bearing witness to medicine from the prurient horror of earlier periods to a state of calm reassurance. The site of surgery was already tellingly known as the operating theatre, but the spectacle was now less the Roman amphitheatre than the didactic milieu of the nineteenth-century stage.

Television now obviates the need for a public gallery in the hospital, but has brought back a little of the sense of strange fascination, if not actually disgust, that such displays once bestowed. We might well be horrified at the film of reconstructive facial surgery or the separation of conjoined twins that the documentary promises, but we can't quite look away. It is possible to feel a palpable sense of the uncanny (Freud's *Unheimlichkeit*) at such moments, a queasy state of suspension that returns us to reality feeling slightly but distinctly changed. What we are experiencing once again is the psychic weightlessness induced by confronting our most disabling emotional responses, intermingled – in the case of surgery, at least – with a sudden, unbidden intimation of our own mortality.

The grotesque has been a cultural obsession since the days of the Roman circus, when it was as intimately connected to investigations of the human body and its destructibility as came to be the case in public anatomical demonstrations. Mortality, which creeps discreetly up on the viewer of televised surgery, was more explicitly the theme of the spectacle when savage and unpredictable death became a matter of mass entertainment.

It is not known exactly why the gladiatorial contests came to be such an integral part of the cultural life of classical Rome. One theory is that the practice of making captives fight each other had been absorbed from the Etruscan culture of central northern Italy. Contests in which slaves, prisoners of war or condemned criminals were painstakingly trained to engage in mortal conflict with each other, or with wild animals, until one or the other prevailed – more often than not through the final exhaustion of his opponent – were the most widely attended of all public spectacles. Perhaps something of the cathartic nature of the tragic theatre attached to the circuses too: by providing a display of unconscionable cruelty and terror, the state ensured that its citizens were reconciled to the duties and privations that life in the Roman Empire thrust upon them. The difference, of course, was that the circuses offered real blood, dismemberment and death, not the stylised enactment and poetic descriptions on offer in the theatres.

Classifications of the different styles of gladiatorial fighting were as meticulous as the divisions of gymnastics. Not all fought with the sword (*gladius*) after which they were named. The *Retiarii* were armed with tridents and nets, hoping to enmesh their adversaries helplessly before finishing them off. Thracians used a curved scimitar rather than the classic short sword, and defended themselves with a small round shield, unlike the long, rectangular shield of the *Sammite* and *Mirmillo* fighters. It was these latter two that wore the visored helmet lately seen again on Russell Crowe. We know too that gladiators were by no means exclusively the fit male combatants dear to the film industry. Women and the physically handicapped were occasionally pressed into service as well. What was wanted, though, was not the quick dispatch of the helpless, but a prolonged, tantalisingly unpredictable contest, which would begin with formal passes between the protagonists, the infliction of light but copiously bloody flesh-wounds, and proceed to a frenzy of mutual assault. Every fight contained within it a moment in which the natural reluctance of the contenders to participate became a bitter struggle for survival, and it was at this point that the crowd became engaged with the action. The final stages were shambolic butchery, but the fight was generally stopped short so that the crowd could pronounce their verdict on the loser. If he was deemed to have taken part to the limit of his abilities, he might be spared, literally living to fight another day once he was patched up.

Despite the ban imposed on gladiatorial contests by Emperor Constantine in AD 325, under the influence of the Christian Church, they continued in more or less flagrant defiance of the law well into the next century, proving as unsusceptible to abolition by administrative diktat as the riotous Bacchic festivals had once done. There was, and perhaps is, an inexhaustible public appetite for the spectacle of death and mutilation, of the sufferings of others. Perhaps horror at the plight of the grievously injured gladiator contained an intimation of the wafer-thin boundary that separated one's own existence from the primordial violence of general human fate. In the circus, one saw life and death being played out in accelerated form, one giving place to the other in a bestial summation of the mortality to which all were eventually subject. Then again, straightforward sadism – at once indulged and absolved by its manifestation in crowd form – no doubt drew people to the arena. After the demise of the contests, attendance at public executions served this function, but the crowds that watched criminals hang or have their heads severed were by no means entirely of one mind. Today, the impulse flickers on in the *corridas* of Spain, southern France and Mexico, licensed displays of bestiality half-sanitised by the occasional serious injury or fatality sustained by one of the toreadors, as if the consequence of their own risk somehow makes it a fair fight.

The chance to see the repulsive, the terrifying and the unworldly still exercises a powerful lure on human curiosity, even though, after the Romans, we may need it to be clothed in some other apparel than sheer entertainment. In place of the catharsis by which Aristotle sought to explain tragic drama, though, the Enlightenment substituted the totem of scientific understanding. Visitors to the von Hagens exhibition were told in the programme notes that they were there to deepen their comprehension of human physiology, not to gawp, slack-jawed, at the sight of real dead bodies with their entrails on view. The same motivation officially explained the interest of Victorian audiences in freak shows, and of small-town American folk in the specimens of disordered humanity that the travelling circuses hid within their curtained booths. The fact that many of these spectacles were faked only seems in retrospect to have rub visitors' noses in their own prurience. 'Come and see the woman born without a body!' my grandmother remembered a circus barker calling to the crowds, and the affronted reaction of a woman nearby who piously murmured, 'It's a sin to let her live.'

The greatest freak show ringmaster of the twentieth century, the cartoonist Robert L Ripley, whose newspaper cartoon strip of oddball facts and disturbing spectacles first appeared in the *New York Globe* in 1918, understood better than anybody since that there is an insatiable public predilection for controlled revulsion. Many of the exhibits at the Ripley museums, which are still open today, in his birthplace of Santa Rosa, California, and on the Blackpool seafront in England, refer to trifling oddities of the kind that provoke nothing more than momentary bemusement. A carrot pulled from the ground in Chile was found to have the precise shape of the country itself. As these bald, inconsequential facts multiply, one finds oneself thinking 'Well, what of it?' The real business of the Ripley industry, however, as its founder often declared, was humanity, the strangest spectacle the planet had to offer. By the time our blood is running cold at tales of Hindu self-mortification (though never, oddly, the Roman Catholic variety), at infants that came to light with one eye-socket, no eye-sockets, double pupils or twenty fingers, at men with horns, women with their breasts on their backs, and tribes where men's legs wither prematurely because they consider it effeminate to sit down, we have arrived at the agenda's principal business. Monitors show videos of people cramming their mouths with cockroaches, or hammering six-inch nails into their nostrils, and perhaps we might ask ourselves what it is within us that wishes to know all this. Not just the physical detail of it, but our own inability to rise above an interest in it, compels us to a powerful sense of disgust. It isn't telling us how congenital defects, or 'pranks of nature' as Ripley preferred, are either corrected or surmounted in the lives of those who have been afflicted with them, but rather inviting us to stare (as we were brought up not to), with the retracted upper lip of Darwin's physiognomics, at the world of human suffering. In this sense, Ripley was an impeccable situationist *avant la lettre*, understanding that in contemporary experience the world exists solely for us to gape at.

In one contemporary instance – the treatment of the circus freaks in Tod Browning's iconic 1932 film *Freaks*, we can perhaps read a possible redemption of the disgust response. *Freaks* in particular, in didactically inverting the moral expectations of its audience, remains a spellbinding exploration of human otherness. 'The love of beauty,' proclaims the film's opening caption, 'is a deep-seated urge which dates back to the beginning of civilisation,' before going on to demonstrate, over its short duration, that the beauty it celebrates is of the moral and not the physiological kind. Its cast of microcephalics, conjoined twins, the limbless and the genderless, emerge as its heroes, passively but perceptively aware of the capitalist racket in which they are participating. It is generally read as a critique of the almighty Hollywood studio system, well into its stride by this time, which was already treating its contracted stars like the deformed exhibits of the circus. In the light of this, its financing and distribution by MGM, the one studio more wedded than all the others to expensive celebrity gloss ('More stars than there are in the heavens!'), seems a remarkable piece of commercial bravery, were it not for the fact that the widespread critical revulsion that attended its release provoked Louis B Mayer to withdraw it from circulation, writing the project off as a straight loss of $164,000. It remained in the MGM vaults, unseen, for decades, and was only rightly restored to the public by means of a tentative airing at the 1962 Cannes Film Festival.

Although not many of the participants retained much affection for Browning after the debacle into which the project turned, the achievement of *Freaks* for modern audiences is that it seems to restore some semblance of dignity to people for whom accidents of nature had been made into the substance of a career. The plot, which is not devoid of a classic dash of MGM romance, reminds us that, when we have finished grimacing and retching, we might come to see that disgust as a response to the mere physicality of other human beings, as distinct from what we perceive of their actions and motivations, is an emotion worth overcoming. It is possible for a full-sized woman to fall in love with a man less than three feet tall. 'Believe it,' Robert Ripley would have challenged us, ' – or not!'

9

I AM DISGUSTED

When Judith Dufour collected her daughter from a London poor-house in 1734, she knew that at least the poor wretch would have new clothes. The child of an unemployed mother who spent most of her time too drunk to find work had hardly enjoyed the best start in life, but in handing her over to the institution, Judith had at least ensured that the pitiful tatters in which she was wrapped were replaced by something better. The child would be washed, fed and tended for a short while before being returned to a parent who might now be in a position to make a greater effort on her behalf. Many children and babies went into – and occasionally came out of – such brutal institutions as a result of being orphaned or abandoned by mothers who, themselves deserted by unscrupulous sexual partners, found themselves with no means to care for them. Judith Dufour's plight was that of many of the urban poor, destitute, often homeless, in the middle of one of the most affluent and populous cities in the world. What was unusual about her case was her motive for reclaiming her daughter.

Barely had Judith and a woman companion taken the child out of sight of the poorhouse than they strangled her. Having done so, they stripped her body of every last stitch of its new clothing, disposing of the little corpse by throwing it into the street ditch, where it would have settled among the stinking mass of animal entrails, blood and excreta. Within a short time, they had sold the infant's clothing on the street, and used the proceeds to buy a decent quantity of what they really craved – the strong, cheap, crudely perfumed spirit that, along with a little moulding bread to soak it up, formed almost the entire diet of many of the city's poor. Judith and her friend were not just drinkers, or alcoholics, as we would now see them. They were gin addicts.

It is often thought that the early eighteenth-century English obsession with gin was largely a working-class phenomenon, but its widespread use among the poor and destitute of the cities only constitutes the most lurid evidence of what was in fact its near universal saturation of society. Everybody drank it, the only difference being that the better off bought the official product of reputable distilleries such as Booths, established in 1740 and still going strong today, while the poor drank whatever they could afford. Most of the privately produced spirit, which was cooked up illicitly in back rooms, attics, cellars, and even in prisons and poorhouses, was made in evasion of drink duties introduced in 1729. Even so, spirits were still taxed more lightly than domestic beer and cider or imported wines, as a result of an Act of Parliament of 1690, which had established the principle that anybody was entitled to distil. Behind the Act lay a conscious antagonism of the French, whose precious cognac and *eau-de-vie* might be elbowed out of the commercial picture if enough patriotic Englishmen took to making 'British brandy'. Since grain products were the only raw material available for distillation, some form of rudimentary white spirit was the inevitable result of freelance efforts.

Gin had been popular in England since soldiers fighting in the Netherlands in the Thirty Years War had brought back a taste for it, and the accession of William of Orange to the English throne after the unseating of James II had led to a substantial increase in imports of the real thing. What dribbled off the stills in the cellars of London, however, and was peddled in the streets from wheelbarrows, bore very little relation to the genuine article. While the recipe might, if you were lucky, be on nodding terms with what in Holland was considered a medicinal tonic – juniper berries having a reputation as a diuretic in an era when the idea of purging the body of unwanted secretions was very much at the forefront of medical thinking – the original bathtub gin was largely concocted from a medley of noxious substances. An ingredients list from a work entitled *The Publican's Daily Companion*, published well after the gin disaster had abated, includes 'Oil of vitriol [sulphuric acid], Oil of almonds, Oil of turpentine, Spirits of wine, Lump sugar, Lime water, Rose water, Alum, Salt of tartar'. Not only the fact that these foul potations were being swallowed, but also the quantities in which they were taken, horrified novelist Henry Fielding, who in a piece of earnest social analysis of 1751, reported of the gin drinkers that:

Many of these wretches there are who swallow pints of this poison within the twenty-four hours: the dreadful effects of which I have the misfortune every day to see, and to smell too.

As well as being poisonous, illicit gin was cripplingly strong. Home distillation does not end, as the official process does, with rectification and adjustment of the alcohol potency, but by bottling whatever trickles off the still. Some of it was sold in the streets still warm.

The widespread toxicity to which people succumbed in drinking poorly produced gin had been aggravated by the Gin Act of 1736, which raised the duty on gin, but more importantly made it illegal to purchase it in anything but bulk quantities, in order to discourage abuse. Once it had been effectively removed from the financial ambit of society's marginals, their only available resort was to poisonous contraband. The Gin Act provoked persistent rioting against its privations, a level of unrest that finally forced its revocation after six years on the statute books. It was all the more hated because it was well known that parliamentarians themselves were often so obstreperous, or else incapable, with gin that proceedings of the House had to be suspended to give Honourable Members the chance to sober themselves up.

The better known of William Hogarth's celebrated pair of engravings, *Beer Street* and *Gin Lane*, published in the same year as Fielding's moral treatise, shows gin as the agent of social disintegration that it had by then become. The skeletal remnant of an inebriate, all fleshless skull and protuberant ribcage, glass in one hand, flagon in the other, sits collapsed at the foot of a flight of steps, at the top of which a nursing mother, still cackling with paradoxical vitality, has let her baby (in what we might take to be a deliberate echo of the Judith Dufour case) topple unnoticed from her grasp. Behind a wall to her right, a gnarled figure grapples over a bone with a snarling dog, while in the background, the jug-shaped sign outside the Kilman Distiller's premises is shadowed by one next door in the form of a coffin. Part of the upper wall of the building outside which it hangs has fallen away to reveal the dangling corpse of a hanged man in a garret. We are studying not just a landscape of moral squalor, but one of physical illness and death as well. You didn't need to have read the reports of the city hospitals to know that this was the inevitable consequence of the gin habit. The evidence, for Hogarth as much as for Fielding, was by then all around. If it wasn't drunken wet-nurses suckling half-starved babies on doorsteps, it was the sight of emaciated beggars puking helplessly into the gutters, school-aged children casually tossing back a morning glass to assuage their hunger, and everywhere the pitiful calls of the impoverished trying to sell whatever possessions they had left – worn-out craftsmen's tools, battered and blackened kitchen utensils – to scrape together the vital penny or two that would buy another briefly satisfying dram.

It wasn't just the doleful cost in adult ill-health and infant mortality that gin was exacting that sounded the alarm for Fielding,

Samuel Johnson and others. What seems to animate much of the more indignant polemic of the time was the unashamed evidence gin-drinking offered of a general public craving run riot, an appetite that had spun out of all rational control, making its victims forget their most basic human duties. That a mother could tear the clothes from the body of her own murdered baby, and sell them for another hit, was only the most glaring example of behaviour that was going on in a thousand less appalling ways all over the city. What had happened to people? It was as though they had been taken over by some mysterious force that rendered them incapable of seeing the harm they were doing to themselves – and to the reputation of England abroad. European visitors to the British Isles could scarcely believe the state of overt, raucous befuddlement under which London seemed to operate. Whether it was parliamentarians roaring at each other by guttering torchlight in the House of Commons, or actors on the Covent Garden stage stumbling and dithering as they forgot their lines, before audiences too lubricated to sit still long enough to hear them, both business and pleasure seemed to take place under the handicap of permanent crapulence.

The general aim was to become drunk as quickly as possible, and stay in that condition for as long as possible, by constantly topping up the level of unmetabolised alcohol in the system. To this end, it has been reliably estimated that Londoners were probably drinking something in the region of two-thirds of a modern bottle of spirits per capita every day, or more than 180 litres a year. (Compare this to current alcohol intake for the UK, which is around 118 litres of beer per annum, 14.4 litres of wine, and only 4.75 litres of spirit.) This colossal consumption took its toll in terms of the then unrecognised conditions of alcohol hepatitis and other liver damage, chronic genito-urinary inflammation, severe toxicity from adulterants, and the associated dietary deficiency – with lack of thiamine leading to psychotic episodes – that all uncontrolled drinking brings in its train. It was during this period that bakeries first began selling bread hacked up into halfpenny lumps, as those who were wasting a large proportion of what little money they had on gin found they couldn't afford to buy the whole loaf. For these people, life itself had become almost valueless. If they were going to be poor, they might be as well be too drunk to notice, and if gin was going to kill them, well then, wouldn't that ultimately be a blessing?

It wasn't until the following century that the psychological aspects of dependency on intoxicants began to be articulated. In the 1750s, it was a mere matter of moral incontinence if you drank yourself into a stupor every day, but what the founding of the homes for inebriates and the ladies' and gentlemen's retreats of the Victorian era indicate is that drunkenness did not disappear with the dwindling of the gin epidemic. It simply became less public. After a brief lull at the close of the eighteenth century, alcohol consumption revived spectacularly in the nineteenth, accompanied now by widespread use of such ancillary substances as laudanum (opiated alcohol) and morphine. The distaste that such habits aroused was more muted in proportion to the relative lack of public display they entailed. The squalid ambience of the old gin shops and drinking dens was replaced by the gin palaces, ornately decorated public houses in which a certain atmosphere of decorum prevailed, and into whose melancholy bosom the working man and woman could retreat at the end of the day, quietly steeping their souls with officially sanctioned liquor, instead of rowdily downing the toxic swill of their forebears. Sunk in self-contemplation amid the ironic décor of gilded mirrors and classical columns, they helped give birth to the persistent myth that, more than any other alcoholic drink, gin is the harbinger of acute depression.

The gin epidemic died out abruptly. It is usually held to have extended its sway over London society for about thirty years, from roughly 1720 to the legislation of 1751 that provided for a sharp increase in taxation. Moreover, whereas the early years had been fuelled by surplus grain, the relative paucity of harvests in the middle years of the eighteenth century meant that very little grain could be spared for distillation. Jessica Warner has offered perhaps the most persuasive argument for its sudden decline, in postulating that, in common with many subsequent epidemics of ruinous intoxicant abuse, the gin craze ran out of steam because the succeeding generation learned the lesson of it. Society, disgusted with the prospect of physical dissolution and infant neglect, realised that things couldn't continue as they had. There were, after all, other forms of drink, and equally patriotic ones such as beer, that didn't produce the devastation that gin had wrought. Both Warner and another recent author on eighteenth-century gin, Patrick Dillon, draw what might seem to be irresistible parallels with drug epidemics of succeeding eras, such as the opium habit of the early nineteenth century, the cocaine craze of the early twentieth, and the depredations of heroin and crack cocaine in North American and European cities of the present day. Warner allows of a more fastidious degree of historical relativity in her approach than does Dillon, for whom the comparison appears to be an exact one, but the truth is that the connections between the gin epidemic and, particularly, the contemporary drug crisis are considerably more tenuous than at first appears. While it is true that much of the gin consumed in the eighteenth century was being privately distilled and sold without licence, and was therefore technically illegal, the product itself was not. Secondly, the consumption of gin had originally been specifically urged on the nation as a patriotic alternative to drinking the imported spirits of the despised French, which can scarcely be said to be the case with heroin or crack. But the principal divergence lies in the sheer ubiquity of the gin habit in Georgian London. We may well flinch at the climbing statistics of registered opiate addicts in the western world, but we are hardly likely to come across heroin being used at polite dinner parties, or openly offered in high street outlets with corporate headquarters in

St James's. In the 1730s, it is recorded, there were certain areas of London, such as St Giles or Holborn, where every fourth building housed some sort of dram-shop, either of the licit or the subterranean variety – and that isn't counting the street vendors who buried bottles of it among the legitimate goods in their carts and barrows, or who, lacking even the recourse of a wheelbarrow, hid it under the layers of their voluminous skirts. A British comic poet of recent years may have insisted in verse that positively everybody is taking cocaine nowadays – but they aren't. Everybody was, however, drinking gin.

It is this now almost unimaginable prevalence that explains, more than any other factor, the delayed reaction to the gin epidemic. It may have petered out quite suddenly in the end, but that it took over thirty years to do so is in many ways the most startling aspect of the whole phenomenon. The reason for this in turn lies, I believe, in the psychological dynamics of disgust. When a situation – in this case objective social conditions – arouses our repugnance, the strength of the emotion reaches a climactic pitch more quickly than any of the other emotions. There do exist such reactions as sudden extreme terror, or – to a lesser extent – anger that reaches a state of acute vituperation within seconds, but these are the exceptions to the expected patterns, in which the former begins as creeping unease and the latter as mild irritation, only intensifying with continuation or escalation of the stimulus. In the case of disgust, though, one either is or isn't. The very word, in its general usage, speaks a level of intensity that seems to admit little, if any, gradation. When we see people wasting away with famine in a country where an unelected dictator has just spent millions on another public ceremony to mark the anniversary of his seizing power, we do not find ourselves progressing from a faint sense of disapproval to firm but moderate disgust, before arriving at full unequivocal revulsion, as the news item unfolds. 'This is utterly disgusting,' we announce decisively, as soon as the headline divulges the outrageous gist of it. Precisely because the response attains this pitch so rapidly, however, an anaesthetising effect takes over. What has disgusted us could simply not be endured if it didn't, and so we then find ourselves becoming strangely inured to its cause, even though – as in the case of the gin epidemic – that cause itself might continually be producing greater squalor. This peculiar rhythm, in which we succumb to pacific tolerance of a state of affairs that had previously moved us to extreme indignation, was caught with incomparable accuracy in the work of Samuel Beckett, particularly in his dramatic works of the twenty years or so following 1945. His characters find themselves stranded in situations of severe privation, which they appear blithely to have learned to endure, until a further noticeable decline creates a moment of sudden panic. It happens to Vladimir in the second act of *Waiting for Godot* (1952), to Hamm in the second act of *Endgame* (1957), and to Winnie in the second act of *Happy Days* (1961), and each time it is followed by the same dogged act of self-gathering that enables the protagonist to continue to tolerate the apparently intolerable. This mood is both an acknowledgement and an indictment of stoical passivity, a dialectically posed argument that the fortitude urged on humanity by a certain branch of philosophy, which runs from the school of Epicurus through the teachings of Christianity and into the modern-day self-help movement, is in itself the occasion for disgust.

Similarly, after some indeterminate period, we awaken to just how much worse things have become. The gradual spread of squalor is as unremarkable as the growth of fingernails in its daily progression, but then one day we see it with fresh eyes (it may not be clear why it should be today), and now we feel disgust all the more intensely, mingled this time with a little self-disgust at our failure to have noticed it before. One day in eighteenth-century London, Captain Thomas Coram stumbled over the half-dead figure of an abandoned baby, and decided something had to be done. That particular something was the establishment of the London Foundling Hospital, under Royal Charter, in 1741, at which some at least of the impoverished or disgraced mothers who could no longer afford to care for their babies were able to deposit them into institutional care, rather than leaving them to expire on the streets. The Judith Dufour case had been one of the many motivations for Coram's tireless lobbying in this cause of both Parliament and the King, the era's outstanding example of pure, disinterested philanthropy.

What complicates disgust as a moral response is that it is almost always driven by anger. Sometimes that anger stems from a painful sense of our own impotence in the face of provocation, and sometimes anger itself turns to disgust at ourselves for continuing to put up with whatever it is that has enraged us, instead of seeking some form of redress. Darwin is sensitive enough to this nuance to note the presence of anger in its facial delineation, so that 'as disgust also causes annoyance, it is generally accompanied by a frown, and often by gestures as if to push away or guard oneself against the offensive object'. This attitude of angry rejection lets us down if, as I argued in the last chapter, it is directed against our own organic beings. Where it addresses our social circumstances, however, it is the indispensable prerequisite for their improvement. And in that momentary spasm of revulsion, not through any administrative act of the authorities, the end of the gin plague was announced.

SADNESS

For in much wisdom is much grief:
and he that increaseth knowledge increaseth sorrow.
Ecclesiastes 1.18

Sad *a.* and *adv.* **1.** Having had one's fill; sated, weary, or tired (of something). **2.** Settled, firmly established, in purpose or condition; steadfast, firm, constant. **3.** Orderly and regular in life; of trustworthy character and judgement; grave, serious. **b.** Of thought, consideration: Mature, serious. **4.** Of persons, their feelings or dispositions: Sorrowful, mournful. **b.** Of looks, tones, gestures, costume, etc.: Expressive of sorrow. **c.** Of times, places, actions, etc.: Characterised by sorrow, sorrowful. **d.** Morose, dismal-looking. **e.** Causing sorrow; distressing, calamitous, lamentable. **5.** Deplorably bad.

Sad *v.* **1.** To make solid, firm, or stiff; to compress. **2.** To make sorrowful; to sadden.

Sorrow *sb.* **1.** Distress of mind caused by loss, suffering, disappointment, etc.: grief, deep sadness or regret; also, that which causes grief or melancholy; affliction, trouble ... **4.** The outward expression of grief; lamentation, mourning; *poet.*, tears.

Melancholy *sb.* **1.** The condition of having too much 'black bile'; the disease supposed to result from this condition. **b.** The 'black bile' itself; one of the four chief fluids or cardinal humours of obsolete physiology. **2.** Irascibility, sullenness. **3.** Sadness and depression of spirits; gloom or dejection, esp. when constitutional. **b.** A vexation. **c.** A state or mood of melancholy. **d.** A tender or pensive sadness.

Darwin's physical indicators: raising of the inner ends of the eyebrows; drawing down of the corners of the mouth; slowing of respiration; slowing of circulation; pallor; muscular flaccidity; drooping of the eyelids; hanging of the head; contraction of the chest. In extreme cases: violent and frantic movement of the arms and torso; motionless passivity; rocking to and fro; spasmodic respiration; choking (*globus hystericus*); crying; screaming.

10

TO BE SAD

If our linguistic resources truly reflected the wealth of human experience, we would have as many words for sadness as the Inuit have for snow. There would be a word to describe the nauseously surging feeling that accompanies bereavement and the ending of relationships. There would be another for the intimation of helpless empathy felt towards the parents whose children are buried somewhere under earthquake rubble. A term for the almost subliminal lowering of the spirits that attends a darkening of the midday sky in July would be indispensable, as well as a more intense one for the sight of the postman passing the gate, or the 'No new messages' announcement in the inbox, for one who is awaiting a longed-for reply. Arching over and above all these localised descriptors would be a term – perhaps 'sadness' or 'unhappiness' will do here, after all – for the ontological condition that appears to have defined our species for all time, a presumptive state of disappointment only occasionally illuminated by short periods, moments even, of unexpected happiness. Strung between these moments like connective tissue, unhappiness remains the same, imprinted in our DNA and having no need of external stimuli to make its lugubrious presence known.

Sadness has been felt to be so much a part of our constitution for so long that it features as a central theme in nearly all religion, philosophy, politics, economics, psychology and the arts. Attempts to account for its apparent status as our default frame of mind and mode of being, and to formulate ways in which we might manage to ward it off, have animated a significant portion of all discursive endeavour throughout history, and while New Age cosmologies and complementary therapies are today's fashionable solution, the dilemma remains. A uniform grey is our natural colour, susceptible at best to being changed temporarily with entertainments, intoxication, or the sibling rivalries of hard work and sensuality, but always seeping back to define us again.

The fact that there is so much sadness in the world, and that it accumulates in individual lives like moss on damp stone, was accepted not just by the classical tragedians, but by philosophers too. In the Greek schools of Stoicism and Cynicism, the exercise of practical mental discipline is brought to bear on the thinking person's dissatisfaction with his life, so that – by adjusting his expectations of what it will deliver– he comes to accept that he who doesn't wish for much can hardly be disappointed. Much the same attitude of mind was arrived at on the other side of the world by the Prince Siddhartha Gautama, who achieved world-historical enlightenment via a near-death experience following self-starvation. Both the Stoical Epicurus and the Buddha define the unhappiness of existence as arising from unfulfilled desire, and conclude that if desire can be restrained, or even quelled altogether, humans might stand a chance of attaining a modest contentment with life. 'The existence of desire as a human fact,' wrote Parisian existentialist Sartre some two dozen centuries later, 'is sufficient to prove that human reality is a lack.' For Sartre, that intimation of lack is what in itself generates unhappiness, whereas for Buddhism and the Stoics, we can choose whether to desire or not, and if we choose not to, we shan't be unhappy.

The notion of lack is a crucial one in the attempts that religion and philosophy have made over the centuries to explain the persistence of unhappiness in human affairs. To the Judaeo-Christian tradition, suffering is the price paid by humanity for displeasing God. It arises directly from the lack of notice that our race has paid to his divine will, starting in the paradisiacal garden, in which a single seed of the infernal has been planted in the shape of one item of proscribed flora. Human knowledge, and the striving after it, is what brings doom to the race for evermore, forcing us out of Eden into a cold, comfortless world from which we must permanently seek shelter, precisely because we now lack the direct protection of our Creator. To the woman is handed down the sentence of pain in childbirth, to remind her that all future begetting of human existence will mark the introduction into the world of further potential for suffering. It will be in God's name that the temporal law presumes to act when it institutes exemplary punishments for blasphemy, because the denial of the deity, or the maligning of his name, only compounds the original offence of which all are guilty. It was by something like this process of reasoning that the deliberate infliction of suffering, as instanced in the predations of the Inquisition, took its cue. If suffering flowed in an unbroken line from original sin and the myth of the Fall, then acts of specific infraction that contravened the will of God must be subject to chastisements that would, by ingenious design, intensify the individual's innate spiritual unhappiness to an unbearable physical pitch. Some faithful servant of the medieval Christian Church invented, for example, a mechanical claw that would tear her breasts, one after the other, from a woman accused of adultery. Such depravity achieved its aim twice over: it made its victims wish they had never been born, but it also further darkened the spiritual landscape in which all of humanity dwelt. Much as we all have to live with the knowledge of Auschwitz, so we all have to live with the crimes of religious piety – both having arisen from the way in which certain ideologies and institutions of our species came to view the world.

Freud too locates all unhappiness – or melancholia – in a sense of lack, but ascribes it not to the primary sense of something missing, but to the loss of what we had once enjoyed, a sense that arises in earliest infancy, as we are gradually separated from the maternal bond. The loss of a loved one through bereavement or physical distance, all sundering of close relations, is what sustains the melancholy under which we all must live. By introjecting the lost object of our affections, he argues in *Group Psychology and the Analysis of the Ego* (1921), we create unwittingly the conditions of the ego's depreciation. And love itself, as we must not be surprised to learn, is a psychological construct, albeit an uncommonly powerful one, that springs from the impulse to protect whatever sexual ties we have formed. A recent writer on clinical depression, Andrew Solomon, who owes a fair debt to Freudian analysis, opens a monumental work on the subject of unhappiness by articulating much the same point:

Depression is the flaw in love. To be creatures who love, we must be creatures who can despair at what we lose, and depression is the mechanism of that despair.

Like much else in the literature of psychoanalysis (in which, as Theodor Adorno remarked, nothing is true except the exaggerations), this version of events constitutes one aspect of the problem as the root point, from which all else then branches forth. But there isn't always a sense of loss, as opposed to mere lack, in sadness. It often seems to the sufferer capable of overriding immediate circumstances, arising from some unseen source, like the elusive trickle in the rainforest from which the mighty river flows, and disregarding the necessity, upon which the laws of physics insist, for every perceptible phenomenon to have a cause. It gains much of its deadening power from its appearance when not expected, and from its tendency – unlike, say, fear or anger or disgust – to linger on indefinitely. Why can't it just come and quickly go like disgust? Why does it feel like the stuff of which we are made?

To address these questions by following the precepts of the Buddha, one would strip away what are seen as life's inessentials, and live in a state of desireless subsistence. But for many, to achieve that would in itself require a great deal of cumulative loss, and hence spiritual desolation. This is not to deny that many in both east and west have adopted the Buddhist lifestyle with what they claim is a certain degree of inner satisfaction. Whether the sense of self-deprivation becomes easier to bear with time is a point the rest of the world must take on trust, but it has to be said that nothing about the ascetic life looks especially tantalising to those not so disposed, and we are still left with the utter solipsism of the Buddhist state of mind. The world can just rot while you sit under your notional banyan tree, ascending majestically through the *janas* to a contentless bliss.

The Christian Church, by contrast, requires of its adherents a more or less compulsory happiness that is drawn from God's salvific mercy, but is at least intended to reconnect to the sublunary world in the form of good works and forgiving love. St Augustine acknowledges, in Book 10 of the *Confessions*, that all human beings want to live a happy life, but insists that happiness lies only within the mind and the memory. It is not, he feels, a commodity that can be apprehended by the physical senses. That joy can at least live in the memory ('for even when I am sad, I remember my joys') might seem a comfort, until it transpires that the fact that those joys have passed suggests that they were not the real thing. Moreover, one often blushes to think back on things that once seemed enjoyable:

For I have been plunged into a sort of joy even from foul deeds, which joy I now abhor and execrate as I recall it, and at other times from good and virtuous things. This latter joy I recall with desire, although perhaps the things are no longer present. Therefore, with sadness do I recall past joy.

Once again, though, it is loss, however construed, that occasions sadness, and robs us even of that evanescent joy we might experience in recalling a time of happiness. In a world where all is ephemeral, only that which is immutable and true can be the source of genuine happiness. Rejoicing in God's existence renders the need for any other sort of joy superfluous. Indeed, 'there is no other. Those who think that there is another such life pursue another joy and it is not true joy.' In this respect, as in many others, Christian theology has inherited the anti-materialist orientation of Platonism. Why God can't allow his creatures to partake of earthly joy without having to subordinate their every impulse to the magnification of Him is never satisfactorily explained by St Augustine. A few pages later, he torments himself with the excesses of fine dining and intoxication, begging the Creator not to let such temptations come near him. This is one of the curious ways in which the supposedly more beneficent Christian God turns out to be rather more autocratic than his Hebrew predecessor, who, according to the Psalmist, gave us bread and wine in order both to satiate and gladden us. Whatever pleasure wine has brought us, though, is unmasked by Augustine as no true gladness, only an abhorrent and execrable delusion – although tellingly, his passage on those who find happiness other than in Christian worship closes with the admission that at least 'their will is not turned away from a certain image of joy'. The ascetic solution to this has its place in Christianity too, in the monastic tradition, but is no more capable of answering King Lear's objection – that, without a certain measure of sensual enjoyment, 'Man's life is cheap as beasts' ' – than is the example of the Buddha.

If we are unhappy because we have absented ourselves from God's presence, we might equally feel that we are unhappy because the world he created for us isn't a particularly pleasant place. Leaving aside for a moment the question of whether we aggravate that state of affairs through our own reprehensible conduct, the fact remains that shocking things happen all the time, and do not trouble to discriminate between those whom they befall. Writing in the latter half of the eighteenth century, David Hume takes up the argument from design for God's existence – that there must be a Creator because everything seems to work just so – by suggesting that if that were the case, it wouldn't preclude the possibility that the world we are living in now might have been an early, abandoned, faulty prototype. There could be another very similar, but considerably more efficient, model in the next universe, but one in which creatures who looked remarkably like ourselves were enjoying the full blessings of this dotty inventor's final, refined patent. Hume's mock-Platonic treatise, *Dialogues Concerning Natural Religion*, published posthumously in 1779, accords with the theological view in one respect at least: humankind is dismayingly good at contributing to its own unhappiness, but, as he sees it, by inventing unnecessary terrors and predators in the forms of superstitious fears to plague it. For the rest, though, the world God has designed is so supremely efficient at denying us any happiness that we scarcely need to bother making it worse. Shakespeare's intimation of the tragedy that attends childbirth, with the infant yelling in horror and the mother crying in agony, is pictured as the preface to a life in which 'Weakness, impotence, distress' attend our every step, until we die in pain. 'Life's a bitch,' as Monty Python's Brian has it on the Cross, 'and then you die.' So why don't we end it all? Because we are too scared, says Hume. ' "Not satisfied with life, afraid of death." This is the secret chain, say I, that holds us. We are terrified, not bribed to the continuance of our existence.' When one of the interlocutors in the dialogue, Cleanthes, dubiously asserts that there is at least more of happiness than of misery in the world, and that therefore there must be a benevolent God, the objection is raised: 'Why is there any misery at all?'

In chapter 11 of the *Dialogues*, Hume posits that there are four principal causes of human misery. Firstly, there is the mystery as to why physical pain has to be one of the motivators for self-preservation, when the mere sense of a diminution in possible pleasure would do just as well. Why should hunger be a matter of irritating lack, followed by discomfort and then torture? Why cannot the sight of the escaping blood announce the necessity of attending to the wound, but it must be accompanied by searing agony as well? Secondly, the world is animated by arbitrary general laws, chance and contingency, and is only very marginally and unreliably subject to human volition. Thirdly, while the rigours of existence must somehow be borne, there is no corresponding robustness in the human spirit to withstand them. Our natural attributes are frugal compared to what we must do even to maintain a state of bare equilibrium, so that all labour and effort are precisely that, a gargantuan toil that leaves us too spent to enjoy fully the respite from want they have bought. And finally, there is the question of what a later century would have termed the malevolent universe. Hume doesn't put it quite that strongly, but castigates what he calls the 'inaccuracy', 'immoderation', and tendency to ruinous extremes, at work in nature, which delivers earthquakes, hurricanes, floods and epidemics to us, against which we can offer only minimal resistance. It is these phenomena, the lineaments of external reality, which bring about human unhappiness, Hume argues, and not some inherent fault in ourselves, either through our wrong-headed insistence on desire, or our deficient appreciation of God's majesty. We need look no further for the proof of life's anxiety and tedium than the fact that we incessantly look forward, eventually to a life beyond life provided by religious belief. So, in a deft dialectical twist, he turns the theological argument back on itself. The mere fact that we are expected to look ahead to a better existence than the present one rather speaks against the architect of both of them.

Against Hume, the distinctly forbidding figure of Søren Kierkegaard – representing that great oxymoron of modern philosophy, a Christian existentialist – arises like Colonel Kurtz from the primeval mud. Although in his first major work, *Either/Or* (1843), he argued that the cure for unhappiness was to yield to despair, since to accept it was in some sense already to have got the better of it, he later came to adopt the more ascetic position that despair itself was the problem. In *The Sickness Unto Death* (1849), he allows that despair is both a defect and a privilege. It is, he says, a privilege in the sense that it represents our capacity for the objectification of our condition that is denied to other creatures. In an unlikely echo of the atheistic Schopenhauer, he argues that the despair one feels over the loss of a loved one is essentially despair for oneself, at the pitiful life one must now lead. The whole question of unhappiness is, for Kierkegaard, bound up with notions of self-perception and self-objectification. '[W]hen whatever causes a person to despair occurs, it is immediately evident that he has been in despair his whole life.' But which is worse: to be in conscious despair, or to realise that one had been in despair without knowing it? A few pages after this assertion, he contends that the most horrifying aspect of unhappiness is that one might not be aware of it. This, though, is the theological rather than the philosophical Kierkegaard. Many might settle for being unhappy without realising it, but when we don't realise we are unhappy, it is really because we haven't let God into our hearts. The piety undermines what is otherwise a penetrating insight into the potential that unhappiness, especially clinical depression, possesses to make us feel that this – this grey, morose, affectless feeling of living against the grain – is the way it really is. Andrew Solomon puts this point in a magnificent line: 'The present tense of mild depression envisages no alleviation because it feels like knowledge.' Happiness, in this intimation, is not just always elsewhere; its existence is a present and enduring myth. The adolescent's illusion, according to Kierkegaard, is that the future is going to be great; the adult's is that the past was. What both seem to lack is the potential for a dynamic present, so that the despairing individual cries out that 'the only thing that can save me is possibility!' – a possibility she has, however, ceased to believe in.

The bleakest formulation in all of western philosophy of the doctrine that human existence is futile is to be found in the work of Arthur Schopenhauer. It runs like quartz through rock in much of his later work, and is particularly succinctly expressed in chapter 46 of the second volume of *The World as Will and Representation* (1844). Enlarging upon Hume, he teaches that we are as inextricably enmeshed in a tangle of misery and pain as if we had signed a bad contract without reading the small print. Our pleasures are illusory, because there is no sensible intimation of them as pleasures, as compared with the gnawing authenticity of pain and disappointment. There is actually only pain and no-pain. It is indeed possible to recall times at which we must have been happy, but the tragedy is that we can't see them as such at the time. This is because, as he argues in an essay in his late *Parerga and Paralipomena* (1851), our lives are like pictures done in rough mosaic, whose outlines are only distinguishable from a distance, in this case the retrospective view. We strive after certain goals, either those we have chosen for ourselves or, if we are less lucky, those that sheer necessity has ordained for us, only to discover that the labour of struggling towards them wasn't worth the pitiful reward they deliver. Each life is heading in the inevitable direction of final illness and death, whereupon we return to a bottomless infinity. Organic suffering is exacerbated by the vileness of human nature, which cannot bear to see what it falsely imagines to be the happiness of others without trying to tear it apart, and also by the economic laws of society. These keep the greater part of the world in abject poverty, struggling for mere survival, are responsible for such monstrosities as the slave trade, and ensure that the vast mass of humanity know little more than agonised subsistence:

[T]o enter at the age of five a cotton-spinning or other factory, and from then on to sit there every day first ten, then twelve, and finally fourteen hours, and perform the same mechanical work, is to purchase dearly the pleasure of drawing breath.

If we sense the faintest hint of the political in this last illustration, we need not be deceived. 'Socialism' won't work either, says Schopenhauer, firstly because it can do nothing to redeem the lives of the millions who have gone before, and secondly because it can't offer anything other than less arduous working conditions, and more time for the individual to pursue fruitless ambitions of betterment. And nor can it save us from death. The argument is not just a static meditation, but acquires polemical force in its stark suggestion, supported by Sophocles, Euripides, Byron and others, that not to have been born at all is the best solution. If this is true for every individual, it follows that it would have been better if the world itself had not come into being. It quite simply 'ought not to be'. Much criticised for the inspissated gloom of his work, Schopenhauer reserves his most withering scorn for the descants of optimism and pantheism. If life is a gift, then it is a piece of largesse one might politely have declined, had one had the opportunity of examining it beforehand. To the nature poet who objects that not everything in the world is abhorrent, since there are mountains and streams, Alpine paths and lush green valleys, he retorts, 'But is the world, then, a peep show?' There may be beautiful things to goggle at as we lurch towards annihilation, but that is scarcely more than saying that the flames that consumed condemned heretics burned a lovely shade of orange.

When Theodor Adorno, towards the end of his life, attacked western philosophy for having 'hardly noticed' the mass of human suffering, he was not suggesting that it hadn't been explored in the works of Hume, Kierkegaard and others. What he meant was that it hadn't been compassionately enough understood, and more precisely that the possibility of its abolition had been passed over as a utopian dream, as incapable of realisation as human beings are of avoiding sin. It is not finally in the textures of suffering itself that we despair, but in its indomitable constancy in our lives. The disaster of philosophy, charged at the middle of the nineteenth century by Marx with its own futility, is that it appears to rest solely on a process of rationalisation. It represents a number of possible ways of seeing the faulty world, without holding out to humanity the means for material intervention in it. As Marx states in the *Theses on Feuerbach* (1845): 'The philosophers have only *interpreted* the world, in various ways; the point is to *change* it.' For Schopenhauer, the mere attempt is risible. For Marx, the impulsion of history demands it. Human life is indeed a nightmare, but it will not be so for ever, because the structures of society that make it so can be overthrown. The task that any true philosophy or theory must undertake is to supply the progressive forces in society with their inspiration to act.

Now that Marx is out of fashion, contemporary philosophy appears to offer us only a kind of radical subjectivism. The world means what I choose it to mean, much as Lewis Carroll's Humpty Dumpty uses the English language. Francis Fukuyama has decided that history is over (give or take the odd global crusade against terrorism, perhaps), while Jean Baudrillard can declare, only half-facetiously, that the (first) Gulf War didn't happen. Thus we can be sure that philosophy is less interested than ever before in the only aspect of human existence about which it could usefully say something – universal unhappiness.

Schopenhauer begins one of his late essays by stating that the starting point of all philosophy is 'the inexplicable'. As soon as any aspect of reality can be explained, it passes into science, a body of disciplines that doesn't especially feel the need for philosophy. The question of whether human unhappiness is an inexplicable given, or whether by contrast it can be explained and abolished, is indeed a crucial one. If we incline to the former view, there seems little point in philosophy attempting to address the issue of suffering, since to do so will be just as productive of bafflement as the old chestnut about whether the tree falling unobserved in the forest makes any sound. On the other hand, if the impulse to avert suffering prevails, because we realise that this involves a greater degree of spiritual responsibility, then universal sadness will at last become the most urgent philosophical theme of all.

11

I MAKE YOU SAD

One of the complexities that any study of the physiological basis of the emotions must confront is that they can be produced by artificial, or non-spontaneous, stimuli. A penetrating exercise of the imagination can produce anger or sadness, even though the intellect is aware that the data it is being presented with have no objective reality. Many actors use precisely such a method (the Method, as it was once colloquially known) to give psychologically convincing representations of the emotions their characters experience. Recollections in tranquillity often have the same effect. Awaking from a melancholy dream, we can find our mood set in low gear for the greater part of the morning. Evoking the memory of an emotionally significant event often brings back the emotional atmosphere that accompanied it, so that tears spring readily to our eyes once again, or our pulses quicken with angry defiance. (I can even find myself blushing again at the remembrance of some acute, but long-gone, embarrassment.) It is in the arts, though, that the most powerful engines of instilled emotion are to be found, and indeed, at least according to the Romantic view, this is their chief function.

It is quite possible that the earliest forms of music, played on primitive instruments sounded by the wind and by the blows of fists and sticks, were the first aesthetic manifestations that seemed to chime with humanity's natural disposition. Unlike cave art, we cannot now encounter them, can only guess at how they must have sounded and what resonances they might have created in the souls of those who made and heard them. To the young Friedrich Nietzsche, however, there seems no doubting the matter. Music, he argues in his first published work, *The Birth of Tragedy* (1871), lies at the wellspring of aesthetic creativity, and is the only begetter of the earliest of the ancient art forms to which we still have some kind of access – tragic drama.

Tragedy is the most closely theorised literary form of all. In its first ascendancy, in the Greek amphitheatres of the fifth century BC, it represented the fullest extension of the creative faculty, and took its place alongside religious ritual and philosophical discourse as one of the three highest achievements of the human spirit. Not quite everyone felt at ease with this consensus, as we shall see presently, but the prolific output of its three foremost exponents – Aeschylus, Sophocles and Euripides – represents perhaps the most gorgeous efflorescence of artistic potential of the classical era. Their lives overlapped, and they worked in productive rivalry with each other in the staged dramatic competitions that punctuated the Athenian cultural calendar. The interest, in these rival versions of the tales of Hellenic mythology, was not in the outcome of the familiar plots, so much as the poignancy of their characterisations, the richness of their language, and – above all – their efficacy in representing human emotion. All the most highly regarded extant plays won prizes, although the unexpected failure of Sophocles to take the palm when *Oedipus Tyrannos* was first presented in around 425 BC (the top prize went to a set of plays by the long-forgotten Philocles, an upstart nephew of Aeschylus) reminds us that the inexplicable jury decision did not have to wait for the Oscar ceremonies to come to full fruition.

Precisely because so much has been written about tragedy as an art form, the popular perception of it in our own time is riddled with misconceptions and fallacies. George Steiner's early work, *The*

Death of Tragedy (1961), for example, asserts that all tragedies end badly, with some calamity – generally death – overcoming the principal character or characters. This proposition admits of so many exceptions in the classical theatre alone as to render the whole thesis of the book rather suspect. Indeed, its bombastic central case, that tragedy is no longer conceivable in the modern theatre because plays aren't about noble personages any more, and because the audiences no longer subscribe to a body of unchallenged religious belief, has been meticulously dismantled in a recent study by Terry Eagleton. To look at the events of tragic drama merely as the depiction of the misfortune of particular individuals is to overlook its origins in sacrificial ritual, and the purgative function that such ceremonials were expected to perform. Arising from these expiatory acts, Greek drama represented a way of examining human fate, as well as a sometimes subversive commentary on the attitudes and actions of the gods. It also offers a certain philosophical purchase on the life human beings have to live, as well as inspiring emotional release in its recipients through the representation of emotion. And while it is true that many works contain a didactic conclusion, usually in the divagations of the Choruses, that one is better off living the unspectacular life of a nobody than being caught up in the dynastic blood-feuds of royal houses, the audiences are not thereby being invited to see themselves as immune from suffering. The epic poet Homer, in whose long shadow all the classical dramatic poets wrote, already taught that all human life, mere existence, is tragic. This idea has survived through the ages to contemporary theatre, reaching perhaps its most concentrated distillation in Samuel Beckett's 1969 'dramaticule', *Breath*. We hear a cry of anguish, and then the amplified sounds of human breathing as the lights fade up and down, with decent haste, on a rubbish-strewn stage.

It is hard to imagine what a Platonist would make of *Breath*. It isn't exactly poetry, and might therefore escape the censor's attentions, but nor does it conform to the devotional or heroic credentials required of works of art. In the notorious Book X of *The Republic*, Plato famously proposed banning poets, including those writing for the stage, from his ideal city-state, unless they confined themselves to producing either hymns of praise to the gods or heroic encomia to great men. Many are the somersaults that have been turned in attempts to explain this embarrassing bit of philistinism, but the fact is that Plato was as deeply hostile to art as the English Puritans were. The philosopher-kings who would run the Republic would happily bin the *Oresteia*, but would look favourably on an epic paean to, say, Plato.

The argument against art is misconceived on virtually every count. We are told that what the artist produces by mimesis, or representation, is at third remove from reality, as if that statement in itself serves to invalidate it. Everybody knows perfectly well that a painting of a bed, to take his example, is not the same thing as the bed the carpenter makes, and similarly – despite those people who attack actors in the street for the reprehensible things their characters have done in the soap opera – we are all aware that the images on the screen have been carefully crafted to make it look as though they are real. Plato castigates artists for pretending to a knowledge of technical or political matters that can never be put to practical application, which certainly traduces the efforts of a Leonardo or a Václav Havel, but is in any case nothing more than a precursor of the reactionary argument that says that you should never criticise anything unless you could do it better yourself. Art fools the gullible, thinks Plato, who are thus as ignorant of the real world as the artist is – but fools them into what? Into believing in its reality, or into believing that it has anything apposite to say about the world? If lectures at Plato's Academy tended not to command the kinds of audiences that Sophocles did, that only confirmed what the philosopher-kings always suspected – which was that they were wasted on the ignorant rabble. It is old elitism, except that in the fifth and fourth centuries BC it was wearing its very first coat of paint.

Dramatic art, for Plato, is contemptible because it appeals to the less noble side of our natures, the expression of emotion and the bemoaning of suffering, at the expense of the higher virtues of reason and restraint. It has a corrupting effect in that it catalyses and manipulates the emotions that we should be learning to master. Pity for others' sufferings encourages pity for our own, so that eventually we are at the mercy of our emotions, instead of allowing them to wither. The same point can be applied to the work of comic dramatists such as Aristophanes, who cynically provoke our laughter. For Plato, then, neither sympathising with the sufferings of others, nor seeing the absurd side of the human lot, is acceptable. Each instinct must yield to a granite-faced anaesthesia, in which the death of somebody dear becomes as much the focus of cold, objective reflection as the activity of insects under a stone. The troubling Book X of his masterwork is generally accepted to be an addendum, intended in pugnacious emphasis of points made only in passing earlier on. Towards the end of the dialogue, he allows that poetry will be given a chance to defend itself at the bar of Platonic authority, with the promise that it will not be banished if it can prove itself socially useful. In the meantime, while the philosopher-kings wait to be propelled to power, Plato informs them of their duty:

Our theme shall be that such poetry has no serious value or claim to truth, and we shall warn its hearers to fear its effects on the constitution of their inner selves, and tell them to adopt the view of poetry we have described.

But the message barely penetrated beyond his immediate circle of sycophants, and there is still more truth about the way the world works in a single dithyramb of Euripides than there is in the entirety of Platonic philosophy.

Euripides was not in favour of stifling emotion, and nor were any of the tragic poets, since one of the points of the theatre is that it allows our indignation at the movements of human destiny full spate. The lamentation song in *Electra*, from the dramatist's middle period, in which the heroine relives the death of her murdered father and her separation from her brother in exile, is a case in point:

> Cry, cry for my labour and pain,
> cry for the hatred of living . . .
> Come, waken the mourning again,
> bring me again the sweetness of tears . . .
> Father, the maenad song of death
> I cry you among the dead
> beneath the earth, the words I pour
> day after day unending
> as I move, ripping my flesh with sharp
> nails, fists pounding my clipped
> head for your dying.

A chorus of Argive peasant women enters, and expresses anguish at her obvious suffering, but counsels humility and reverence before the gods on Electra, if she is to stand any chance of living to see 'gentler days'. This is swept aside as a pious homily:

> Gods? Not one god has heard
> my helpless cry or watched of old
> over my murdered father.
> Mourn again for the wasted dead,
> mourn for the living outlaw
> somewhere prisoned in foreign lands
> moving through empty days,
> passing from one slave hearth to the next
> though born of a glorious sire.
> And I! I in a peasant's hut
> waste my life like wax in the sun,

thrust and barred from my father's home
to a scarred mountain exile
while my mother rolls in her bloody bed
and plays at love with a stranger.

What intensifies her plight, and that of the brother who may be 'moving through empty days' as she says, but who may equally well be dead, is the sense that it is not simply a matter of past wrongs, but of their continuation into the present. Her mother has taken her father's killer, Aegisthus, as a lover, and in that standing insult to his memory, the pain of past events is prolonged. Shakespeare will return to this precise dilemma in the action of *Hamlet*, but the instructive point in Euripides' later plays is that the time for paeans of devotion to the gods has gone. No dramatist could quite bring himself to say 'There are no gods', but Euripides is the first to suggest that, if they are there, and can preside calmly over a series of grotesque catastrophes like this, who needs them?

Electra is a fascinating example, not least because it is one of the myths for which we have extant treatments by all three of the great tragedians; it forms the action of the second play in the *Oresteia* trilogy of Aeschylus, and is the subject of an eponymous play by Sophocles. Euripides' play is perhaps the most provocative of the three, in the sense that it offers the most complex psychological study of the heroine's story. Neither Electra, nor her brother Orestes, are especially likeable characters. Their mourning, which proverbially becomes Electra like no other tragic figure, seems to have a mercenary undercurrent to it: there is much lamentation over the lost privileges of palace life, while the forced marriage to a peasant farmer Aegisthus has decreed for her (on the grounds that breeding beneath her station will prevent her from producing any male heir capable of avenging his grandfather's death) is hardly the living hell both she and her brother believe it to be. When Orestes shudders out loud at the thought of his sister having to submit to the sexual attentions of a peasant, she tells him that the farmer – a spotless, unassuming, bucolic soul who emerges as the real hero of the piece – hasn't laid a finger on her. She remains a virgin, which leads the affronted Orestes to wonder whether her husband is blind to her beauty. In fact, he has remained circumspect because he knows that she has married him unwillingly. When Orestes concludes that the poor peasant must be terrified of his brother-in-law coming one day to avenge Electra's honour, she replies that that might be part of it, but it is also because he's a nice man. They could be talking about the pedigree of a farm animal, and that sense of a void of incomprehension between the unfortunate nobles and the contented simpletons is not lost on the audience. Indeed, it sits well with the lament that Orestes offers to a world out of kilter:

> Alas,
> we look for good on earth and cannot recognise it
> when met, since all our human heritage runs mongrel.
> At times I have seen descendants of the noblest family
> grow worthless though the cowards had courageous sons;
> inside the souls of wealthy men bleak famine lives
> while minds of stature struggle trapped in starving bodies.

That can ring true enough with everyone, and yet only moments before, the valiant brother has uttered this sentiment:

> Uneducated men are pitiless,
> but we who are educated pity much. And we pay
> a high price for being intelligent. Wisdom hurts.

This too is the view of the Preacher in the Old Testament book, Ecclesiastes, for whom the search for knowledge can yield nothing but trouble.

We run the risk of falling into an error akin to that of George Steiner if we simply see tragedy as tragic because it involves calamitous events befalling the nobility. The plays represent only the most lurid examples of the malevolent force at work in human affairs, and that sweeps everybody – great or humble – before it. In *Electra*, particularly, with its concluding double murder, in which first Aegisthus, and then their mother Clytemnestra, are butchered like heifers by the avenging siblings, there is hardly a feeling of the world being set to rights. Both express their remorse in the immediate aftermath of the carnage, and the final twist is that the pair are to be separated again by order of a *deus ex machina* who appears above the farmer's cottage to pronounce judgement on all. Electra is now handed in marriage to Orestes' comrade-in-arms Pylades, who hasn't opened his mouth throughout the action but is rewarded at the end with somebody else's wife, while the Chorus is left to opine that anybody who can get through life's rotten journey without encountering 'trouble on the road' must be leading a very charmed existence. Emily Vermeule, in the introduction to her 1959 translation of the play, states cogently:

Electra cannot be dismissed as wilful or perverse. It is a planned demonstration that personal relationships, human or divine, are inescapably fraught with indecency and that justice can be as ugly as crime.

This is the true tragic vision, a disposition that refutes not only Platonic theory, but also the Nietzsche of *The Birth of Tragedy*, who sees the decline of classical culture as devolving almost entirely upon Euripides, in whose works tragedy has become mere psychology. For Nietzsche, it is because the drama ceases to speak directly to the audience's intimation of tragic universality, and starts being about the misfortunes of particular individuals, that it forfeits its relevance. Nothing, in the case of *Electra* and of all the late plays of Euripides, could be further from the truth. Instead, the choruses frequently advise the spectators that the disasters they see un-ravelling before them are emblematic of the general sum of human fate.

It was Aristotle, in the *Poetics* and also in the *Politics*, who offered the notion of catharsis to Plato as the best way of constru-ing the necessity of the emotional ravages that tragic drama wrought in its audiences. The usual bill of fare at a dramatic presentation was three tragedies and a satyr play, the last the vulgar parody (hence 'satire') of the events of one of the foregoing pieces. Whatever tears the tragedies had drawn forth could be washed away in raucous chuckles as the satyr actors lampooned the suffer-ing and wailing of the Electras and Antigones. It was not only this knockabout comedy, though, that provided emotional relief. The tragedies themselves, in the view of Aristotle, acted as a purgative for the emotions. Only this could explain the age-old paradox that seeing ghastly and upsetting events in drama can give pleasure. The explanation lies not in some untapped sadism, but in the psycho-logical mechanism by which powerful emotions such as pity and fear can be safely released in response to fictional stimuli. There is just enough of a suggestion of the therapeutic about it for Aristotle's definition of catharsis to have become widely accepted as the legitimate reason for our interest in the macabre and the gruelling. It is said that early performances of the *Oedipus Tyrannos* had such a shocking effect on their audiences as to cause some pregnant women to miscarry. If these accounts are only par-tially true, they should leave us in no doubt that the case for cathar-sis is a valid one. Nor does it matter that we already know the out-come of the story. That sense of inevitable doom is what makes the unfolding of the action all the more minatory. We know that Clytemnestra will kill Agamemnon, that Macbeth will kill Duncan and Burnam Wood come to Dunsinane in the form of Macduff's avenging army, and we can pretty well guess, as we gaze up at the cinema screen, that the babysitter who has unwisely climbed into the car in the garage at night will be duly throttled by the bogey-man waiting in the back seat.

Much as the sense of smell is held to be the one most instantly evocative of nostalgia, so that the smell of a certain dish cooking wafts us straightaway back to childhood, so music, in its only imperfectly determinable way, is richly productive of emotional response. But how do we account for this?

An impressionistic or programmatic piece, it is true, may work at a fairly obvious level. Told that we are about to hear the aria of the desolate princess whose lover has died in battle, for all that it may be sung in a language we don't understand, we set our emotional recep-tors accordingly, and wait to be affected in the prescribed way. When a passage in a work of chamber music has the same effect on us, clearly some other repertoire of pre-verbal, and extra-representational, responses is being called into play. Darwin describes this effect when discussing the physiological impact that emotional feeling can have. Emotions frequently cause muscle tremor as well as tears, and so, in apparent imitation of these effects, does music:

Music has a wonderful power ... of recalling in a vague and indefinite manner, those strong emotions which were felt during long-past ages ... And as several of our strongest emotions – grief, great joy, love, and sym-pathy – lead to the free secretion of tears, it is not surprising that music should be apt to cause our eyes to become suffused with tears ... Music often produces another peculiar effect. We know that every strong sensa-tion, emotion, or excitement ... all have a special tendency to cause the muscles to tremble; and the thrill or slight shiver which runs down the backbone and limbs of many persons when they are powerfully affected by music, seems to bear the same relation to the above trembling of the body, as a slight suffusion of tears from the power of music does to weep-ing from any strong and real emotion.

That tingling along the spine in response to some especially evocative passage of music is indeed both a physiological and emotional effect. But in what specific ways does it achieve this?

The late string quartets of Beethoven furnish many examples. Their combination of expressive intensity and formal innovation has long marked them out as seminal, anticipatory works. The late quartets are a crowning achievement, dating from the final, torridly productive years between 1823 and 1826, in which Beethoven was experimenting with the classical sonata form. These are by no means uniformly, or even predominantly, sombre works. The thematic material ranges expansively, often within individual movements, modulating from studied reflection to momentary exhilaration, allowing space in the middle of the most hopelessly yearning moods for the abrupt swagger of a little march, which might essay a defiant *da capo* before a more measured stateliness returns. There is very little of outright despair in the late quartets, which will surprise those who, venturing towards them for the first time, and knowing that these works issued from the composer's final, abyssal deafness, expect the atmosphere to be bleak, comfortless, grief-stricken.

In April 1825, while at work on the Quartet no. 15 in A minor, Beethoven fell seriously ill with acute abdominal pain. He had oedema, a severe accumulation of fluid in the tissue ('dropsy', in old-fashioned medical parlance), almost certainly related to the liver cirrhosis and lead poisoning that, between them, were to contribute to his death two years later. What existed up to that point of the A minor quartet were sketches for the first two movements, a restless, intermittently brooding Allegro with much use of dotted rhythms, and a shorter, busy waltz movement. The third, and central, movement is entitled 'Hymn of Thanksgiving to the Deity, in the Lydian mode, from one who is convalescing'. It is constructed of two entirely different, alternating elements, the opening, solemnly treading A-minor chorale, and a shift into D major for a more fleet-footed theme in 3/8, entitled 'Feeling new strength'. These represent the twin poles of the composer's recent physical condition. After prompt medical intervention, the abdominal crisis had been swiftly resolved, and it was relief and gladness that led Beethoven not only to express his gratitude to God, but also to compose and conjoin two passages that illustrated the human continuum of good health and bad, along which, in either direction, all our lives must inevitably shift. The more conventional practice might have been to leave the two moods sundered, with a gloom-laden, sickly movement followed by some form of chuckling scherzo. What Beethoven does is to stitch these two states of consciousness together, and not merely so that one follows the other, fatuously suggesting providence triumphing over adversity, but so that they alternate, the ill-health giving place to recovery, which must then, in time, submit to another morbid episode. The interweaving of these states of sickness and health is transformed by the music into a mutually informing whole, representing an apparently deeper understanding of the relation between human suffering and relief, one that is worthy perhaps, in Christian terms, of the God who dispenses and then ameliorates these conditions. It is much the same point that Kierkegaard would make a century later (with regard to despair rather than physical illness), in *The Sickness Unto Death*, where he argues that most people have too little consciousness of themselves to have any conception of inner consistency, so that bleak periods are punctuated by periods of relief, with no idea of 'putting everything together'. In the central movement of the Quartet no. 15, Beethoven puts it all together, for himself and for his listeners.

The opening theme is a sedate chorale, contemplative and expressive of utter resignation, advancing through thickened harmonic progressions in stately minims, all four parts in absolute formation, but interspersed with a plaintive melodic passage that descends through the instruments from the wounded pleading of the first violin to the low groan of the cello. The plea goes nowhere, trailing off always into those sombre, long chords, but what animation the passage contains is located in the ebb and flow of its dynamics, the painstakingly swelling *crescendos* returning abruptly to tentative *piano*, mirroring the drastically decelerated rate at which the invalid's life is lived, each deceptive stirring of vigour the prelude to a relapse into inevitable forbearance, and the correct state of patient acceptance that gives the willing subject of medical attentions his name. There is a paradoxical sweetness in the whole passage that seems to memorialise as well as lament the mortal condition of its author, subtly preparing the ground for the return to vitality that abruptly interrupts it at the destabilising modulation of the thirtieth bar.

Darwin's musicological consultant, the Mr Litchfield of his fourth chapter, advises him that it isn't the specific elements of a melody, the absolute pitch of its constituent notes or the loudness or softness of the passage, nor indeed even its timbre, that works its effect on us. It is the relative association of these elements, the fact that, in Beethoven's piece, the first violin's opening middle C is followed by an aspirational leap through a sixth to A, a momentary fall back to G, and then a second, successful attempt on a sustained high C, a full octave spanned in the first four notes, that establishes the pathos of this initial motif. 'A tune is always the same tune,' states Mr Litchfield, 'whether it is sung loudly or softly, by a child or a man; whether it is played on a flute or on a trombone.' It is a point we might have hoped to see Darwin dispute, since, for example, it seems precisely the elegiac quality of the violin that plays the opening theme of the central movement that is so constitutive of its emotional resonance. That impact is based in turn on the actual arithmetical resonances to which each note was known, by the nineteenth century, to correspond. Why any particular succession of such vibrations, however, should set up specific emotional responses in the listener remained a mystery. Mr Litchfield ends his communication with Darwin by cautiously positing a theory:

'[I]t is possible … that the greater or less mechanical facility with which the vibrating apparatus of the human larynx passes from one state of vibration to another, may have been a primary cause of the greater or less pleasure produced by various sequences of sounds.'

The writer's assumption was that Darwin's query related to the emotional effect of vocal music, and he suggests, persuasively enough, that sudden passages of coloratura, or any that require great vocal exertion on the part of the performer, will have the strongest impact on their hearers. Darwin further quotes the work of a German physiologist, Hermann Helmholtz, whose important study, *Théorie Physiologique de la Musique*, published in Paris in 1868, had postulated that musical sound is so productive of emotional reaction because it is the origin of all human communication. Our first vocalisations were musical tones, the variety of which encompassed the repertoire of all the important physical and emotional states and the evolutionary cultural advantage conferred by being able to communicate them to one's peers. This rudimentary form of vocal performance may, in Mr Litchfield's words, 'be taken as the primary type of all music', bequeathing its indelible character as the means by which a range of emotional data may be broadcast, and even invoked, in those who hear it. There are, of course, no voices in a string quartet. And yet, in another sense, there are. They have become transposed, to be sure, to the sounds that strings of cured cat's intestine make when agitated by tautened strands of horsehair, but when they describe a melodic sequence, they are speaking (or singing) some form of regular sentence, its grammar and semantics residing in the intervals and temporal progressions between its constituent notes, and when they come together in simple harmonic utterance, they stand for the inarticulate cry that speaks the body's, and the spirit's, condition. Beethoven's third movement is, after all, a *Dankgesang*, a song of thanks. Not only our first pains, but our first gladness and our first courtship rituals, were expressed, according to Helmholtz, vocally, and although they have become technically and formally instrumentalised in the guise of musical instruments, we cannot be surprised, on consulting Beethoven's score, to find that the first marking that he gives to all four parts at the outset of the third movement is 'sotto voce'. These are, lest we be uncertain of the point, real voices.

The orchestral composer has a far greater number of voices at his or her disposal, some of which lend themselves to evocations of melancholy more readily than others. There are few more precise intimations of bottomless grief than may be had from the cello, nor of wistful regret than from the oboe. Can a tuba be introspective? In tandem, they can seem to represent not just one or two voices engaged in animated, private conversation, but the Babel of tongues in a crowd. When one singular discourse is being articulated, the composer may choose to confine it to a particular section of the orchestra. The celebrated Adagietto from Gustav Mahler's Symphony No. 5 in C sharp minor, viscerally familiar from its extensive use in Luchino Visconti's 1971 film of Thomas Mann's *Death in Venice*, is such an instance. Scored entirely for strings, its ravishing textures, the pathos of its *pizzicato* reflective spells, and its sublime use of dynamics, represent an apogee of direct emotional expression. Although the Fifth Symphony sounds so indelibly cinematic to our ears, it is worth noting that it was begun in 1901, and that it, and indeed Mahler's whole œuvre, belongs to that last period of unsullied innocence in classical music, before the foundation of the film industry as a mass entertainment medium. Once composing for the films was established as a specific art form with the advent of sound pictures in the late 1920s, all cinema music sounded like Mahler, the cascading strings and weeping woodwinds evoking the rise and fall of Greta Garbo's bosom and the shiny tracks of Mary Astor's tears.

Helmholtz also established, to Darwin's approval, that certain types of sound are productive of certain states of mind. This is demonstrated at the most basic level. When a member of a community finds herself or himself in mortal danger, the scream they emit is loud, prolonged and high, so as to carry far to others and give notice of the need for assistance. Because of the way the internal cavity of the human ear is shaped, such piercing cries have the greatest interior resonance, a resonance that carries beyond the eardrum and into the deeper being. By the same token, in music, high notes often produce the strongest impressions. A sudden flight above the surrounding register, the re-emergence of a previously announced theme an octave higher, have the effect of heightening one's sense of engagement with the music. The songs of Sammy Cahn and Jule Styne, swing jazz composers and librettists, frequently feature an abrupt upsurge into a higher register, an operatic flourish beautifully rendered in the 1940s by the young Frank Sinatra, and by such interpreters as Doris Day. One's heart rises correspondingly with the pitch, and teeters on the verge of breaking with the vibrato. Judy Garland's finest recordings capture the same feeling even more exactly, and gain emotional authority from that sudden break in the voice that she made all her own, and that sounds precisely like the crumbling of stoical resolve.

In these latter instances, at least, we have returned to the direct impact of vocal tones on the listener. Not all such impact is derived from deliberate deployment of vocal technique, however, *pace* Mr Litchfield's assertion that the most affecting performances are those that involve some exercise of demanding vocal force. Singers in popular music, which has not traditionally been as concerned with technical virtuosity as classical music, often achieve a similar degree of emotional resonance with considerably more limited resources. The comforting drone of Leonard Cohen's vocal style, allied to his formidable lyrical gift, can produce exactly the kind of muscle tremor that Darwin spoke of almost a century before Cohen's first recordings were made. Often accused of wilful morbidity, Cohen has replied by insisting that 'seriousness is deeply agreeable to the heart'.

The point was once undeniable, but has perhaps lost force in a media culture increasingly given over to the tone and techniques of relentless pastiche. The German singer Nico, first known for her recordings with the Velvet Underground in the late 1960s, also has an apparently (often literally) flat style that might seem at first to be able to do nothing more than declaim, but in songs such as 'I'll Be Your Mirror' and on much of her solo work – particularly the album *Chelsea Girl* (1967) – there is a fragility that brings the improbable subtleties out of the rather hackneyed, shop-worn songs she covers. These are voices that undermine our traditional notions of how emotional affectivity should function, while at the same time asserting the truth that the capacity for emotional communication does not reside exclusively with the most obviously gifted.

Returning to the question of the emotional release afforded by drama and music, there is a suggestion in Aristotle's *Poetics* that catharsis is something only ordinary people have to undergo. No self-respecting philosopher-king would have need of such histrionics, and it is with that suggestion that he tries to sweeten the pill for the fastidious Plato. Whatever objections the old prude may have raised to Aristotle's assertions, it wasn't finally for Plato to decide the issue. Catharsis theory has impacted on western aesthetics ever since. If nothing else, what Aristotle's argument suggests is that the point of deliberately arousing strong emotions is so that they may be dissipated. We are not meant to leave the theatre or concert-hall distraught, but to have put the sadness safely behind us. The point would be made many times in the succeeding centuries, as, with notable poignancy, in the opening pages of Goethe's early novel, *The Sorrows of Young Werther* (1774):

[T]he pains people endure would be less if only ... they did not put so much imaginative energy into recalling the memory of past misfortune, rather than bear an indifferent present with equanimity.

Life is indeed tragic, but we need to learn to let the specific occasions of our distress recede securely, one after the other, into temporal distance. Or as Homer Simpson more succinctly puts it, 'Everything looks bad if you remember it.'

12

I AM MELANCHOLY

There have only ever really been two ways of dealing with adversity, one of which is stoical fortitude, the other a lapse into melancholy. The former was represented in antiquity by the mercurial Socrates. His 'serenity of countenance', according to Aelian, survived 'what misery soever befell him', for all that, inwardly, he was said to be much tormented by that ill humour consequent upon the intimation of mortality. Montaigne cites the instance of his own contemporary, Charles de Guise, cardinal of Lorraine, who, while attending the Council of Trent, received news of the deaths, first of his elder brother, and then of his younger. He bore both of these shocks with awesome forbearance, displaying no outward sign of grief, until a further message brought him tidings of the death of one of his men, at which point he 'gave himself over to grief and sorrow'. Those who concluded that only this last death had really touched him had misconstrued the situation, Montaigne advises us; it was rather that this latest intelligence simply opened the floodgates on a reservoir of previously stifled despair. The stoic is not immune to melancholy. He only attempts to forbid it dominion over his soul.

The opposing temper figures in the scriptures as one who is burdened down with the cares of a world steeped in perturbations, sickness and sorrow. Speaking of a great teacher who is to come to humanity in the guise not of an avenging prince of heaven but that of a suffering servant, the prophetic Book of Isaiah characterises him as a 'man of sorrows, and acquainted with grief'. He will be nothing to look at, we are warned – 'when we shall see him, there is no beauty that we should desire him'. Quite the reverse: he will be 'despised and rejected of men', as the melancholy often are. From these opening verses of Isaiah 53, the medieval world derived its image of Christ himself as the Man of Sorrows. To take the troubles of the world upon one's own shoulders and surrender to a melancholy aspect was thus to essay an honourable, if fractional, imitation of the suffering of Christ.

Nobody, it was held, was born melancholy, but some very definitely had it thrust upon them, generally in the form of bereavement, the loss of a beloved without whom there seemed little possibility of joy in life. To these people, the further accumulation of ordinary afflictions, great and small, offered sustenance for that heaviness of spirit that now appeared to have become their natural disposition. In an interesting paper written in 1915, 'Mourning and Melancholia', Freud noted the structural homology between the psychiatric state known as melancholia and 'the work of mourning', the sense of etiolated bereftness that follows the death of somebody close. In both states, the suggestion that anything good could happen, restoring some point to living, is only the wisp of a delusion.

In these extreme emotional states, something like a *rigor vitae* sets in, in which the sufferer becomes immobilised, incapable of action, frozen in life rather than death. This emotional paralysis or petrifaction is what turns the Theban queen Niobe into a rock, after the gods Artemis and Apollo punish her for the hubris of her fecundity by killing all her daughters and sons. After much shedding of tears, she turns to stone, although the stone, in the *Metamorphoses* of Ovid, continues to shed tears. There is a further analogy, suggests Montaigne, between the grief-stricken and the lovelorn, and he quotes from an ode by Catullus, in which the lover enumerates the physical dysfunctions he suffers through his adoration – 'Love snatches my senses from me' – inviting us to see the contiguity in aching devotion with desolation.

From the ancient theory of the four humours or essential bodily fluids, comes the proposition that chronically unhappy persons were suffering from an excess of black bile, 'melancholy' being the literal Greek name for the substance. Too much blood made one sanguine, too much phlegm phlegmatic, and too much yellow bile choleric, but a superfluity of dry and cold black bile rendered the victim affectless, given over to an unearthly spiritual autism in which, through the noxious distillation of one emotion, sadness, all the other emotions were subsumed. What was being identified was clinical depression, but the idea that it had some physiological derivation, which we now know to be centred in neurochemical activity in the brain as opposed to some dark splenetic secretion, has an eerie prescience.

The melancholic takes an apparently unnatural interest in his own extinction. Having lost the will to live, perhaps through the death of another, he becomes, as Keats has it in his address to the nightingale, 'half in love with easeful Death', calling him soft names like the endearments one pours upon a lover. As there is no more cure for life's travails than there proverbially is for love, one's own demise is the only comfort looked for: 'Now more than ever seems it rich to die,/ To cease upon the midnight with no pain.' Addressing this failure of the normal instinct for self-preservation, Freud postulated that, only when the sufferer has come to objectify her own ego to the extent that the rest of us only objectify phenomena in the external world, does the impulse to destroy the self arise. 'In the two opposed situations of being most intensely in love and of suicide,' Freud writes, 'the ego is overwhelmed by the object.'

The manifestations of the melancholic state are many and various, and include the physical ailments as well as the low-spirited temperament. Robert Burton warns us in *The Anatomy of Melancholy* that its modes of presentation encompass St Vitus's Dance (Sydenham's chorea), hydrophobia (or rabies), states of physical extasis, and lycanthropy, which last causes those upon whom it preys to 'run howling about graves and fields at night, and ... not be persuaded but that they are wolves, or some such beasts'. According to the eleventh-century Persian medical writer Avicenna, this affliction is most likely to occur in February, a dry, cold time of the year.

By the time of the Renaissance, melancholy had shed some of its aetiology and acquired the dimensions of a dignified spiritual state. In a world of sorrows, to be carefree and merry could easily seem like the disposition of an idiot. Sadness and sorrow take on a certain elegance in the literature of the period, and in English culture in particular, the Jacobean epoch that followed on the demise of Elizabeth I in 1603, itself traumatic for the nation, was distinguished by a certain cult of the morbid. Pallid reflection replaced the heroic Elizabethan mode, comfortless cynicism was the prevailing tone of the tragic theatre, and sartorial fashion began to tend towards the sober. In the poetical works of John Milton, born into this London culture of studied detumescence, the words 'sad', 'sadness' and 'sorrow' are ready at hand, informing the entire desolate atmosphere of *Paradise Lost*, intensifying the apprehension of that 'sad overthrow and foul defeat' that 'Hath lost us Heaven'.

At the time Montaigne was writing, however (the 1570s), the affectation of sombre reflectiveness was a cultural pose worthy of scorn: 'I neither like it nor think well of it,' he declares, 'even though the world, by common consent, has decided to honour it with special favour.' He sees no convincing reason why such qualities as Wisdom, Virtue and Conscience should of necessity take sadness as their natural habiliment. In contemporary Italian usage, he notes, *tristezza* signifies not the reflective sadness of the French *tristesse*, but something more like wickedness, an inimical danger to Virtue rather than its apposite. By putting on the distracted, ponderous air of tormented genius, those in thrall to *tristesse* hoped to persuade others of their bottomless spiritual depths, even their kinship with divinity. What they missed was the enfeebled nature such a posture imbued, in contrast to Montaigne's own intellectual temperament, which, he tells us, he thickens and toughens with the abrading force of argumentation. There are no such arguments in *tristesse*; its proponents already know the world has won.

Albrecht Dürer's copper engraving of 1514, *Melencolia I*, portrays the frustrated seeker after knowledge, typified by the figure of the alchemist, wearing the expropriated wings of an angel, surrounded by the apparatus of his fruitless quest – the crucible, the balance, the compasses, the hourglass. A cherub averts his commiserating gaze, a skeletal hound slumbers in ignorance. Somewhere in the distant background, the sun of knowledge dawns over a broad, calm sea and a rainbow arcs across the sky, but none of the figures in the foreground, sunk in their benighted lassitude, sees it. To be a seeker after truth, the picture tells us, is to submit to spiritual gloom. It is precisely the affectation of that cast of mind to which Montaigne, later in the same century, so dismissively objects.

The fashion for assuming a state of melancholy offended Montaigne, at least partly, because it seemed a parody of the mental state induced by genuine affliction. If one went about pretending to be desolate, then surely enough in time, life would give one something to be desolate about. Extreme mourning over a bereavement perhaps represents the true measure of anguished consciousness. This was demonstrated in the latter half of the nineteenth century by Queen Victoria's descent into a forty-year period of mourning after the death of Prince Albert. The years from Albert's death in December 1861 until her own in January 1901 were marked by a mixture of sombre forbearance and an effluvium of private grief, which latter, as she vouchsafed in a letter to her eldest daughter, was unaccountably 'soothing to the bruised heart and soul'. She grieved for the nation as much as for herself, feeling that it had lost a tender patriarch, the agony of his passing personally accentuated by the fact that she was absent from his bedside for a moment when it occurred. At the bar of Brooks's Club in London, even the champagne paid its last respects, acquiring a stout ale coat of black livery, in which guise it was christened Black Velvet.

Victoria's mourning was very much in keeping with the tone of the times. The literature of the late nineteenth century is populated by catastrophically dejected creatures, from the fragmenting landed gentry of Anton Chekhov's plays to the yearning heroines of the short stories of Elizabeth Stoddard, America's presiding muse of existential disappointment. Laura Calton, the young widow and mother of a stillborn boy in Stoddard's '"Me and My Son"', sits alone at a window contemplating a sunlit world of crushing tedium:

What made ordinary people contented, she wondered – those who read no novels, had few new dresses, and never came across attractive men? . . . Was it her doom to walk up and down Main Street for the rest of her life, to see that Cummings had a peck of clams outside his door, or a basket of cocoa-nuts [sic], or, on the bench at Begg's Emporium, Tom Frost and Jem Cole smoking, and disputing whether the wind was hauling round, and what the minister 'went on' to say the Sabbath before?

Her husband's death, and the slight anticlimax of his will, have left her in a 'dreary melancholy, which she believed was to last till some fatal disease should seize her and carry her off'. In 'Waiting at the Station', Mary Sage intends to write a book entitled *Dissection and Analysis of all Human Disappointment through Emotion*, if only she can rouse herself from languorous anomie long enough to pick up the pen.

Stoddard's stories frequently take place in hot, dusty summer, with the prevailing conditions providing an ironic backdrop to the heartsick lethargy of the central characters. Laura Calton readily acknowledges that Thoreau or Emerson, those bracing apostles of the American landscape's wide open spaces, would each have delighted in the vista of radiant sky, mountainous white clouds and distantly susurrating sea that is entirely wasted on her; and yet something about the scene recalls for us the brilliant, unnoticed sea of Dürer's alchemist. It is the banality of broad daylight that makes the sorrowful vision so bitter. Asking whether there may not be some organic ebb and flow to the rhythms of depression, Freud observes that the gloom of the melancholic's daytime is often oddly ameliorated towards evening, as though the mood were obeying some somatic elimination of toxins that took place by degrees as the day wore on. This rhythm prefigures the final passing of the condition, and reminds the wretched of the earth that even sadness can have an end.

JEALOUSY

Jealousy is the sister of love, as the devil is the brother of angels.
Marie Françoise-Catherine de Beauvau

1. Anger, wrath, indignation. 2. Devotion, eagerness, anxiety to serve. 3. Solicitude or anxiety for the preservation or well-being of something. 4. The state of mind arising from the suspicion, apprehension, or knowledge of rivalry: a. in love; b. in respect of success or advantage; c. in biblical language, said of God: Having a love that will tolerate no unfaithfulness in the beloved object. 5. *dial.* Suspicion; apprehension of evil; mistrust.

Darwin's physical indicators: none

13

TO BE JEALOUS

Jealousy is the uninvited interloper at the banquet of the emotions. It was denied its true status as a basic emotion by many researchers, including Darwin's acolyte Paul Ekman, and yet most people would identify it as a central emotional state. Great works of literature that occupy unassailable places in the canons of both popular esteem and the academies turn on precisely this theme. For Freud, at least, our emotional and sexual lives begin in jealousy, with the infant's tussle with the parent of its own sex in an attempt to compete for the attentions of the other. Our search for a sexual partner in adult life is thus a continuation by other means of the desire to find a love that is both unconditional and indivisible. Now that Freud's theories are no longer the perceived wisdom, this concept of primal jealousy has receded somewhat from contemporary psychology.

The difficulty Ekman has in accepting jealousy as an emotion, a difficulty Darwin himself didn't find, arises from the fact that their work is based upon a study of physical manifestations of emotion. In his general introduction, Darwin had acknowledged that there were certain states that did not appear to have corresponding facial expressions, and he asks 'Can guilty, or sly, or jealous expressions be recognised? though I know not how these can be defined'. If there is no involuntary facial evidence of this state of mind, can it truly be said to exist as an independent emotion? Ekman concludes not, allowing however, that it may be a complex of other emotions.

Darwin remained troubled by the point, and felt that writers and painters did too, in the sense that they must rely on imprecise metaphorical devices to illustrate the envious or jealous countenance. Shakespeare uses conflicting descriptions of the physiognomy of jealousy or envy, as either 'pale' or 'black', or as 'lean-faced Envy in her loathsome ease' (2 *Henry VI*, III:ii), or the 'lean and hungry look' that the envious conspirator Cassius wears in *Julius Caesar* (I:ii), or as in the much-quoted bestial image of jealousy as 'the green-eyed monster which doth mock/ The meat it feeds on' in *Othello* (III:iii). In this last and most famous of all images of jealousy, it is worth noting that the epithet applies not merely to the colour of the beast's irises, but to a quality of its vision. Just as a sharp-eyed person sees things sharply, so the monster sees things greenly. Green was established as the colour of jealousy long before Shakespeare was writing, perhaps because it is also the colour of immaturity, inexperience, newness. We are 'green with envy' at somebody else's success or possessions because we haven't come to emotional maturity in such matters. It is also the colour of sickness and nausea, and the jealous are nothing if not emotionally sick. Painters must rely on some physical object, a theatrical prop as it were, to depict jealousy or envy, since it can't be precisely drawn on the face in the way that sadness, anger and fear can. It would be wrong however to make facial expression the sole indicator of an emotional state. It is after all possible to burn inwardly with furious rage, without betraying the slightest flicker of it in the face. In the case of jealousy, moreover, it seems wilfully perverse to insist that it can't be a true emotional state when its casualties are all around us.

Looking back to the etymology of the term, we note that it is effectively an Old French variant of 'zealous', but with the difference that the jealous are powered not just by enthusiasm but by anger. The dictionary gives us first wrath and then devotion as definitions, and to characterise jealousy in the way that modern psychodynamics understands it, as wrathful devotion, would not be too far off the mark. It is indeed a compound emotion, but not to be disqualified for that, any more than green should be disqualified as a colour because it is compounded of blue and yellow.

The obnubilation thickens when we consider, as we must, the typological difference between jealousy and envy, the latter often seen as more an attitude of mind. How bold this dividing line is seems questionable, and to the degree that some homology between the two states can be identified, so we can account for the widespread confusion between them. Jealousy is generally regarded as a state of emotional or sexual possessiveness, in which the affected individual tries, under real or imagined provocation, to protect the object of his or her desire from being claimed or tempted by another. Envy is defined as a case of wanting for oneself some material commodity, or general state of affluence or happiness, that another enjoys. The wanting, however, is often seen as reprehensibly devoid of any intent to expend personal effort in acquiring it for oneself. More simply, envy is the feeling we have towards those who have something we haven't got, whereas jealousy involves not wanting them to have it either. While jealousy – for all that, at its extreme manifestation, it may become a disorder – can be seen as an understandable and even noble feeling, envy is quite the opposite, a mean-minded, resentful squalor of the soul. Ekman, like Darwin, in finding the two states equally unreadable, already partially conflates them: 'Sexual jealousy is what we most often think of, but there can be jealousy involving rivalry and loss which is not sexual.' But that, precisely, is envy – a solecism Darwin does not commit (but which, problematically, the OED compilers did allow). Jealousy is in a sense the personification of envy, its transposition from the realm of the material to that of the human, and as such it is always either sexual or sentimental. There is nothing sentimental about envy. While jealousy may be about the desire to get naked, envy is just naked desire. Both, however, are emotions.

*

At the heart of envy is often the perception of inequality, as seems to be the case with its first scriptural exemplar, Adam and Eve's eldest son, Cain, whose story is affectingly told in the fourth chapter of Genesis (1–15). When his younger brother Abel's offering to God is inexplicably preferred above his by the Creator, he descends into an angry depression, only to be told by God that if he hasn't done well, it must be because he is sinful. Talking the matter over with his brother doesn't satisfy him and, consumed with zealous wrath, he becomes history's first murderer. There are two dynamics at work here. One consists in whatever it is about Cain's character that leads God to refuse or, as the Authorised Version has it, not to 'respect' his offering. This initially seems rather mysterious. Cain is a farmer, a 'tiller of the ground', while his brother is a shepherd. When they make their offerings Cain's is of 'the fruit of the ground', while his brother offers God the pick of the newborn flock, 'the firstlings', and 'of the fat thereof' – the meat. God graciously accepts the latter, but rather choosily declines Cain's grain or root vegetables, like somebody who has been invited to one too many vegetarian dinner parties. If the meat is intrinsically better, can it be that the farmer will always appear to God lower down the spiritual pecking order than the tender of livestock? The gloss generally given on this aspect of the story follows that cited in a single verse of the apostle Paul's epistle to the Hebrews:

By faith Abel offered unto God a more excellent sacrifice than Cain, by which he obtained witness that he was righteous, God testifying of his gifts: and by it he being dead yet speaketh. (11:4)

It isn't the content of the offering, but the way in which it is made, that has displeased God. He doesn't deem it to have been made 'by faith', out of a true devotion, but judges it to be a perfunctory gesture, made in an attempt to placate the irascible figure who has just evicted his parents from Paradise. Three emotions are called forth in Cain: first furious anger, then melancholy, and finally – the bitterest pill of all – consuming jealousy. Matters are not helped by God's cruelly disingenuous questioning of Cain ('Why art thou wroth? and why is thy countenance fallen?'). He is told that if he behaves appropriately, he will be accepted, and if not, he will lay himself open to temptation, when 'sin lieth at the door'. This suggests that brand of petty officialdom that insists, while introducing some new curtailment of civil liberties, that if you toe the line, you'll have nothing to worry about, which turns a harmless platitude into something more menacing, and anyway constitutes no justification for the curtailment. What undoubtedly twists the knife for Cain is that the brother who is preferred is his junior. God's favour has already overturned the primogeniture on which the world was implicitly founded. Intervening in the familial relations of the very first family, he tells Cain that if he keeps his nose clean he will enjoy a position of authority over his brother – 'unto thee shall be his desire, and thou shalt rule over him'. The world's first crime therefore issues from the corrosive force of sibling rivalry.

Cain's attempt to discuss the matter with Abel comes to nothing. The younger brother is not granted a single word of dialogue in the whole story – perhaps his sense of security in his own faith is too great for him to take issue with his elder brother's mundane objections – but at any rate, Cain is not placated. While they are hard at work in the fields, he kills the golden boy he has come to hate, presumably with a blow from the very implement with which he cut the offering that was flung back in his face. God reappears, and asks what has become of Abel. 'I know not,' Cain demurs. 'Am I my brother's keeper?' Now he has compounded his actions. Not only has he committed fratricide, but he is the first character in the Bible to answer back to God. The disputatious stance, coupled with the bare-faced lie, which together add up to the most daring disavowal of responsibility in world mythology, are sufficient for him to be cursed for the rest of his life. Nothing will grow for him in the ground that he has profaned with his brother's blood, reducing him to the life of a vagabond for the remainder of his days. Even now, under sentence, he appeals, telling the great judge with some pathos, 'My punishment is greater than I can bear.' For this final piece of boldness, he is rewarded with a kind of commutation. Nobody shall attempt to kill him, for all that his reputation will go before him. It is almost as though, in his final defiance, he earns the respect from God that his harvest offering had failed to win. And then out he goes from the Lord's presence, to that land of banishment 'east of Eden', where we imagine him frittering the rest of his days kicking his heels with James Dean.

In a recent work of pop theology, Andrew Knowles accepts St Paul's reading of Cain and Abel's story. It is the less than pious mood in which Cain has offered his grain that dooms him, and the commentator hazards a more specific guess as to the precise cause of offence. It is a 'grudging', even 'phoney', offering, not merely made in the wrong spirit, but made by one who doesn't genuinely want to make it at all, so that it is stained with the character of falsehood. It is as though God would rather not have had an offering so insincerely meant. Mindful perhaps that this makes the deity sound a trifle prissy, Knowles strengthens the imputation against Cain even further: 'his heart is hostile', we are told. From 'grudging' to 'phoney' to 'hostile' is a formidable trajectory by any standards, and all the more remarkable for being achieved in a single act. The fact is that none of this is present in the Hebrew text. Cain's gift is not described in any more negative terms than is Abel's. We have only God's own word for it that it was beneath him, but that of course is the word that cancels out all others. Knowles is undoubtedly correct in identifying the theme of the story as envy. It is indeed that intolerable perception of inequality that precipitates the action, and makes Cain the first rebel, not to mention a true son of his mother. Another commentator draws the lesson from Cain's tale that 'rebellion leads to bloodshed', which it certainly has done throughout human history, but one would want to ask what it is that provokes that rebellion in the first place. Rebellions and revolutions, and all the stirring-up of trouble known proverbially as 'raising Cain', are not created *ex nihilo*. They generally arise only after a prolonged period in which their makers have tried, to the limit of their tolerance for privation, to live with systematic disregard, and when after vainly seeking allies among the more favoured classes, as personified by the pure and silent Abel, they realise their only hope of salvation lies in going it alone.

George Steiner's preface to the Everyman Library edition of the Hebrew Bible of 1996 worries honestly at the questions raised by Cain's tale. Like many another example of God's unfathomable wrath – his instruction to Abraham to kill his son Isaac, the utter gratuitousness of his treatment of Job – the narrative constitutes a 'provocation' that, like these others, continues to trouble the religious conscience:

No amount or ingenuity of textual criticism can answer satisfactorily the question of God's preference of Abel over Cain ... What possible abyss of motiveless preference, of the injustice of divine love, generates that first act of homicide and of fratricide in which all of the dark of future history is figured?

It is precisely the 'gentler, less destructive' offering that God has rejected. But if we read the story as just one of the mythical accounts that the Book of Genesis offers of the creation of the world, and of the actions and events that determined its subsequent course, instead of pondering the sublime motivelessness of its Creator, we might stumble on enlightenment. Is not the moral to which the story points us that envy, which follows from the felt evidence of injustice as surely as *beth* follows from *aleph*, is generative of hatred between those who should be close? If so, it is a teaching that applies as readily to the social and economic fields as it once did in the devotional. The inequities of wealth distribution and privilege on which the global economy is founded will not cease to inspire destructive envy in those below the upper echelons, as long as they are falsely seen as fundamental to universal well-being. Any political representatives who speak out against this dispensation are accused of callously exploiting people's consciousness of their own inability to rise higher. Ever since envy was declared to be one of the seven deadly sins, the attitude of wanting for oneself what others have can only be seen as a moral lapse, particularly because it is presumed that one wants to have it without exerting any effort in procuring it. In fact, what many desire is simply the introduction of equality. The British and American right-wing press used to refer to socialism as 'the politics of envy', as if ostentatious displays of wealth and privilege (often themselves acquired without the slightest expenditure of effort) could instil anything else in their less favoured spectators. In any case, the opposite of being envious of the better off is meekly accepting that one has no right to such benefits, an attitude of mind unlikely to attract many adherents outside the ascetic communities. For this reason, the concept of the 'politics of envy' underwent some prudent revision in the 1980s, when the theory of 'trickle-down' economics was first promulgated during Ronald Reagan's presidency in the United States. The desire to have what others have was now supposed to be a motivating factor in capitalism's dynamic, with the conspicuous spending of the more fortunate held to generate some eventual tenth-hand beneficence for those at the bottom of the pyramid. Thus, talk of envy was quietly dropped by conservative ideologues. If, as was asserted by Michael Douglas's Machiavellian financial broker Gordon Gecko, in Oliver Stone's defining film *Wall Street* (1987), greed was now good, then the corollary it dragged in its wake was that envy too was a fit state for the human soul. Like money, it helps to make the economic world go round.

*

Defined in contradistinction to envy, jealousy can only ever be sexual jealousy, the experience of being the losing horse in competitive romance, or of unwillingly ceding one's established sexual partner to the attentions of a rival. But is not this tussle over individuals as sexual commodities not the precise equivalent of material envy? The objects of our amorous attentions are in themselves material bodies after all, albeit desired in a different way to consumer goods. If, however, we feel that the dignity of romantic love and its transactions lies outside the world of the marketplace, then we should reproach ourselves with the thought that sexual jealousy always risks importing it back into that realm. By inwardly growling like guard dogs when somebody else appears too familiar with them, we effectively reduce our partners to the status of material possessions, and the legitimate desire and love and concern we feel for them become commodified into the currency of exchange.

A philosopher in the field of aesthetics, John Armstrong, argues that jealousy proceeds from a fundamental aporia, or contradiction, in the human condition. On the one hand, we in the west tend to believe in the version of sex promulgated by the Christian tradition, that sexual congress only acquires meaning and value when underwritten by the capital of love. (The financial metaphor slips into his argument too: 'The Christian view accepts that we do invest sex with special moral and emotional significance not accorded to other activities and thinks that we are right to make this investment.') Sex without love is both unfulfilling and ultimately degrading because we are reducing ourselves to some sort of purely animal function. The alternative view, which exercises a simultaneous, countervailing influence on us, says that sex is simply another form of physical pleasure, akin to a strenuous round of badminton or the appreciation of good food. On this latter view, whatever potential it has for our degradation lies precisely in our taking it too seriously. Why, therefore, should sexual fidelity be the measure, or even one of the measures, of whether love is genuine?

Armstrong contends that most of the difficulties we encounter during the course of a long-term monogamous relationship arise from the destructive tension that obtains within this moral polarity. The former view takes jealousy very seriously, as the honourable response to a situation in which love's contract is breached by one of its signatories, while the latter desires that jealousy be abolished, so that the mass of our physical impulses, while not being denied gratification, could be safely fenced off from the separate arena of love. There are only two possible courses in love, thinks Armstrong: one is to renounce any extra-curricular opportunity for sexual satisfaction, while the other is to indulge it but keep it hidden, at least until a decent interval has elapsed, following which it can safely be referred to almost in passing.

Why, though, should it matter that somebody who is attached to another might go off from time to time, even systematically, and have satisfying physical relations with others? The answer lies in what Armstrong calls the 'hinterland of sex', by which he means all the significative physical manoeuvres that surround the act itself. Participants in open relationships claim that it is 'just sex' they are engaging in, and nothing more. We might insist that nothing in human affairs is ever 'just' anything, especially with regard to sexual behaviour, the allusiveness and complexity of which are in direct proportion to our elevation of it to such an exalted status in our lives. If this 'just-sex' that goes on in the interstices of non-monogamous relationships really possessed that undifferentiated lack of any moral or emotional impact that its practitioners claim for it, one would want to know what it is then that keeps drawing them back to it with such obsessive regularity. If it were of no greater interest than 'just' taking the bus to work or 'just' loading up the washing machine, then perhaps our sympathies are owed to those who find themselves repeatedly having to carry out such a monotonous chore. The fact is that it is as remarkable to them, and hopefully as rewarding, as all sexual encounters are, which is why

HUMANITY: AN EMOTIONAL HISTORY

it is so singularly pursued, and with every act of supplementary sex that takes place in an open relationship, the perpetrator is saying, 'At this moment, given this choice, I would rather have sex with this other person than with my partner.' While it is technically possible to commit the sexual act without further preamble, and then walk away from it, what in fact happens is something more, an exploration – however brief and hurried – of the hinterland:

This is the sensuality of a caress, rather than of intercourse. It is, as it were, the hinterland of sex which is most powerfully evocative of intimacy. Many people who feel intense jealousy at the thought of their partner having sex with another say that it is not intercourse itself which is the focus of their anguish, so much as what they imagine to come before and afterwards. It is these passages of sensual closeness which most directly tie sex to love.

There may not be love, but there is the acting out of the physical rituals associated with it. What comes 'before and afterwards' may well be 'imagined' by the aggrieved partner but is not thereby to be dismissed as imaginary. Somebody else is discovering with delight just what physical stimuli your lover responds to in the prelude to sex – they are the same ones he responds to with you – and he is now submitting to that discovery with the collusive kindness that he once bestowed on you. The particular excruciation of which sexual jealousy is composed lies in its amalgam of certainty and ignorance. One knows full well what physical activity is taking place, more or less, but both the setting and the identity of the other remain concealed.

If it is possible to attain a truly beatific state in which one simply doesn't mind what sex one's own partner has with whom, or how often (and I confess I have yet to see any convincing example of it), then the question would arise as to the point of relationships. Why does an open relationship have to think of itself as a relationship at all? Why is it not just another episodic moment in the continuing stream of sexual *jouissance*? What is there in it that makes both parties keep coming back to it? For the great mass of humanity, on the other hand, those who want one constant partner, whom they love, to come back to them in the sense that they never truly go away, the sexual conduct of the other will always be a matter of legitimate concern. What they need to see, if an infidelity takes place, is not that there is necessarily some underlying fault in the established relationship – that foul bit of ideology with which women have been encouraged to forgive the errant male, since if she was giving him what he wanted in the first place, he wouldn't have been tempted to stray – but that in the strongest relationships, trust is renewable. It is only renewable, however, on the basis that the other is not one's sexual possession, and that a corresponding infidelity won't 'even things up', since either of these principles returns us once more to the notion of emotional exchange as commodity exchange. Some may feel that trust is not infinitely renewable, any more than a market can expand indefinitely. But then this brings us to the heart of the argument. Human relations are not subject to market forces, and assuming love doesn't wither, infinitely renewable is precisely what trust is. Its serial fracture and repair can't be made the *modus operandi* of an entire relationship, but when it is necessary – and although the hurt might scream in every corpuscle, so that the very thought defies belief – love affairs heal better than bones do.

14

I MAKE HIM JEALOUS

The great question that has worried Shakespeare scholars over the centuries with regard to his only entirely domestic tragedy, *Othello*, has been: why does Iago do it? Among the critics of the early twentieth century, the redoubtable A C Bradley in the vanguard, the riddle came to assume almost Sphinx-like significance. The delineation of the villain's character memorably set down by Samuel Coleridge in the previous century, that in Iago's soliloquies we hear 'the motive-hunting of a motiveless malignity', could no longer suffice. One may choose from a handful of such motives offered in the text: that Othello is suspected of having slept with Iago's wife Emilia, that he has overlooked Iago in appointing Michael Cassio his Lieutenant while Iago has had to settle for the less exalted rank of Ancient (or Ensign), that he harbours a racist distaste for Othello's hard-won reputation. Or one might see that these are the red herrings we are invited to consider while the single-minded campaign of destruction he wages against the General takes its effect. Generations of school students poring over the text are now encouraged to wave the question aside with the answer that 'We don't know and it doesn't matter', which doesn't thereby banish the interpretative puzzle. Meanwhile, what is arguably the more pressing question has too often been overlooked: quite apart from Iago, why does Othello do what he does?

It is specifically established in the play, although perhaps too late for the point to carry full credibility, that not the least of Othello's qualities has been precisely that he is immune to jealousy. Having realised she has mislaid the charmed handkerchief upon which the action of Act III turns, Desdemona tells Emilia that she worries that its loss will put him to 'ill-thinking', for all that he is made of 'no such baseness/ As jealous creatures are'. It isn't clear at this stage whether she knows the full story of the handkerchief's supernatural powers (having been entrusted it by his dying mother, Othello has given it to his wife in the belief that it retains the power to keep him besotted with her, as long as she doesn't lose it), but more poignantly than any such exotic occultism, it was his first gift to her. Emilia seems surprised that Desdemona should not consider Othello to be prone to jealousy, but the faithful wife insists 'I think the sun where he was born/ Drew all such humours from him.' To which, if the action allowed us to pause, we might want to reply by asking her how she can be sure. It would be hard to know what the test of immunity to jealousy might be, other than the obvious one of seeing whether the examinee rose to some specific provocation. In any case, although she doesn't yet know it, that provocation has just been poured into his ear in the previous scene by the trusted Iago, a comrade-in-arms 'of exceeding honesty'. Speaking his own epitaph in the final scene, Othello describes himself as having loved 'not wisely, but too well', adding that he was 'not easily jealous, but, being wrought,/ Perplexed in the extreme', perplexed enough indeed to have just strangled his blameless wife. More than the irrelevant tokens of Iago's resentment, this notion of Othello's being too noble to have been prey to baseless jealousies is the play's great decoy, what Alfred Hitchcock used to refer to in his own film plots as a 'McGuffin', some apparently significant object, observation or occurrence that turns out to be wholly misleading or irrelevant. We are asked to believe that Othello is of such iron-willed resolution that only some scheme of diabolical Machiavellian intricacy could trap him in its snares, and yet at the same time we see him coming to a state of boiling rage at the mere suggestion, unfounded as he himself sees it to be, that his wife has been unfaithful to him. The most telling aspect of the whole deception is that Iago informs him, prior to unburdening himself of this shameful suspicion, what the theme of it will be. After dodging for several minutes Othello's insistence that he speak his mind, a process that builds to a furious 'Ha!' of exhausted patience from the General, Iago finally shows his hand – 'O, beware, my lord, of jealousy!' – giving its monstrous name to the beast to which Othello will now obediently fall prey, even before he has heard the sketchiest detail of the charge.

The truth is that the play's hero is acutely prone to tortuous jealousies; this indeed is his *hamartia*, or tragic flaw, in the language of Aristotle's theory of tragedy. As we see him struggling to control himself, the point is made plain, and his weakness in this regard enables Iago to get to him. The ruin of Desdemona couldn't matter less to Iago, although it is interesting to note that in the source-tale on which Shakespeare based his play, a preposterous little saga of 1565 by one Giraldo Cinthio, the Ensign's motive for engaging in the plot is his murderous resentment of a woman who has spurned his advances. When the Moor, convinced of her infidelity, comes to kill her, the Ensign assists him in the deed. They bludgeon her to death together and make it look like an accident. For Shakespeare's Iago, only the fact that Desdemona is seemingly as chaste as the world takes her to be is of any instrumental significance to him. But is she?

One of the thematic preoccupations of the mature Shakespeare is the hiatus between being and seeming, and the concomitant tragic truth that the world is full of people who are adept at appearing to be virtuous and well-intentioned, when all manner of unsuspected maleficence seethes within them. It becomes apparent that her husband is not the only man who might have tried his luck with Desdemona had the opportunity arisen: Cassio himself, unjustly impugned as the adulterer in Iago's plot, clearly harbours his own powerful attraction to her, as does the ridiculous Roderigo, and even Iago himself ('Now, I do love her too'). She is the rock on which their own hopes of sexual preferment have been dashed, and she knows it well enough. As to the theory that Desdemona rather likes Cassio herself ('tis apt and of great credit,' says Iago, when working it into his plot), we have the evidence of our own eyes in the extraordinarily flirtatious kissing game she enacts with Cassio, upon which Iago pronounces his own aside, at the opening of Act II. This immediately follows her extended verbal flirtation with Iago himself, in which she begins by inviting him to say how he would praise her poetically, and then encourages him to create aphoristic little rhymes about the sexual fortunes of women, using all the possible combinations of fair, foul, wise and foolish. His opening address to her, which portrays her as combining fairness and wisdom, runs: 'If she be fair and wise, fairness and wit, / The one's for use, the other useth it.' This, the product of some prior mental effort, is not the empty-headed compliment of courtly wooing, but contains a rather pungent imputation. She gets what she wants in life by making use of her good looks, but her only response is 'Well praised!' Her acceptance of the accuracy of the charge, for that is surely what it is, recalls Socrates' reply to the stranger who accuses him in public of being full of every kind of vice and foulness – 'You know me, sir!' All this verbal foreplay and kissing takes place, we should recall, when nobody is quite certain whether Othello's ship has landed safely in port in Cyprus. For a woman supposedly anxious for her beloved's safety, she seems remarkably easily distracted, and is so again, at an even more crucial stage in the proceedings in Act IV.

Here, having been sent to bed after dinner on Othello's orders, not long after he has hit her in front of her cousin, the Venetian dignitary Lodovico, she awaits his presence, and some possible explanation of this ghastly turn in her husband's affections. As

Emilia prepares her for bed, Desdemona suddenly announces that she is rather taken with Lodovico: 'This Lodovico is a proper [i.e. good-looking] man.' Emilia readily agrees. 'He speaks well,' Desdemona adds, to which Emilia appends the intensifier she seems to want to hear. 'I know a lady in Venice would have walked barefoot to Palestine for a touch of his nether lip.' And then, as though caught in her distraction, Desdemona begins to sing a melancholy song of love, in which a poor soul sits repining under a sycamore tree, an attitude she had curiously escaped for a moment, distracted as she was by how gorgeous her cousin has become. Does she know that her marriage to Othello is doomed, and is she already pondering his replacement? And who exactly is this 'lady in Venice' that Emilia speaks of? Might she be referring immodestly to herself, or is there some oblique intention to implicate Desdemona?

Considering these issues in a recent work on Shakespeare, Frank Kermode puts the point no more strongly than to say that there is a faint lack of moral clarity about Desdemona's part. This seems to suggest that there is something indistinct, the outline of which we can't quite make out, which might lend credence to Othello's mental breakdown following the suggestion of her infidelity. However that may be decided, we are surely on firmer ground in seeing that it is not only Othello who is infected with ruinous jealousy. Iago himself seems to feel it in his very fibre, not only in his having been passed over for promotion by Othello, but in the approbation that Cassio now enjoys in the post he feels should have been his. 'He hath a daily beauty in his life/ That makes me ugly,' he tells Roderigo, prior to setting him on to murder the Lieutenant. If he has felt anything towards Desdemona in the past, it is gone now, except that he would have preferred it if, himself being slighted, he had not had to endure the sight of anybody else enjoying her. Almost contemporaneous with *Othello*, and exploring the same emotional themes as Shakespeare's play, Robert Tofte's 1615 translation of the sixteenth-century Italian philologist Bernardo

Varchi's *The Blazon of Jealousie*, identifies the kind of jealousy that Iago is suffering from, as being 'when we would not have that anyone should obtain ... that which we wish and desire to obtain'. The effect is a kind of negative dog-in-the-manger syndrome, in which because we do not possess the object of our affections, we wish for nobody else to possess it either. Iago's suppressed rage at the union of Othello and Desdemona takes the form of the sexual disgust with which he tries to infect others, principally Roderigo, Cassio, and Desdemona's father Brabantio. The mismatch in both age and racial origin between the recently married pair seems to him particularly vile, and he resorts to bestial imagery in imagining it. 'Even now, now, very now,' he tells Brabantio, who has been awakened in the middle of the night to hear that his daughter has married without his consent, 'an old black ram / Is tupping your white ewe', the repeated 'now' making the scene all the more discomfitingly present to contemplation. Even while we speak, they're at it. The revulsion of it recalls a little of Hamlet's anguish at the thought of his mother in the throes of sexual congress with her fratricidal brother-in-law, the difference being that Iago has become consummate at what Freud termed transference. He uses his own burnished reputation in order to turn the full force of his disgust on the black General. 'I am not what I am,' he announces triumphantly in the opening scene, an intentionally scriptural pronouncement that recalls the thundering tautology of the Old Testament Yahweh, 'I AM THAT I AM' (Exodus 3:14), in order to establish for the audience his elemental malevolence, and then a short while later, and rather more to the point, 'I hate the Moor.' The greatest weapon in his armoury – greater even than the natural prurience of others, on which he knows he can rely – is his profoundly Machiavellian (one might even say Schopenhauerian) understanding of the limits of human benevolence:

I have looked upon the world for four times seven years, and since I could distinguish betwixt a benefit and an injury, I never found a man that knew how to love himself. (I:iii)

Self-doubt may be seen to be the meat that jealousy mocks as it feeds on it, and it will be meat to Iago too in his scheme. Notwithstanding his great military prowess, and his evident indispensability to the Venetian state, and indeed the fact that Desdemona has made a free and unharried choice of him in marriage, Othello is still able to succumb to the melodramatic suggestion that there are doings afoot that he did not suspect. Despite his rank, there are aspects of Venetian society that remain alien to him, including perhaps, as Iago suggests, the notoriously public sexual incontinence of its young women. Once in the state of crazed suspicion, then, what assets one is in possession of start to be undervalued. He may seem to have it all, Iago contentedly notes, 'But riches fineless is as poor as winter,/ To him that ever fears he shall be poor.'

There is a striking sense about the play, particularly from the pivotal Act III, scene iii onwards, that all the characters are enmeshed in a factitious doom arising from their own lack of self-belief. Even Iago, triumphant as his plot rolls on without obstacle, knows that in the end he is likely to be discovered, and when he is so, has nothing to say. His insouciance contrasts with the frothings of the evil Moor, Aaron, in the early tragedy *Titus Andronicus*, who, when captured and accused of foul deeds, chooses the moment of his ascent on the makeshift scaffold to enumerate a few of the even fouler, undetected crimes he has committed. Still alive at the play's end, he is led away fulminating at the contemptible nature of a world he loathes. The 'malcontent' was a stock figure in the Elizabethan world, which accepted that there were some people who appeared to have no faculty for seeing the benevolence in creation, and whose life's work it was to undermine it. Iago is just such a character, but now dressed in the richer, more psychologically subtle livery of the mature Shakespeare, and his life's work is done once he has completed this single act of treachery. (This is why we can safely consign to the dustbin of literary analysis that rather naïve suggestion that Iago is, in some allegorical sense, the Devil incarnate.) But while in *Titus*, much mocked now for its Grand Guignol crudery, the characters upon whom Aaron preys are largely blameless innocents, in *Othello* everybody seems to have some part to play in the disaster that befalls them. They are left trapped and struggling, like flies in a bottle, by the emotional storms their sexual conduct appears to have unleashed. The entire ambience is infernal, a mood caught by the apocryphal observation that in the names of the married couple, Shakespeare has hidden their true natures. He has inherited Desdemona's name from the Cinthio original, but Othello is his own coinage. Stanley Cavell, arguing that the play has some of the Manichaean starkness of the medieval morality play, makes this point in a work of 1979:

It is against the [background of the] tradition of the morality play that I now go on to call attention – I cannot think I am the first to say it out loud – to the hell and the demon staring out of the names of OtHELLo and DesDEMONa.

'From Heresy, Jealousy, and Frenzy, good Lord, deliver us.' Thus a venerable English proverb, nailing the three demons most likely to turn the heart of the devout from the path of righteousness. The rage of jealousy is capable, as Shakespeare has shown us, of turning spiritual probity to maleficence. Once succumbed to, it enmeshes the sufferer in a deadly cycle of moral decline, its symptomatology helpfully spelled out by Robert Burton: 'Those which are jealous, most part, if they be not otherwise relieved, proceed from suspicion to hatred, from hatred to frenzy, madness, injury, murder, and despair.' As an affliction, jealousy has always had something of the demonic about it in folk cosmology. Erasmus, in the sixteenth century, reports a story in which a demon was blamed for the fire that destroyed a German village in 1533. The fiend was popularly believed to have fallen in love with a young woman there, raining down its vengeance when it grew jealous at the sight of her having sexual relations with her man.

By the turn of the seventeenth century, Burton and his contemporaries were able to refer not only to the classics, but also to more recent historical examples of incidences of sexual jealousy. Acts of mutilation, directed as much against themselves by the suspicious as against the bodies of their rivals, are common. Amestris, wife of the Persian king Xerxes, is said to have unleashed a rage of unimaginable violence upon the wife of her brother-in-law Masistes, upon discovering that a cloak she had made for Xerxes was being worn by Masistes' daughter, with whom Xerxes was having an adulterous dalliance. She ordered that the mother's breasts be chopped off and fed to the dogs, as a preamble to the hacking away of her ears, lips and tongue and the flaying of her skin, while the daughter herself got away with merely having her nose slit. Castration was a frequent recourse, institutionalised in cultures such as Ottoman Turkey, where eunuchs were retained to decoy the sexual longings of women in the seraglios. It was also practised in rather a different fashion in the west, when certain newly-wed men, such as the baker of Basel, cited by Burton, were driven to sacrifice their own sexual competency to prove to themselves the devotion of their wives. If she would stay uncomplainingly with one so discommoded (or of such obvious mental instability, one is tempted to add), then she must really love him. The Turkish concubines, meanwhile, might safely disport themselves with emasculated African natives without inappropriate desires ever entering their elaborately coiffed heads. Even phallic items of food, such as cucumbers and carrots, were sliced up before being carried in to them.

Burton allows, as does Shakespeare, somewhat contrary to the tendency of the *idée reçue*, that men may fall victim to possessive jealousies just as easily as women. Robert Tofte, in *The Blazon of Jealousie*, colludes in the prevailing view that there is even a certain physiological type that predisposes to the jealous temper. They are likely to be red-haired, sallow-skinned, dark-eyed, shrill-voiced – and of course female. The examplar of such suspicious, doubting hags was Juana la Loca (Joan the Mad), the Spanish queen who reigned over Castile and Aragon in the first half of the sixteenth century, and who harboured such consuming misdoubts of her husband, Philip, that she was sent to Ximenes, Archbishop of Toledo, for psychiatric treatment. A form of violent rages were her stock-in-trade too. During her husband's absence on diplomatic business in Flanders in 1504, she began to repine and sicken, refusing food and company, and finally, despite being pregnant, took sail in inclement weather and a turbulent headwind to track him down. Even when her surprise appearance was kindly accommodated by Philip, she still felt there was something she wasn't being told, and finally seized – accurately, as far as we know – upon a young female courtesan as the likely mistress and temptress of the king. She beat this woman savagely, dragging her about and cursing her, and tellingly shearing off all her long hair, which was not honest Spanish black but incriminating blonde, the very colour of carnal seducement. For this outrage, Philip slapped her and had her confined to her room, where she promptly went on hunger strike again.

Her convulsions of jealous frenzy persisted throughout their short marriage, up until the moment of Philip's untimely death from illness at the age of twenty-eight, when she was carrying his sixth child. After a period of several weeks' black-clad mourning, the old suspicions returned. Even in his death, she couldn't persuade herself that somebody might not be attempting to deprive her of him. She had the coffin opened to make sure his body hadn't been substituted and, as the winding-sheet was removed, fell to kissing the enrigored feet in an ecstasy of necrophilia, until she had to be, first gently and then forcefully, propelled from the vault. *En route* to its final resting-place in Granada, the coffin was opened again on her orders, so that she might check once more that the corpse it contained was that of her late beloved. The journey to Granada was undertaken nocturnally, to minimise the risk of any competing attention. It was made known that no women must come near the cortège, and rests were taken at monasteries rather than convents. As the tortuous progress continued, she had the coffin opened again and again, perhaps less for fear of substitution now as just to gaze in plain rapture on the stinking, beautiful remains. She was to live for another fifty tedious years, hovering in a twilight state between the lucid reason of she was in periodic possession and descents into wildly disordered rage, in which state she would refuse as of old to take sustenance before witnesses, only eating her dry bread and niblets of cheese when there was nobody to see her.

What fascinated Shakespeare was the facility with which those so predisposed to this state could be unravelled, like frayed woollen garments, by the malevolent interventions of others. But authentic jealousy needs no such exterior will. It can strike the sufferer by the force of mere circumstance. What its victim fails to see is that the motivation for his possessive anger has stopped being the unconditional love that Othello claims to feel for Desdemona, but has become that peculiar alloy of love and hatred that is jealousy's natural element. Victims of jealous rages are not the 'women [and men] who love too much' of Californian therapist Robin Norwood's bulging casebook, but people who have allowed their love to become blended with hatred.

A much talked-about recent study of the phenomenon was Adrian Lyne's 1987 film, *Fatal Attraction*, in which Glenn Close plays Alex Forrest, associate editor with a large publishing company, who, following a weekend of adulterous fun with one of the company lawyers, Dan Gallagher (Michael Douglas) finds that she can't just forget about him as he returns to his family. After cutting her wrists in front of him, she progresses to breaking into the married couple's house and killing his daughter's pet rabbit, in order to exercise a demonic vengeance on him. Much of the debate that the film generated centred on the moral question of whether a man who commits adultery deserves everything that is coming to him, including a psychotic woman attempting to destroy his family and kill him. Many on both sides of the Atlantic found themselves answering in the affirmative. The more interesting point the film raises, however, is whether Alex is already mentally disturbed before her weekend sexual encounter, or whether it is just the closure of that encounter in itself – the prompt withdrawal of sensual fulfilment after it has been briefly but thoroughly tasted – that tips her over the edge. It has to be said that nothing about her character, as we are at first introduced to it in the film, suggests that she is anything other than lonely. A little more of her likely mental state is revealed, however, in the scene in which Dan jokingly plays dead while they are out in a park, and her reaction is one of blind panic. She explains herself by recounting the traumatic effect that her father's death had on her, a story that turns out to be untrue. She has manipulated his sympathies in order to extract an immediate, quite disproportionate, revenge. Displaying the classic symptoms of pathological jealousy, she doesn't want anybody else to have her lover if she can't have him, and although she wants to be with him, she also cannot stop herself from making his life intolerable. The agony that jealous people have to contend with is not simply the tantalising mental business of knowing, or suspecting, that their beloved is with another, but realising that the way they themselves are behaving is utterly counter-productive of any kind of sympathy. It is the knowledge that, while trawling through his pockets and possessions in search of evidence of his affections having wandered, the jealous lover is doing the very thing that might make them wander. If you have to slash yourself with broken glass in order to secure his sympathy, then perhaps it wasn't naturally forthcoming in the first place, and the hardest lesson of all for the jealous to learn is that the flow of neither blood nor tears is reason enough in itself for their suit to be heard.

A relatively recent phenomenon, borne out of possessive obsession, is that of stalking, which has resulted in the formulation of laws to deter it. An all-consuming fixation on another person can affect almost anybody, not just film actors and tennis stars, and can be characterised as a self-deluding belief that the object of one's attentions might secretly reciprocate them, but is just unable to show it. This state of mind has been recognised since 1927 as de Clérambault's syndrome, after a French psychologist who identified it in a woman who had persuaded herself that her love for the King of England, George V, was mutual. She stationed herself daily outside Buckingham Palace, and convinced herself that, although His Majesty was constrained from any public acknowledgement of his feelings for her, he knew she was there every day, and secretly communicated with her by altering the position of the curtains. The case is cited in an addendum to Ian McEwan's novel *Enduring Love* (1997), in which the central character, a scientist, is stalked by a gay man he has fleetingly encountered while attempting to give assistance at the scene of a ballooning accident. What is intended to make tales such as these the more unsettling is that the infatuation that triggers the pathological behaviour may strike its sufferer in a moment. Those who doubt whether the old romantic chimera of love at first sight can feasibly exist should not be in the least deceived about the possibility that instant infatuation can be very real. De Clérambault characterised the condition as typically episodic, comprising a phase of hopefulness followed by a phase of simmering resentment, a movement that we can observe in both Othello and Alex Forrest.

The psychologist David Smail has suggested that we too readily pathologise uncontrolled jealousy, seeing it as the fevered product of a disordered emotional state, whereas in many cases all we are witnessing in individuals in the grip of such turmoil is the cathexis that some actual previous grounds for suspicion have wrought in them. Clearly, somebody in the grip of de Clérambault's syndrome has no objective grounds for their condition, but when one partner in a relationship finds himself or herself having been deceived, the thought that it might happen again is very difficult to dispel. Reduced to a state of extreme paranoia by too many unexplained (or less than convincingly explained) absences, the betrayed partner finds his or her vision of the beloved taking on the sickly green tint that Iago manages to instil in Othello. What such individuals have lost sight of is the degree to which relationships need to be founded on a symbiotic balance of love and faith. If Othello, the suspicion already gnawing at his innards, hadn't shoved away his wife when she was trying to soothe his headache, she wouldn't have dropped the fatal handkerchief in the first place. If we are not careful, our jealous actions will help to bring about the very outcome we dread. In its final extremity, a relationship poisoned by jealous suspicion is almost invariably incapable of salvage, and the best result for both parties may well be its swift demise, although strangling one's lover and then stabbing oneself may not be the most constructive way of achieving it. The love in such a relationship has died because an antibody with which it cannot coexist has been introduced, and which will finally turn the whole emotional complex to hatred. The name of that foreign body is contempt. It is what causes Othello, in the midst of his destruction, to compare Desdemona's precious, but finally ambiguous, honesty to the scent of carrion that attracts flies in the slaughterhouse.

15

I AM JEALOUS

The young Johann Wilhelm von Goethe's first expedition into prose fiction, *The Sorrows of Young Werther*, written in his mid-twenties when he had already established a reputation with dramatic works and lyric poetry, is the founding text of romantic fatalism in the form that we continue to recognise it. In epistolary form, it is the tale of a bookish young man, passionately engaged in the great intellectual questions of the day, most notably that of whether suicide is a heroic act, who falls in love at a country ball with a young woman, Lotte, who is promised to another. While Albert, her intended, is away putting his affairs in order following the death of his father, Werther and Lotte enjoy what is in effect a phantom courtship, played out against the gorgeous idyll of high summer in the country north of Frankfurt, and composed of radiant tableaux rather than narrative episodes:

I often sit up in the fruit trees in Lotte's orchard, using a pole to get at the pears on the topmost branches. She stands below and takes them as I pass them down.

Even when Albert rejoins Lotte, there is no hint of personal animosity between the men. He is a 'dear and honest man whom one cannot help liking'. More, 'I cannot help esteeming Albert. His tranquil evenness of manner is in marked contrast to the turbulence of my own disposition, which I cannot hide.' For a while at least, accorded the unexpected mercy of not being asked to witness the stolid Albert kissing Lotte in his company, Werther is able to be relatively urbane about the situation. But not for long. From the first, the tensions at work in the divergent temperaments of the two men give notice of the manner in which the dam will break. If Albert seems a likeable plodder to the overwrought Werther, by contrast, '[h]e sees me as a man of some sensitivity'. It is hard not to sense the egotism lying behind this remark, but then there is another, more antinomic element in the state of affairs that perhaps should give the sensitive soul a little more pause for trepidation.

[H]is own triumph is augmented by my attachment to Lotte, and the joyful warmth her every action produces in me, and he loves her all the more.

To the deprived in love, the success of the rival can only ever be tainted by an attitude horribly close to gloating, and by means of this imagined sadism, the nightmare is brought inexorably to light. In due course, Lotte marries her Albert, and Werther – as he records meticulously in letters to his friend Wilhelm – slips into a maelstrom of self-hatred. Finally resolved on his own destruction, Werther sends a note to Albert to ask if he may borrow his pistols for a journey he is ostensibly about to undertake. Albert has just returned home from a rather trying day crowded with obstructive bureaucrats and bumpy roads, only to find a mountain of correspondence to deal with. Glancing at Werther's note, he curtly instructs Lotte to take the pistols down and send them on, with best wishes for a good journey. Lotte knows perfectly well what is going to happen, but to the husband who has had a pig of a day and is busy at the escritoire scratching out replies to his letters, her tremulous dithering is only further cause for exasperation. Despite the fact that Albert has been lured some while before into a lengthy discussion with Werther on the merits of suicide as the heroic deed of a forceful will, his request for the pistols fails to sound the warning bell. Werther duly shoots himself in the middle of the night, dressed to the nines in his much admired, fashionable blue and tan ensemble, characteristically making a bit of a hash of it, so that he is found by his servant the following morning in gouts of blood and brain tissue, but with his heart still beating. The servant raises the alarm, and runs to tell Albert and Lotte, she crumpling unconscious at her husband's feet on receiving the dire news. Werther dies a few hours later with his eldest and favourite brother's kisses on his lips, and is buried under cover of darkness late that night, in a hasty proceeding bearing all the solemn lack of ceremony reserved for a suicide's obsequies. 'No priest attended him.'

That this short novel should have exerted such an immediate and deep-rooted emotional effect, not just in its native Germany but wherever it appeared in translation in Europe, seems barely credible to an age steeped in postmodern irony. Not just the intensity but also the variety of its manifestations makes for one of the great stories of Romantic literature. Young people of refined aesthetic temperament, or perhaps those who simply aspired to such refinement, began to mimic Werther's incontinent, exclamatory style in their own writing. Men affected his faintly bizarre, co-ordinated country wear of powder-blue and shimmering tan. People flocked from all over the continent to the villages of Wetzlar and Garbenheim, where the real events on which Goethe's text is based had taken place. There they were treated to mournful displays of memorabilia, some of it emblematic, some of it (like the mound of earth dug by a wily innkeeper and passed off as the unmarked grave of the doomed Werther) quite obviously fake. Nobody cared to remember that Werther was a fictional character. What mattered was the cult of tortured sensibility that his 'case' was paradigmatic of. But there was more. It is one thing to have followed in your idol's footsteps, but the Werther cult turned rather more macabre, unleashing a wave of copycat suicides. In a revisionist account of the events following the first publication of the book, its recent English translator Michael Hulse has argued that 'there is little evidence that Goethe's novel prompted a suicide epidemic', and that the story was at best exaggerated, at worst a complete myth. What is truly at issue here, though, is overlooked in this sceptical stance. The question as to whether a literary work could trigger a spate of suicides may well remain unresolved, but that there was such a spate is not in doubt. Morbid self-reflection, accompanied often by the desire for annihilation, was very much in tune with the prevailing cultural mood, and in the wake of the book's appearance, the dank aesthetic of suffering despair that it had encapsulated had seeped out into almost every corner of the European landmass.

Even if the suicides were not to be attributed solely to the influence of *Werther*, many firmly believed they were. Chief among them was the young author himself, who quickly came to bemoan the naïveté of those who 'believe you need to turn poetry into reality, re-enact such a novel, and even shoot yourself'. Recalling the novel's disastrous effect some years later, he clearly remembered that 'what occurred at first among a few took place later among the general public'. If the unthinkable had come to pass, and a work of fiction had spawned these baleful social consequences, then perhaps *Werther* can be identified as the first text in the debate as to whether a lurid work of art can inspire its recipients to imitative behaviour. Can a horror video inspire small boys to abduct and kill an even smaller one? Would *A Clockwork Orange* have led to the creation of murder gangs, had its director not withdrawn it from general release?

On a hard winter's day in 1778, a young noblewoman, Christine von Lassberg, ended the misery occasioned by her lover's abandonment of her by drowning herself in the river Ilm in Weimar. The spot she chose was just behind Goethe's garden. She went to her death with a copy of *Die Leiden des jungen Werthers* in her pocket. Another young woman, Fanni von Ickstatt, flung herself from a tower of the Frauenkirche in Munich. The connection may have seemed more tenuous, but a tragic poem that appeared shortly after the event clearly blamed her self-destruction on *Werther*. So axiomatic did the malign influence of the novel come to be that when the Theological Faculty of the University of Leipzig, the city in which it was first published, petitioned the City Council to ban it, the request was granted. In certain countries such as Denmark, it came to be subject to a nationwide proscription.

What ensured the book's fame, and kept it popular on the continent so that imitations, burlesques and tributes to it would continue to appear for many years, was the degree to which it legitimised self-lacerating melancholy, both philosophically and psychologically. It successfully married the grandiloquent effects of the *Sturm und Drang* aesthetic to the introspective inwardness of the Prince of Denmark. Much of its saturnine temper could be said to be drawn from Act III of *Hamlet*, the meditative pallor and the heartsick fatalism. But it transforms the languid ambivalence of Shakespeare's Prince into something like the gnashing and wailing urgency of Job, who bemoans the wretched fate of humanity at the hands of a tormentor god. And the emotional device Goethe utilises is not just unrewarded love, but love gratinated under a bubbling top-layer of red-hot, curdling jealousy.

That in itself may have led some of its contemporary readers – and a considerably greater number of its later critics (W H Auden finds Werther a 'horrid little creature') – to despise the solipsism and the self-dramatising of its protagonist. In basing the work closely on a real incident, however, and partly on his own, still keenly felt experience of unrequited love, Goethe has done his best to accord the emotional travails of his hero a certain *gravitas*. It is there in the prefatory note to the text:

I have diligently collected everything I have been able to discover concerning the story of poor Werther, and here present it to you in the knowledge that you will be grateful for it. You cannot deny your admiration and love for his spirit and character, nor your tears at his fate. And you, good soul, who feel a compulsive longing such as his, draw consolation from his sorrows, and let this little book be your friend whenever through fate or through your own fault you can find no closer companion.

This unashamed blurb sets the tone concisely and forcefully before we have even dared peep at page 1. You will be grateful. You cannot deny. The story is framed as an edited account being published by a disinterested commentator, the occasional irrelevant footnote sustaining the illusion, a strategy intended to confer authority on that opening note, in which not just our admiration of Werther but our love for him, and our grief at his downfall, are invoked with a dutiful sense of piety. This isn't just 'If you have tears, prepare to shed them now'; it is 'Give in to the pain, you know you want to.' And so Europe did, from the girl in the ribboned white dress teetering on a church parapet and seeing the unforgiving ground come leering up to meet her, to General Bonaparte, who took *Werther* with him on the Egyptian campaign in 1798, confessing to having read it no fewer than seven times. What profundities of self-justification was he looking for?

This active celebration of jealousy and lovelorn self-sacrifice returns us to the cultivation of sadness. The precise German term for the radically melancholic temperament in which the novel is situated was *Empfindsamkeit*, a kind of yearning, doomed sensitivity turned art movement, in which we see the upturned eyes appealing to a merciless heaven for a respite that won't be granted, the hands clutching at the breast as if holding the wrung-out heart in an exterior clasp of protection, the cheeks raked with silver tracks, the breath coming in chunks. It gained an easy passage into the visual arts, where its tremulous introspection made for many a mawkish portrait of private grief, and it threw up several contenders for the title of poet laureate of the new misery. (In the moment following a thunderstorm at a ball where Werther has first met and danced with the gorgeous Lotte, when she, turning tearfully from the window and the rain-bathed countryside, puts her hand over his and utters the magical endearment, 'Klopstock!', she is doing no more than naming one of the patron saints of *Empfindsamkeit*, the nature poet Friedrich Gottlieb Klopstock.) In *Werther* – although a later age may struggle to see it through the forests of exclamation marks – *Empfindsamkeit* was given its most authentic expression, and it gained that authenticity to the precise degree that it celebrated the transports of the sensitive youth in the grip of a mighty jealousy.

That the end result of all this shameless emoting should be a certain *froideur* is perhaps not entirely surprising. What great tidal wave of aesthetic enthusiasm doesn't issue in its temperamental opposite? Shivering misery enjoyed a good forty-year run in the intellectual culture of the mid–late eighteenth century, and there are only so many narratives of premature death, smashed ambition and thwarted hope one can take without borrowing a pair of pistols. So it is that we detect the unmistakable impression of reflections from maturity in Goethe's own assertion in the auto-biographical *Dichtung und Wahrheit* (1811–14), begun nearly forty years after *Werther*, that the emotional and intellectual climate created by *Empfindsamkeit* at least gave everyone his chance to play Hamlet.

To the age of sentiment, the bluster of sexual jealousy was an unmistakable part of the landscape of sensitivity. Its ability to possess the lovelorn individual utterly was the raw material of the sentimental temperament, and one that survived intact into Romanticism and even up to the present day. Its paradigm of noble suffering may have been coarsened in our own time into the frizzy-haired visage of Glenn Close haunting the careless adulterer Michael Douglas, but the murderous rage her tenacity unleashes in him conveys itself with scarcely less force today than it did in

Goethe's youth. So powerful is the sense of empathy with it that, two centuries after his novel appeared, psychologist David P Phillips coined the term 'the Werther-effect' for the sympathetic rash of suicides that may follow upon harrowing news of the unnecessary sufferings of others.

It was always likely to take something fairly momentous to edge the first great personality cult in modern European literature out of the foreground of attention, and so it did. After fifteen years of Wertherism, young Europe was suddenly to find a new outlet for its emotional zeal in the eruption of revolutionary ferment in Paris. What now impelled the fury of the volatile masses was not jealousy, but the legitimate envy of a dispossessed class that had grown tired and violent under a regime of ostentation and privilege. Notwithstanding its very different political springs, it may not be too fanciful to suggest that at least some of the outraged sensibilities at work in the upheaval of 1789 had been educated in a feeling for the injustice of needless suffering by the emotional travails of Goethe's hero. He is badly treated by his colleagues, and he feels radically alienated from society. More than either of these factors, though, the image that disaffected eighteenth-century youth was bequeathed, in the luckless Werther, was of the furiously soliloquising boy grinding his teeth to powder at the vile injustice of a world that has delivered his rightful sexual inheritance to a chump. Who wouldn't, under such provocation, tear an absolute monarchy to pieces?

CONTEMPT

Pride that dines on vanity, sups on contempt.
Benjamin Franklin

1. The action of contemning or despising; the mental attitude in which a thing is considered as of little account, or as vile and worthless. 2. The condition of being contemned or despised; dishonour, disgrace. 3. Object of contempt. 4. Law. Disobedience or open disrespect to the authority or lawful commands of the sovereign, the privileges of the Houses of Parliament or other legislative body; and esp. action of any kind that interferes with the proper administration of justice by the various courts of law.

Darwin's physical indicators: uncovering of the canine tooth on one side; derisive smile or laugh; partial closure of the eyelids; turning away of the eyes or of the whole body; turning up of the nose; contraction of the nasal passages; wrinkling of the nose; snort or nasal expiration; protrusion or raising of upper or both lips; tightening and stretching of one corner of the mouth; snapping of the fingers; flicking away of an imaginary tiny object; biting of the thumbnail.

16

TO BE CONTEMPTUOUS

If, as we saw, disgust often appears to be symbolically indicative of the taste of something foul in the mouth, so contempt – its close relative – is more suggestive of offensive odours. Darwin's physiognomic description refers to the wrinkling of the nose, the wilful contraction of the nostrils, and the tilting back of the head that accompanies it, all of which tend towards closing the nasal passages to, or withdrawing them from the immediate site of, some unpleasant smell. The sharp downward breath through the nostrils, together with a sudden retraction of the head, made when somebody nearby behaves boorishly, suggests a desire to expel any of the air that may have carried that person's scent into one's sensorium. In tilting back the head as though to look up, however, the eyes remain focused downwards, as though to eliminate the offending personage from sight, contributing to that haughty demeanour known as 'looking down one's nose'.

'Contempt' is the past participle of the old verb 'to contemn', now confined to archaic literary uses, and which has its root in the Latin verb *temnere*, to despise or disdain. To hold somebody in contempt is to regard them with scorn, and at the same time hardly to regard them at all. Contempt hovers between a desire to ignore the offending individual, and the desire to make it plain to him how worthless he is – in effect two quite different strategies. Something of this contradiction is suggested by the synonymous verb 'to slight', which expresses both the intention of treating an offending party as though they were of no more than 'slight' account, and yet also implies a conscious desire to insult. A person whom one ignores in the course of a chance passage in the street has not simply been left out of account; they have been taken into account to the extent that they are being informed that they are of precisely no account.

In addition to the universal expressions that Darwin identifies – the retracted lip, the derisive smile, the peering downwards from the tilted head – are various culturally specific gestures of contempt. The Dakota tribe of North America have an elaborate gesture that begins with a clenched hand being held to the breast, which is then thrust outwards towards the offending person with the fingers spread. It mimics, suggests Darwin, the action of throwing something away, or letting it carelessly drop. In the eastern Mediterranean, flicking the thumbnail off the upper front teeth is still a common gesture, but one that is recalled as early as the opening scene of *Romeo and Juliet*, when Sampson, a member of the Capulets' retinue, announces his intention to insult a party of the Montagues' men: 'I will bite my thumb at them, which is disgrace to them if they bear it.' Less current now is a habit familiar to the Victorians of miming the rolling and flicking away of some tiny, indeterminate object (a ball of dry snot, perhaps?) to indicate that one couldn't care less for the person referred to. Snapping the fingers, as in the old American phrase 'I don't give a snap', was also expressive of caring nothing. All these gestures are marked again by the dual character of contempt. 'I couldn't care less about you, except that I care enough to let you know it.' There is a difference between not being concerned about something, and being concerned to express one's defiance of it. In the 1990s, chic inversion of the normal expression of calculated contempt, 'I couldn't care less', gained currency – 'I could care more.' Uttered with the right tone of suppurating disdain, it expressed the full force of one's scorn, where its antecedent phrase seemed to suggest only shrugging vacuity. (The correct emphasis was not solely, as some read it, on the 'more', but on the 'could' as well. Thus enunciated, one broadcast one's ability to be more concerned, but the simultaneous disinclination to be so.)

As a world-view, contempt is not an especially attractive trait; it is distinctly adolescent. The unreconstructed villains of Elizabethan drama, including Shakespeare's Aaron in *Titus Andronicus*, Iago in *Othello* and Edmund in *King Lear*, are all characterised by their contempt for the world, an attitude often tellingly found alongside ascetic austerity. Not content simply with despising the mass of humanity, they feel compelled to set in motion actions and schemes that will bring ruin and misery to those who don't share their malevolent outlook. It is possible, as Shakespeare knew, to progress from one state to the other, as the hero of *Timon of Athens* does. Repelled by the mercenary parasitism of his so-called friends, Timon retreats to a lonely spot outside the city gates, where lying prone in a pit and claiming to desire nothing, he execrates the whole stinking dung heap that is humanity, at great and otiose length. The paradigm is the lamentation of Job, scorned by God when brimful of piety, offered nothing in his scrofulous distress but the deity's heartless accusations and bombastic reminders of his own limitless power. God's scorn for the world lets him treat even his faithful servants like dirt, and although Job is restored to health in the end, his own servants and children – murdered in the opening chapter of the book – are simply forgotten.

Contempt for the world has a firm place within the Christian tradition. It was the defining attitude of the Gnostic and Johannine sects in the early years of the Church's foundation, and it has been the guiding spirit of the monastic communities, particularly those closed orders that have no contact whatsoever with the outside world, ever since that earliest Christian era. Richard Webster traces it to a verse in Luke's gospel, in which Jesus is quoted as saying:

If any man come to me, and hate not his father, and mother, and wife, and children, and brethren, and sisters, yea, and his own life also, he cannot be my disciple. (14:26)

What Jesus appears to require of his followers is that contempt that God himself shows in his treatment of Job, and that Shakespeare's malcontents also display. Much exegetical labour has been expended on the precise weight that should be given to 'hate', but the import of the words remains clear. Religious devotion is more important than family ties. The point gains continuity from its echo of the Old Testament counsel of separation from the family, in Micah:

Trust ye not in a friend, put ye not confidence in a guide: keep the doors of thy mouth from her that lieth in thy bosom. For the son dishonoureth the father, the daughter riseth up against her mother, the daughter in law against her mother in law; a man's enemies are the men of his own house. (7:5–6)

To this jaundiced view, one might object that a person's enemies should first be looked for among those who exploit their labour, imprison them for political dissent, torture them in the name of faith, or otherwise hold their lives in contempt.

William Ian Miller argues that the erosion of feudalism, indeed the development of democracy itself, arose from the spread of contempt as a mental habit among the underclasses. In medieval society, contempt flowed only one way, from the sovereign down through the landed classes to the lower orders, to be rewarded by an upward flow of deference and respect. 'Contempt,' Miller states, 'is the emotional complex that articulates and maintains hierarchy, status, rank, and respectability.' With the circumscription of the powers of the monarchies, first in England and then in the rest of

Europe, and the concomitant formulation of civil law, this obligation of deference was progressively weakened, with the eventual result that 'the contempt of the people that once was a prerogative of high-Toryism is now readily available to everyone'. Note that contempt now becomes a universal human right, as inalienable from the general populace as the right to vote, which was its greatest benefaction. The French dissident thinker Alexis de Tocqueville, sojourning in the newly spawned American Republic, noted the comparative absence of social paranoia among the people, compared with that of the British, where the loosening of social stratification had created a state of high anxiety among the privileged classes as to how they were perceived from below. Miller appears unsure whether the democratisation of contempt is an entirely healthy social phenomenon. If the price of universal suffrage is that everybody is entitled to be sniffy about everybody else, have we not bought it too dearly? Then again, to hear the withering tones of the professionally *enragé* can often seem weirdly comforting, as Miller discovers when reading an interview with the rap artist Ice-T: 'Let me tell you something about the masses. You ever watch wrestling? Hulk Hogan and all that, guys jumping off the ropes? And the arena's always packed? Those same people vote, man.' That such a sentiment might as easily have been expressed at a reunion weekend of Ivy League alumni suggests to Miller that even rap isn't quite as oppositional as it likes to think.

Where I think Miller's argument falls short is in suggesting that contempt became an emotion expressed by the masses at such a recent historical juncture. It may have come as a surprise to the Roman dramatist Plautus that servile obeisance was the only cast of mind available to the low-born, comic protagonists of his plays. Equally Montaigne, who discusses the ambiguities loaded into social hierarchy in the *Essays*, is a rich source of instances from antiquity of the famous unease in which the crowned head has traditionally lain. The dazzling pomp of imperial state is nothing but acting, he avows, underneath which is the same afflicted, irascible human constitution with which the rest of us must deal, and he forces us to train our penetrating mental gaze on the bejewelled poltroon. '[D]raw back the bed-curtains and look at him: he is but a commonplace man, baser perhaps than the least of his subjects.' Baser because, following a motto in Seneca, his happiness is plated in gold, unlike the true inner blessings of the humble. The Roman emperor Julian the Apostate is commended for his repudiation, as reported by Ammianus Marcellinus, of the coerced approbation his courtiers show him. 'I would be prepared to be proud of such praises,' he is said to have remarked, 'if they came from persons who could dare to condemn and censure any actions of mine when they were contrary to justice.' The insecurity of the high-born derives from his inability to know whether the deference he is paid is merely lip service or is genuinely felt; if the former, then the fawning subject is actually getting away, even if unwittingly, with offering a disdainful insult to his prince. This, incidentally, explains why all members of royalty (down to our own day, perhaps) prefer equestrian sport to direct competition with other humans, because the horse knows no patronising duty to let them win – 'it will throw a king's son as soon as a porter's'. When *noblesse oblige* extends to courteously mimicking the physical defects of the great, so as not to seem to be in possession of presumptuous soundness of body, the division between deference and contempt has been all but erased. Thus did attendants upon Alexander the Great twist their heads to one side, tortoise-like, as he did, while flatterers of the tyrant Dionysius:

used to bump into each other when he was present, stumbling against whatever was under their feet and knocking it over, to suggest they were as short-sighted as he was.

The followers of King Mithridates of Pontus, whose heart's desire was to be hailed as a learned physician, offered themselves up as laboratory subjects, allowing him to open up and cauterise their limbs so that he might demonstrate his imagined medical genius. Surrendering a leg to possible gangrene to slake a monarch's *amour propre* is at least preferable, thinks Montaigne, to ceding one's soul. Either way, only contempt, however privately harboured, can result from such acquiescence.

The post-revolutionary era of the twentieth century added a new level of complexity to feelings of contempt. It was now necessary, if you believed in any kind of radical politics, to master the emotion to the extent that you tutored yourself out of feeling it towards the economically disenfranchised, and reserved it only for the bourgeoisie and the embattled gentry. In theory, it should be possible to turn it into something like its obverse, which was pity for the fate of the dispossessed in a world in which capitalism seemed to be careering towards apparent collapse. For many, though, this was a political ideal too far, as George Orwell was to discover when slumming it with the owners of a Lancashire tripe shop in 1936. The filth and squalor in which the Brooker family live is partly attributable to their economic status in a part of the Empire that was cheerfully being allowed to rot, and yet for all his educated, middle-class egalitarianism, Orwell can't help rebuking the needless lack of hygiene all about him. Was it really necessary to leave a brimming chamber pot under the table while you ate your morning bread and scrape? An entire bestiary of noxious comparison is called forth to describe the inhabitants of the Wigan slums: they crawl around their back kitchens like 'black beetles', the one son of the Brookers whom he meets is 'a large pig-like young man'. What the family feeds its lodgers is, by Orwell's standards, 'uniformly disgusting', even when it doesn't involve cow's stomach, although the regimen of bacon and egg for breakfast, tinned steak pudding with boiled potatoes and then rice pudding in the evening, with a later supper of Lancashire cheese and cream crackers, isn't exactly, for the period, the nadir of deprivation that he took it to be. If he felt any greater contempt, it was, decently enough, for the likes of himself – left-wing bourgeois intellectuals who, in their Fabian zeal to vanquish the ignorance of the proletariat, have only succeeded in creating an ignorant political vacuity where there ought to be socialism. At the close of *The Road to Wigan Pier* (1937), he warns, with cold prescience, that fascism would come if we didn't get socialism right. Yet even then, he sneers, it will likely be a fatuously British version of state tyranny, making do with 'cultured police-men' where Germany had 'Nazi gorillas'.

The self-tormenting acerbity of Orwell's writing in the 1930s, teeming with contempt for virtually everything with which he comes into contact, tells us something of what this most easily per-formed of all the spontaneous emotions had become. Once you retreat into nothing but contempt for the world, you cease to see any practical means of altering it. Once the only basis for an ecumenical vision of humanity is not that we all worship the same God, or harbour the same desire for security for ourselves and our families, but that all hold each other in equal and universal con-tempt, then there is no telling what will happen. Contempt is not the lifeblood of democracy, but of permanent conflict.

17

I HOLD YOU IN CONTEMPT

Contempt as a social attitude, as opposed to a philosophical disposition, arose within British society in the later eighteenth century,
during the period of the first great expansion of entrepreneurial
dynamism among the rising bourgeoisie. As the middle classes
acquired economic power, so too a certain cachet came to accrue to
them, and the dual system of class divisions, by birth and by
material worth – with which the British lived uncomfortably at
least until the closing stages of the twentieth century – was given a
laboured and difficult parturition. The recognised structure of
society, once thought to be as celestially immutable as the pre-
Copernican universe, which placed the nobility in the heavenly
realm, with the artisanal tradesmen and their families a fair way
below them, supported by a murky nether region of uneducated
labouring folk, began to be replaced by the notion of society as a
greasy pole, up which anybody with the means and the wherewithal
to make something of themselves might shinny. With growing
wealth came access to education for the children, a commodity that
it had not previously been thought necessary to waste on them. If
the view from the bottom of this pole seemed daunting enough, the
view from the top was not without cause for alarm. A lady of the
quality, Caroline Norton, put the point with heartfelt anguish in a
letter of 1841:

I am not sure that in the overeducating of the classes who never can have our *leisure*, what ever else they may obtain that is ours, we have not destroyed all our companionship with them; they stand too close for our comfort or theirs; they climb just close enough to our level to prevent their looking up to us; they elbow us, and we have no longer room to stretch out our hand in fellowship with them! [Emphasis in the original.]

What had seemingly kept society harmonious until social mobility began in earnest, was that the better off should have this clearly demarcated area of *Lebensraum*, so that they could dispose themselves towards the less fortunate as and when they so chose, and not have to feel themselves jostled within their own well-tended precincts by the *nouveau riche*. Tellingly, the writer of these sentiments argues, familiarly enough, that under the old dispensation everybody knew where they were, and the arm's length at which the parvenus and the chancers could be held also doubled as the extended hand of social amity. With the democratisation of social access has come an unnatural proximity, and hence the lament that the aspirant classes are too physically close to their betters, so that one can almost smell the infrequency of their toiletry hovering about them, mingling with the raw onion on their breaths. The most excruciating aspect of all, however, is that they no longer feel the need to look upwards. A man who had made a fortune importing wine from the Canaries, having perhaps started out in the business doing no more than humping barrels about, might now look the likes of Mrs Norton full in the face, so directly that she may find herself unable to repress her instinct to tilt it aloofly away. If objective social distance was being dissolved all about you, it might prove necessary to reinforce it at a personal level.

The intricate tracery of social signals, by which the British evaluated each other in polite society from the late eighteenth century, became a subject of both fascination and repulsion to foreign visitors. Americans in particular expressed themselves baffled by these codes, responsiveness to which seemed to require the sonar sensitivities of the pipistrelle. That they often articulated their bemusement in stridently emphatic tones reflects the degree to which they themselves fell foul of them. The proper cultivation of proficiency in these matters could only take place within the peculiarly deadened atmosphere of what became known as British reserve, which to many overseas observers looked merely like unsociability – and, when it was justified in specious terms by the etiquette manuals of the day, sounded even more like it. To maintain one's distance, keep one's cards close to one's chest, until any newcomer within one's habitual circle had had chance either to prove himself or to give himself away, established the means by which the Mrs Nortons of fashionable society ensured that the besieged security of their own positions was maintained. Indeed, many would argue that such behaviour is by no means extinct in Britain today. In continental Europe, nothing like this social fluidity was to be found, and the aristocracy treated its servants and labourers with not much less overt superiority than they had done before the fall of the Bastille. Only in England did their counterparts find themselves having to employ subtler means to ring-fence their social territory from those who so shamelessly wished to share it. To the French nobleman passing through, it was difficult to tell who was of the best society and who was not, while to the American visitor of the 1820s, bringing all his rough-and-ready, newly minted classlessness with him, it was a reminder of everything that the world's first unabashed democracy had fought to shake off:

The art of cutting especially, a filthy bud of English growth and nourished by the insolence of Aristocratic pride, is unpractised and unknown across the Atlantic, as indeed every where but in England alone.

If cutting – the deliberate turning away of the gaze from somebody who knew that you had recognised them, but to whom you just didn't want to be seen talking – seemed a particularly chilly mani-festation of British reserve, its practice was to be explained by the insistence on a sacrosanct space that the leisured classes could con-fidently occupy. Writing in the *Edinburgh Review* in 1822, Francis Jeffrey painted a picture of gentility finding itself physically assailed, in the places it had traditionally called its own, by the unruly ranks of the aspirant. Some time around the 1760s, the writer argued, an 'incredible increase of forwardness and solid impudence' among those of less exalted birth, but recently acquired social status, had meant that 'a herd of uncomfortable and unsuitable companions beset all the approaches to good com-pany, and seemed determined to force all its barriers'. An English gentlewoman who married an Italian, among whose people the co-ordinates of social hierarchy were more securely plotted, blamed the authorities for complacently presiding over the social flux to which Britain had now been subjected:

Our government has left so narrow a space between the upper and under ranks of people in Great Britain, that if our persons of condition fail even for a moment to watch their post ... they are instantly and suddenly broken in upon by the well-employed talents, or swiftly-acquired riches, of men born on the other side of the thin partition.

Here the writer, Hester Lynch Piozzi, is thrown into that particular slough of crestfallen despond that often attended the British when they travelled abroad and discovered that there were aspects of the home country that compared unfavourably with other cultures. She can't quite make up her mind whether the 'space' that ought to sep-arate her from the aspirant is a borderline between higher and lower regions, or whether it is a 'thin partition' incapable of with-standing contiguous intrusion. The statement moves from the old cosmological schema of above and below to a more tellingly domestic scenario, in which the undesirables are people who have just moved in next door, rowdily knocking through as the neighbourhood around them goes bang.

With the onset of the Victorian era, these attitudes had become entrenched, to the extent that entire systems of etiquette were built around them. You may no longer have been able to tell from the cut of a man's coat, or the conversational tones he adopted, whether he was of any station, but his picking up a fork to eat his asparagus when all about him were using their fingers would certainly decide the question. In the mid-nineteenth century, the concept of snobbery was first elaborated, and it is interesting to note the semantic contortions it has undergone since then. Over the last hundred years or so, snobbishness has come to mean the *de haut en bas* superciliousness of the upper classes, their anachronistic presumption of superiority in a society whose manners are more earthily democratic these days. To the Victorians, it meant precisely the opposite of that. Snobs were those people who were besetting Mr Jeffrey's approaches to polite company and breathing all over Mrs Norton. They were the aspirant bourgeoisie, the excluded, the socially desperate. To students at Cambridge, snobs were the townies, the local yokels who were outside the intellectual caste of the university. Those who truly belonged in the upper echelons wouldn't be seen dead near a snob. One of their most contemptible traits, however, was that they sometimes took it upon themselves to act as though they were superior to others, precisely because they wanted to be part of the class that could with impunity behave in such a way. In the 1840s and 1850s, it wasn't necessarily clear whether somebody described as a snob was simply being condemned as a member of the lower orders, or whether he was somebody whose expressed views and modes of behaviour marked him out as having a crudely imitative regard for those of higher station. The grotesquely fawning Uriah Heep in *David Copperfield* is in the latter sense a classic snob, but then so, in the former, is Abel Magwitch in *Great Expectations*. If one of the characteristic habits of snobs was obsequious flattery of those held to be above them, that very attitude only confirmed that they themselves were of lowly rank. The word 'snob', as far as we can tell, originally referred (in the 1780s) to a shoemaker, or more specifically the shoemaker's apprentice. It may be that the change in meaning derives from the apprentice's desire to please his master, which the cringing behaviour of social snobs was thought to resemble. Thomas de Quincey, in a piece of social anatomy written in the early nineteenth century, tells us that, during a workers' strike, those who held out for the cause were known as 'nobs' (the gentility, as it were, of the struggle), while those who broke the strike by returning to work for lower wages were taunted as 'snobs', contemptible suckers-up to the proprietorial classes.

From being the lowest of the low, snobs rose, no doubt to their delight, up the social scale. They had started out as mere tradespeople, before becoming members of a newly enriched class who did their level best to blend seamlessly among the gentry, before eventually becoming the gentry themselves, the kinds of people who might these days let you on to their land for a pop festival, but who would still refer to you over high tea as 'the great unwashed'. During the period of their self-establishment as a class, which exactly coincides with the ascendancy of the militant bourgeoisie, and from whose ranks they issued, they perfected all manner of tricks to ensure that their social status became fluidly undeterminable. Not the least effective weapon in their armoury, as Darwin is ready to observe by the 1870s, was a haughty peering down their noses at those who had neither the means nor the desire to rise as they had.

The disdainful gaze still underpins social stratification in many cultures around the world. Powerfully wordless, it acts as a means of marking off members of the élite from the lower orders without recourse to language. In other forms of hierarchy, its use is institutionalised in words as well as glares, from the sergeant major's snarling on the parade ground to the chanting stand-offs between rival gangs of football supporters. A diminutive pop idol leaving a restaurant to find a phalanx of photographers awaiting her is as adept at the curled lip and the muttered 'Fuck off!' as a crinolined lady alighting from a carriage once was at putting the doorman in his place. All of these attitudes and articulations are about reminding people in one's immediate vicinity that they are not fit to breathe the same air as oneself, and that one shouldn't have to stoop to the indignity of reminding them of this. It can be heard every time somebody of some modest level of public achievement, asked for identification at a security barrier, responds by asking of the punctilious official, 'Don't you know who I am?' To which the only logical answer would seem to be 'Obviously not'. As the Ceauşescus were being led to their summary execution in Bucharest in December 1989, it is said that Elena turned on a soldier who tried to take her by the arm, spitting out, moments before she and her husband were to be sprayed with machine-gun fire, 'Don't you know you're not allowed to touch me?'

Darwin would have had no trouble in recognising in Elena Ceauşescus's snarl of indignation the spontaneity of a true emotion. In considering its prevalence in societal behaviour, however, we must question whether contempt is an emotion, as distinct from a cultivated state of mind. We are surrounded today by casual expressions of contempt, and since much of this represents a contrived stance, we are not dealing with a genuinely reactive emotional response. Real contempt (like Madame Ceauşescus's) has at its heart pure, molten hatred, the intimation that hell is other people, a reaction not readily enactable in quite the ways that casual contempt is, and therefore not as legibly present on the face. For me, then, what Darwin is talking about is the calculated expression of a distancing instinct, generally in the interests of social exclusion. In a world that contains so much to be authentically contemptuous of – nepotism, cruelty, dishonesty and hypocrisy – true contempt, like jealousy, leaves no physiognomic trace.

*

The observation that 'Hell is other people' is probably the only piece of undiluted existentialist thought that has passed into popular consciousness. It comes from Jean-Paul Sartre's one-act play of 1944, *Huis Clos*, translated into English as *In Camera* and, later, *No Exit*. It was first performed in Paris in May 1944, three months before the city's liberation from the Nazis. The action of the drama concerns three characters who are shown into an elegant Second Empire drawing room by a rather sullen valet, and realise that they must spend eternity there in each other's company, since the place is a department of Hell that has been reserved solely for them. A South American journalist, Garcin, claims to have been killed while defending the freedom of the press, but turns out to have been rather more of a poseur who has been shot while trying to flee his country. Inez is a lesbian who has died when her lover Florence asphyxiated them both with gas, after Inez killed Florence's husband. Estelle, who died of pneumonia, is a type that the era knew as a vamp, a vacuous and sexually voracious socialite who killed her baby for fear that it might interfere with the way of life to which she was accustomed. There are no mirrors in the room, and nothing to function as a reflective surface, so the characters are forced to contemplate each other in perpetuity, their only relief being occasional personal visions of what is going on in the world they have left behind. Initially relieved to find that there are no red-hot knives or other means of physical torment in Hell, they come to realise that simply being cooped up here with each other for all eternity is going to be quite unbearable enough. In one of her visions, Inez sees Florence entertaining a man on the very bed in which her own affair with her had been conducted. An attempted liaison between Garcin and Estelle is mocked by the relentless Inez. The night in which they might enjoy some secrecy will never fall, and in any case, none of the characters – while they all yearn to feel genuine emotions – is capable of them. 'Human feeling?' sneers Inez. 'That's beyond me. I'm rotten to the core.' It is left to Garcin, in the closing moments of the play, to utter the flash of insight that has dawned on all of them: 'Hell is ... other people!' There is no need of torture when they must put up with each other for ever. After the concluding grim silence, in which each of them lets this knowledge sink in, Garcin bursts out with a cheery 'Oh well, let's get on with it!'

Such is the philosophical import of *Huis Clos*. Its characters circle each other warily, in the kind of diplomatic *pas de trois* that they would have exercised in the earthly world, before realising that in Hell, all need for pretence is gone. The nightmare is that anything your interlocutor says to you is rendered instantly transparent, its ulterior machinations laid bare at the very moment of its utterance, so that there is no need even to feign taking it at face value. Not only do you know that what the other person has said is riddled with insincerities, but you are also aware that they know the same thing of you. This is why the play ends with a thickening silence among the three protagonists.

In one sense, Sartre's view accords with that of Schopenhauer, that the world is nothing other than what each person's perceiving will makes it out to be. It is just that Sartre has taken the point to its obvious conclusion, which is to realise that billions of different takes on the world don't add up to a colourful patchwork, as the traditional liberal view has it, but lead to an incessant state of embattled mutual incomprehension. Nor is it simply a matter of how we see the world. Inasmuch as that depends on self-formation, the laborious construction of the self that we undertake from the moment we begin to rationalise about the world, so the potential for further antagonism is deepened. The world that we look out on is not an inanimate landscape after all, like the blasted vista that Beckett's Clov sees through a telescope from his ladder at the window in *Endgame*, but is instead teeming with other people, each one representing another possible hindrance to our own self-realisation. Without human agency, the world might have gone on sedately turning in its orbit, its life forms breeding and dying out to some fathomless rhythm, as it progressed towards a peaceful extinction. As soon as it played host to a species that came to consciousness of itself and the world around it, the possibility of infinite conflict was admitted. No two members of the species would ever have quite the same apprehension of the world, and so to the extent that each consciousness of reality was different, all these different perceptions must inevitably clash. They can't live harmoniously because they can never be in agreement about the nature of the place they are living in. All each can do is fashion its environment in a way that seems to make sense to itself, thus inventing itself along the way, and in so doing making its own versions of those it sees around it. The person you think I am is wildly at variance with who I know myself to be, whereas your disobliging reluctance to be what I think you are causes me a mass of unnecessary grief.

Existentialism, as Sartre reassures us in the Introduction to his major contribution to it, *Being and Nothingness* (1943), doesn't trouble itself any longer with the tremulous doubt of Descartes – 'How do I know the world exists?' It accepts that it does, and proceeds to interrogate it from the point of view of its phenomenal appearances. For an existentialist, the individual is essentially free, and yet doomed to frustration because its dearest wish is to dominate and possess other free individuals. The existentialist doesn't consider whether there is a hidden reality behind the world of appearances, since simply to perceive the world is to grasp it. Added to the anguish created by the unmalleability of others is the anguish wrought in us by this apparently meaningless freedom. We can do what we want to try to improve things, and yet all exercises of that freedom fall flat, resulting in a dull, unfulfilled state, in which we become acutely conscious of everything that we lack. Not even the emotions ring true: one acts out the role of being sad, for example, much as the café waiter performs his role as the occasion requires. A customer clicks his fingers, so we present him with the bill. A close friend dies, and we stand and look solemn by the grave-side. We don't have to, but this seems to be what is expected. The price we pay for this freedom is the existential angst of knowing that 'Every belief is a belief that falls short; one never wholly believes what one believes.' Crowning the entire predicament is the unavoidable truth that if everything in the phenomenal world is what it banally appears to be, then the same must be true of both our perceptions of others and of ourselves. In other words, we are nothing in particular, and all the relations and transactions that take place between us are stained with the character of falsehood, to the extent that they are predicated on the facile belief that things matter.

Relationships themselves are tragic, because they must inevitably fail. We have the sense of needing another person in order to stop the gap of that nothingness through which the wind is howling at our centre, and yet when we try to form a relationship with another person, it turns out that, far from being the means to our comple-tion, relationships amount only to conflict, as each person fails truly to understand the other. Every time a character in a soap opera utters the familiar aphorism, 'Women! Can't live with 'em, can't live without 'em!', he is articulating one of the central tenets of the existentialist view of human relationships. The picture is further complicated anyway by the fact that each individual is involved in a whole set of different relationships, at varying levels of intensity and complexity, so that there is the interaction between the relationships to consider as well. This is why the proprietors of the Hell to which Sartre's characters have been consigned have pro-vided not for one mismatched couple to spend all eternity together, but for three of them to occupy the same infernal drawing room. That way, whatever liaisons take place between two of them will be subjected to the ruthlessly evaluative gaze of the other, and the potential for rivalry between two in competing for the attentions of the third is infinite. There is a language of deception at the heart of all human relationships. It deceives because it involves the conviction that the commitment embarked on is a noble endeavour, whereas in truth it unavoidably entails the desertion and traducement of others outside the relationship. We cast off our closest friends once we become immersed in the one relationship that feels more serious than those that have gone before it. Often some form of public contractual ceremony seals our final estrangement.

If Sartre were right, it would be so much simpler if one existed in a state of sublime singularity like God, untroubled by the existence of others, incapable even of hypothetically positing their existence. But we don't. We are, tragically and inescapably, we. And it is the inexorable plurality of our kind that makes the world as much a hell for us as it is for the dramatis personae of *Huis Clos*. (A curiously overlooked point about this excessively familiar dictum, '*L'enfer ... c'est l'autre!*', is that what is really meant is '*L'autre ... c'est l'enfer!*' Sartre isn't attempting to say something about the nature of hell, but about the nature of other people – namely, that they are constitutive of hell.) The quote may sound like nothing more than the disgruntled moan of someone stuck on an underground train packed with commuters, but hell is not just *some* other people. It is a question of otherness itself, so that in even the most apparently benign of circumstances, the presence of these others in our lives contains the potential for disaster. Every friendship is a disguised impediment to our own self-realisation, every emotional relationship a ticking time bomb. If only we could do without these others, or there were some remote corner of the world to which we could escape that would be free of their influence, then we might stand a chance of happiness. But no: we are stuck with each other on a shrinking planet.

If all this sounds like a rather odd view for a self-professed Marxist to hold, the answer is that it was. The bleakness of Sartre's existential world-view, imbibed from Heidegger with echoes of Nietzsche, is irreconcilable with any coherent project of radical, transformative, emancipatory politics. At the heart of *Being and Nothingness* and *Huis Clos* is the insistence that this is just the way things are. As a philosophical creed, which considered itself to have given a fully rigorous account of existence, it is shamingly riddled with inconsistencies. Not the least disabling of these is the question that, if hell is other people, and there is nothing other than this hell in which we are all imprisoned, and there never has been, what exactly is the problem? How do we know what other life there could possibly be? It is true that, inasmuch as there is such a thing as desire, then human existence must acknowledge the presence of lack, but desire is capable of fulfilment, as Sartre grants. In its fulfilment lies its abolition, of course, but this doesn't preclude the possibility of further fulfilled desires. To say that one never wholly believes what one believes doesn't undermine the nature of belief, as is evidenced by the fact that people go on believing in things, be they failing relationships, Sartrean existentialism or God. Not every relationship that falls under public scrutiny is destroyed thereby, and not every commitment involves the desertion of another, since it may well have been the conclusion of one such previous liaison that has created the possibility for the new one. What seems to underpin the Sartrean view of human relations is a form of naïve perfectionism, in which, because present realities so often fall short of the ideal by which they are measured, so they cannot be anything other than a source of the most poignant misery. Your lover and you might have had a dream of living a carefree existence, but found yourselves instead having to put up with financial impediments, monotonous work and too few holidays. That hasn't rendered your relationship meaningless, however, nor need it lead you to conclude that it would have been better not to have set out on this road together in the first place.

What is most damaging about the philosophy articulated in *Huis Clos*, however, is that the idea that other people are hellish seems to do away with any chance of solidarity between us, whether of the political or of the emotional kind. This suggests that we could only hold the rest of the world in contempt, which doesn't exactly help. Sartre's rejoinder to this was to say that, just because you don't want the world to be a certain way doesn't mean it will obligingly change itself. Perhaps mutual contempt is our inescapable fate. But not only is this a strange philosophy for a socialist to expound, it was also a very peculiar one to arise from a Europe then still mostly in the grip of fascist occupation and engaged in the most vitally urgent war in history. If democratic humanity had been as paralysed before the evidence of overwhelming malevolence as are Sartre's pathetic cardboard characters at the end of *Huis Clos*, then the game would indeed have been up. In fact, they somehow contrived to get over their ineluctable existential distaste for each other long enough to drive out Nazi occupation all over Europe. Mutual contempt was a philosophical luxury they managed to forgo.

Contempt is a highly corrosive state of mind. It was in recognition of its damaging power that laws against contempt of court came to be formulated, forcing even democratic societies to resort to force to compel the successful operation of a certain minimal level of consensus, without which the stronger would be able to prey at will on the weaker. 'History will tear the verdict of this court to tatters,' Hitler declared as his sentence for the Munich *putsch* of 1923 was handed down, and so it did. If an abstract social institution like a law court cannot survive contempt, then how much less likely are vulnerable, injurable human beings to be able to survive it? Even if we do find the idea of co-operating with others disagreeable, we have no choice but to proceed as though it weren't, because the opposite is the kind of genocidal inferno that might just live up to the name of hell, and in as much luridly present reality as would make the setting of *Huis Clos* look like nothing more than the faintly dull drawing room that it is.

The whole ethical debate turns once again on the question of whether there is any such thing as genuine altruism, as opposed to some kind of delusional self-gratification, so that the woman who jumps into the freezing canal to save the drowning boy only does so because of the warm feeling of congratulation she will receive for her heroism, from herself as much as from the boy's parents and the local press. What people who draw the latter conclusion – with a sigh of Sartrean despair – have missed is that it scarcely matters what the motivation was when measured against the hugely countervailing outcome that the boy's life was saved. If our actions contribute to the sum of human happiness, we can perhaps be allowed the inner glow of satisfaction that accompanies them, however smug. Indeed, just as the exhilarating sensation of cool water flowing down our throats on a hot day is the reward for the parched thirst that led to it, so, by the same token, motivating our selfless actions by rewarding us with that glow of self-satisfaction may well be the cleverest trick evolutionary psychology has yet played on us.

18

I AM TREATED WITH CONTEMPT

Apart from its role in bolstering hierarchical social orders, contempt's celebrated provenance is, as the old saw has it, in familiarity. This proverb of seemingly ancient lineage is conventionally attributed to Aesop, in whose collection of *Fables* it forms the moral to the story of 'The Fox and the Lion':

When the Fox first saw the Lion he was terribly frightened, and ran away and hid himself in the wood. Next time however he came near the King of Beasts he stopped at a safe distance and watched him pass by. The third time they came near one another the Fox went straight up to the Lion and passed the time of day with him, asking him how his family were, and when he should have the pleasure of seeing him again; then turning his tail, he parted from the Lion without much ceremony.

Familiarity breeds contempt.

At first glance, the moral may simply seem to be that repeated sightings of the Lion have cured the Fox of his fear, as a phobic may be cured by exposure therapy, but that doesn't necessarily amount to contempt. There is something, though, about the airy badinage in which he engages the Lion that hints at scorn, or the emboldened demeanour of those who finally stand up to bullies. The turning of his tail, the unceremonious departure at a moment of his own choosing, is what seals it. The Fox is not just unafraid of the Lion now; he holds him in disdain.

The emotional reaction of contempt is an obvious natural resolution of what was previously fear. As children, when the light in the bedroom is turned on, and we see that the hulking shape in the corner of the room was just an odd fold in the curtains, we allow ourselves to feel superior to what had seemed, moments earlier, to be the minatory nature of our surroundings. Mingled with relief is also a feeling of contempt at ourselves for having been so craven before what is now so obviously harmless. If this were all the author of the fable intended, the point would be a relatively uncontentious one, for all that its insistence on the perishability of fear might come to have subversive political resonance – Aesop himself, Herodotus tells us, was a slave on the island of Samos in the first half of the sixth century BC. The element of fear, however, isn't evidently essential to the moral, which simply states that it is familiarity itself that engenders contempt, including presumably familiarity with the everyday. When a Latin translation of some of the *Fables* was prepared in the first century BC by the Roman poet Phaedrus, the moral of this tale would have chimed with a contemporary Roman proverb, *Cotidiana vilescunt* ('the everyday makes things common'). If everything that is familiar to us – which is to say everything with which we come into contact each day – is likely to become contemptible, then perhaps we are nearing the answer to the question as to why most people live unhappy lives.

Translated into Latin, *Familiaritas contemptum parit*, Aesop's moral became an eternal verity of no more controversial a stamp than the notion that words are less meaningful than deeds. Despite its pessimistic ring, it appears to have passed easily enough into the ambit of Christian theology. It is cited by St Augustine in the *Confessions*, in the writings of Pope Innocent III in the first decade of the thirteenth century, and it appears in the work of the great Italian Renaissance scholar, Angelo Poliziano. In each of these cases, though, it seems to be a bit of worldly wisdom, mentioned *en passant*, but often subjected to qualification. While it may be true that familiarity breeds contempt, due devotion to God is a virtue of which one will never tire, because at heart, as Augustine declares, we all want to worship him, whether we admit it or not. Augustinian man is not so much *Homo ludens* (the playing animal) as *Homo laudans* (the praising one). In any case, the role that this emotion plays in Augustine's writings is linked to the extent to which he holds the world, or his former godless life, in contempt. For the less devout, the proposition that the familiar becomes the boring is itself a boringly familiar truism, and yet one that poses a potent challenge to us. If a life staled by repetition does indeed become objectionable to the person who must live it, and if this is a universal truth, why are we such creatures of habit?

Our working lives may impose formidable demands on us, not just weighty obligations, but also the unvarying structures in which those obligations are to be discharged, adding to the stress of the workload the tedium of the changeless working hours and the daily confinement to the same desk and chair. And yet we add more invariant patterns to these, in the way we conduct our relationships and plan our leisure, so that, even released from obligation, we repair to the same bar in the evening, watch the same TV programmes each week, and go through the same routines every year on our birthdays. Indeed, as Wittgenstein reminds us in the *Tractatus Logico-Philosophicus* (1921), in the way we perceive time itself, we have forgotten that it too is an invention of our own:

We cannot compare a process with 'the passage of time' – there is no such thing – but only with another process (such as the working of a chronometer).

When we are stuck behind a desk for a predetermined portion of each day, time drags by, mocking us with the funereal procession of each minute on the clock. Stuck with nothing in particular to do on an inactive Sunday afternoon, we find the sense of empty time frittering past even harder to bear. It demands to be filled, and yet not with what will fill it again on Monday morning. The handmaiden of contempt is boredom, close kin of existentialism's nausea, that faintly seasick feeling of alienation at a world that appears to commend itself so little to us.

Boredom as a cultural theme is no older than the mid-nineteenth century. Its first great literary exemplars are women caught in loveless marriages – Flaubert's *Madame Bovary* (1856), Tolstoy's *Anna Karenina* (1874) and Nora Helmer in Ibsen's play *A Doll's House* (1879) – whose lives catch fire only through illicit sexual liaisons, or the promise at least of some life outside the marital straitjacket. When Emma Bovary is able to stand before her mirror, following her seduction by the charismatic Rodolphe, and declare to herself in triumph, 'I have a lover', the words mark not the breakdown of an established life, so much as the start of the new one for which she has been yearning. Very often, the boredom of the nineteenth-century leisured and middle classes reached the catastrophic pitch that it did because they had no idea how to find a way out of it. The characters of Anton Chekhov's plays are caught in a vortex of ennui so thickly encircling that, other than the odd burst of youthful enthusiasm, such as Konstantin's ambition to revolutionise the theatre in *The Seagull* (1895), or the anguished desire of the *Three Sisters* (1905) to get to Moscow, they cannot see what might transform, or even mitigate, their lassitude. There is something both tragic and richly comic about the impasse in which Chekhov maroons his characters. Idle bickering, sententious philosophising and pallid grumbles about the uncertain state of one's health are their conversational stock-in-trade, the aimless blather occasionally punctuated by somebody leaping to their feet in frustration – 'God, I'm so bored, bored, bored!' – but then subsiding back into the morass of indolence. The English writer William Gerhardie, who lived in Russia in the early part of his life, owed a considerable debt to Chekhov, as is evidenced by the title of his first novel, *Futility* (1922). George Bernard Shaw's best play, *Heartbreak House*, first performed in 1920, is saturated with Chekhovian anomie, as a group of affluent, witty but inert individuals engage in disputatious ironies, against the tumultuous European bloodletting of the Great War. Sartre comments in his autobiography *Words* (1964) that, as a growing child he felt his isolation made him into 'a glass palace in which the budding century beheld its boredom'.

There are wastrels and do-nothings in the eighteenth-century picaresque novel, but these are characters content not to spend their time profitably, usually for misanthropic reasons. Characters fallen into a state of cold-hearted resentment at the world populate Dickens's fiction, but this resentment gives them something to focus on. Ebenezer Scrooge has a nice line in sharply argued contempt for the life around him (his riposte to Bob Cratchit that the fact that his Christmas Day off only comes once a year is a poor excuse for theft has unanswerable moral force). Miss Havisham amuses herself with the company of Estella, and derives exquisite vicarious pleasure from attempting to engineer the wreckage of Pip's emotional hopes through her. Perhaps in the figures of the decrepit Smallweeds in *Bleak House* (1853), ancient and ignored, propped up on sofas, bitterly complaining and throwing the occasional cushion at each other, we can discern terminal disenchantment, but this is the pitfall of old age that awaits all the poor – to be old and useless in a world too preoccupied to notice you. Radical boredom is the privilege and curse of the leisured classes. When domestic servants and other more advanced forms of technology have delivered aching, empty hours of unoccupied time to you, the problem of what to do with it looms ever larger. It is for the women of the affluent classes, still largely excluded in this decisive era from careers outside the home, for whom the business of having no particular business that isn't already taken care of by housekeepers, cooks, gardeners, wet nurses and governesses, comes to seem such a curse. The tedious inertia of the lives of Jane Austen's titled ladies bears eloquent witness to the point.

Not even the intervention of two world wars resolved the problem of boredom in the modern psyche. Indeed, following the Great War, it seeped through all social classes, until it could be applied as readily to the frustration of John dos Passos's factory workers, who were less menacing to the rest of society if they could be seen as just bored rather than angry, as it could to the pointless flitting of Scott Fitzgerald's gadflies. After the Holocaust, radical boredom returns in the numbing parodies of conformity and repetition in the work of absurdist dramatists such as Eugène Ionesco (*The Bald Prima Donna* and *Rhinoceros* are representative, if now largely overlooked, works of the 1950s), in the blank canvases of high minimalism, like Robert Rauschenberg's white paintings of the early 1950s, and in the public avowal of Andy Warhol in the following decade that he was 'bored with everything'. Boredom, with a catalytic admixture of fury, is the motivating mental state of 1970s punk rock, its irrepressible anthem being the Buzzcocks' 1976 song of the same name. 'Bored Teenagers' (1977) by the Adverts drained the studious ironies from the Buzzcocks' version of boredom, and poured the lathering fury back in. 'We're bored out of our heads,' the song climaxes in a throttled scream, 'BORED OUT OF OUR MINDS'.

But as opposed to what?

Ennui, it sometimes feels, is the price we pay for living without fear, and without having to struggle for survival, but it can reduce us to nothing more than an alienated bundle of organic functions, resulting in a keen sense of contempt at our own impotence. A central philosophical reaction against it is Nietzsche's admonition in *The Gay Science* (1882) to the great of soul to 'live dangerously', forsaking the transient distractions of bourgeois culture, and the momentary physical satisfaction of intoxicants ('Does he who is enthusiastic need wine?' he snaps), in favour of a great affirmation of life itself, with all its terrifying contingencies and challenges. The old philosophy won't do ('Plato was a bore,' he informs us), any more than the old-time religion will. 'In truth there was only one Christian,' he declares in *The Antichrist* (1895), 'and he died on the cross.' There is little point in aiming for salvation, since 'In heaven, all the interesting people are missing.' Yet Nietzsche never quite tells us what it is we should be doing with our time. Retreating to the Alps and penning increasingly slim volumes of incendiary philosophy seems a good bet, but how much of that can society – or the publishing industry – tolerate? The conception of a will to power in his work is very much a hierarchical view of the ideal world, not that distant finally from Plato's ghastly vision of a well-regulated polis run by philosopher-kings, who muse on the world while slaves wash their robes for them and swill out their latrines. The *Übermensch* is he who rises above sentimental religion and damp-eyed pity for the sufferings of others, but what he is to do with his overweening superiority remains hard to establish. Back in Turin, on return from yet another recuperative visit to Sils-Maria, Nietzsche saw from his window a delivery man pitilessly belabouring his horse in the street and, overcome with anguish at the cruelty of the scene, suffered the critical mental breakdown that left him incapable for the final twelve years of his life. Whoever the *Übermensch* was, it wasn't him.

Nonetheless, the exhortation to live dangerously passed into popular parlance, as did no other dictum of Nietzsche's. A political leader in the UK announced in 1999 that his party would begin to live 'a little bit dangerously', and when pressed as to what that little bit of danger might entail, replied that it would involve espousing policies of 'social justice and European integration'. Even for a mainstream political leader, this seems to stretch the notion of danger to the point of semantic vacuity. A computer services website urges us to live dangerously by deleting expired emails, so as to clear our inboxes. We can be reasonably sure that Nietzsche had something a little more dynamic in mind than throwing away old correspondence, and perhaps even riskier than the chances taken by the 'seat belt grouches' who, according to one US automotive manufacturer's website, live dangerously by neglecting to fasten their safety belts on short car journeys. The last sort of dangerous living, in a very literal sense, involves flirting with the possibility of death or serious injury. For Nietzsche, however, dangerous living comports a different kind of risk. It means living against the grain of one's established society and its mores, like Mary Wollstencraft openly living with and having a child by a man to whom she wasn't married, or Quentin Crisp parading through the Pimlico of the 1930s in dyed hair and make-up. It means, finally, making one's own life, or in the two cases just cited one's sexual morality, into an ideology, which then often ceases to feel dangerous when it has been accepted by others as one's stance. In any case, such assertions of personal integrity have a habit of becoming disappointingly unremarkable with the passage of time. F Scott Fitzgerald observes that in our youth our principles are the mountain peaks from which we declaim, while in later life they become the caves in which we hide. Only if we subject our lives to the possibility of constantly renewed risk can we be said to be living dangerously. After a while, its very predictability negates it, since it depends crucially on its being something we wouldn't normally do.

Are there enough things in the world that we wouldn't normally do to allow for a form of life that is all risk and no dully bourgeois consolidation? Scott Fitzgerald has one of his characters state that we spend the first part of our lives trying to cope with what life throws at us, and the remainder wishing it would throw something at us. It is during that remainder – generally thought to arrive with the establishment of our first long-term relationship – that one may eventually cry out for risks taken, and having failed to find them, succumb to the condition now given the name of anhedonia. Literally an absence of pleasure, anhedonia is not to be confused with depression, although it is nearly always one of the symptoms of depression. It refers to that curiously anaesthetised state in which one ceases to derive any enjoyment from activities and stimuli that would previously be guaranteed to produce pleasure. Its recognition as a psychiatric symptom dates back as far as the 1890s, although throughout most of the twentieth century it was ignored in favour of the more lurid symptomatology of depression – unhappiness, fatigue and disrupted sleeping and eating patterns. Anhedonics may not be miserable, but they are subject to the peculiar anxiety caused by discovering that a night out in their favourite restaurant leaves them oddly unsatisfied, or that some unexpected piece of good news is only blankly registered. The condition is none other than nineteenth-century boredom, accorded its aetiology at the time in the emergent science of psychiatry, but then later identified in the socio-cultural realm as ennui – later, anomie and angst. It is a state of pervasive emotional frigidity, particularly disturbing for the impression it gives – like classic depression – that it must be impossible to recover from, just as the colours in a garment, once faded with repeated washing, won't ever be restored to their former lustre.

When all the other likely candidates for the cause of anhedonia have been ruled out, the most obvious culprit will be the dreariness of the routine into which the sufferer's life has been moulded. When each day brings nothing but more of the seemingly interminable same, the spirits in all but the most Panglossian of individuals will eventually refuse to rise to meet it. That fact returns us to the question of why, even left to our own devices, we arrange our lives into the kinds of familiar patterns that can only, in the last analysis, occasion contempt. The answer, as so often, is embedded in the question, in that critical clause 'in the last analysis'. Forms of life that become stale and repetitious to us were once replete with novelty, and we clung to them over time as long as that novelty, or some brightly coloured reflection of it, continued to hold. There is nothing ignoble about the desire for structure, against the sort of ceaseless flux and spontaneity that the operations of multinational capitalism, for instance, have delivered to working people. These patterns are tolerable partly because they appear to us as a bulwark against chaos and unpredictability, and partly because, by their seamless insinuation into our lives, their apparent monotony can be more lightly borne. Moreover, the allure of security is very often only enhanced when one considers its opposite, as personified in those people who profess to live their lives according to the principle of unfettered spontaneity. The idea may start out in the form of deciding to fly to Acapulco tonight, rather than going home and watching television like the other drones, but as often as not unravels amid a series of aborted, foolish ventures. Such people, in their fetishisation of spontaneity, only seem to be giving voice to whatever bit of nonsense enters their heads next. Proposing the flight to Acapulco, they know they can rely on the other person to veto it, since it is neither practical nor affordable, thus forcing the other to cast himself in the role of eternal killjoy, while they – the true shooting stars – are tethered against their will to an earthbound existence. Considered in these terms, spontaneity is about as appealing as a dose of irrationalism, itself held out as a therapeutic recourse from the stodgy certitude of reason.

The sustaining structures of the familiar, however, are strung together across a series of more or less critical snagging points, moments at which the mind suddenly cries out for rejuvenation. Finding it not to hand, we slip into contempt at ourselves, for realising the truth of Socrates' famous dictum that 'the unexamined life is not worth living', but being so impotent at finding the escape route. There is such a thing, however, as too much introspection, even though the critical mind may snarl at the very idea.

W H Auden commented that while Socrates' postulation was broadly true, nonetheless the life too closely examined could not be lived at all. There has to be some living going on between these bouts of examination, and it is in those periods that we manage not to notice that, although we are seeing it come home to us for the thousandth or the ten thousandth time, the face of our beloved still restores the shine to a day that had all but lost it.

SHAME

Conscience is the mark of shame of an unfree society.
Theodor Adorno

1. The painful emotion arising from the consciousness of something dishonouring, ridiculous, or indecorous in one's own conduct or circumstances (or in those of others whose honour or disgrace one regards as one's own), or of being in a situation which offends one's sense of modesty or decency. **2.** Fear of offence against propriety or decency, operating as a restraint on behaviour; modesty, shamefastness. **3.** Disgrace, ignominy, loss of esteem or reputation. **b.** An instance of disgrace. **c.** *spec.* Violation of a woman's honour, loss of chastity. **4.** What is morally disgraceful or dishonourable; baseness in conduct or behaviour. **5.** A fact or circumstance which brings disgrace or discredit (*to* a person, etc.); matter for severe reproach or reprobation. **6.** A person or thing that is a cause or source of disgrace. **b.** A thing which is shockingly ugly or indecent, or of disgracefully bad quality.

Darwin's physical indicators: blushing; averting of the gaze; turning away of the face; covering of the face with the hands; partial or complete closing of the eyes; involuntary movements of the eyes; unnatural brightness in the eyes; affectation of manner.

19

TO BE ASHAMED

Literature's greatest demystifier is the small boy in Hans Christian Andersen's 1837 tale, *The Emperor's New Suit of Clothes*. He has been brought by his father to see the Emperor's grand procession through the city streets and, standing amid the awestruck ranks of the credulous, he alone points out that the head of state is nude. The premise under which the swindlers have taken pecuniary advantage of the vain Emperor is that the apparel they will fashion for him is of such incomparable finesse that those who are dull-witted, or in some sense elevated above their station, will not be able to see it. Nobody wants to admit that of themselves, and so all affect to be amazed at the gorgeous colours and the craftsmanship of their work. Once the boy blurts out that the Emperor – whom we must imagine as an arrogant, corpulent buffoon – has nothing on, a ripple of enlightenment breaks through the crowd, until only the central figure in the procession, and his immediate entourage, are left apparently still insisting otherwise. Depending on which translation one consults, the Emperor himself either secretly knows that they are right, or else uncomfortably suspects that they might be ('for it seemed to him that they were right'), but continues as though undaunted on his spectacular promenade, because to admit otherwise would be to admit his own gullibility. He has no choice but to see it through, while all around him see through it.

The metaphor that Andersen's fable employs in order to puncture the pomposity of the self-adoring Emperor is a telling one. Nakedness will shame him because it is funny. A bit of current folk wisdom advises those facing some daunting ordeal, whether it be before the job interview panel or the magistrate's bench, to imagine their inquisitors in a state of undress. This, it is held, will deflate their perceived status, although it is hard to see why inward amusement, as opposed to plain distaste, should be the effect. What this strategy depends on, however, is the sense of debasement that nakedness is thought to confer on the naked, a debasement that renders them at least ridiculous, and perhaps even shameful.

We do not have to look too far to find the mythical origins of nakedness as shame; like so much else, it is traceable to the Book of Genesis. However, the notion that shame begins when we fall from grace, and attain consciousness of our exposure *as* exposure, losing our blissful ignorance of it in some act of self-demystification, is not quite what the legend of the expulsion of the happy couple from the Garden of Eden is about.

Adam and Eve begin their sedentary, paradisiacal lives in a state of unknowing: 'And they were both naked, the man and his wife, and were not ashamed' (2:25). After the serpent has persuaded Eve, and thus Adam, to try the forbidden fruit, 'the eyes of them both were opened, and they knew that they were naked' (3:7). They stitch together fig leaves to cover their genitalia. Our interpretation of the story must turn on the subtly different Hebrew words translated by the same English word 'naked' in the King James version. In the second chapter, when they are unashamed at their physical condition, the word used is *arowm*, which simply denotes an unclad state, bareness. By contrast, their realisation of their nakedness is indicated by the word *eyrom*, to be or to make bare, in other words, instead of being simply a prior descriptive state, their nakedness is now something to which they have been subjected. They are the passive objects of a process, an act of exposure. Paradoxically, they had been clothed, in that they were beings of divine light clad in human nakedness, whereas now that they understand good and evil, they have become mere human beings, attired in nothing. Having been, in a sense, uncovered, they must now conceal their nakedness. A further layer of complexity is added by the quality attributed to the serpent above all other of God's creatures, that he is very 'subtil'. The Hebrew word thus translated turns out to be *aruwm*, almost identical to, and lexically derivative of, the *arowm* that describes the nakedness of Adam and Eve. By a slight metaphorical shift, their innocent nudity is also the craftiness or cunning of the serpent, by linguistic association probably with some idea of smoothness, as in plausibility. In other words, it is the very lack of affectation that conceals the malevolence of intent. Even when the serpent directly gainsays the warning uttered to her by the Creator, Eve is not minded to contradict him. Indeed, beguiled by the serpent's suave, naked plausibility, she even misquotes God, saying that she and Adam have been commanded not merely to avoid eating the forbidden fruit, but to steer clear even of touching it, on pain of death. When the serpent replies that she will certainly not die, he has perhaps seen his entry. Indeed she won't die from merely touching it, but her correction on that point stands to her – as the serpent well knows it will – for an assurance about eating it as well. The fate of humanity thus hangs on a deception, made possible by the fact that, just as being natural is sometimes said to be the ultimate pose, being naked can be the ultimate disguise.

As a result of this fatal lapse, nakedness becomes a matter of shame. Its inextricable connection with that emotional condition lies in the fact that it exposes not the generality of the body, but specifically the organs of procreation. Henceforward, these must be covered. The very word for 'garment' in Hebrew, *le-bush*, derives from the primitive root *buwsh*, meaning 'shame', indicating that the act of clothing oneself arises out of this sense of age-old guilt. The Koranic account of the Creation is drawn in much less picturesque detail than the Judaic version, but the text does lay down very specific guidance as to the correct dress to be adopted by devout Muslims. Nothing in it, it is worth noting, sanctions the total swathing of women in the *burka* insisted upon in fundamentalist communities, but it is said that she should take care to cover her breasts, and that both sexes should hide those parts of themselves that might give sexual excitation to the other. The lesson of the casting out from Paradise is again one of erotic awakening. Tellingly, the Koran represents the forbidden fruit not as an apple (which wasn't indigenous to the biblical lands, and isn't in fact specified in either the Hebrew or the King James English), but a banana. The physical symbolism of that fruit in a legend about sexual enlightenment can scarcely be lost on even the careless reader, the more so since '*banan*' is a common Arabic vulgarism for the penis. The message is clear: nakedness is shameful because it refers explicitly to the sexual.

A further indiscretion arises in Genesis, when Noah, having planted the world's first vineyard after the Flood, drinks of the wine of it and ends up in a lolling state of inebriation. When his youngest son Ham stumbles in on him in his tent and sees him naked, he goes to tell his elder brothers, and Shem and Japheth, observing a propriety that their father has abandoned, walk backwards into the tent so as not to compromise themselves by witnessing the scene, carrying a 'garment' that will conceal the old man's shame. The word here is not *le-buwsh*, however, but *simlah*, the word for an undergarment. They don't just throw the first thing that comes to hand over their father, but the first item that he should properly put on if he is going to dress himself. (Interestingly, the word for an over-garment, *beged*, means 'treachery' or 'deceit', so that clothing is at all levels implicated in moral corruption. It at once hides the shame of nakedness, but is itself the means by which we give a semblance of ourselves that may deliberately be intended to mislead.) When he sobers up, Noah places a curse on his son Ham for telling on him, by making Ham's own son Canaan 'a servant of servants'. Not only has nakedness once more been the cause of a curse that will descend through the generations in perpetuity, but it is now also attached to drunkenness, thus inscribing a lasting shame into the use of intoxicants. Ham, it is generally understood, is the father of the African races (his grandson Nimrod became the founding emperor of Babylon), one of the dual meanings of his name in Hebrew being 'black'. In some rabbinical commentaries on the tale of Noah's family, it is suggested that his apparent lack of indignation at his father's nakedness is reflected through the ages in the lesser inhibition that native African peoples have about being naked, living as they do in some of the hottest regions of the earth. The other meaning of Ham's name is 'hot' or 'heat'.

Where does our facility for shame originate? What mechanism is at work inside our minds to induce the hot flush, and that peculiarly physical sensation that the shame of being naked or drunk imparts to us? In particularly acute episodes of shame, we might be overcome by a feeling of wanting to escape the boundaries of our own body. This reminds us that the emotions are not merely physical in the sense that they can be read from facial expressions, as Darwin shows, but that each also has its own subjective physical sensation. Even more than in jealousy, shame makes one want to step out of one's own skin (whereas fear, by contrast, makes us wish to shrink back within it), in order to dissociate ourselves from the being that has been convicted as guilty before the world.

We would not have a sense of shame if we didn't have a conscience, and conscience itself arises in the context of the violation of taboos. Conscience is what Immanuel Kant proposes should be the normative mechanism driving all our actions in the world; as the 'categorical imperative', it represents the linchpin of his moral philosophy. If our behaviour were governed by the consideration of how it would be if everybody were to behave in this way, the cause of humanity's greater good would be well served. Although he is represented in philosophical history as one of the great questioners of the theological tradition, there is more than a waft of ecclesiastical incense detectable in many of Kant's formulations.

A more nuanced consideration of the way conscience operates is to be found in Sigmund Freud's important work, *Totem and Taboo* (1913), in which he points out the peculiarly contradictory character of the notion of taboo in its earliest cultural manifestations. What is taboo is simultaneously the sacred and the unclean. Religious taboos surround and protect the deities, so that ordinary mortals may not approach them or touch them, for fear of falling foul of their supernatural power. The diseased, the infectious and the polluted are also to be avoided, lest the unfathomable power of what ails them should infect oneself. Eventually, the moral weight of the concept would shift towards the latter orientation, elevating, for example, concerns about food hygiene into religious tenets in the Judaic and Muslim faiths. Freud posits that the origins of conscience lie in the sense of guilt that arose from violating a taboo. He argues that it is characteristic of the subjects of taboos that they are aspects of life to which we feel emotionally ambivalent. We are both fascinated and repelled by the gods, as also by whatever is forbidden, and the psychic conflict that this creates reaches its apogee, in the minds of disturbed individuals, in the form of obsessional neurosis. The neurotic patient who maintains a painstakingly thorough regimen of cleaning or checking behaviour fears falling into the grip of contradictory temptations, as though the endless self-examination and applications of cleansing lotion were designed to edge aside the temptation to let himself become dirty. Despite the appearance of almost maniacal control, obsessive-compulsive behaviour contains at its heart the anarchy of unbridled anxiety. Neuroses of this kind, according to Freud, represent the workings of conscience run riot, but exploring their internal psychic mechanism also illuminates the inherent conflict in all consciousness of taboo, the simultaneous attraction and repulsion we feel in its presence. That consists in the realisation that what is forbidden must always, in some sense, be what is desired. In the earliest legal codes, there could have been no need to prohibit acts that nobody was capable of committing. Returning momentarily to Eden, we come across sexual awareness being made the consequence of eating the fruit of the Tree of Knowledge, so that the manifestations of sex – the lure of its unconquerable desires, the non-procreative ways in which it can be practised, and the state of nakedness that seems its primary element – are henceforth subject to ambivalence, and to the repression to which ambivalence is perpetually attached.

Ours is not the first age to have to engage with nudity in places we were not traditionally used to finding it. Walking in Scarborough in the summer of 1858, Lady Rothschild and her daughters, Constance and Annie, came upon a scene of bathers worthy of the work of Ingres:

Here is complete absence of costume, as in the garden of Eden before the fall of man, and hundreds of ladies and gentlemen look on, while the bathers plunge in the foaming waters, or emerge from them.

The daughter who so recorded this startling tableau in her journal thought there was only one thing for it, spoiling the lightly appealing poetry of the description with a Victorian sniff: 'I really think the police should interfere.' Naked bathing is scandalous to the Rothschild *mademoiselles* precisely because it appears to be done without guilt, when the natural habiliment of nudity ought to be shame. And yet what could be more natural than to enter the water unclothed? Not only Ingres, but painters of the later nineteenth century too, Cézanne in particular, took nude bathing as a theme, while a few years before the Rothschilds had their unseemly encounter in Scarborough, Gustave Courbet painted a pair of women bathers, in which a rather weighty figure *au derrière* emerges on to a riverbank in thick forest, caught in the act of pulling a drying cloth around her formidably muscular buttocks. Its celebration of illicit sensuality is quite clear: her companion, still fully clothed but gazing deliriously at her, stretches forth her arms in ecstasy, one hand clutching at the satisfyingly thick shaft of a nearby branch. Without the peasant headscarf, her adoring head, lolling sideways in frank rapture, could be the head of Mary Magdalene drinking in the beauty of Christ.

The shame of nakedness is the theme of representations of the story of Susanna and the Elders, which depict the Apocryphal tale of two elders of the church who, having been aroused by the beauty of a magistrate's wife walking in her garden, spy on her while she is bathing. Rubens painted several versions of it, in which the viewer's expected moral indignation at the assault upon virtue is complicated by the evident enticement represented by the comely female nude. A letter to the painter from his associate Dudley Carleton, English ambassador to Holland, anticipates with crude relish the alluring prospect of a Susanna the artist was currently embarked on. Notwithstanding the voluptuary opportunism of the ambassador's attitude, the centre of gravity of the tale concerns virtue assailed. The elders, excited beyond endurance, demand sexual favours from the chaste Susanna, threatening her with false indictment as an adulteress if she doesn't accede to their lusts. Its most affecting seventeenth-century treatments are the two versions by Rembrandt. In the earlier one, dating from around 1634, Susanna is shown preparing for her toilette, and turns towards the viewer, an expression of injured perturbation on her face, her feet maladroitly stepping into her slippers, while she pulls a sleeve of her discarded garment over her pudenda. In a later version, dated to 1647, the elders are doing rather more than looking lasciviously on. One white-bearded old duffer, who should know better, watches from the background, while a younger colleague is caught in the act of attempting to extort compliance from the virtuous wife. Her cringing posture is retained from the original, but now she has been accosted at the moment of entering the bath, her right foot having just been placed in the water when the hand of the interloper intrudes to pull the shift away from her back. This time, her startled gaze importunes as well as accuses the onlooker, daring us to intervene rather than simply wait, goggle-eyed, for the garment to fall.

By contrast, Michelangelo's early sixteenth-century scene of naked soldiers disporting themselves in the river Arno during the course of the war between Pisa and Florence is a celebration of the pleasure of nudity. Although it was much studied and copied by his contemporaries, Vasari's *Lives of the Artists* of 1550 records that at some stage while it was kept in the Great Hall of the Medici Palace in Florence, it was torn to shreds. The soldiers have been surprised by a call to arms, in what will be the Battle of Cascina, and run from the shallows of the river. It is a frenetic picture of extraordinary mobility, in which some of the men are shown hastily throwing on pieces of armour, some buckling on their cuirasses, others taking up their arms just as they are, while one or two on horseback are already engaging the enemy. One old man, his head garlanded with ivy against the throbbing sun, struggles to pull snagging stockings over his sodden feet, his mouth twisting with the helpless exertion of it. Crowds of nude soldiers dash towards the fray, drawn in every conceivable anatomical attitude, some kneeling, some fallen and lying prone, some dramatically foreshortened, some with detailed features, others left as ghostly outlines, a few strokes of the carbon enough to suggest a tautly contorted body. The general reaction to it, so striking in its reverential tone for what was after all a non-devotional work, hints at the incalculable aesthetic loss we have suffered by its destruction. Vasari torments us:

[. . .]artists were amazed when they saw the lengths he had reached in this cartoon. Some in seeing his divine figures declared that it was impossible for any other spirit to attain to its divinity. When finished [in 1506] it was carried to the Pope's hall amid the excitement of artists and to the glory of Michelangelo, and all those who studied and drew from it, as foreigners and natives did for many years afterwards, became excellent artists . . .

Happening upon a similar scene in Italy during the Second World War, the British poet F T Prince had reason to recall Michelangelo's work. 'Soldiers Bathing', written in 1942, describes a group of combatants stripped and disporting themselves in the sea. The true liberty of their nakedness is being restored to them, as a sense of respite from war washes away its shame and its vulnerability. The poor bare forked animal of *King Lear* is invoked, but now

> Conscious of his needs and desires and flesh that rise and fall,
> Stands in the soft air, tasting after toil
> The sweetness of his nakedness: letting the sea-waves coil
> Their frothy tongues about his feet, forgets
> His hatred of the war, its terrible pressure that begets
> A machinery of death and slavery
> Each being a slave and making slaves of others: finds that he
> Remembers his old freedom in a game
> Mocking himself, and comically mimics fear and shame.

The poet is explicitly reminded of Michelangelo's work, in which their naked bathing has restored to the soldiers their appetite for the war, so that running from the waves they are filled with a kind of sexual frenzy, 'hot to buckle on and use the weapons lying there'. The theme returns us to the archetypal votive image of nakedness, that of the Crucifixion, 'the obverse of the scene', concrete enactment of the intimidating love the Creator reserves for his incorrigible, wayward progeny. All oblivious to this, and ready once more for the fighting, the soldiers restore themselves to their martial roles:

They dry themselves and dress,
Combing their hair, forget the fear and shame of nakedness.
Because to love is frightening we prefer
The freedom of our crimes.

The streak of red in the western sky becomes at the close the blood of the pierced Messiah as the poet muses on the 'strange delight', 'strange gratitude', that strikes him at the reminder of humanity's capacity for destruction, 'as if evil itself were beautiful'.

If they have been able to forget the shame of their nakedness while splashing about in the sea, the soldiers have managed momentarily to overcome the inherited curse of their own physicality. From the 1840s on, as an alternative to public bathing, hydropathic establishments offered a middle-class, cultured constituency the chance to liberate themselves from their customary confinement by undergoing perspiration treatments in steam rooms, followed by a dip in a deliciously shocking, ice-cold plunge-bath. Accounts of these remedies, as popular with women as they were with men, unequivocally emphasise the sensuality of the treatment. 'A powerful reaction,' reported one well-bred society lady, 'and a high degree of exhilaration and vigour are the result.' It is compelling how often the shame and the vulnerability of nakedness are washed away by the body's contact with water, the most immediately sensual of the four elements, and the one in which – as we now know from palaeontology – our own origins, in common with all other land mammals, certainly lie.

One Talmudic account of the expulsion from Eden story calculates that the length of time Adam spent in Eden amounted to no more than twelve hours, with Eve joining him only at the midpoint. If God only allowed us half a day in Paradise, it might be thought that we would long since have forgotten what it was like. But, much as our marine origins compel us towards the water's edge, so the vestigial apprehension of some state before the Fall, in which our bodies were the sites of freedom and possibility rather than shame, haunts us still. It is only that, having disported ourselves in the Edenic rivers when we can, we will always then return to the banks and fall gleefully upon the waiting weaponry.

20

I SHAME YOU

The emotional dynamics of shame are extremely complex. To be discovered to have committed a moral or legal wrong is to feel its corrosive intensity, the more so because the perpetrator is doubly guilty: of the act itself, and of trying to conceal it. Then again, shame may be imposed from without upon a person, for an act that seems to others objectively free of moral taint. To a lesser degree, it may be felt in isolation, where the evidence and the consequences of a guilty act do not come to light. Although, like most emotions a negative one, it is thought to be made honourable by an act of public contrition, but equally, it too can become pathological, issuing in debilitating shyness, unfounded fear of ridicule and obsessive-compulsive behaviour. We see the cycle of inherited shame at work in the savagery of Heathcliff's family in *Wuthering Heights*, and in Lady Macbeth's futile hand washing. Akira Kurosawa's 1952 film *Ikiru* (*Living*), which depicts the mental disintegration of a man told that he is terminally ill, is a poignant study in the dynamics of shame. In all these contexts, it is the inner sense of nakedness that powers the emotion, and that can sustain it beyond its original occasion.

The intentional infliction of shame through public humiliation of criminals and malefactors has been practised in jurisprudential systems since ancient times. It speaks to the desire of the mass of society and its institutions for a perfect atonement, encapsulated in the adage that justice should not only be done, but be seen to be done. We should not necessarily think of the desire for manifestations of public guilt as having died out in Europe with the gradual abandonment of public physical chastisement in the latter half of the nineteenth century. Even now, justice must be public, or it is nothing. The convicted felon may now be taken down to serve his sentence away from the gaze of society, but the trial itself still takes place before an audience of both interested and neutrally observing parties. Just as the public galleries at the court are full, the proceedings may well be televised in many countries, and will certainly be reported in the press. There is an appetite in the UK for witnessing the bureaucratic dispatch of cases even as minor as motoring offences, with the verdicts and sentences being noted in the local newspaper. Public interest may be thought to go hand in hand with the jury system, and the right to be tried by one's peers, but this doesn't quite explain the psychological factors at work in those who turn up merely hoping to witness the proceedings. It is as though justice itself is a delicate bloom, which if not conscientiously tended would wither and lose its allure. The utopian hope in the ideal of justice is that all malfeasance may be put right, and that this will contribute to its eventual demise. To this end, those who contravene the law must publicly pay the price for their subversion of the moral order.

In earlier times, a public shaming was often inflicted in addition to a custodial sentence, but it was available on its own where it was felt that imprisoning a felon did not quite meet the peculiar nature of the crime that had been committed, or where the severity of the offence was not sufficient to merit detention. In England, there were three main instruments of public humiliation. The pillory and stocks were the two most often resorted to, and were of such unremarkable status that they formed part of the public furniture of every market town and village in the land, by act of law from 1405. Stocks, which had been introduced by the Romans in Britain, were reserved for the lesser offences, such as minor drunkenness, defiance of a public official, and – in some communities – missing church. They stood on the ground and consisted of two lateral beams, the upper of which could be lifted, pierced by a pair of holes in which the legs of the miscreant would be inserted before the beams were locked together. Some versions contained four holes, so that restraint of the arms could be practised as well, which would have resulted in acute physical discomfort. The sentence, which could be up to a whole day, was usually for one or two hours only, but was always to be carried out on market day, when the streets were at their busiest. Passers-by were expected to pour scorn and insults upon those imprisoned in the stocks, and often resorted to flinging missiles. With their hands free, the victims were able at least to put up a rudimentary defence against the stones, lumps of wood, rotten vegetables and clods of mud that were hurled. While never officially abolished, the stocks had more or less fallen into disuse by the midpoint of the nineteenth century, although an instance is recorded of them being used in Rugby as late as 1865.

The pillory was retained for more serious infractions, often those involving some form of deceit, such as the forging of legal documents, selling short measures of provisions, cheating at gaming or, most seriously of all, perjury. A statute of 1256 prescribed its use for lying under oath. It consisted of a vertical post with a crossbeam lying on top of it, into which were cut holes for the head and hands. Convicts would spend anything from an hour to a whole day in this device, enduring the taunts and missiles of the crowd, the sentence often repeated on consecutive days, and often embellished with some particular indignity specific to the nature of the offence. A dishonest merchant's provisions – the underweight sacks of fuel or spoiled meat – would typically be burned at the foot of the pillory, so that he was forced to choke on the fumes of his livelihood literally going up in smoke. In London in 1364, a seller of putrid wine was forced to drink a deep draught of his own foul merchandise, before having the rest of it poured over his head while he stood in the pillory. The symbol for liars was a whetstone, a block of turned stone used for sharpening blades, which would hang heavily about the miscreant's neck. Alternatively, a wooden sign or placard detailing the nature of the offence would be hung on him for the enlightenment and amusement of passing strangers.

What is especially instructive about these punishments is that they cannot work without the willing participation of the public. To this end, stocks and pillories were always sited in particularly busy areas, such as the market square or beside the village green. The most famous pillory in London in the seventeenth and eighteenth centuries was at Charing Cross. There, in 1700, two convicted homosexual men were ruthlessly pelted with mud and shit from the streets until, it was said, their features could no longer be discerned beneath the coating of filth. The punishment depended on a certain level of consensus. Yet, when, following an Act of Parliament of 1637, the pillory began to be used for misdemeanours such as slandering the government or unlicensed publication of seditious or dissenting material, during the reign of that most self-regarding of monarchs, Charles I, the complicity of the crowds in the spectacle could no longer be relied upon. Daniel Defoe was sentenced to the pillory in 1703 for his pamphlet, *The Shortest Way with the Dissenters*, in which he satirised the Anglican Church's intolerance of Christian unorthodoxy. The Church prosecuted, and Defoe was fined and sent to Newgate prison, but not before being placed in the Charing Cross pillory. The action backfired, however, when Defoe was greeted on what should have been his ignominious arrival by a hearty ovation from the crowd. After his head and hands had been secured, his supporters garlanded the pillory with flowers, while others threw flowers at him instead of the usual missiles, and cried their encouragement of the dissenter rather than hurling the expected ritual invective.

Defoe was at least spared the torment of many sentenced to this form of humiliation, who had nails driven through their ears to pin them against the board, in hope that they might tear them off in their pathetic attempts to dodge the stones. If they were still wholly, or partially, attached at the completion of their ordeal, they would be cut away. This was the fate in 1637 of the puritanical dissident author William Prynne, who also had his nose split open and both of his cheeks branded with the initials 'S.L.', for 'seditious libeller'. He tells us in his journal that the hangman, having 'burnt one cheek with a letter the wrong waye, he burnt that againe'. Eventually, in 1816, the pillory was restricted to use for perjury only, and was finally outlawed altogether in 1837.

Shame was not restricted to use against living felons. In the third method of public shaming widely practised, humiliation was intended to extend beyond the moment of death. For the most serious capital offences, such as treason, hanging was considered (as modern-day tabloid apoplexy would have it) too good for the convicted, and their asphyxiated, broken and often sectioned bodies were hung up to public view on the gibbet, a wooden structure that resembled the hangman's gallows. There, their bodies would dangle and fester, as a public example to the law-abiding, often until they rotted down to the bone.

The great exploration of nineteenth-century shame is Nathaniel Hawthorne's *The Scarlet Letter* (1850). Its heroine, Hester Prynne, is introduced to us as she is led from the prison house to the pillory. Somewhat surprisingly, as the action is set in the vengeful Puritan New England of the mid-seventeenth century, the scaffold she ascends is not being used for execution. Its alternative purpose is dire enough, however, as the narrator explains:

The very ideal of ignominy was embodied and made manifest in this contrivance of wood and iron. There can be no outrage, methinks, against our common nature, – whatever be the delinquencies of the individual, –

no outrage more flagrant than to forbid the culprit to hide his face for shame; as it was the essence of this punishment to do.

Hester is required to stand on the platform, at shoulder height above the multitudinous crowd, and face their righteous judgement for a prescribed period, before being returned to her cell. Having been sent ahead to the American colonies by her husband, himself detained on business in Europe, and having waited two years for him to follow on, she has had sexual relations with another man, and given birth to a child. The psychic mechanism of exemplary punishments such as these is as readily understood by the author as it must have been by those who devised and ordained them:

In our nature, however, there is a provision, alike marvellous and merciful, that the sufferer should never know the intensity of what he endures by its present torture, but chiefly by the pang that rankles after it.

It is the memory of the humiliation undergone that will live on, enduring unbearably in the mind long after the immediate moment has passed. Somehow adding to the bitterness of the ordeal is the crowd's morbid silence. We are told that Hester could have taken the usual taunts, the judgemental scorn and hatred, in her stride, but what she is faced with is a kind of awed, silent gravity, a mood in which they seem to sense the full ghastliness of her plight. The stately presence of the Governor, in the company of judges, generals and priests, commands a respectful solemnity in those attending, denying Hester that attitude of defiance that is the shamed criminal's last resort of dignity:

Had a roar of laughter burst from the multitude . . . Hester Prynne might have repaid them all with a bitter and disdainful smile. But, under the leaden infliction which it was her doom to endure, she felt, at moments, as if she must needs shriek out with the full power of her lungs, and cast herself from the scaffold down upon the ground, or else go mad at once.

The further mark of her shame, which she must carry about with her for ever, is a letter A, made of bright-red cloth, stitched to her clothing with gold thread. Standing for the name of her crime, Adultery, this is the shameful badge that gives the story its name ('... she will be a living sermon against sin, until the ignominious letter be engraved upon her tombstone'). In a religious universe that has put a total ban on graven images, on unnecessary decoration and ostentation, the only commodities that may be so arrayed are sins. Every time she leaves her lonely cottage on the edge of town, accompanied by the illegitimate daughter Pearl, she is dogged by the accusing stares and mud-slinging of her erstwhile neighbours, who can literally read her sin in the single, incandescent letter that glows from her breast. The letter keeps intruding into the consciousness of those around her. Like any facial disfigurement to which the gaze of the other keeps helplessly returning, it literally cannot be overlooked, reminding the one who bears it that, even if she can live with it, others can't. A terrible moment occurs when Hester sees her baby's eyes distracted by it for the very first time, as she bends over the cradle. When she goes with Pearl to the Governor's house to plead that her child not be taken from her, there is a moment when she notices herself reflected in the breastplate of a suit of armour in the entrance hall:

... and she saw that, owing to the peculiar effect of this convex mirror, the scarlet letter was represented in exaggerated and gigantic proportions, so as to be greatly the most prominent feature of her appearance. In truth, she seemed absolutely hidden behind it.

And so she is. Moments like these recall to her how, no matter how sanguine she may have become, the rest of the world will always view her (and her child) through the medium of this vivid red mark, the cathexis of her shame.

The Scarlet Letter, and its implied critique of Puritan morality, reminds us of one of the concealed truths about the emotion of shame, which is that – somewhat like fear – its natural life expectancy is short. Precisely because the felt intensity of it is so unendurable, it doesn't of itself endure. We cure ourselves of shame by forgiving ourselves, the more quickly as those whom we have offended are unlikely to provide the absolution we crave. Hester is, almost from the moment of her release from prison, ready to live with herself for what she has done, even though the estranged husband to whom she is still wedded turns up just in time to see her exhibited on the platform. She is especially militant in the matter of Pearl's welfare, refusing to allow the stain of shame to trickle down to the innocent child, and she dresses her daughter not in the sombre, earthy habiliments of the Puritan drudge, but in bright, gaudy clothes of her own embroidery. The colours reflect her own stigma: when she takes Pearl to her meeting with the Governor, the girl is arrayed in scarlet and gold, transmuting the very colours of her own ignominy, by moral alchemy, into the gorgeous apparel she sees the headstrong child as deserving. This perhaps explains why the judicial process has to make the question of not just guilt, but of the shame and contrition of the convicted, into an administrative matter. If there is no shame, the law has not achieved as complete a victory as it requires and, in an era when a crime was also first and foremost a sin before God, there is no proper repentance before the Almighty. The scarlet letter is thus a means of sustaining that shame beyond its natural term, indeed even beyond the death of the sinner, so that her soul may be saved, and that others will think twice before treading the same disastrous path.

The inculcation of shame is not now overtly a concern of judicial proceedings. Restorative justice – whereby offenders are encouraged to meet those from whom they have stolen – is a more advanced means of achieving both restitution and, more optimistically, reform. What seems to have replaced induced shame in recent times is the vogue for self-indictment, in which public avowals of one's own shame are an indispensable element of atonement. These range from the public confessions of Chinese Communist Party officials, who are regularly expected to own up to having failed the proletariat by lapses into bourgeois self-seeking, to the tearful *mea culpas* of philandering televangelists such as Jimmy Swaggart. America's most famous recent adulterer, for whose actions a presidential impeachment inquiry was established, underwent the public shame of being closely questioned on TV about the technicalities of this adulterous affair, finally confessing to and atoning for what he had at first so circuitously denied. There is thought to be some cleansing operation at work for the convicted individual in these cases, a hope that by making one's transgressions (real or imagined) known before an audience, a due process of exculpation has been undergone. But do these displays of shame not more obviously serve the spectators, just as they did in the days of which Hawthorne writes? Party members in China may shudder inwardly at the dramatised apologies of their regional secretaries (a spectacle of great piquancy in a culture where the apologetic manner in itself involves a terrible loss of face), while at least some who saw Swaggart bawling his eyes out on the mainstream news shows had a healthy chuckle at his performance. The net effect of public contrition, however, is to make the observer feel that there but for the grace of something (be it the Politburo or God), go they.

V A C Gatrell's great work on public execution in England during the eighteenth and nineteenth centuries, *The Hanging Tree* (1994), is profoundly instructive about the complex interplay between sympathy and retribution at work in these spectacles. Juridical authority in Georgian England could never wholly rely on the deference of the public before its solemn ceremonies. Anne Hurle, sentenced to death in 1804 at the age of twenty-two for having forged a letter of attorney, was hanged in the old-fashioned way, from a tripod scaffold erected in the yard of the Old Bailey. She and a fellow prisoner, Methuselah Spalding (indicted for an 'unnatural crime', probably homosexual relations), were driven by cart to the gallows, where nooses were fixed about their necks and the cart driven from beneath them. The first reaction of the crowd was mass jeering, as they saw they were to be deprived of the more spectacular, but costlier, trapdoor hanging, with its awe-inspiring plunge into eternity. At this display of rowdiness, 'the sheriff in a loud voice described to them the impropriety of their behaviour, after which they were silent'. The respectful silence was only momentary, however, giving way to groans of horror at the manner of Hurle's death: '[s]he gave a faint scream, and, for two or three minutes after she was suspended, appeared to be in great agony, moving her hands up and down frequently'.

What was there of shame in the arsonist Charles White's hanging? He tussled unceasingly on his way to the platform, kicking out at the executioner and managing to shake the hood off his head, and when the trap dropped, he struggled with such tenacity that he succeeded in getting his feet back on to the edge of the hole above him, freeing his hands from the restraints, so that he could hold on to the rope above his head and relieve the pressure on his throat. The hangman had to knock his feet away, and then pull down on his legs until the neck vertebrae snapped. From cheering the condemned man's indomitability, the watching crowd turned to shrieking with repulsion as his engorged and exposed face swung before them in continuing agony. To see the features of the hanged was to be reminded too nearly of his or her expiring humanity. In any case, at no stage in such a gruesome fiasco as this – and there were many other such incidences, even after execution was carried out privately – could anybody involved in the proceedings be said to be overcome by what should have been the didactic contrition of the victim. The problem is that in insisting on too much humiliation in the guilty, the shaming process becomes dangerously counter-productive. If, as I have argued, every negative emotion must have its corresponding positive moral virtue, then the heroic obverse of shame must surely be something like Charles White's defiance, a defiance that his fellow human beings could not help but admire.

The Treaty of Versailles is history's most catastrophic example of the shaming process backfiring, but the risk of setting in motion a cycle of revenge through punishment is still apparent in the continuing unrest in the Middle East. What drives defiance in these contexts is a sense of honour, the need to right perceived wrongs, the restitution of balance. The unpalatable truth is that, if we are ever to free ourselves from continuous retribution, whether it be on a personal level or in relation to current international conflicts, a certain amount of shame must be accepted, indeed even shrugged off, to prevent the cycle of violence from continuing, *ad infinitum*. Our hope in this endeavour should be to recall that the shame we feel for personal causes naturally wishes to be short-lived, and that not much of human benefit can accrue from an entire community taking upon itself a collective, unexpungeable shame, for evermore.

Some condemned to public execution went to their deaths stone-cold sober and unrepentant, declining to mutter humble prayers, but facing their fates with bravado. In those convicted, even of the worst crimes, it is hard not to feel a quiet regard for their courage *in extremis*, which attained a pitch beyond what most of the rest of us will ever have to summon. The same attitude in disgraced politicians today, however, reminds us that a measure of shame (whose name is cried in the British Parliament when a Member verges on tastelessness or a lack of compassion) is what constitutes true bravery in the face of guilt. Not all humiliation is unwarranted, even if for some, as we shall see in the next chapter, its merits have been raised to the level of a fetish.

21

I AM SHAMED

After Thomas Becket's assassination in Canterbury Cathedral in December 1170, at the hands of agents of Henry II, the monks and priests tending his decapitated body for burial came upon a detail of his innermost life that none had previously known or suspected. Underneath his archiepiscopal habit, which had been sent to him by Pope Alexander III, he had for several years since his enthronement been wearing a hair shirt. Coarsely woven from goats' hair, it was a garment specifically designed to cause major irritation to the wearer's skin. Every movement of the body within it would be an abrasive, scratching penance, a reminder that, although designed to receive pleasurable sensations, the skin could also be an organ of torment, the more acute because of its extensive surface area. In Becket's case, the abrasion was heightened by the fact that the secret garment was crawling with lice. To the stoicism he had adopted in his suicidal confrontations with the King, he had added the forbearance of living with the fact of being eaten alive, day and night, by exponentially multiplying bloodsuckers.

The desire to suffer, to bring down shame and humiliation upon oneself, predates that more recent historical phenomenon known as masochism, first identified in the 1880s by researchers in the field of sexual diversity. Throughout the Christian era at least, suffering has been elevated to the level of the sublime, by a theology more or less explicitly founded on the denial of the flesh. One way of denying oneself even the accidental pleasure that the body sometimes delivers was deliberately to pursue acts and practices that guaranteed discomfort, even pain. The individual who chose this path was not only mortifying the sinful flesh, but imitating the example of the Saviour, who had yielded up his own life amid intense suffering for the sake of humanity. Addressing the specific question of martyrdom in his tract *Ad Martyres*, Tertullian defiantly asks of the pagan Roman governors: 'For who is not incited by the contemplation of it [i.e. willingly borne persecution] to inquire what there is in the core of the matter? And who, after having joined us, does not long to suffer?' Indeed, there was no shortage of candidates among the first Christians, beginning with the apostles themselves, all but one of whom died martyrs' deaths. Stephen's death by stoning is recounted in the Acts of the Apostles. As he sank to his knees under the pelting, it is recorded, he continued to pray for the souls of the angry mob. James, the son of Zebedee, was put to the sword on the orders of King Herod about ten years after Christ's crucifixion. Others were themselves crucified: St Peter upside down (at his own request), St Andrew on the transverse cross that bears his name, St Bartholomew after first being flayed alive. Their readily surrendered lives form the bedrock of the Church's first claim to divine revelation, still inscribed in the Catholic Catechism in the words, 'Martyrdom is the supreme witness given to the truth of the faith.' How can the articles of Christianity not be true if those who knew Jesus went to these lengths in testifying for him?

There is more than simply religious fervour in these accounts of martyrdoms. Many through the generations have found the accounts of them exercise a strange, compelling fascination for the excess of natural suffering they describe, as well as the peculiar notion of willingly accepted agony. As a child, the Austrian aristocrat Leopold von Sacher-Masoch experienced a terrible thrill on reading of the passionate sufferings of the martyrs and the confessors. He wondered what it would be like to be in their position, to welcome a tidal wave of extreme pain into one's body instead of cravenly seeking to protect it all the time. What he was stumbling towards was the revelation, elaborated in the novels he wrote as an adult, that pain could be rewarding, not just spiritually but sexually. In the most famous of these, *Venus in Furs* (1869), his narrator Severin is contractually bound to a woman, Wanda, whom he encourages to treat him cruelly during the preordained term of an erotic liaison. He recounts the stories of the Christian martyrs to her during their periods of greatest intimacy, implicitly inviting a comparison between his own contrived sufferings and those of the apostles. Sacher-Masoch seems to recognise that there may not be the same nobility in such suffering, but the welcoming of it is what joins Severin to their example.

Something of the same ambiguous attitude is reflected in the figure of Roger Chillingworth, the physician in *The Scarlet Letter*, and the adulterous heroine Hester Prynne's estranged husband. Going about under an assumed name, he bears the full knowledge of who it was who cuckolded him.

In a word, old Roger Chillingworth was a striking evidence of man's faculty of transforming himself into a devil, if he will only, for a reasonable space of time, undertake a devil's office. This unhappy person had effected such a transformation by devoting himself, for seven years, to the constant analysis of a heart full of torture, and deriving his enjoyment thence, and adding fuel to those fiery tortures which he analysed and gloated over.

Meanwhile, his wife's erstwhile adulterous lover, the sickly but much admired priest Arthur Dimmesdale, speaks of his own need to be recognised as worthless:

'Had I one friend ... to whom, when sickened with the praises of all other men, I could daily betake myself, and be known as the vilest of all sinners, methinks my soul might keep itself alive thereby.'

Had he been living in latter times, he would have found a number of urban nightclubs capable of supplying just that need. The end result of Chillingworth's and Dimmesdale's self-torment may be the opposite of what the Christian martyrs achieve, but underlining their actions is a radical voluntarism, the satisfied acceptance of pain and ignominy.

Running through Hawthorne's narrative is the persistent acknowledgement of shame, whose shadow falls upon all three of the principal characters. The very word is uttered like an incantation throughout the novel, and its accompanying expiation consists in that 'positive and vivacious suffering', the 'long and exquisite suffering', evoked in the chapters in which Hester takes her daughter for a walk in the primeval forest. In the pre-civilised, Edenic environment of the forest, shame's potency is rapidly eroded to the point where Hester and her child's father can begin to make peace between and within themselves, and Hester can tear off the scarlet letter and throw it away, at least for a time. The forest in the novel is a typically late Romantic construct, a New World setting in which the moral tenets of the Old might be symbolically cast off. Twenty years later, Lewis Carroll let Alice wander through this same environment, as the Wood where things have no names, in *Through The Looking-Glass* (1871). Just as Hester's little Pearl is attended, in all her knowing purity of heart, by an extraordinary bestiary of docile woodland creatures – a partridge and its young, a benignly cooing pigeon, a squirrel that flings a playful nut at her, a sleepy fox, even an amiable wolf that offers its head to be patted – so Alice too is accompanied by a friendly fawn that, on emergence into the daylight at the end of the sylvan path, suddenly recalls their respective identities and bounds away in startlement.

Back in the real world, however, there is shame to be experienced once more. But what would this 'vivacious' and 'exquisite' suffering entail? The answer, in the psychological mood of the mid-nineteenth century, lay in its sensuous enjoyment. Before the

pioneering German psychologist Richard von Krafft-Ebing purloined the latter half of Sacher-Masoch's name to denote a sexual
predilection for pain and humiliation, the novelist himself had
preferred the studiedly Romantic term 'supersensualism'. It was
intended to evoke a state of heightened receptivity that could be
brought on by willingly undergoing tactile experiences that our
evolutionary lives have taught us to shun. If suffering can be seen as
'vivacious', life-affirming, instead of morbid, some release into a
previously unexplored sensual life might be afforded. The nineteenth century is the era in which, for the first time, the devotional
term used for the sufferings of Christ, the Passion, begins to be
truly ambiguous.

In Krafft-Ebing's monumental *Psychopathia Sexualis* (1886),
masochism is defined as going hand in hand with what was then
thought to be its complementary perversion, sadism – the sexual
urge to inflict pain rather than receive it, which takes its name from
the Marquis de Sade. Freud at first accepted Krafft-Ebing's dual
definition, erroneously declaring in the *Three Essays on the Theory
of Sexuality* (1905) that masochism is an offshoot of sadism, the
other side of the same troubling impulse. By the time he came to
write the 1924 paper 'The Economic Problem of Masochism', however, he had openly disavowed this earlier view, and acknowledged
that there were indeed cases of what he now called 'primary
masochism', people whose desires had only ever tended in the
direction of wishing to undergo pain. He identified three types of
masochism: erotogenic (in which the pure sensation of pain itself is
sought for reasons of sexual arousal), feminine (in which the male
subject wishes to take on what is seen as the traditionally passive
female role) and moral. Moral masochists are those who simply
want to be found guilty, even where they have perpetrated no
wrong. They are suffering from the overdeveloped conscience that
western civilisation has wrought in many of us. This strain of
masochism may have loosened its connection with the explicitly

sexual, but it involves the same willingness to expose oneself to torment. Such people can be identified by the way in which they are likely to forget whatever has been troubling them as soon as a new cause of guilt presents itself. It should be noted that, in all cases, Freud is talking about masochistic men. To early psychoanalysis, there is nothing particularly remarkable about women wanting to be passive victims; it is only a psychosexual problem where it pertains to males.

According to Freud, the psychic struggle in which masochism develops is between the ego, which may not be conscious of wanting to suffer, and the superego – cast as our lives progress in the roles of parental authority, the judgements of the external world, and finally a sense of our own inescapable destiny – which exercises a regulatory, necessarily prohibitive, influence over the ego. What Freud calls a '*a cultural suppression of the instincts*' is at work:

[T]he suppression of an instinct can – frequently or quite generally – result in a sense of guilt and . . . a person's conscience becomes more severe and more sensitive the more he refrains from aggression against others.

This instinctual renunciation, forced upon us by external powers, is what creates our sense of ethics and therefore our conscience, which in turn demands a further, and often excessive, renunciation of instinct. We are all at the mercy of two countervailing but irresistible instincts, given the names, in Freud's work, of Eros and Thanatos, the life and death drives. Contained within the death drive is the natural urge to destroy, which must find its occasional and healthy outlet. Freud's suggestion in the 1924 paper – and it is very much, as he owns, a speculative postulate – is that masochism is a part of the death instinct that has escaped, because of the overweening influence of the moral conscience of the superego, from what he terms normal destructive urges. This, precisely, is its danger. The urge turns on itself. Where it is linked to erotic factors, the subject's self-destructiveness brings with it 'libidinal satisfaction', resulting in a (male) individual who prefers to be on the receiving end of sexual initiative rather than taking responsibility for it, who has taken on what is presumed to be the woman's desire to be violated.

There are many assumptions in Freud's argument that seem risible in an age when most consensual sexual proclivities are, if not fully accepted, then at least well on the way towards that status. But Freud's ideas represent a rather more advanced stage of thinking than is evident in many of those who followed him. Erich Fromm argues in *The Anatomy of Human Destructiveness* that masochists are those who don't react to what he calls 'normal stimuli', finding it difficult to initiate excitement, and only able to experience it when it is forced upon them. On this view, a masochist would be somebody who hoped to live a life free of sexual stimulation, a view that our awareness of modern sexual practices makes it easy to refute. 'Both the sadist and the masochist', Fromm announces, 'need another being to "complete" them.' This may make one wonder what it is about this dysfunctional pair that is so at odds with ordinary sexual relations. Are the partners in a relationship that is entirely consecrated to 'normal stimuli' therefore wholly autonomous from one another?

Richard Webster, upon whom nobody who valued their own intellectual reputation could pin the label 'Freudian', puts the more persuasive argument that many people do simply suffer from Freud's 'moral masochism', manifested as a need to confess, to own up to infractions and misjudgements as though their sanity depended upon it. There are many instances of patients who mutilate themselves out of a sense of their own guilt, often focused on a form of shame at their own excretory functions, and can only achieve alleviation through the act of self-indictment and the receipt of some sternly judgemental absolution. Manifestations of this neurosis include the resort to the Catholic confessional and the psychoanalyst's couch, but it is also found in many of these cases that masochistic sexual practices can fulfil the same function. If the need to confess, to have one's badness acknowledged – and punished – by others, is so strong, then the relief of such an overloaded conscience brings a pleasure comparable to the relief of sexual satisfaction. Nathaniel Hawthorne – whom Webster rightly celebrates, alongside Dickens and Dostoevsky, as 'one of the greatest anatomists of guilt' – doesn't explicitly make the link between shame and pleasure, but it is nonetheless there, in all three of the main protagonists of *The Scarlet Letter*, hinted at in their tumultuous emotional lives.

Addressing the fundamental question of why we so enjoy tragic art, Terry Eagleton suggests that perhaps the apparent sadistic pleasure taken from watching the sufferings of others, and the aesthetic enjoyment derived from it, lies in its role as a displacement activity from the masochistic satisfaction we secretly crave.

What if we would rather confess our enjoyment of another's agony than acknowledge the shaming truth that the destruction we most revel in is our own? Could our wryly conceded sadism be yet another mask for the death drive?

A resounding 'yes' would have been Freud's answer to this, but the question, which has worried many thinkers since Aristotle in the *Poetics*, is somehow always more complicated. To the extent that seeing the sufferings of others in the great works is unbearable, so to the same degree, we are not merely revelling in their pain, but undergoing it with them in some empathic sense as well. The twin emotions that classical tragedy expected us to feel, according to Aristotle, are terror (*phobos*) and pity (*eleos*), the latter being what Walter Kaufmann, in *Tragedy and Philosophy* (1968), translated as 'ruth', that is, the opposite of ruthlessness. We cast off – for the duration of the play or the film anyway – the hardened exterior with which we habitually react to the miseries of strangers. We remember our common humanity and our shared capacity for suffering, and find ourselves wishing, in that utopian moment only art can create, that things were not inevitably so. None of this, it has to be said, sounds much like sadistic enjoyment. Indeed, it would be hard to imagine anybody going to the theatre in order once more to see King Lear carrying the lifeless body of his only faithful daughter into the final scene and relish the feeling that it serves the old fool right.

Reconciling suffering and the pleasure that can be gained from it says less about suffering than it does about pleasure. It isn't necessarily odd that a state of physical atonement should be satisfying; it is distinctly more peculiar to find that one's repertoire of pleasures should include physical pain or discomfort. Novelist and critic Anita Phillips, in *A Defence of Masochism* (1998), has argued that we make a sort of category error if we imagine that the masochist simply finds pain pleasurable, in some looking-glass inversion of ordinary sensual experience. Pain is still painful, discomfiting; at the moment one receives it, one wishes for an instant that it wasn't happening. However, Phillips says, the fact of being on the receiving end of it, in the circumstances in which it is administered, are what is erotic to the masochist. To those who live and work entirely in the intellectual realm, it can offer a dose of bracing reality. For Phillips, the sting of pain is a commodity 'that no sophisticated intellect can defuse or deflate'. For someone in her milieu, it is the ultimate bit of rough, not in the sense of dating somebody who would rather eat fish and chips on the seafront than sit in the dining room of the Grand Hotel, but a mode of sexual conduct in which the life of the mind can be truly suspended, while one is oneself suspended in handcuffs, waiting to be flogged. Simultaneously preposterous and delicious, masochistic sex appears scandalous to the uninitiated because, as Freud already intimated, it seems to refer to death and decay, to the mortification of the will. That said, any idea that it is a purely self-referential kind of sensuality, that one could inflict it on oneself in the privacy of one's own bathroom, is absolutely to miss the point, according to Phillips. It depends on a complicit partner who will act within certain pre-agreed boundaries, but will continually surprise, alarm and terrify. (It also helps enormously if the other person isn't simply a boring sadist, because they are the people who don't want you to have fun.) In this erotic symbiosis, we learn that:

[o]ne of the messages of masochism is that one should do one's suffering in company, rather than being alone with it. The enemy is not suffering, but disconnectedness . . .

Phillips argues that, far from being an admission of self-contempt, masochism can only really properly be practised by those who have power in their own non-sexual lives. For those with responsibilities, it represents a holiday from decision-making, and she suggests that this could explain why so many senior politicians and judges engage in masochistic sex games. Bondage, claims Phillips, is one of the healthy ways of learning emotional attachment and trust. If you love the partner who is playing the role of your tormentor, you will love him or her the more for exercising both severity and kindness towards you. Moreover, the post-orgasmic state is immensely heightened by having added to its condition of thrilled exhaustion a whole series of other localised sensations of ebbing pain, stinging and prickling, together with the unearthly feeling of tactile sensation returning to those parts of the body that had gone numb through impeded circulation. One now feels bound to the other in a way that transcends both ordinary cuddling and the silly paraphernalia of restraints and chains that had concretely symbolised the bonds between you moments ago. In this state of pure physicality, the doubled tenderness of the embrace that follows is like no other.

If, however, one reacts to the idea of masochistic sex with unease, the source of that perhaps lies in its normalising of abusive power relations. We can fairly take Phillips's point that not all devotees of masochism are pathetic victims in the rest of their lives, but many are, and there must be many of those – Freud's moral masochists among them – who cannot achieve satisfaction in any other way. Masochistic relationships contain the evident danger that, as the physical pleasure involved in them becomes psychologically addictive, so one comes to reconstruct one's own identity in ways that are considerably less conducive to empowerment, within not just the masochistic relationship, but also the circumstances of one's non-sexual life.

Secondly, masochism is still seen as what writers like Phillips and the theorist of gay sexuality Jonathan Dollimore call 'transgressive' sex, this practice too will in due course assume the same level of normality towards which homosexuality is progressing. One does meet straight young men who, more or less earnestly, seem to wish they were gay, which was certainly not the case in my own school-day nightmare of the 1970s. Sooner or later, many people will want to be masochists, or at least try masochism. The problem remains, however, that the constructed fantasies of masochists are anything but conducive to enlightened social attitudes. The subjugation of women, the repression of minority ethnic groups, the depressing preponderance of Nazi iconography in the literature, are not themes that sit comfortably with being sexualised within mainstream culture, when such cost has been expended in ridding ourselves of them. That these are only games doesn't quite absolve these fantasies of their moral ambiguity. Phillips claims that there is nothing inherently contradictory in playing at being tortured and being a vocal member of a human rights pressure group. Yet if repression is thrilling, how can it also be morally outrageous? Is it morally unproblematic to devote one's emotional life to an activist from a neo-fascist party, just because he is good-looking? 'Masochistic pleasure,' according to Phillips, 'does not merely reflect inequalities and unfairness, however; it *eroticises* them', a claim that could also stand, unqualified, in condemnation of it. Towards the close of her book, she notes with barely a pause for reflection that recent history has seen socialism 'well and truly annihilated', suggesting with a sigh of Fukuyamian relief that there will now be nothing to stand in the way of the flourishing enactment of privilege and power within sexual relations. To some, this might seem a rather heavy price to pay for a relatively modest increment in sexual liberty. The deepening of trust between partners is what sanctifies it, because, as Phillips avers, '[b]ondage is not much fun if there is nobody around to untie you'. Indeed not. Centuries of economic exploitation, and the cauterised emotional lives it produced in a great mass of humanity, already testify to that. None of this is intended to suggest an approval of the judicial attitude that saw a group of consenting adult men engaging in sado-masochistic sex in Sheffield in 1990 arraigned in court and given custodial sentences, which were upheld, shamefully, by the European Court of Human Rights. The right to consenting sex ought to be sacrosanct.

There is a fairly heady quotient of straightforward objectification in masochistic sex, and this, I think, is its most damning quality. It may indeed be the case that, between two established lovers, the bond of trust is deepened and complicated in all sorts of productive ways by this mode of sexual behaviour. As a first preference between those who have never met, however, there seems something strangely sterile about it. The excess of physical pleasure – *jouissance* in the present vocabulary – that is supposed to contain release appears rather one-dimensional when the partners involved have no other business to transact than ritualised humiliation. I am not making a moral point about casual sex, which has a perfectly honourable place in human experience, but when the only activity on the agenda is highly stylised role-playing, I wonder whether the potential for a richer, more emotionally nuanced sex life isn't being forfeited. This isn't a sin of course, just a shame. As Anita Phillips reminds us, 'The masochistic pose is one of exaggerated servility, the body language speaks of weakness and even shame.' Quite so. It is just that many, perhaps most, people have spent a significant part of their lives learning to overcome shame and the debilitating lassitude it carries within it. More liberating than willingly undergoing this painful emotional state is the attitude of Poly Styrene, the greatest vocal stylist of the punk generation, who launched her brief career in pop with the rebel yell, 'OH BONDAGE! UP YOURS!'

EMBARRASSMENT

Better a blush on the face than a blot on the heart.
Miguel de Cervantes

Embarrass 1. To encumber, hamper, impede (movements, actions, persons). **b.** *pass.* Of persons: To be encumbered with debts; to be 'in difficulties'. **2.** To perplex (in thought). **3.** To render difficult; to complicate (a question, etc.).

Embarrassment 1. Embarrassed state or condition, *esp.* of pecuniary affairs, circumstances, etc. **b.** Perplexity, confusion of thought; hesitation; constraint arising from bashfulness or timidity. **2.** Something which embarrasses.

Darwin's physical indicators: blushing; averting of the gaze; turning away of the face; involuntary movements of the eyes; partial or complete closing of the eyes; awkward or involuntary muscular movements (twitching); rapid heartbeat; irregular breathing.

22

TO BE EMBARRASSED

A man whose wife has left him, and who has been stymied in trying to commit suicide when the high window from which he wants to jump won't open, drops in on an old friend for solace. The friend, a sports journalist, is hosting a card game amid the spectacular squalor of his apartment, where potato chips cascade on to the floor, the sandwiches contain an unidentifiable green substance, and the rising midsummer heat has coated everybody with a thick film of sweat. With the card-players swiftly dismissed, the journalist takes his suicidal friend out to a late-night delicatessen.

While sitting and discussing his plight, the abandoned husband Felix Unger (Jack Lemmon) notices that his sinuses are beginning to silt up, as a result, probably, of the over-efficiency of the air conditioning. This necessitates an elaborate unblocking procedure, in which he massages the sides of his neck while emitting a series of explosive sneezes, accompanied by a crescendo of guttural cries. Eventually, we imagine that everybody else in the place has been stopped in their tracks by this performance, and has turned to stare. The excruciating discomfort of the moment is written all over the habitually inscrutable face of his friend Oscar Madison (Walter Matthau). A man who has no compunction about inviting guests into a pigsty of an apartment is momentarily overcome by an emotion quite foreign to him. Indeed, the import of the whole scene, coming early as it does in *The Odd Couple* (1968), is to signal to us that Felix is a character so impossible to put up with that he can even reduce the thick-skinned Oscar to a state of squirming embarrassment.

There are people – the thick-skinned and hard-faced, the highly self-regarding – who claim to have no capacity for embarrassment. Such people often insist that they don't really know what it means, and indeed, of all the emotions we encounter in this survey, embarrassment is the one most resistant to definition. To some extent, all the emotions, in that they are primal states of feeling, are difficult to define in any but their own terms, but whereas one can, for example, describe fear as a sense of being inwardly churned up by the presentiment of danger, embarrassment is much less apprehensible. Could this be because, unlike fear, it isn't after all a primal emotion? We can imagine Palaeolithic peoples in the grip of mortal terror, rage, even unhappiness, but not quite embarrassment. Did the hunter who unleashed his spear at the fleeing gazelle, only to see it rebound off the trunk of a nearby tree, find himself wishing the earth would swallow him up as his mates broke into a snigger? Embarrassment is surely a much later cultural construct, born of the refinement of social manners in Georgian England. Its earliest recorded usage in the modern sense dates only from 1774, but it had passed sufficiently seamlessly into the literary discourse of the early nineteenth century for Sir Walter Scott to be able to describe one of his virtuous maidens as being in a state of embarrassment. No synonym will henceforth serve its place. So what is it, in fact?

Intending to meet it head on, compilers of dictionaries seem to find themselves flailing about, not knowing where to look for the analogical phrases that will precisely capture the state of embarrassment. The *Shorter Oxford* offers 'Perplexity, confusion of thought; hesitation; constraint arising from bashfulness or timidity', which comes reasonably close without quite pinpointing the acutely discomfiting feeling of loss of face that it always entails.

The *Collins Concise* gets a little nearer in identifying 'confusion or self-consciousness', the latter surely an indispensable element. To embarrass somebody is to 'disconcert' them, it suggests. What both lack is any acknowledgement of the circumstantial stimuli. The *Oxford*'s 'bashfulness or timidity' are good enough reasons to be embarrassed, but what is described are character traits. What about that which embarrasses the bold and the headstrong? Those who claim to be incapable of embarrassment may be less prone to it, but surely each has his or her Achilles' heel, as is demonstrated on reality TV programmes that put people in compromising social positions to see how they will react. Interestingly, spectacles such as these are quite unwatchable to many, for whom a controlled dose of administered embarrassment possesses neither the thrill of aroused fear nor the satisfaction of released anger, but is simply, ineluctably, embarrassing.

Darwin discusses embarrassment at length in *Expression*, without quite being able to bring himself to name it. He talks of shame and guilt, which are quite different, though related, entities, but even when he is clearly focusing on situations where no other word will do – such as accidental breaches of etiquette, or the flustered feeling one has when somebody mishears a remark of ours as something grossly offensive – the word itself is missing. This is unfathomable, in that by the time the book was written, the terminology of embarrassment had already been in currency for around a century. It was hardly a new coinage, and must at least have occurred to the writer, and yet it is as though it is somehow too pallid or too frivolous a term to denote the mysteriously powerful sensation of which Darwin's chapter otherwise speaks so eloquently.

Before we proceed any further, let me risk showing myself up by essaying a workable definition of this elusive commodity. To be embarrassed is to be placed in a temporary state of suspension by the unwanted scrutiny – sometimes critical, often not – of others. It is to be involuntarily placed at the epicentre of a particular social moment, and is marked by an overheated, prickly sensation of excruciated unease, a feeling in which the very carapace of one's being seems to crack and collapse in on itself. For a few seconds, we are as helpless as if all our major joints had been disarticulated, and to meet any one of the burning pairs of eyes focused on us would only defer the longed-for recovery. What makes that recovery all the harder is that the condition we are in is quite likely to have been painted luridly on our faces in throbbing crimson. As Darwin rightly points out, this is an emotion that feeds on itself, so that concentrating on not blushing only increases the likelihood of doing so, precisely because it intensifies the very phenomenon that causes embarrassment – attention to the self. There is some evidence that blushing may affect any part of the body on which attention, especially critical attention, is fixed, so that a woman learning the piano is said to have reported that when her teacher stood behind her while she was playing, her hands blushed.

Darwin satisfies himself that blushing is trans-cultural, or at least that, among races where it doesn't seem spontaneously to occur, it can be instilled by social example. One of his respondents informs him that the Chinese tend not to blush (even though they have a verbal usage, *tōng hóng*, that connotes the idea of reddening from shame). It is also reported, though, that those Chinese who had been employed as domestic servants by European families blushed very readily and profusely, especially when their personal appearance was criticised. For some reason, this appears to have been a source of surprise to those uncouth enough to have provoked it. According to the Book of Jeremiah, the Jews are a non-blushing race. When confronted with their abominations, 'they were not at all ashamed, neither could they blush' (6:15). Notwithstanding this, the author of Ezra cries out, 'O my God, I am ashamed and blush to lift up my face to thee' (9:6). In either case the King James version is a translation of another of those words, kalam, that denote a general state of shame or humiliation. There is nothing, etymologically, to link it to the reddening of the face. Respondents informing Darwin of the physiological characteristics of black Africans tell him that, while no red tone may be seen when they are embarrassed, there is a noticeable darkening of the skin, which is how facial flushing is registered in high-melanin skin pigmentation. It is noted that very young children do not blush, only learning to do so at around the age of two, while young adults blush more than the elderly, women more than men, and each sex more in the company of the other than among its own.

It is not just aversive attention that triggers the discomfiture of self-consciousness; excessive praise can have the same effect. Finding oneself singled out before others for some acclamation is not often a pleasant experience, especially if it is strongly felt that one doesn't seriously merit the plaudits being heaped on one. It is impossible to control blushing, not simply because any attempt to do so guarantees that one's face will disobligingly colour up, but also because the blush has always already started before one is aware of it. Blushing is often followed by a brief, unnatural pallor, as too much blood flows back out of the facial capillaries, so that the whole process resembles the ebbing and flowing of a fever, all distilled into a lightning moment of pure psychical ill-being.

Both shame and embarrassment, while they are productive of anxiety within the individual, are also characterised physiologically by a state of muscular lassitude. While anger and fear are high-tensile states that tend to tauten the muscles, embarrassment and shame are accompanied by a feeling of things drooping, withering away, dissolving as one tries to retreat from one's sense of self. The muscular armature of the facial arteries relaxes, allowing blood to flow rapidly into the capillaries, the concentration of which causes reddening of the skin. In some people, the face flushes evenly; in others, there may be a visually fascinating sequence, perhaps beginning on the forehead or in the centre of each cheek, before radiating downwards or outwards. Some people blush only on the face, but the reddening can spread over a large tract of the upper body in others.

The evolutionary point of blushing remains hard to determine. When blushing from embarrassment, modesty or excessive shyness, the face is mimicking the reaction produced by the effect on the circulation of such external influences as standing too near a powerful source of heat, or drinking too much alcohol. In these circumstances, the warning of potential danger thus conveyed is all the more forceful for being so graphically legible, but why would it be useful for oneself or others to know that one was embarrassed? Darwin suggests that the involuntary reddening of the face is a means by which we let others know that we realise we have committed some social transgression or breach of etiquette. We are not shameless in our error, but readily acknowledge it in this non-verbal way, so as not to be thought responsible for insouciantly undermining the unspoken rules of social engagement. Assuming the fault is not especially grave, a verbal apology is not generally thought to be necessary, when the lividly flushing face and averted gaze are already eloquent enough. Darwin's argument may be convincing, but it only fits those cases where we can accept that we have been, however inadvertently, at fault. Where simple shyness, social timidity, an excess of modesty, or finding oneself the object of unaccustomed attention, are the cause of blushing, it is hard to comprehend what the point of it is. In all these cases, the physical manifestation of embarrassment can be radically disabling, since facial colouring always brings with it that state of mental confusion that is rightly cited in the dictionary definitions. For a few moments, we are completely lost for words, unable to get our bearings or remember what it was we intended to say, and equally incapable of composing our thoughts sufficiently to resolve the crisis. It is this aspect of embarrassment that marks it out as such a relatively recent historical development.

A couple of Darwin's contemporaries, his compatriot and consultant Dr James Crichton Browne and a German pharmacologist, Professor Wilhelm Filehne, suggest that the extremity of blushing is what also accounts for the mental confusion experienced during acute embarrassment, and that the same effect can be produced under the administration of a direct physical stimulant. Both Crichton Browne and Filehne point to the mental befuddlement of patients given amyl nitrite, a deep inhalation of which causes intense facial flushing and, after an initial moment of potent stimulation, a state of helpless mental disequilibrium. Both the psychic and physical stimuli appear to act on the same vaso-motor centre of the brain, producing the muscular relaxation that leads to blushing. Only when blood begins to flow back out of the facial capillaries are the mental faculties capable of re-orientating themselves. That a mental hiatus is an essential ingredient in embarrassment is lexically indicated in the word itself. Even before the notions of self-consciousness and discomfort under attention creep into the definitions as the causes of embarrassment, the condition itself is referred to as a suspension of mental functions, a blockage, literally an 'embarment' (from the Old French *embarrasser*, meaning to bar the progress of, to impede, or to hinder). In its French nominal form, *embarras*, it contains the idea of immobilisation through superfluity, so that, on entering the wine merchant's and being faced by shelves groaning under an *embarras de richesse* or an *embarras de choix*, one is temporarily unable to make a selection. In English, we are merely spoiled, in the sense of being pampered, by so much choice. In French, one is embarred, rendered inutile, before it. (A picturesque southern American borrowing of the nineteenth century uses the French term '*embarras*' to refer to a point in a river where navigation has been made difficult, embarred, through an accumulation of driftwood.)

There is an undoubted connection between shame and embarrassment, although it is a relatively tenuous one. While the reasons for which we experience embarrassment tend to be notably less drastic (committing a *faux pas* at the dinner table, or finding oneself short of the right money at the corner store), the difference is not simply one of degree. There may be embarrassment in our public shaming, but not necessarily shame in our being embarrassed. A sense of exposure is common to both, but to be embarrassed is not as inwardly directed an emotion as is shame. It doesn't cut one off from the social world, but marks a momentary rupture with it. It represents a loss of self-esteem without guilt.

To the Japanese, the face has two generic dispositions, each with its own term. *Tatamae* is the public face that one shows to the outside world and in formal company, while *honne* is what one normally hides inside, one's true feelings. The same duality once applied in British society, reaching its apogee of refinement in late Georgian and Victorian times, but the distinction now operates at a much more subconscious level. Today, in Britain, we are encouraged to voice our feelings more, to be more upfront, with the result that we are more prone to moments of embarrassment. In Japan, this emotion is still regarded as something to be foreseen and headed off, so that a man who has recently been made unemployed will continue to dress for work, leave the house at the same time and take the commuter train as always (even if he is going to while away the day in a café reading the newspaper), so as to spare his family any embarrassment.

In all the circumstances discussed so far, the face reddens in that it is seen, and not just seen but scrutinised, focused on, by others. This raises the question as to whether embarrassment can ever be a wholly private emotion. Can one blush when alone? Is it possible to avoid embarrassment if one's face is obscured? Do we blush if accused of some insensitivity over the telephone? The answers seem to be in the affirmative. Some of Darwin's own respondents, women particularly, claim they have no immunity from blushing in the first two of the above contexts, leading him to detect an error in Act II, scene ii of *Romeo and Juliet*, when Shakespeare has Juliet say to her lover, 'Thou know'st the mask of night is on my face; / Else would a maiden blush bepaint my cheek.' Another correspondent, gallantly stepping into the breach in the dramatist's defence, suggests that the text does not necessarily disagree with Darwin's point, but rather implies that Juliet's blush is hidden by darkness, not that the darkness has prevented it. Her construction doesn't quite sustain the point, though: she doesn't say 'If it weren't dark, you would see me blushing', but 'If it weren't dark, I would be blushing'. It is possible, though, to blush without witnesses, as Darwin affirms, which would suggest that embarrassment can be felt under self-scrutiny as much as under the scrutiny of others, perhaps not quite as readily, but certainly as intensely when it does happen.

There is a persuasive case to be made that the life of our emotions has become externalised, publicised, over the course of the last century. Whereas once we dealt with our feelings internally, confiding the abrasions and scars life left on us to personal journals or close kin, or otherwise taking them with us to the crematorium, we now feel increasingly comfortable about openly demonstrating them. What it misses is the less busy traffic that has gone by in the opposite direction. Some of what was once expressed publicly has become internalised. This is surely the case with a phenomenon like social rage, at least to the extent that it gets bottled up and eventually implodes in the form of traumatic stress. Phobic fear, too, is very often a condition with which one suffers in silence and solitude. It strikes me that embarrassment, that apparently most public of emotions, can also fit this pattern, for precisely the reasons that Darwin intimated. Lacking for any external judge, we supply the role within ourselves, as is evidenced when one blushes at the mere recollection of an embarrassment. This may well be healthy, healthier at least than not having any such faculty at all, but like all other emotions, our facility for feeling embarrassment can become overdeveloped. We know from the fieldwork of Paul

Ekman that embarrassment is, as Darwin theorised, trans-cultural – as are the other emotions. Whereas in other cultures, however, mental discomfiture and blushing may communicate anger, or a feeling of being overwhelmed by events, western society appears to have invented a whole new category of experience for it to symbolise. The feeling of being studied or appraised by others, and of being unworthy of their approbation, or else anxious at what inadequacies they will discover, is very much the creation of an entrepreneurial, but still economically hierarchical, society. If we expect to be judged on the evidence of our relative success in life, as opposed to what Martin Luther King referred to as the content of our characters, then we must constantly expect to be found wanting. Even the empire-building plutocrats of this world must expect to be embarrassed from time to time by their lack of intellectual resources, or their anaesthetic indifference to culture, while those who still struggle to pay the monthly bills, or have spent several fruitless years trying to reinvent themselves in a new career, won't lack for opportunities to examine their lives and find them wanting.

If embarrassment is entirely about misplaced modesty, we would be better off without it. If it originates, like the term itself, in a sense of feeling stuck, impeded, then it issues an obvious challenge to us to overcome it. But where it is a way of reminding ourselves that we have a responsibility to others, it can only be – despite all its inhibiting potency and scarlet face-paint – the evidence of an advance in human civility. As Darwin points out at the opening of his chapter on the topic, monkeys don't get embarrassed.

23

I CAUSE YOU EMBARRASSMENT

All the emotions, as we are noting, are capable of active infliction. Fear may be harnessed by state institutions for the maintenance of civil order; anger may be provoked by those organisations that seek precisely to subvert that order. Embarrassment is quite as suscepti- ble to being used in this way, but the contexts in which this might happen, as compared with the deliberate inculcation of public shame, remain at the level where the individual interacts with his or her immediate society. In this respect, it resembles the infliction of jealousy. It is possible for our proclivity for embarrassment to be exploited against us as a form of social punishment, but it will be our peers who so exploit it.

Since embarrassment is so embarrassing to look upon, why would we want to instil it in others? There are two primary explan- ations for this. One is that social decorum depends on everybody observing the same codes of conduct, with the clear implication that to break any one of these codes, even inadvertently, is tanta- mount to letting the side down. That mechanism necessarily involves a voluntary shouldering of the capacity for embarrass- ment. One might also cause embarrassment in others for one's own pecuniary gain. That an individual's capacity for embarrassment can be converted into instant financial return for another conjoins the currencies of embarrassment and cash, as is evidenced by the fact that the state of monetary paralysis is referred to as being financially embarrassed. In a starkly simple mechanism, threatening letters, promising to reveal anything from a foolish peccadillo to a major crime unless an insurance payment against exposure is forthcoming, are sent to the victim. The malevolent intent of these letters, couched though they often are in the language of solicitous courtesy, is what led to their being indicted as 'black mail'.

As she turned thirty-five, Harriette Wilson, Georgian society's most famous blackmailer, began to dream of a rather more salubrious life than that she had thus far enjoyed. She hadn't exactly been lacking for excitement up to that point. As the most renowned and sought-after purveyor of sex in London, she had a client list that a Covent Garden hooker would have given her best suspenders for. The gentry came to her in flocks: earls, dukes, marquises and sundry other members of the House of Peers paid her generously for her imaginative, professional service. Nor was she was averse to taking on the better class of tradesman. For every Marquis of Worcester, there was a self-consciously fumbling doctor, telling himself it was purely out of medical interest that he was palpating her ample breasts; for every Duke of Argyle, there was someone like the lust-crazed Oxford Street haberdasher named Smith, who found himself in financial hot water when unable to redeem the substantial sum Harriette had run up in his shop on credit. It was a life that couldn't go on for ever though, and as she turned her thoughts to securing herself financially through the years of a long, eventful retirement, she realised that she needed to turn one final trick that would underwrite that future life she envisaged for herself. Prostitution was all very well for young girls, but Harriette had her dignity, as well as her expansive tastes, to consider. She rather fancied Paris.

The solution was both simple and ingenious. She would publish her memoirs, a no-holds-barred account of the foibles of a swathe of Regency society, relating the life of a high-class courtesan in as graphic detail as public decency would tolerate. Such literary works were not unknown. The Georgian period had produced other accounts of the unacknowledged, seamy underbelly of polite society in the capital, catering more or less explicitly to the literate public's prurience, some running to successive editions. Even though by 1824, when Harriette sat down to write hers, there was a distinct whiff of the puritanical in the air – faint enough during George IV's reign, to be sure, but nonetheless gathering strength – still, she could be confident that hers would sell, for one straightforward but explosive reason. She intended to name names.

The plan was to publish the work in instalments. A quondam coal merchant and bookseller, Joseph Stockdale, with premises on Opera Colonnade, was to be her conduit. Stockdale's normal stock-in-trade was the kind of merchandise you didn't necessarily wish to be seen purchasing, books and prints of the kind that a generous nature might term 'erotic', but which looked to the unrefined eye like unabashed pornography. He had done particularly well out of a print listed in his catalogue as 'a Magnificent Painting of the Redemption of Coventry by the Countess Godiva'. When Harriette came to him with her proposal, his nostrils must have twitched at the scent of money. An uninhibited account of the sexual dealings of the notability could hardly fail to sell. The author would receive not just a percentage of sales, but at the publication of each instalment, a payment of funds from those whom she gave notice of exposing in the next. It was open to the dukes and earls to buy themselves out of her book, by responding positively and promptly to a letter that typically ended:

... if you [would] like to forward £200 directly to me, else it will be too late. Mind I have no time to write again as what with writing books, & then altering them for those who pay out, I am done up – frappé en mort.

The audacity of it may seem to have begged defiance, but instead it constituted sufficient of a threat for most of those she contacted in this way to pay up without demur. Harriette's advice to them to be expeditious in the matter suggests that some may unwisely have tried to play for time, and then found themselves named in print before they had even begun to negotiate with her. Those of classical education and cultured sensibilities who had bought sex from her must have winced at the unpuncturable affectation of the gutter French (she was after all the daughter of a Swiss clock-mender, who now fancied herself in the role of chic Parisienne), even as they hastily raised the demanded cash. As well as protecting their own reputations, they were of course also thinking of their families. There was clearly no legal way of stopping publication, because Harriette was well-versed enough in defamation law to know that the best defence against a charge of libel is that what you are saying is true. All that those who chose not to give in to the blackmail could hope was that nobody would be interested enough to keep buying instalments of the book, but that was utterly forlorn. They sold like hot penny buns, devoured greedily precisely because their *dramatis personae* were the great and clearly not-so-good of London society. And then there was the tiresome fact that the damn things were so entertainingly written.

Harriette turned out to have a prodigious gift as a mimic, catching the tone and diction of well-known figures of the gentry to the life. The era's most celebrated novelist, Sir Walter Scott, caught this side of the writing well, noting in his journal in December 1825:

She must have been assisted in the stile [sic] spelling and diction though the attempt at wit is poor – that at pathos is sickening. But there is some good retailing of conversations in which the stile of the speakers so far as known to me is exactly imitated.

Scott had met her some years before at a dinner party, and remembered her as a 'smart saucy girl with ... the manners of a wild schoolboy'. The fact that even he couldn't resist a glance at the final published version of the *Memoirs* indicates the degree to which they had seeped into the consciousness of literary London. It was with a distinct note of self-approval that Harriette observed, as her sales began to match those of the author of *Ivanhoe*, 'Now we are the two greatest people in Europe! Scott in his way, I in mine! Everything which comes after us will be but base copies.' Scott is a little too harsh in his judgement of the book. The wit in it is often rather telling, for all that one doesn't have to take the dialogue as a verbatim account of what actually passed between the author and her clients. In many places, the pathos is clearly ironic, and in others laid on so thick that one forbears to read it as anything other than the self-dramatising of a good storyteller, something that neither Scott, nor his even more illustrious successor Dickens, was above. Here she is, apparently distraught, after one of her more devoted paramours, Lord John Ponsonby, has deserted her:

Then I suddenly recollected his parting kiss. Gracious God! could he have left me? My brain seemed absolutely on fire. I flew to the window, where for years I had been in the habit of watching his approach. It is not high enough, thought I, and would but half destroy me. I will go to him first, and my trembling hands essayed, in vain, to fasten the ribbons of my bonnet under my chin; but no, no, I will not risk her happiness. I am not really wicked, not so very wicked as to deserve this dreadful calamity. We are sent into the world to endure the evils of it patiently, and not thus to fly into the face of our God. If he is our Father, and I kneel down to Him with patience, this anguish will be calmed.

I locked my door, and then prostrated myself, with my face on the floor, and prayed fervently for near an hour, that, if I was to see Ponsonby no more, God would take me, in mercy, out of a world of such bitter suffering, before the morning. I arose somewhat comforted; but stiff, and so cold that my whole frame trembled violently. I swallowed some lavender-drops, and tried to write; blotted twenty sheets of paper, with unintelligible nonsense, and wetted them with my tears.

No figure in Harriette Wilson's *Memoirs* bulked quite so large as the hero of Waterloo – Arthur Wellesley, Duke of Wellington. Her procuress, Mrs Porter, had set up the first encounter, reporting that Wellington was ardent of meeting her, and while Harriette affects in the narrative to be as indifferent to him as to any other new client, she recognises openly his pecuniary value. In due course, he became her lover, conveniently replacing the Duke of Argyle, who had not long before returned to Scotland, as her chief paymaster. Although she appears to have regarded him rather sourly – his sombre, predatory look leads her to compare him at one point to 'a rat-catcher' – Wellington became besotted with her, and must have found it tormenting to be threatened with exposure in the *Memoirs* along with every catchpenny tailor and teenage undergraduate marquis she entertained. He was possibly the only named party to threaten to sue her over the book, but Harriette's response was defiance incarnate. She simply added more incriminating detail. On receipt of her final ultimatum to cough up or face the indignity of publication, Wellington is said to have gathered his wits about him, and uttered the celebrated line, 'Publish, and be damned!' Harriette's recent biographers, Valerie Grosvenor Myer and Frances Wilson, have argued that this particular exchange, for which there is no documentary evidence, is unlikely to have taken place, and was perhaps retailed as a way of shoring up Wellington's own buffeted dignity. The fact is that Harriette needed no encouragement to publish, and knew her audience well enough by that time to know that the Wellington passages would be the most lucrative of the whole work. People queued ten deep outside Stockdale's premises when they first went on sale. The dialogue captures the Duke's staccato maladroitness with the language of the boudoir: ' "You should see me where I shine," Wellington observed, laughing. "Where's that, in God's name?" "In a field of battle," answered the hero.' The reader is invited to delight in the mordant facility with which the author maintains the upper hand. We learn that the Duke pines and sighs for her 'by the hour', talks non-stop of her miraculous beauty, and pursues her across the West End without thought for his reputation. On one occasion, she relates with relish how Wellington made a beeline for her on his return from an expedition to Spain, only to find that he had been beaten to her by the handsome Argyle, whereupon 'my tender swain Wellington stood in the gutter at two in the morning, pouring forth his amorous wishes in the pouring rain, in strains replete with heartrending grief'. The detail is both gratuitous and cruel, anticipating the tone of the modern scandal-sheet by well over a century, and helped to ensure that the first edition of the book went into at least twenty printings, with further pirated editions contributing to the general sense among the *beau monde* that Harriette Wilson had become a public nuisance.

It wasn't all plain sailing. Returning from one of her flits to France, Harriette found the wife of one of her victims lying in wait for her on the pierhead at Dover. Before she knew what was happening, she had been knocked to the ground and had handfuls of her hair torn out. Notwithstanding such hazards, the *Memoirs* succeeded in making it possible for their author to carry out her cherished dream of retiring to Paris, where she settled peacefully into a tranquil life, writing execrable novels. She died at the age of sixty, on a return visit to London, where she was pleased to note that the British were now succumbing to a certain piety in social relations. It would be a long time before a woman might again fashion a career for herself out of her own instincts as she had, turning from the role of courtesan to that of best-selling writer, but, as she would by now be the first to admit, the century could quite well rub along with just the one Harriette Wilson.

*

Not much has changed in the psychological mechanism of black-mail in the nearly two centuries since Harriette Wilson's *Memoirs* were published. The technology has developed of course, and is more obviously visual than in Wellington's day. Compromising photographs or videotape threaten humiliation for the victim by the distinctly more painful means of being seen in the wrong circumstances, so that the literary talent of a Harriette Wilson in relating a tale of indiscretion is no longer always needed. For the detached onlooker, this may seem a shame. As her painstaking notes to her former clients attest, Wilson's extortion scheme required imagination and effort, whereas simply setting up a hidden camera and then threatening one's victim with revelation of his activities, as recorded *in flagrante delicto*, demands comparatively little mental exertion. Indeed, anybody now setting out to extort money from a careless party by offering simply to inform on him to his relatives or to the authorities may be unsuccessful. In an era when our every trip to the cashpoint has been recorded on CCTV, the threat of merely verbal exposure may be something of a paper tiger. 'Where is the evidence?' the victim might justly demand. Why should the mere word of a hostile individual be taken at face value? We recall Darwin's locating the source of embarrassment in being the unwilling recipient of visual attention, and must conclude that the present times are potentially much more lucrative for the blackmailer than were the 1820s.

The technology may have advanced, but the psychological dynamics have not. Blackmail is predicated on the evident fact that there is nobody in the world who doesn't have something – maybe not a particular act, but more generally a trait of character, or peculiar personal habit – that they would rather remained private. Arguably, human life would be intolerable without a certain minimal level of such privacy, because the exposure of it is so compromising. It is the brute capitalism of blackmail that is so insidious, in that it puts a price on an individual's privacy – and an ever-increasing one at that. Police advice to the victim is not to give in, partly on the grounds that blackmail can be an open-ended process. The Wilson affair is unusual in that, where Harriette's threats succeeded and cash was forthcoming, she was satisfied with one payment. It is quite rare today for blackmailers to fade back into the darkness on receipt of a single handout, precisely because money can rarely be made with such ease, and because no extra effort is required for future subventions, only a repeat of the same threat. Notwithstanding the sterling advice to stand up to such pressure with Wellingtonian firmness, it remains the case that few victims have the wherewithal to defy the threat at its first occurrence. The initial attempt at blackmail often works just because of the shock of realising that anybody at all knows what one has done.

Just as blackmail was big business in the Georgian era, so the question of what we are entitled to know about those who have made a career of thrusting themselves into the public eye for profit has today become a burning ethical issue. The tabloid scandal-mongering of recent times is nothing new. It has its origins in the work of those gossip columnists who created an industry in the early years of Hollywood, recognising that just as there was an insatiable appetite for details of the stars' careers, so there was also a thirst to know what these individuals got up to in their personal lives. The first, and arguably still the greatest, of their genre were Louella Parsons and Hedda Hopper.

Parsons, so the legend goes, owed her career to the fact that she was present on William Randolph Hearst's yacht in November 1924, when the media mogul allegedly shot the film producer Thomas Ince for becoming too familiar with Hearst's partner Marion Davies. Everybody who had been invited on the cruise in celebration of Ince's birthday, including box-office goldmine Charlie Chaplin, was paid off in some way to keep the crime secret (in some versions it was Chaplin himself who was on more than platonic terms with Davies, and Ince was simply unlucky enough to get caught in the crossfire), and Parsons' reward was her tenure in perpetuity as Hollywood columnist on the Hearst newspapers. She specialised in a forensically precise style of vicious put-down, was mistress of the vinegary aside, and presented a public front to match. Mamie van Doren, one of her regular victims, recalls her 'pinched face and raptor eyes', and it is certain that many of the studios' biggest stars lived in genuine terror of what might be retailed about them in Parsons' columns.

Hedda Hopper's style was more flamboyant, as befitted her background. Where Parsons had clawed her way up through the placid backwaters of local journalism, Hopper had been a chorus girl and minor film actress. Her column on the *Los Angeles Times*, which was also widely syndicated, tended to have less obvious personal malice about it, but she was quite as indiscreet as Parsons when it came to spilling the beans. There was a little more of the eccentric maiden aunt in Hopper's personality – she cultivated a conspicuous taste in preposterous millinery, and doted on certain of the B-list celebrities – and she often seemed to consider herself to be in the same game as the actors themselves, whereas Parsons knew that she was an outsider, feeding the public taste for ritual humiliation in much the same way that the Puritan fathers of New England had persecuted the real-life Hester Prynnes.

While many purported to disapprove of the gossips (Parsons is dubbed by Kenneth Anger as 'The Paganini of Piffle'), readers nonetheless hung on their every prurient word, and once the post-war era ushered in a much less fastidious approach to privacy, the way was open for a publication wholly devoted to steamy revelations. *Confidential* magazine launched in 1952, explicitly aimed at a readership that was fascinated by the lewd lives of the entertainment industry's luminaries. It was the first publication to declare openly that the simpering, corpulent glam pianist Liberace was homosexual, and not merely in a closeted way, but hungrily, predatorily so. An article bylined to one Horton Streete, and titled 'Why

Liberace's theme song should be "Mad About The Boy" ', told the ghastly tale of the star's relentless, apparently open harassment of a good-looking PR agent in the kind of indelibly vivid, unpunctuated prose style that was minted to serve this new genre:

[T]he pudgy pianist's many faithful fans would have popped their girdles if they had witnessed their idol in action last year in an offstage production that saw old Kittenish on the Keys play one sour note after another in his clumsy efforts to make beautiful music with a handsome but highly reluctant young publicity man.

As a result of this 1957 story, Liberace successfully sued the magazine for libel, somehow managing to turn a sound alibi that he had been in another city at the time of one of the alleged assaults on the publicist into evidence backing his central claim, derided universally ever since, that he was straight as a die. The Liberace case, risible though it was, marked the start of a backlash by the stars against gossip journalism, and in its later years the magazine became a tame shadow of what it had been, its lurid coverlines diluted from the likes of 'Anthony Quinn caught in the powder room' to the sort of homespun consensualism in which the women's weeklies traded – 'The terrible tensions that spoil Christmas'. For its first five years of publication, however, it got away with an extraordinary level of sniggering, bullying bravado, all for twenty-five cents a month. Its self-conscious parody of the slick style of such industry creations as *Variety* was to prove a thoroughly durable one, recognisable today in the hugely entertaining www.popbitch.com internet site.

Gossip doesn't always have to destroy a star's livelihood, even where true. In his first *Hollywood Babylon* book (1975), scandal connoisseur Kenneth Anger argues that Mary Astor was the first star whose career survived exposure of her personal life. In 1936, during the course of a custody battle, a diary was introduced as evidence, in which Astor had recorded, in the overheated language of the more carnal type of romantic novel, her sixteen-month affair with the playwright George S Kaufman. There was much gasping, panting and plunging, and as it was all read out in court, the affair became the columnists' premier talking point. Not too long before, this kind of information had led the studios to strike an actor off their books without hesitation, but Warner Brothers, to whom she was contracted, correctly judged that the public was more entertained than horrified by what was being revealed, and Astor went on to make some of the most celebrated films of her career – *The Prisoner of Zenda* (1937), *The Maltese Falcon* (1941) and *Meet Me In St Louis* (1944).

What Mary Astor's case demonstrates is not that embarrassment is necessarily conquered by defiance, but rather that it is something one can survive. Blackmailers rely on the fact that their putative victims will be unable to cope with being exposed. By its very nature, blackmail has always first to be the announcement of an intended hostility, not the hostility itself, with the result that it gives its victim the chance, under duress to be sure, of releasing the information in his or her own way. It may be dismaying enough to find oneself conforming to another's agenda, dancing to their tune, but to pay them in coin or in kind for their silence is to be truly imprisoned in their will. In any case, the consideration that the payment buys, the blackmailer's continued discretion with respect to your privacy, is only the most lethal parody of kindness, beside which a red face and a dose of public contrition seem positively beneficial.

24

I AM EMBARRASSED

An apocryphal tale is told of a visiting African dignitary who, dining some years ago with the Prince of Wales at St James's Palace, and not entirely versed in the paraphernalia of the table, picked up his finger bowl in both hands and drank from it. As a ripple of sympathetic embarrassment travelled around the company, the Prince picked up his own fingerbowl and calmly followed suit, so that the dignitary was unaware of having done anything impermissible.

For the English, the dinner table is an arena where many of our social embarrassments are played out. Not only the question of eating etiquette, but such issues as the topics of conversation, the compatibility or otherwise of the guests, individual dietary requirements, and the arrangement of the seating plan, are all potential causes of discomfort. The attempt to produce a solution to all these thorny issues at once is inevitably condemned to failure. A successful dinner party is an exercise in minimising the likelihood and intensity of such failure. The politest occasions demand a degree of willing co-operation from the invitees that must be sustained at least until such time as the intake of wine has produced a certain *laissez-faire* among the company. At this point in the evening the loudly braying reactionary may be called an idiot, or the overly loquacious actress whose boyfriend is treating her like dirt may be bluntly asked why she doesn't just leave him, without causing the proceedings to judder to a halt. What is demanded of the participants is a kind of social choreography that doesn't apply when the occasion involves standing in a crowded room drinking. Iris Murdoch, in one of her novels, refers to a moment, arriving during a dinner party, at which each guest stops talking to the person on his or her right and starts talking to the person on his or her left. If this moment is not properly co-ordinated, one guest will be left stranded, putting on an exaggerated show of being preoccupied with removing the skin from a piece of fish, while waiting desperately for a lull in the conversations on either side.

It is often avowed that the codification of table manners, refined to a level of punctilious precision by the British in the nineteenth century, created a mechanism of social exclusion by which the well-bred could be easily distinguished from the hoi polloi. This was felt strongly by students from working-class families who arrived at Oxford or Cambridge University by way of some northern grammar school, and found themselves evaluated more readily than by their accents on whether they knew at dinner in halls which glass to pour the water into, or whether they knew how to slice the cheese. Learning to trifle with one's food, as opposed to eating hungrily, seemed *de rigueur*, while the boy who rose from the table between courses to go to the lavatory when the high table was sitting was told in no uncertain terms by the head steward that there were no circumstances – literally none – in which this was permitted. Better to vomit into a tissue, or pass out face first in the soup, than offend the Rector by quitting the scene before him.

While such age-worn customs continue to handicap those who are not fluent in them, the formulation of table etiquette was intended originally to achieve exactly the opposite. Much as school uniforms are held to mask the degree of privilege among the pupils' backgrounds by making everybody look the same, so table manners, in the sense that they were a code that theoretically all could learn, covered up whatever differences in upbringing obtained among those present. If each negative emotion does indeed possess its concomitant moral virtue, that of embarrassment would be social *politesse*. In a society that esteems a proper way of doing virtually everything – from walking along the street to opening a newspaper – embarrassment is the emotional consequence of not getting it right. That at least was the case when and where a critical level of social consensus could be assumed. As long as you knew how to butter your bread, a Victorian society hostess might well tolerate you volubly anticipating the day when the working classes would rise up and obliterate the bastions of privilege. The Victorians enjoyed a maverick, and welcomed a finely judged quantum of dissidence in a personality, although the matter of going a little too far was an ever-present threat. Equally, one could be too proper: it was said of the sternly patrician Liberal Prime Minister William Gladstone by his great rival Benjamin Disraeli that he lacked a single redeeming defect.

Armed with knowledge of the right ways of taking food in formal company, one may gain admittance to almost any society foreign to oneself. Much is made of the variant customary practices that distinguish one eating culture from another. In Muslim or Hindu company, one must beware of taking food with the left hand; in Japanese business circles, one would never pour *sake* into one's own cup but wait to be served by a neighbour; while in Chinese society, to turn a piece of steamed fish over in the serving dish is considered distasteful, as it seems to portend the capsizing of the fisherman's boat. And yet, as the historian of table manners Margaret Visser has argued, what is most striking about a comparison of cultural etiquettes is the degree of similarity between them. There is generally a pronounced preference for cleanliness, as being next to healthiness, and an atmosphere of due consideration for others. A group eating together is universally thought of as a social or familial unit, the integrity of which must not be breached by any ill-judged behaviour. The preference for using the right hand for food eaten with the fingers is not wholly specific to eastern societies. Even in the west, one learned to carry out some functions with the left hand and some with the right, as is noted in the caricaturing of left-handed people as 'cack-handed'. When a meal is being held as a form of honour or celebration, it is incumbent on the participants to eat copiously; otherwise, restraint – especially in those gastronomic cultures where each diner serves himself or herself from a communal bowl or pot – is the most seemly way of proceeding. Mostly, these mores are transmitted down the generations in the course of upbringing, but it would be wrong to think of them as unwritten rules. The practice of prescribing collective civility by setting down its terms is an ancient one.

One of the earliest, and most spectacularly successful such documents in western history is the sixteenth-century etiquette guide of the Dutch scholar Erasmus, *De Civilitate Morum Puerilium* (*Civil Behaviour for Boys*), first published in 1530. It was, for a century and more throughout Europe, the standard work on the subject. Dedicated to a prince's son but intended for all who would aspire to achieve something akin to that nobility, the text advises the would-be debutant what standards will be expected of him if he is not to reveal himself to be of the common stock. Cleanliness above all is insisted upon, particularly in the fingernails and teeth. There is a time to spit, and a time not to, and it is important to be aware, when the moment is propitious, that there is a right and a wrong way to spit. If eating with one's hands, it is advisable to wash them first, using some scented infusion such as camomile or rosemary. Try not to use the whole hand when taking food from the communal pot; the better classes manage with just the thumb and the first two fingers. Gummy fingers should not be wiped on tunics. Touching the head or hair while eating is unsavoury (head scratching is the behaviour of lunatics), as is prising particles of trapped food from between the teeth with fingers or knife. Farting or vomiting are unhelpful, but as suppressing them can be physically dangerous, it is as well to be discreet as one can in one's expulsions. Emunctuation requires a particularly circumspect approach:

To blow your nose on your hat or clothing is rustic, and to do so with the arm or elbow befits a tradesman; nor is it much more polite to use the hand, if you immediately smear the snot on your garment. It is proper to wipe the nostrils with a handkerchief, and to do this while turning away if more honourable people are present. If anything falls to the ground when blowing the nose with two fingers, it should immediately be trodden away.

This advice was being given at a time when the use of a handkerchief among boys of the classes for whom Erasmus was writing was relatively rare. The preferred method of evacuating the nose was to stop off each nostril in turn with a finger while exhaling sharply downwards through the other, much the same technique as is used today by footballers on the playing field and people whose use of cocaine has attained a critical pitch of frequency. Giovanni della Casa's almost contemporaneous Italian etiquette manual, *Galateo* (1558), is similarly preoccupied with the complexities of correct handkerchief use, advising that '[n]or is it seemly, after wiping your nose, to spread out your handkerchief and peer into it as if pearls and rubies might have fallen out of your head'. That fascinatingly unpleasant habit seems to have stuck, for it is still being sternly cautioned against in Jean-Baptiste de la Salle's posthumously published French guide *Les Règles de la Bienséance et de la Civilité Chrétienne* of 1729: 'After blowing your nose you should take care not to look into your handkerchief. It is correct to fold it immediately and replace it in your pocket.'

Rules of etiquette also extend to placement at the dinner table. The best seats at the table were those nearest to the host, and it would have been a considerable *faux pas* to assume a place higher up than one was going to be accorded. Christ's admonition in

Luke's Gospel to the guests at a Sabbath meal in the house of the Pharisee not to scramble for the best seats is a parable about humility, but it also has some practical philosophical force, in the manner of Epicurus, about lowering one's expectations of life. Bagging a place near the host, you are quite likely to be asked to move down, and suffer the humiliation of being seen to do so. Humbly sitting in the lowliest place, by contrast, the chances are you will be encouraged to move up, and feel duly gratified when you are. 'For whosoever exalteth himself shall be abased; and he that humbleth himself shall be exalted' (14:11). Hierarchies of seating remain, in those Oxbridge dining halls and also at weddings, where the top table is reserved for those nearest and dearest to the bride and groom, so that any who feel that they should have been included on it but have somehow been passed over have been rather publicly slighted.

Much embarrassed self-consciousness may result from being made the centre of attention at the table, because it instantly turns fellow-diners into an audience. The birthday girl knows that all eyes are upon her already, but when the staff have been secretly instructed to dim the lights and bring her a flaming Sambuca at a particular moment, her delight will be mingled with awkwardness. Many were those who resented being toasted, for much the same reasons. The clergyman and social commentator John Trusler, writing in 1791, demanded to know, 'What could be more rude and ridiculous than to interrupt persons at their meals with unnecessary compliments?' Trusler's great work, *The Honours of the Table* (1788), is an engagingly irascible English attempt to codify what constituted acceptable behaviour in the context of eating. His later *System of Etiquette* (1804) returns to the subject of superfluous toasting with some venom, noting – prematurely – that the custom was now 'exploded' among polite society. Where it persisted, it could safely be taken as indicative of those who were frankly no better than they should be. Trusler's jaundiced view of social relations provides a diverting snapshot of an era when such matters were being refined to the point of caricature, and it is perhaps fitting that the latter work should contain advice on the correct way to behave when challenged to a duel.

Much of the cantankerous resentment in works like Trusler's, a tone that persisted into the etiquette manuals of the early twentieth century, may be attributed to the fact that the British didn't and still don't want to eat with people they don't know. Those who embarked on the Grand Tour through Europe in the early part of the nineteenth century were often dismayed to find themselves having to eat in *table d'hôte* fashion in hotels and restaurants along the way. Instead of the curtained booth seating they were used to in English taverns, they had to find a place at one shared table. Here, they were subjected to all the variation in table etiquette that cultural differences allowed for, often jostling elbows with a number of other nationalities. Even more extraordinary was the discovery that other people expected to talk while they were eating, discussing anything from the political situation to what they had seen while out walking that day. The conversation, as bemused travellers' reports attest, often had a cacophonously competitive edge. In Normandy in 1818, the writer of historical romances Anna Bray observed in some bafflement that:

[c]onversation seemed as much the object of attention as their repast; the whole party spoke together, and made a most unceasing voluble noise.

It wasn't that the English, who gained an unshakeable reputation in Europe for taciturnity in company, didn't want to talk. It was just that they considered it proper to eat first and converse afterwards, or at least wait until the dessert stage was reached and more wine was served before opening up. At those establishments where they could get away with it, particularly in the British boarding houses where the *table d'hôte* system was a necessity, more aristocratic guests often asked to be served in their own rooms, enduring a cramped and incommodious meal alone, rather than suffer the indignity of having to sit next to somebody of lower social rank who was bellowing his appreciation of the lovely countryside. In the United States, such requests would often be met with mute incomprehension. If the President himself was happy to eat in whatever company there was, why should the frosty-natured British be cloistered away?

One of the most acute observers of social manners in the early nineteenth century was Harriet Pigott. A spinster of modest independent means, she ridded herself of her troublesome family as she neared forty by travelling, first reinventing herself at the most *soigné* London dinner tables, and then gaining admittance to the salons of fashionable continental Europe. Essaying her own version of the Grand Tour through France, Belgium, the Netherlands, Switzerland, Germany and Italy, she recorded her experiences in a journal of pellucid wit and vivacity. If there was one race in Europe that had the reputation of being more suffocatingly class-ridden even than the British, it was the Germans, and yet even here, as Harriet noted on her passage through Baden-Baden in 1818, there was evidence of far greater social lubrication than at home. Members of the nobility sat in unembarrassed proximity to ordinary folk when dining in the inns. It almost seemed as though it were the very rigidity of class distinctions in continental society that permitted this rubbing of shoulders and sharing of food and drink. All knew their place within the hierarchy was secure enough not to be threatened in any way by something as transient as communal eating. In Britain, by contrast, where there was much greater fluidity between economic groups in society, there was a greater need to fence off one's own social status by insisting on distance from those on the lower rungs. This claws-out attitude sat particularly ill when British travellers imported it to foreign settings. Even when entreated to do so, the English traveller refused point blank to dine:

at the same convivial board with those of inferior rank, though he is almost certain to meet with others of equal and superior station to himself; for all etiquette of this nature is waved [sic], – the Prince and the untitled hero mix in social converse . . .

But mixing was the last thing on the English gentleman's mind. '[T]he waiter,' Harriet Pigott could have informed him, 'who generally carves each dish at the sideboard, also assigns your place at the table, from the date of your arrival.' Not if the English visitor had anything to do with it, he didn't.

What made this insistence on distance all the more peculiar was that private social occasions in England often had exactly the opposite character. Where no dinner was offered, but rather an 'at home', the guest list was typically huge, so that the entire elite of the county might appear to have been invited to circulate around somebody's home. The success of such occasions was measured, as one astute commentator noted, 'by the difficulty of breathing and moving about'. Etiquette ruled that nobody was entitled to address anybody to whom they had not been presented, and yet managing to get presented to anybody in such a stifling fray was next to impossible. Joseph Blanco White, the self-exiled Spanish poet, essayist and religious dissenter who arrived in England in 1810, remarked that invitees to these soirées were often doing nothing more than what distant relatives at a funeral would be expected to do back in Spain – put in an appearance:

The host stands at the door of the drawing room and spends two or three hours shaking the hand of those who manage to reach him through the throng, 'very pleased to see you' and hoping you will go as soon as possible.

When one did snatch a fragment of conversation with somebody one recognised among the crowd, it was often limited to Dr Johnson's celebrated formula of a comment on the weather, still so familiar today, with perhaps a perfunctory inquiry after the health of the other, before the crush impelled one on down the hallway. Maintaining a genteel demeanour amid the jostling and shoving was a challenge in itself, but one managed as best one could. The available seats being quickly claimed by those too infirm to withstand the press, the rest were left grimly circulating from room to room, saying nothing mostly but merely appraising the attire of their fellow guests, and returning the odd glance with a vacant nod. Such an ordeal passed for a social occasion in London for the better part of a century from around the 1730s through to the early Victorian era. It was familiarly known, for reasons not hard to fathom, as a 'rout', or later and more colloquially still, a 'squeeze'.

One's heart goes out to the anonymous writer of 1808, cited in the *OED*, who commented, 'The weather is getting terribly hot for squeezes.' But not the least problem with such gatherings was that the conditions in which they were held militated against cultivated mannerliness. A heatwave could only make matters worse, and so indeed could the opposite extreme of temperature. It is worth recalling that the formulation of social manners arose at the same time as a significant improvement in the quality of life within private residences. It was only from the early eighteenth century that households managed to keep themselves reasonably warm in winter. Prior to the invention of the draught chimney with its curved flue, low mantelpiece and narrow hearth, there were only the old, vast, medieval-style fireplaces with seating inside on either side of the fire, and a straight chimney big enough for two sweeps to climb. Only the area immediately in front of these fireplaces received any heat, so that a particularly cold winter was agonising to endure, and often saw off frailer members of the family. Nor were the privileged necessarily much better off in this respect. There may have been a fireplace at either end of the Hall of Mirrors at Versailles, but even together they could not warm more than a fraction of the colossal interior. Dining in the company of Louis XIV in February 1695, the Princess Palatine, shivering in her furs, wrote that the wine and water at the King's table froze in their glasses. The French historian Fernand Braudel dates the revolution in domestic heating in Europe to around 1720, and it is surely with this gradual thaw that the refinement of manners really began. In the Princess's case, refinement meant leaving beside the plate the new-fangled fork that the King didn't much favour, and eating delicately in the old style with a knife and fingers.

Today, whatever vestiges of table manners have been taught us in the home during infancy are required less and less in public. It may still be as well to know them and observe them in somebody else's home, but there can be no particular need to maintain a decorous front in most restaurants and hotels. Both the management approach, which is increasingly in favour of casual familiarity in the North American style ('Hi, I'm Andy, I'm going to be your wait-person for tonight, and I'd like to tell you folks about some of the good things we've got for you'), and also the table design, invite us to do away with the old proprieties. Often there is no side plate for the bread, so that one is expected to spread a mass of crumbs on the table, and the first sightings have now been made of Londoners sweeping them on to the floor, rather than getting them stuck to the elbows of their jackets. Elbows will quite likely be rested on the table because the acoustics of many modern brasseries – especially those that can accommodate hundreds at a sitting – are such that you cannot hear what your companion is saying unless you lean forward amid the din. The same knife with which you have just buttered your bread is apparently now to be used for the first course, and where once each course was cleared when everybody at a table had finished, it may well now happen that each plate is taken away individually. Many people quite unselfconsciously eat with their fingers in restaurants, returning to a state of unpretentious delicacy of which Louis XIV would heartily have approved. These phenomena do not mark a decline in civilisation. If anything, they represent an advance beyond a time when everybody had to be taught a certain code for fear that they might behave like animals, or do something embarrassing such as speak excitedly across the table, or sympathise excessively with a companion's tale of woe. Ultimately, in these circumstances, nothing was more likely to cause embarrassment than the expression of emotion itself. Embarrassment can so easily be the emotional reaction unleashed by the emotions of others, which is why the system of manners was conceived against it. If there is an antidote to emotion, it is etiquette.

SURPRISE

There is no surprise more magical than the surprise of being loved.
Charles Morgan

1. *Mil.* The (or an) act of assailing or attacking unexpectedly or without warning, or of taking by this means; formerly also in a more general sense, seizure (of a person, a place, or spoil). 2. The (or an) act of coming upon one unexpectedly, or of taking unawares; a sudden attack ... c. An attack of illness; a sudden access of emotion. 3. Something that takes one by surprise; anything unexpected or astonishing. b. A fancy dish, or an ingredient of a dish, a present, or the like, designed to take one by surprise. 4. The feeling or emotion excited by something unexpected, or for which one is unprepared; the feeling or mental state, akin to astonishment and wonder, caused by an unexpected occurrence or circumstance, alarm, terror, or perplexity, caused by a sudden attack, calamity, or the like.

Darwin's physical indicators: opening wide of the eyes; raising of the eyebrows; transverse wrinkling of the forehead; opening of the mouth; protrusion of the lips; sudden oral inhalation; clucking of the tongue; raising of the arms, with palms outwards and fingers separated; clapping of the hand over the mouth.

25

TO BE SURPRISED

We may be surprised to find that surprise has a place in the emotions elaborated by Darwin, listed as one of his basic six, alongside fear, anger, happiness, sadness and disgust. Is surprise an emotion, as opposed, say, to an involuntary state of mind? Both Darwin and Paul Ekman are in no doubt that it is, not least because in its spontaneity and limited duration, it has the structure of an emotion, and it is also profoundly facially expressive. Unexpected good news, the clandestinely arranged party, the radiantly sunny March morning that breaks the long dank spell: all deliver the inner glow of satisfaction that the successful outcome of something planned can do, and this pleasure is reflected in the face. There is a surplus in it as well that derives from the apprehension that the unpredicted happy event is somehow unearned. In that sensation, our belief that the world can be benign is restored to us.

Surprise has undergone a noticeable semantic shift over the centuries. While it can still denote something either pleasant or unpleasant, its centre of lexical gravity has moved from one side of the fulcrum to the other. It was originally very much the state occasioned by a nasty shock. In military parlance, it meant an unexpected raid or ambush. Its Latin root, *sur-praehendere*, refers to seizure, sudden apprehending. Around the late seventeenth century, it started acquiring a greater accretion of positive connotations, so that the 'surprise' at a dinner party announces an unimagined treat, some bit of extraneous luxury, a *bombe surprise* perhaps. These days we most often assume a surprise to be something gratifying. If it isn't, then we tend to add a qualifier. The hefty gas bill was a 'nasty surprise', not just a surprise, and is in fact more accurately rendered as a 'shock', a 'blow', or a 'bombshell'. The word itself in English, once accented on its prefix, now blooms into its second syllable like a sudden sunrise. 'I have a surprise for you.' Is any statement more instantly effective in quickening the pulse?

The giving of gifts is the most common ceremonial form of surprise. Even when we expect to receive one, the carefully chosen gift is like a reassurance, because it is the concrete form of another's concern for oneself, and their sense of who the recipient is. The apposite gift is a pleasure to receive because of the congruence it establishes between the sort of person the recipient wants to be seen as, and the perception the giver has of them. Dressed up in shiny paper, it arrives from some unimaginable beyond, where the thought and effort that have gone into its choosing have the dignity of being concealed. Furthermore, it violates the exchange principle, on which the rest of our lives must seemingly turn. It is handed over to its recipient only because she is who she is, and some moment has come to celebrate the fact.

Not all present-giving lives up to the selfless ideal. The annual ritual of Christmas is a testing time, at which one must decide whom to give to – the office colleague? the next-door neighbour? – and then judge whether what (if anything) is received in return is commensurate with one's own effort. In Tudor England, the whole process was elevated to the status of a social lubricant, so that there was a constant traffic in all manner of commodities, representing acknowledgements of past favours and hopes of future preferment. Privy Councillor Lord John Dudley Lisle ingratiated himself with Anne Boleyn by presenting her with a lapdog on which she came to dote. So fond of it was she that when it died in a fall, nobody wanted to be the one to relay the tragic news to Her Grace. Lisle's letters, a collection of which was published in 1983, are an invaluable source of detail as to the social mores of the period. The inventory enumerated of gifts given and received suggests that, even though the act of giving had itself become formulaic, no imaginative exertions were spared when it came to deciding what to give. Food and wine remained an obvious choice, and Lisle lists quails, cranes, haunches of venison, oranges and barrels of wine changing hands, but live animals and birds were also a frequent resort. Not only toy dogs, such as the unlucky Purkoy presented to Henry VIII's consort, but sporting dogs – bloodhounds, greyhounds, mastiffs and water spaniels – and more exotic creatures such as marmosets and other monkeys, as well as puffins, parrots, hawks and songbirds, might be given. A bolt of satin or a coral necklace might appeal to one's vanity, a silk purse to one's practical nature, books to one's intellectual pretensions, or an object described as the tip of a unicorn's horn to one's fantastical credulity. What firmer token of devotion was there than an item of gold jewellery, nor one more likely to issue in the receipt of like benefit? If you were very privileged, you might be gifted with the fruit of some exotic plant or tree, grown in a hothouse far away from its native soil. Elizabeth I was sent the fruits of the tamarind tree planted in the gardens of Fulham Palace by the Bishop of London, setting the tone for a tradition of royal horticultural benefice that included the stunted pineapple grown in the Duchess of Cleveland's glasshouse and triumphantly presented to Charles II.

This highly formalised giving, in which every gift announced its donor's hopes of favour, constituted a corruption of the basic idea. Prior to the sixteenth century, the culture of gift-giving was limited to midwinter. Marking the winter solstice with festivities dates back at least to Egyptian times, and probably earlier. The pagan festival of Yule, the feast of light generally celebrated on 21 December, marked the moment from which the days began slowly to lengthen. Light was returning to the world, after a period in which organic life had all but stopped, save for the evergreen trees that preserved the hope of vernal rebirth. Christianity adopted the winter solstice celebrations to mark the birth of Christ, and in AD 567, the Council of Tours instituted the Twelve Days of Christmas, in which each day, from Christ's birth through to the Epiphany, was to be consecutively marked with festivities. It was not until the sixteenth century in Germany, however – the time at which Tudor England had turned the giving of presents into a complex social and political strategy – that the modern version of the Christmas festival was formed. And just as Yuletide had involved present-giving, as a way of gladdening one's kith and kin at the defeat of winter, so the Christian calendar allowed its adherents to mark the end of the period of abstinence and contrition that was Advent by resorting to the indulgences of gifts. In the Baltic cultures, there is the tradition of New Year bucks, when from Christmas Day until the Epiphany or Twelfth Night (6 January), young men of the community go from house to house with their sheepskin coats on inside out, disguised as reindeer. They bring benevolent wishes to the families on whom they call, dispensing hopes for a successful and happy coming year, in turn receiving small tokens of the community's gratitude. In Sweden, the feast of St Lucy (Santa Lucia) is observed on 13 December by similar arrivals. A young girl in a white gown and a crown of candles emerges from the darkness of the early hours, usually between two and four in the morning, bringing a tray of saffron buns and piping-hot coffee to some unsuspecting family. Her blazing crown symbolises the earth's coming re-emergence into light. Something of these customs lives on in the Scottish practice of first-footing on New Year's Eve, but at the heart of the midwinter tradition is the more widespread cultural construct – itself northern European in origin – personified as Santa Claus, indiscriminate dispenser of gifts, who presides over the Yule festivities as a less anarchic incarnation of the medieval Lord of Misrule. What could be more excitingly subversive than making free presentations of objects to others?

In Judaic cosmology, too, the winter feast of Chanukah is known as the Festival of Lights. It commemorates the victory of the Maccabees under Judah in driving the Syrian forces of King Antiochus, who had tried to insist on their apostasy, out of the temple at Jerusalem. During the course of the rededication of the temple, a tiny bowl of oil was found and lit in traditional honour to Yahweh. It was estimated that there was fuel for less than a day's flame, but somehow the oil continued to burn for eight days, which became the prescribed duration of the Chanukah festival. From the moment of sunset on the first day, menorahs (the traditional nine-branched candlesticks) are lit, friends and family pay seasonal visits, the house is decorated, and festive foods are eaten. These last should customarily include *sufganiot*, a type of deep-fried dough-nut filled with jam or date jelly, and *latkes*, the highly seasoned pancakes of shredded potato and onion. There is also giving and receiving of presents, to mark the renewal of faith.

The contemporary version of Christmas is largely an invention of the mid-nineteenth century. While the practice of bringing evergreen boughs into the house, or of garlanding a tree in the marketplace, are an ancient Germanic tradition, the origin of today's purple tinsel and fibre-optic specimens lies in the cultural cross-pollination effected by the Hanoverian takeover of the British throne in the early eighteenth century. The German court brought its festive customs to England, and when at Christmas 1846, Victoria and Albert were depicted for the *Illustrated London News* standing around a baubled fir tree with their then three children, the model was set for the rest of fashionable society to imitate. And imitate it did, piling layers of real-silver tinsel, twinkling candles and gaudily wrapped gifts on top of the royals' homespun simplicity.

In any case, the example had already been set by the greatest fabulist of the time, Charles Dickens, whose *A Christmas Carol* had been published to extravagant acclaim three years earlier. Such was the immediate success of the work that Dickens was prevailed upon throughout most of the rest of his career to produce a regular supply of Christmas stories, obliging the public demand for them more or less up to the time of his death in 1870. He may never quite have recaptured the spellbinding moral force of the tale of the miserable old skinflint who awakes reformed on Christmas morning, after being visited during the night by revenants of his buried past, dingy present and likely future, but it is to Dickens that we owe our image of a Christmas that sputters on in card designs and popular myth. His is the domestic interior lit with glimmering candles, the lambent fir-tree, the steaming punchbowl, the hot pastries stuffed with dried fruits, beef fat and sweet spice, the wassailers bellowing carols at the door – a vision of utopia at home that made the heart of one tucked up in bed on Boxing Day night ache with melancholy at its passing. And at the centre of the whole sumptuous ritual were presents, presents done up in silver and gold paper, with bows and posies and tassels attached, intended to crown the spectacle with gratuitous charity. No token of Mr Scrooge's Damascene conversion is more plangent than his presentation to the Cratchit family of the last turkey in the shop, big as a small boy, and a gigantic metaphor for the last chance gratefully grabbed at. Filmed over a hundred times, its central character's most exact interpreter remains Alastair Sim, graduating from embittered misanthrope to chortling merrymaker in the Renown studio's 1951 cinema version.

The exchange of presents requires a minimum level of happiness in both parties. They are an objectified form of one's sense of well-being at an important moment in the calendar. The more modern idea that one might give another a gift in order to cheer him up is quite alien to these celebratory rites, as is any sense of duty. One gives presents because the time inspires one to do so, not out of a sense of obligation. Exactly that dreary character now stains our mutual present-giving at times like Christmas, when the necessity of everybody giving to and receiving from everybody else can create both resentment at the amount of time and mental effort required, and despair at the expense. If imagination fails completely, the final recourse in deciding what each person should receive is to decide what one wouldn't mind getting oneself, with the implicit proviso, as Adorno acidly observes in *Minima Moralia* (1951), that one isn't quite as lavish in buying for others an item with which one would have liked to treat oneself. Most of us have at some time given presents in just the opposite spirit to this, taking time to find something that will truly delight the receiver, so that he will not feel cruelly scrutinised when he opens it, but will respond with spontaneous gratification. It is the almost childlike memory of this delight, in both receiving and giving, that makes us mournfully aware on Christmas morning that there was once more to the exchange of presents than the polite smile and the stock formula ('Ooh, *just what I wanted!*'), and that whatever it was that made that possible has been lost in adulthood.

One consequence of the duress of present-giving in the modern era has been the multi-million pound gift industry. Items specifically manufactured to be given as gifts began to crowd department stores in the 1940s, until they became so numerous that they required their own shops. Airport shopping malls are largely given over to them, especially in the departure areas, where it is presumed that you will want to grab some novelty article or duty-free merchandise for the folks back home, as a token of the holiday from which you are now returning. Where once the holiday gift was a piece of the unfamiliar location that you had spent a week discovering, it has now become indistinguishable from the Christmas present, another bit of passive extortion from the friends who were left behind. A small catalogue that drops from the magazine section of the Sunday newspaper makes a fetish of the utter lack of use value of the merchandise it offers, and one can well see why. Among its attractions are mugs that allow office workers to select their tea or coffee preferences by sliding a series of aluminium bands (saves the bother of speaking), a six-foot-wide sphere of inflatable cushions for rolling about in, a rack that sits across the bath and holds a wine glass, book and candle, glasses that glow, coasters that flash, novelty cuff links, a ballpoint pen that doubles as a vibrator, a toy gun that shoots ball-bearings at cartoon targets, intended specifically for under-occupied company directors, and much more besides. Many of the gifts grouped under the ghastly category of 'Lifestyle' assume that you have all but lost the use of your limbs, other than to fasten on novelty cuff links of course, while the sales pitch – that the recipients of these pieces of expensive junk will be highly paid CEOs – tells the casual reader more about the distribution of responsibility within modern corporate organisations than could a month of trade union meetings.

At the bottom of the whole racket, suggests Adorno, is the uncomfortable truth that we don't know what to give people because we don't actually want to give them anything. The equation could just as easily work the other way, so that we don't want to buy a present just because we can't think what to buy. The mental effort involved feels onerous enough for the problem to seem insoluble, and conscience as well as idleness dictates that it was better to give nothing than to give something inappropriate. We learn the pungency of disappointment at such presents in early infancy, when the torn-off wrapping reveals not the hoped-for paintball kit but some dully instructional board game, and then, like the twin masks of classical theatre, surprise presents the obverse of its wide-eyed, gasping, happy face. Not wishing to provoke such a reaction in those to whom we have to give is the last bit of charity left in functional present-giving. This dilemma is vividly illustrated by Hector Munro, writing in the Edwardian era under the *nom de plume* of Saki, in one of his early comic monologues, 'Reginald on Christmas Presents':

I wish it to be distinctly understood ... that I do not want a 'George, Prince of Wales' Prayer-book as a Christmas present. The fact cannot be too widely known. There ought ... to be technical education classes on the science of present-giving. No one seems to have the faintest notion of what any one else wants, and the prevalent ideas on the subject are not creditable to a civilised community. There is, for instance, the female relative in the country who 'knows a tie is always useful', and sends you some spotted horror that you could only wear in secret or in Tottenham Court Road.

The answer to all the waste and sunken spirits occasioned by clue-less gift-buying lies, as we are now habituated to expect, in making lists. Gift lists were once the sole prerogative of the affianced, but now proliferate at birthdays and Christmas too, whether in written or in verbal form. While they appear to be offering the ultimate consideration, that you may choose your own present within a specified budget, what they are really doing is shifting the mental effort on to the recipient. By the end of his monologue on the sub-ject, Reginald has more or less invented the phenomenon – in 1904:

Personally, I can't see where the difficulty in choosing suitable presents lies. No boy who had brought himself up properly could fail to appreci-ate one of those decorative bottles of liqueurs that are so reverently staged in Morel's window – and it wouldn't in the least matter if one did get duplicates ... And then, of course, there are liqueur glasses, and crystallised fruits, and tapestry curtains, and heaps of other necessaries of life that make really sensible presents – not to speak of luxuries, such as having one's bills paid, or getting something quite sweet in the way of jewellery.

Inviting the recipient to nominate his own present makes the whole process more functional than ever. Buying the gift is then a matter of acting on instructions. Mention of 'having one's bills paid' rais-es the one remaining modern recourse, which is simply to issue money to the recipient to please herself, so that if, hesitating in the gift shop, she ends by buying herself some tasteless item of over-priced table furniture, she has only herself to blame. The gift voucher, introduced after the Second World War, is only a slightly more discreet form of the cash offering. It at least involves the choosing of a card.

What has been forsaken in these present-day rituals is the intention of providing the other with a pleasant surprise. Indeed, the only surprise still possible at birthdays or Christmas is the nasty surprise of receiving nothing, which indicates that the potential giver has either forgotten you, or else is making the even more insufferable statement that you are not quite worth it. On the other hand, the line between the judicious gift and the ostentatious one is often perilously thin: over-generosity blends an element of guilt into the surprise, so that at the very moment that we should be gratified, we find ourselves disarrayed by intimations of inadequacy.

Gifts are worth giving at unexpected moments. Even though their monetary value may be negligible, they re-establish that warmth within human relations without which we become reduced to automata. It is sometimes posited that in an economic climate of superfluous production and excess, in which two or three generations have now grown up in the western world, present-giving is no longer necessary, and that the sterile functionality of Christmas is the true indicator of this fact. Adorno, for one, even writing in the 1940s, doesn't accept this. It is quite simply a lie, 'privately as much as socially, for there is no one today for whom imagination could not discover what would delight him utterly'. Even the junk of the gift industry, if ripped out of its depressing context, can hold the means of such delight, as was discovered by the critic of capitalist reification whose lover brought him a helium-filled, heart-shaped balloon on Valentine's Day. It bobbed about the living room for days before deflating, its value higher than rubies.

26

I SHOCK YOU

It is easy to assume that we are today all but incapable of being shocked by art. Shock disappeared surely, at least in Britain, when the last vestiges of Edwardian morality were swept away along with the old pornography laws and the office of the Lord Chamberlain. Until the 1960s, when these reforms were enacted, the bourgeoisie could be shaken from their smug composure with heartening ease by radical and confrontational works in the theatre, literature and the visual arts. Whether they personally saw the licentious plays or scatological artwork for themselves, or merely read about them, didn't matter. The bait had been risen to, and another earnest late-night television debate guaranteed that the fires of indignation were continually stoked. Now that our culture has moved on from this difficult period, we pride ourselves on our ability to rise above such ritual controversies. But with what justification?

In the late summer of 2003, theatre audiences in London were still capable of being, if not shocked, then certainly unsettled by the spectacle of eroticism between men. A production of Christopher Marlowe's *Edward II* at Shakespeare's Globe Theatre was no more demonstrative in its depiction of the consuming sexual obsession of the King for his paramour Piers Gaveston than previous stagings had been. Gaveston, portrayed with defiant, amoral sensuality by Gerald Kyd, was topless for a significant proportion of the action, and while Liam Brennan's Edward doted on him, embracing and kissing him with hungry fervour, the audience shifted uneasily in its seats, some gasping, others giggling, when the actors came in physical contact with each other. It seemed odd, and then depressing, that while images of homosexuality proliferate in popular culture, the living, breathing evidence of it should still occasion such discomfort.

A similar reaction greeted a production by the Royal Shakespeare Company in 1992 of the German dramatist Frank Wedekind's *Spring Awakening*. Written a century earlier, the play contains a scene in a vineyard in which two teenage boys, who are deeply in love with each other, imagine their future together and kiss. Wedekind's play seeks to show the way in which moral hypocrisy in the adult world destabilises the lives of a group of adolescents in a small German town at the end of the nineteenth century. The work was published in a self-financed edition in Zurich in 1891, but was held to be too flagrantly pornographic to be staged. It was finally put on in a much modified version at the Kammerspielhaus in Berlin in 1906, in a production directed by Max Reinhardt. The author himself played the role of the allegorical Masked Man, *der Vermummte Herr*, who appears in the final scene in a graveyard as a kind of *deus ex machina*, rescuing from the clutches of death a boy whose pregnant girlfriend has died at the hands of a back-street abortionist, and whose best friend has shot himself. Following the Reinhardt production, the play was banned by the Prussian Administrative Court, and only relicensed on appeal after it was found that it was 'impossible not to recognise the piece as a serious work'. What was so unpalatable about it – in addition to the scenes of competitive masturbation and explicit sexual language, its depictions of illegal abortion and kissing boys – was the merciless attitude it evinced towards the unbending moral authoritarianism of its adult characters. The work is dedicated to parents and teachers, and it was an alliance of just these figures within German society that rose up against it. It proved controversial wherever it was staged. A one-off performance on Broadway in 1917 was threatened with being halted halfway through by legal intervention from the City Commissioner. In the early 1930s, it was staged in Britain, again in a single performance by the Sunday Theatre Club in London. The theatre critic of the *Daily Telegraph*, alienated beyond retrieval by what he saw as typical foreign filth, uttered a grateful piety: 'Thank Heaven that we in England have always grown up too slowly and set too much store by childish pursuits and games.' Proof of the slow maturation of the English was offered by the two performances allowed at the Royal Court Theatre in April 1963, only after the Lord Chamberlain had declared that the public could safely see it, on condition that the words 'penis' and 'vagina' were excised from the script, some less juicy substitute could be found for the masturbation game in the reformatory, and that, when it came to the vineyard scene, there was to be 'no kissing, embracing or caressing' between the boys. The play was considered for a production at the National Theatre two years later but, despite the advocacy of luminaries such as Laurence Olivier, the proposal was turned down. '[S]ome poky experimental theatre in Sloane Square' was its natural habitat, according to a theatre spokesman. Only with the Theatres Act 1968, which abolished the post of Lord Chamberlain, and with it his power to censor what appeared on the British stage, were obstructions to an unfettered production of the work finally removed. Yet even in 1992 at the Barbican, Hans and Ernst's kiss in the play's penultimate scene occasioned audible offence for many members of the audience.

Spring Awakening was written at a time when European theatre rediscovered its social mission, chiefly in the works of the late nineteenth-century pioneers of naturalistic drama. Heroic epics, epitomised by the works of Goethe and Schiller, no longer seemed appropriate to an age in which European prose fiction had dedicated itself to the minute analysis of society's ills. If the events and attitudes depicted in the socially critical dramas of writers such as Henrik Ibsen and the young August Strindberg caused disquiet among their first audiences, that was all to the good. There was a lot to be disquieted about. As the boundaries were consciously pushed at (Ibsen brought masturbation to the stage, in *Ghosts*, as early as 1881, when Wedekind was of an age only just to be discovering it for himself), so the parameters of what could be said about sexual morality in western societies were expanded. This was the era when researchers such as Krafft-Ebing were beginning to work out a detailed model of human sexuality, which was causing ripples of interest among those sectors with access to their work. In the aftermath of the Great War, the formal dramatic structures by which arguments and ideas were conveyed were felt to be hopelessly inadequate, and naturalism was subsumed under a wave of experimental theatrical technique, especially in defeated Germany. What came to be known as expressionism was the mode of dramatists such as Georg Kaiser and Ernst Toller, and indeed of the first handful of works (*Baal, Drums in the Night, In The Jungle of Cities*) by Bertolt Brecht. The expressionists retained sexual content in their work, but added to it a harder political edge, a radical demand from a broad left perspective for complete social change. Brecht was to go on to lay the foundations for an entirely new form of politically didactic, tendentious theatre. By the late 1920s, the twin leitmotivs of twentieth-century drama, sex and politics, were in place, and they would never really disappear.

In the period following the Second World War, the desire to shock through a work of art became partly an end in itself. This was certainly the charge levelled among conservative cultural circles. Taking *Spring Awakening* as an example, to write off the reflection upon such matters as teenage pregnancy and homosexuality as mere attention-seeking was to absolve oneself from the need to reflect on what these themes represented. Something of that self-disabling stance can be seen in the reception of the right-wing press in Britain of the socially critical plays of the late 1950s, centred on the success of John Osborne's *Look Back In Anger* (1956).

These were plays, it was said with a barely suppressed groan, with a 'message'. Not being able either to locate or to decode the message then became a reactionary badge of honour, as proud a distinction for those who wore it as the one that displayed your utter lack of credentials in seeing what was represented in abstract painting. Adorno, writing in the late 1960s in his final work *Aesthetic Theory* (1970), argues that people who claim not to know what point modern art is trying to make actually understand it perfectly well, and that if anything it is the work of earlier eras that no longer speaks to them. The anguish everywhere apparent in Beckett's work, for example, is more uncomfortably transparent to a contemporary audience than is the lost language of Elizabethan tragedy. Notwithstanding this, there was a post-war current – especially in the works of conceptual artists from the 1950s on – that sought to make a fetish of confrontation. The efforts of the Vienna Group and of the kinds of poems published by the *New Statesman*, for example, larded with liberating four-letter words *pour épater le bourgeois*, often appeared to be doing scarcely more than marking out their own territory, distinguishing themselves from the suffocating normativity of mainstream culture. While thousands flocked in 1963 to buy a copy of *Lady Chatterley's Lover*, unexpectedly discovering in themselves a taste for the overheated, masculinist stodge of the pre-war era, popular culture was just beginning to assert its own cultivated superiority. 'Your world is not my world,' Bob Dylan is heard to taunt some hapless interviewer in D A Pennebaker's film of his 1965 British tour, *Don't Look Back*.

This post-war version of aesthetic shock, which recalls the gratuitousness of Dada, is the exaggerated version of that strangeness peculiar to all art at its most communicative. 'If one perceives art as anything other than strange,' declares Adorno, 'one does not perceive it at all.' Even where we come back to works that we love and know intimately, what often rescues them from the graveyard of over-familiarity is an aura of otherness that keeps revealing itself.

The comedy of Laurel and Hardy's short films of the early 1930s derives much of its force from the extreme tension between what each of them is doing. While Oliver Hardy's performances seem to stem from the heightened naturalistic acting found in melodrama, Stan Laurel allows himself to get away with less and less, so that even where he has to participate in a few lines of dialogue that advance the plot, rather than maintain the mute puzzlement of his matchless clowning, he speaks them as though reading them from an autocue. One of them is overacting preposterously, and the other under-acting to the same pitch, and it is the utter improbability of such a liaison of styles that produced one of the finest comic partnerships in cinematic history.

Much of the straight acting of the 1930s and 1940s is imbued with a deeply unreal character when seen from the vantage of today's hyper-naturalism, and that is precisely what preserves it now for the fascination of later eras. The mumbling, semi-improvisational style of James Stewart is a case in point, as is the trance-like insouciance of Greta Garbo, and yet both these actors were capable of performances of vivid emotional intensity. A crash course in the strangeness of the wartime cinema can be had from *The Maltese Falcon* (1941), in which, without exception, the performances are, each in its own way, mesmeric: Humphrey Bogart's squirt-gun deadpan, delivered flat as a punctured tyre but with the urgency of a man who now has a train to catch; Mary Astor, all scheming *fatale* beneath the ripped bodice of tremulous vulnerability; Elisha Cook Jnr's staring-eyed psychotic baby hoodlum; the grandiloquently pouting Sydney Greenstreet as the greatest of all Hollywood's English villains, bobbing about the screen in shimmering cummerbund, with his operatic laugh and fluttering, meaty hands; and at the outer limits, Peter Lorre, seething with camp indignation, the hissing, consonantal delivery pointed up by an aura of exophthalmic distraction as pungent as his gardenia-scented calling card. Is there, even now, a suspense film to match it?

If there is an other-worldliness to works of art of the highest rank, however, it is also apparent that this sense can't be achieved merely by causing shock. Many professed to be appalled by British artist Marcus Harvey's *Myra* (1997), an eleven-foot-high portrayal of the famous mugshot of the 1960s child abductor Myra Hindley, rendered in a mass of monochrome children's handprints. The fact that people are morally outraged by a work of art, as were the several Academicians who resigned when it was first exhibited at the Royal Academy in 1997, is a matter of personal jurisprudence, but it tells us nothing about the work's aesthetic value. With Hindley dead, and the initial controversy having abated, the work now hangs – or, rather, leans nonchalantly against a wall – in its permanent home at the Saatchi Gallery, its enormous, intimidating blankness calling us to ponder once more the enormities it faithfully records. The sculptures of Ron Mueck, an Australian-born London artist, are in the direct tradition of photo-realism. Human figures that recall the eerie verisimilitude of waxworks, they derive their freakish power from their unexpected dimensions. A 1999 work, *Big Boy*, is a colossal representation of a kneeling pubescent child, while *Dead Dad*, which premiered at the same 1997 show as Harvey's *Myra*, is an anatomically exact depiction of the artist's deceased father, but scaled down by half and laid on the floor, so that as one prowled around and peered down at it, one was overcome by the feeling of vertiginous guilt that attends us at the death of senior relatives. By contrast, the work of artists like Sarah Lucas, she of the bits of fruit and a bucket on a mattress (*Au Naturel* [1994]), look like inarticulate art-school horseplay.

The shock that some contemporary works seek to instil in the viewer is connected to the trauma of neurosis, and the ways in which we choose to deal with it are strikingly similar to the evasion and repression strategies that Freud described. The shocking endings of the classic productions of nineteenth-century naturalistic drama were often too much for the mores of their societies, and were rewritten to make the whole spectacle more palatable to the times. Ibsen's *A Doll's House* is a prime case: when the rebellious wife Nora finally walked out on her overbearing husband Torvald, slamming the door behind her, there were shouts of protest at the first performances. In a subsequent production the scene was recast. Nora was coaxed back by Torvald, who forgave her for her folly by fondly popping a bonbon into her mouth. In earlier times, great psychological cruelty or tragically premature death were often too hard for audiences to bear. Dr Johnson, who famously thought Shakespeare a rather crude tragedian who would better have stuck to comic writing, felt the death of Cordelia was too awful to pass unedited, while the distinguished playwright and Poet Laureate Nahum Tate, similarly stricken, gave her a happy ending in 1681, in which she was married off to the virtuous Edgar.

Real events, as opposed to the mendacities of art, cannot so easily be edited to avoid offence. The Great War taught the infant science of psychoanalysis a great deal about trauma as a medical condition. In *Beyond the Pleasure Principle* (1920), Freud attempts to theorise the different types of anxiety. Among his categories is what the German text gives as *Schreck*, a state of sudden fright, terror or shock. What distinguishes this condition is that it always comes upon people who are not ready for it. They don't see the approaching peril. *Schreck* is 'the state a person gets into when he has run into danger without being prepared for it; it emphasises the factor of surprise'. In this lack of preparedness, we may say that *Schreck* is fear that lacks a past tense. Anxiety, thought Freud, did not have the potential to create traumatic neurosis, but shock clearly could, and just as shell-shock left many surviving combatants of the European war helplessly traumatised, so the catastrophe itself left European societies in a state of shock. In the immediate aftermath of shock, and perhaps for a long time afterwards, we are deprived of our faculties – in German, *sprachlos* (speechless) *vor Schreck*, or *vor Schreck wie gelähmt* (paralysed). In traumatised individuals, 'an extensive breach [has been] made in the protective shield against stimuli', with some direct damage having been occasioned to the molecular or histological (tissue) structure of the central nervous system. Where they have repeating nightmares about the event that caused their condition, Freud posits, these dreams constitute an attempt to master the traumatic stimulus by imagining back into the primal event a preparedness for fear that wasn't present at the time. This mechanism exists quite independently of the usual dualism of the reality and pleasure principles, and represents a more primitive form of the mental processes by which we try to ensure a minimum quantum of happiness in our lives.

Casting our glance back at those modern artworks that seek to paralyse their audiences through their initial impact, we can see that what these works intend is the reverse of the healing process Freud outlines. Shocking artworks want us to see that not all is well, and that we have strong cause to be deeply unsettled at the course our lives have taken. They want to jolt us out of the apathy that led to the present social and moral state of our existence. Yet this resort has been so overused during the last century that it has become only haphazardly effective. Meanwhile, all the other catastrophes that have befallen humanity since 1918, from bombing raids to concentration camps, napalm to suicide hijackings, have bequeathed a legacy of shock not just to the survivors, but to many onlookers in the global village too. While the art world (including television and the modern cinema) works feverishly on new ways to startle us out of our anaesthesia, we are entitled to wonder what efforts it is making to compensate us, as only it can, for the damage that these real events have inflicted.

27

YOU SURPRISE ME

The physiological mechanics of surprise, as outlined by Darwin, are evocative of strategies the body unconsciously performs to shield itself from danger. The original form of surprise would be the sudden danger from a potentially hostile member of a rival tribe, or a beast of prey, coming upon primordial humans and catching them unawares. The wide-open eyes represent an attempt to perceive as much as possible of one's surroundings by increasing the field of vision, a reflex action that is enhanced by the raising of the eyebrows. Darwin points to the way drunken people raise their eyebrows when trying to focus, in order to counteract the drooping eyelids caused by the muscular relaxation experienced when the body is saturated with alcohol.

The opening of the mouth is ingeniously attributed by Darwin to the fact that respiration is quickened and made more stertorous during a sudden alarm. In order to listen out for the audible evidence of any unseen danger, it may be necessary to quieten the breathing, which is achieved by breathing through the open mouth – even holding one's breath momentarily. A colleague, writing in the *Quarterly Journal of Science* in January 1873, suggests that the open mouth of amazement may be embryonic of a cry, of alarm or of warning to others. Most fascinating of all is the trans-cultural practice of clapping a hand to the mouth, or to some other part of the head, to express astonishment. Reported consistently by his respondents in Australia, southern and western Africa and Ethiopia, among the Amerindian tribes of the western United States, and in India, this gesture remains hard to account for. The philologist and professor of classical philosophy, Theodor Gomperz of Vienna University, in a letter to Darwin of August 1873, proposes that surprises in the prehistoric world would often be accompanied by the need for complete silence in the face of impending peril, and that the hand clapped over the mouth was the means by which the one who heard it simultaneously stopped himself from blurting out any sound, while entreating others in the group to be quiet too. In any case, it is an age-old response, as is witnessed by a verse in the Book of Job: 'Mark me, and be astonished, and lay your hand upon your mouth' (21:5).

In the original Hebrew the word translated as 'astonished' in the King James version is *shamem*, which has a rather stronger inflection than the English, and denotes more a state of being horrified, appalled, desolated, stunned, ravaged. This speaks of the close kinship between the original idea of surprise and extreme shock. Darwin groups surprise and astonishment together in the same chapter in which he looks at fear and horror, with astonishment being the stronger form of surprise, and amazement implicitly stronger still. To be astonished or astounded is to be stunned into a state of mental consternation, extreme wonder. In its Middle English origin, in the now defunct form of 'astoned' or 'astonied', to be astonished is to be deprived of sensation by something totally unexpected, to be stupefied, even to the extent of ceasing to be conscious. Over time, it becomes a state of being simply greatly surprised, as in the King James usage. 'The people,' reports Matthew's Gospel of those who heard Jesus preaching, 'were astonished at his doctrine' (7:28). Via the French *étonner* (originally *estoner*), it refers back to the Latin verb *tonare*, 'to thunder'. English has retained a Jacobean coinage, 'thunderstruck', for that state of being rendered mute and motionless by astonishment.

Among the arts, it is drama in all its forms, from the classical theatre to the modern cinema and television, which requires the element of surprise above any other plot device, as surely as mammals need oxygen. As noted by Aristotle in the *Poetics*, it is the fulcrum upon which the events of the tragic plot are balanced. Conflict is what impels the action on, but it is the surprising event on which it turns. A moment of surprise can be skilfully caught in painting, but what we are privy to is the moment at which the unexpected becomes apparent. In drama, we experience the revelation itself, and its aftermath as well, and – perhaps even more crucially for the sympathetic involvement of the audiences – its anticipation in the preceding events. For Aristotle, the chief importance of the mimetic function of drama is that it represents human action and its consequences, rather than simply reflecting human nature. This is why all dramatic plots (and indeed all narratives) are didactic. They attempt to teach us something about the way the world is constituted by human agency, about the choices we make under the impact of external forces such as chance, or in the ancient Greek world, Fate. At some crucial moment in our lives, the unexpected happens, some realisation dawns on us, and a sequence of events is set in motion.

In very many plays, and this is certainly true of Greek and Roman drama and the theatre of the Elizabethan and Jacobean golden age, the dramatic tension is sustained by the fact that the surprise coming to the character or characters is anticipated by the audience. This is because we have been vouchsafed the critical information by the Chorus or an emblematic figure supplying the choric function, or else just because we already know the story from mythology. None of this softens the resonance of the actual moment of revelation, as is demonstrated when we watch once again a film that we are already familiar with. When the first gull swoops down to take a snap at Tippi Hedren's head as she steers her motorboat into the harbour at Bodega Bay, the moment is still perfectly chilling, no matter how many countless times we have seen *The Birds* (1963), perhaps even more so because we now know exactly what it portends and also because we recall our surprise and horror when we first saw it. This kind of shock is not of the same order as the revelations of classical drama, in the sense that it appears as the randomly malevolent act of a world beyond human deciphering, whereas the moment that takes the vulnerable hero of the Greek tragedy by surprise is part of a preordained fate that could be divined if only the hero would make himself or herself aware of it.

The term Aristotle uses, *anagnorisis*, literally means 'recognition', further defined as 'a change from ignorance to knowledge', which may be of a person, but equally may be of the true nature of another's actions. The surprise consists in the hero's perception of something that had been there all along, and it is especially cataclysmic when the fate of a character turns on it. The most catastrophic revelation in Greek drama is that of Oedipus in the *Tyrannus*, as he realises that the plague that has befallen Thebes is of his own making, and that the sentence he has passed on the person guilty of the pollution must now be enacted on himself. In modern narratives, the surprise more often couldn't have been foreseen by the character on whom it impacts. One fine morning Josef K is arrested and sent for trial, although he hasn't done anything wrong and couldn't have known that 'somebody must have been telling lies about [him]'. One afternoon, for no apparent reason, a woman is attacked by a seabird. One rainy night, another woman steps into the shower at a cheap motel and is hacked to death by a stranger. In Shakespeare's works, a kind of median point is marked between these two extremes, in which the moments of tragic recognition are not necessarily driven by fate, but are still phenomena that could have been foreseen, and their moment of realisation often involves a point of self-discovery. King Lear realises that the elder daughters he has favoured were the two least deserving. On the eve of a foreign campaign, Henry V is driven to murderous vengeance on discovering a plot against him among lieutenants he had thought entirely trustworthy. The generous nobleman Timon suddenly becomes aware, rather like Scott Fitzgerald's Jay Gatsby, that none of the people soaking up his lavish hospitality is in any sense a true friend. There may be varying degrees of subtlety in the psychological colouring of these events, and the reactions they provoke, but they are still identifiably moments of Aristotelian recognition, transitions from darkness into light.

If tragedy relies on instances of dramatic surprise, the same is true of comedy. The farcical confusions, punctured pretensions, mistaken identities and impeded romances in which comic drama has traded since Aristophanes are all about things turning out not to be as they seemed. When the action of a comic plot or sketch makes us smile, it is often because what happens to the characters is not what we or they expect. The rococo machinations of seventeenth-century comic plays are peopled with familiar stereotypes, and yet their attributes are exaggerated and they are forced to contend with circumstances that test them to their limits, thus breaking the bounds of the personae they inhabit. An example to relish is Ben Jonson's *Epicoene, or The Silent Woman* of 1609, in which a misanthropic old miser Morose, whose particular tic is that he can't stand noise, threatens to disinherit his vain but stylish nephew Sir Dauphine Eugenie. With the help of a pair of willing, cynical accomplices, the miserable patriarch is hoodwinked by Sir Dauphine into marrying what he believes to be a taciturn female beauty, whose physical charm is compounded by the fact that she is so modest that she never utters a sound. The minute he is wed to her, her nature changes and she becomes a twittering nag. Sir Dauphine offers to obtain an annulment of the marriage for Morose in return for having his inheritance back. The plot against Morose is revealed in a final scene of crushing cruelty. The wife is nothing other than a rowdy boy in a wig. Now that his fortune has been safely transferred, it only remains for Sir Dauphine to dismiss the old fool, who leaves the stage quite destroyed, with his nephew's words ringing in his ears: 'I'll not trouble you, till you trouble me with your Funeral, which I care not how soon it come.' The play ends not amid peals of laughter, then, but with this venomous note of contempt, in which even the conspirator's accomplices realise they have been duped (neither of these was in on the ruse that the wife was a disguised boy). There is a final, moralising speech by the sidekick Truewit to close the proceedings. Jonson was one of the great didactic playwrights of the day, and used comedy in a way that both entertained the audiences, but also upset their expectations. The sweep of his social vision is Dickensian *avant la lettre*, and that trick of making the laughter die in our throats – which we may think of as a feature of the modern theatre – really begins with his later plays.

One of the key points about comedy is that it deals with ordinary life, rather than the emblematic lives of individuals singled out by fate for special torment. The characters are brought down, when they are, by common human failings, and we are implicitly invited to reflect on these as we see them try to negotiate their way through the sticky situations the plot entails. In a series of films made in the late 1980s and 1990s, Woody Allen has brought a distinctly seventeenth-century focus on social mores and their influence on personal morality to the modern cinema. *Crimes and Misdemeanours* (1989) tells of an ophthalmologist (Martin Landau) who has recently terminated an extramarital relationship with a possessive and potentially vengeful woman (Anjelica Huston). He confesses his predicament to his rabbi (Sam Waterson), who also happens to be one of his patients, and who advises him to come clean to his wife. Realising the world of pain he will unleash if he does so, but under threat of exposure from Huston, he asks his mobster brother (Jerry Orbach) to help. The brother says the problem can be made to disappear with a single phone call, and after some soul-searching, is allowed to go ahead. Soon after, Huston is found dead at home, apparently the victim of housebreakers, leading Landau to descend into a pit of torturous remorse. If this is the crime of the film's title, the misdemeanour lies in the story that centres on Allen's own character, a television film-maker who embarks on his own adulterous relationship with a TV producer (Mia Farrow). At the close of the film, Allen and Landau meet for the first time at a wedding reception at the Waldorf Astoria. Allen is still castigating himself over his own infidelity to his wife, and the consequent loss of his lover to the sebaceously arrogant comedy producer (Alan Alda) about whom he has been making a documentary. But Landau has learned to live with what he has done and, retailing his story to Allen as though it were the hypothetical idea for a movie script, realises that he has made the right decision. Not only has he saved his marriage, and protected his wife from unhappiness, but he has prevented somebody else from acting to undermine it.

In the immediate aftermath of the murder of his mistress, as Landau now relates it, he is stricken with the intimation – surfacing from his Jewish religious upbringing – that he has transgressed an ethical code. He had come to believe that the universe was ethically neutral and that our sense of morality is nothing more than the restless urging of the superego. Once he is responsible for somebody's death, however, the world takes on the ethical coloration of theology. 'It's not an empty universe at all,' he realises, 'but a just and moral one, and now he's violated it.' As time passes, though, he isn't punished, but rather prospers, continuing his life of wealth and privilege. It turns out, gradually enough to be sure, but inexorably, that there is no punishment. His life can continue, as though his part in taking somebody else's away does not in any way have to be atoned for. 'But then his worst beliefs are realised,' Allen suggests, returning to the theme of the ethical vacuum. 'Well, I said it was a chilling story, didn't I?' Landau replies. Allen suggests that if he were making the story into a film, the central character would have to turn himself in. 'Then it would assume tragic proportions.' 'But that's fiction, that's movies,' the doctor counters.

As the luckless Allen is left to contemplate what there is of the morally balanced universe he so cherishes, we too are left with the conundrum. Perhaps sometimes the due prosecution of a crime, and the consequent atonement it should by rights call down, are not necessarily required to bring about a proper redress. What purpose is served, after all, if the doctor chooses to confess to adultery and complicity to murder? How can anybody's lives ever be put back together again after such a revelation? For the permanently self-questioning Allen, such an outcome only adds to the great weight of existential ambiguity, with which it is both necessary and impossible to live.

Having had his nose rubbed in his own predicament by making a shambolic tribute to the hated comedy mogul, Allen's character is denied even the solace of satisfaction in his own work. What he really wants to do is to make a film profile of an aged European moral philosopher, who has spent a career meditating on precisely the questions that it has taken the eye doctor a mere couple of months to resolve to his own satisfaction. While he is at work on his paean to the Alda character, news comes through of the philosopher's death. Now the film that he really wanted to make can never come to fruition. The sage's reflections, spoken in halting *mittel*-European English over transitional passages of the film, are intended to illuminate what is happening in the modern American lives of the principal characters. After the final dialogue between Allen and Landau at the wedding party, the picture closes with a peroration from the now departed thinker. What keeps us going, he suggests over the closing montage, in a world where no especial provision appears to have been made for human happiness, are the essential elements that furnish our day-to-day environment – 'our family, our work, and the hope that one day, future generations will understand more'. But there seems precious little hope of that if actions do not necessarily have consequences, and if moral responsibility is a feeling that can, sooner or later, be comfortably shrugged off. It was possible to run an extermination camp in the centre of Europe, and then go and live in comfortable retirement in South America. Who can understand this? And how much of irreparably damaged life can we devote to trying?

There is evidently a universe of differentiation between comedy that poses questions such as these, and the type that involves a man clattering a small table over when he uncrosses his legs, or alienating a woman on a blind date by giving an offensively demonstrative lesson in how Chinese people like to shovel rice into their mouths. That comedy should have the means to take us by surprise, by raising the questions that are traditionally held to be the preserve of tragedy, is what lends it its dignity, and raises it above the level at which we guffaw obediently at all the usual cues – the slapstick, the loss of clothing, the expletives. Chaos, for example, that hellish medium unleashed by the forces of tragic fate in the lives of such as Macbeth or Brecht's Mother Courage, is also axiomatically funny when it dictates the outcomes of farce or mistaken identity. In many of the most successful modern works of the theatre and cinema, we are driven back to Samuel Beckett's observation that nothing, in the dramatic arts at least, is funnier than unhappiness. We may not know at first whether the hand we clap to our mouths is silencing our shock or stifling a laugh. It is in the ambiguity of such moments, however, that the beginnings of moral enlightenment occur, and all enlightenment, as in the Japanese concept of *satori*, is a flash of surprise, a stroke of thunder.

HAPPINESS

Tomorrow do thy worst, for I have lived today.
John Dryden

The quality or condition of being happy. 1. Good fortune or luck; success, prosperity. 2. The state of pleasurable content of mind, which results from success or the attainment of what is considered good. 3. Successful or felicitous aptitude, fitness, or appropriateness; felicity.

Darwin's physical indicators: smiling; laughing; retraction of the corners of the mouth; lowering of the outer corners of the eyebrows; quickening of the circulation; brightening of the eyes; colouring of the complexion; clapping; stamping; dancing about; crying.

28

TO BE HAPPY

What is happiness? Is it worth striving for? And how do we recognise it once we have it? Is it best to accept whatever comes our way without calling it good or bad, therefore defining oneself as happy or sad? If there is true happiness, how can we be assured of its pedigree without having unhappiness – our own or somebody else's – against which to measure it? These are the questions that have troubled philosophy, and to which religion claimed to know the answers.

What happiness must, irreducibly, depend on is good fortune. To be happy is to be blessed with a quantity of 'hap' in one's life, those felicitous chance occurrences that bring contentment, even ecstasy. The word itself is of Old Norse origin, *happ*, and denotes the quality of good luck. It is possibly related to another dialectal usage, in which to be 'hapt up in bed' is to be securely covered, as is a charmed life by the haps of fortune. That a hap was specifically a stroke of benevolent chance is underlined by the fact that its antonym is a 'mishap'. We might venture therefore to suggest that happiness depends on chance or luck, and that there is therefore little or no point in setting out in pursuit of it. 'Happiness,' says the early Taoist interpreter Chuang Tzu, 'lies in not striving for happiness.' The Old English *hæp* refers merely to good order or right proportion, to what is fitting, convenient or orderly, and this is recognisable in Montaigne's proposition that happiness in life depends on 'the tranquillity and contentment of a spirit well-born and on the resolution and assurance of an ordered soul'.

To the melancholic, the only time to call a man happy was at the moment of his death. Among numerous enunciations of this temperament throughout literature, one need only cite Ovid in Book III of the *Metamorphoses*: 'You must always await a man's last day: before his death and last funeral rites, no one should be called happy.' To those of less saturnine or stoical bent, the road to death may be a haphazard one, but it is strewn perhaps, if we would but look, with haps. Indeed, all occurrences are marked by that character of chance that might just turn out to be fortunate. What happens may well prove happy. In other words, in wanting happy things to happen to us, we are in one sense uttering a mere tautology, but in another, mutely expressing the hope that the operations of chance will favour and not condemn us. The thick black cloud is famously silver-lined, or, as a sixteenth-century saw beautifully expressed it, 'If the Skie fal, we may happe to catch Larkes.'

In what, precisely, will these happy periods consist? Darwin relates the response of a small child, a girl presumably, of a little less than four years old, who, when asked what being in good spirits meant, replied, 'It is laughing, talking, and kissing.' 'It would be difficult,' he thinks, 'to give a truer and more practical definition.' What happiness seems to involve for this child and for Darwin himself is activity, human agency, a sense of exercising prerogatives, rather than merely being in a changeless, passive state of rapture. This attractive, dynamic view of happiness is at odds with both the world-view of eastern mysticism, first being explored in western intellectual circles in the nineteenth century, and of the Judaeo-Christian view, that life involves striving towards some distant goal, set either here or in the afterlife. It seems to say that there can be happiness in the immediate, which is exactly what most of us have difficulty in seeing. It is not so fatalistic that it counsels the wanting of nothing and accepting of everything, but nor is it so unwisely optimistic about the chances of some grand resolution of all human conflict. We take laughter for granted as a byproduct of joyousness – it is the natural element in which high spirits and good cheer announce themselves – but the emphasis on talking is more surprising. And yet can one envisage a happy life without the converse and colloquy of those whom we love? Both familial and erotic relationships are clearly eroding when silence becomes dominant, and when lack of communication leads to the build-up of needless resentment. Kissing may be a little more elusive as a vehicle for happiness, especially at those times of life – maladroit adolescence and decomposing old age – when we feel ourselves most in need of it, but somehow we manage to find even that. What one might wish to add to these elements would be the consumption of intoxicants, unimaginable to a child, and perhaps some regular encounter with art. Thus equipped, we would be in possession of a commodity that appears to have eluded the greater part of humanity for much of the world's history. Is it that we find it hard to know when we are experiencing this emotion, or rather that we grow to be less satisfied with these simple things, and are always inclined to desire more than we have?

It seems probable that the reason we don't tend to define these humble faculties as adding up to happiness is that we retain before us an image of something more akin to exhilaration. There are moments, even periods, of one's life when everything speeds up, events take on a dynamic, unpredictable turn like the montage in a miraculous dream, and the overcast autumnal landscape we move through is suffused with the vividness of spring. At such moments, one's feet seem scarcely to touch the ground. Whether these elated interludes concern love or work, sex or money or travel, they leave a residue of defiance at their passing. If we have been happy, which we assuredly know we have now that the moment has gone, then somehow we have a right to more – or if not a right, then a right to hope. After this, the laughing and talking and kissing will do to get us by, but they don't feel like proper happiness, only contentment.

Such a grand view of happiness is least helpful in answering the question of whether happiness is worth chasing. To posit that there might be some changeless state of final attainment, whether through the acquisition of fame or money, or being able to make all one's own life choices without acceding to external compulsion, is deeply misleading. We would do better to remember that it is in the nature of unhappiness only to be changeless, and to see happiness as an intermittent state – sometimes expected, more often not – that deepens the textures of present life, rather than being a final destination in which, once arrived at, we will surely plan to stay.

For the German philosopher Ernst Bloch, happiness emerges as the reward of enduring hope. His three-volume *The Principle of Hope* (1959), composed in the 1930s and 1940s in America, where Bloch was exiled from the Nazis, finds the glimmer of spiritual cheer in some unexpected places – in the plots of pulp fiction or in the neon lights of advertisements, for example – but it also addresses the complex dialectical conundrum raised by posing that inaugural question, 'What is happiness?' Bloch recalls Nietzsche's scorn for those who live a quiet, safe, soft life, believing that happiness consists in the avoidance of stress, but questions his unequivocal celebration of danger. The call to danger was again being made in Europe when Bloch was writing, but he points out that, no matter how dangerously the Nazis thought they were living, their lives were still far less risky than those of their victims. It is not only fascists, though, for whom the perilous life seems attractive. Settled in salaried comfort, set up domestically with our choice of partner, we find ourselves wondering sooner or later whether this is all there is. Although most of us subscribe to the nineteenth-century utilitarian view – which modestly seeks only the greatest happiness of the greatest number, as distinct from universal liberation – each of us perhaps secretly feels that greater fulfilment might lie in risking it all. For Nietzsche, happiness is a weakness, related to fear as the default state of the passive, timid bourgeois. His call for the new, heroic individual, who was more concerned with being strong than virtuous, achieved its historical realisation in the murderousness of fascist gangs less than forty years after his death. And yet Bloch believed it possible to use Nietzsche's anti-conformism to serve as a model for the kind of radical political action that could secure maximum well-being for all. The end result of unambitious contentment, Bloch states, is not the happiness of the greatest number, 'mahogany cabinets for everyone [and] the sofa corner with the slowly smoked cigar', each being satisfied with his own lot. This state of existence does nothing to alter the underlying structural impediments that ensure that 'the greatest number' is never even a majority. None of this is to deny that in domestic tranquillity and friendship there is much to treasure, especially when we remind ourselves that the alternatives are solitude and indifference, at worst hostility. To malign these ideals is to deny succour to those – the battered wife, the bullied schoolboy – for whom the chance of respite would be the very beginning of a joyous life.

The ideal of contentment through moderate enjoyment of the blessings of a simple life is one that dates back to the teachings of Epicurus in the Greek age, and receives its unblushing advocacy in the work of the Roman poet Horace. When he was around thirty, Horace was given the use of a farm in the Sabine hills by his friend Gaius Maecenas, political adviser to the Roman emperor Octavian. The uncomplicated bucolic idyll of this country life greatly satisfied the poet, who composed many of his odes and eclogues in its praise. These set the tone for the visions of paradise that would preoccupy European art and letters at least until the youthful Nietzsche came to the boil, and which furnish the landscape of many a conception of Utopia. Much of the allure of the pastoral life revolves around the modest sensuality of rustic cooking and Falernian wine, the sacrament of companionship and conversation that carries on through the night; and the tone to which the poet repeatedly returns is that of the entreaty or invitation. Thus, the opening stanza of 'An Invitation to Maecenas', in a slightly soupy nineteenth-century American translation by Eugene and Roswell Martin Field, which preserves something of the untimely, faded character of the poet's vision:

> Dear, noble friend! a virgin cask
> Of wine solicits your attention;
> And roses fair, to deck your hair,
> And things too numerous to mention.
> So tear yourself awhile away
> From urban turmoil, pride, and splendor,
> And deign to share what humble fare
> And sumptuous fellowship I tender.
> The sweet contentment retirement brings
> Smoothes out the ruffled front of kings.

That note of gentle, knowing aloofness, telling us that only when you have wearied of the apparent sophistications of urban life, will you truly appreciate the benign simplicitude of the country, sustains many of Horace's lyrics from the Sabine farm. We don't have to take his word for it, the poet insists, but should go and see for ourselves. 'In Praise of Contentment' sharpens the sentiment further, waving a weary hand in dismissal of the idea of ambition and toil, which fail to repay those who set their store by them, but deliver instead the 'ruffled front' (wrinkled brow) of worry. Moreover, the message is as germane to the lolling poet in the hayrick as it is to one of Nietzsche's soldiers rampant:

> This man loves farming, that man law,
> While this one follows pathways martial –
> What boots it whither mortals turn?

Grim fate from her mysterious urn
Doles out the lots with hand impartial.

Nor sumptuous feasts nor studied sports
Delight the heart by care tormented;
The mightiest monarch knoweth not
The peace that to the lowly cot
Sleep bringeth to the swain contented.

By the final stanza, the tone has become so smug that we might be tempted to leave him to it:

Nay, I'd not share your sumptuous cheer,
But rather sup my rustic pottage,
While that sweet boon the gods bestow –
The peace your mansions cannot know –
Blesseth my lowly Sabine cottage.

At least two aspects of the Horatian idyll strike a discordant note in the post-Nietzschean age. One is the presence of that miserable harpie, 'Grim fate', who dishes out the mishaps, the runs of rotten luck and the devastating tragedies, along with the blessings, with no discrimination between the deserving and the innocent. If she is capable of ruining the pleasures of the cynical city-dweller, why should she not also rain on the grape harvest and strike the lowly cottages with lightning when making a tour of the Sabine hills? The other discomfiting doubt comes upon us when we reflect that the poetic voice of Horace's idylls is that of the seasoned urbanite who has found refuge among the farmers. But what of those brought up in unrelenting poverty in the country who have had a glimpse of the gorgeous lubricity and opportunity that the city offers? Why would they derive any satisfaction from the assurance that theirs was the better life? Or, to put it in terms of the First World War lyric that satirised the likelihood of Midwestern farm boys wanting to go back to life in the cornfields, 'How're you gonna keep 'em down on the farm, after they've seen Paree?'

What we all seek is not that settled Horatian contentment and the refulgence of the simple life, but the exhilarated feeling described earlier, in which life takes on a multicoloured, dynamic aspect, when one discovers that external reality is capable of corresponding to one's hopes. The name for this kind of happiness is joy. 'Joy is the aristocracy of happiness,' says Bloch. '[N]othing can any longer challenge its claim to the status of happy life.' What is more, it vanquishes any need for the pretence of living dangerously, a mode that requires the individual to go on proving himself or herself eternally, for fear of ending up in a state of bourgeois satiety. One can quite comfortably be both joyful and content, but to live dangerously requires a constant confrontation with the world, reducing each of us to the character of 'a bad soldier who judges the success of a battle by his wounds'. Occasionally, one encounters the reactionary notion that too much happiness is undesirable, because it leads to a diminished capacity to appreciate it. 'You wouldn't want nothing but happiness,' a colleague remarked, to which one could only retort that, all in all, one might be prepared to chance it. The sentiment is a late residue of the Protestant work ethic, itself the secularisation of the Christian vision of heaven as the reward for forbearance in the vale of tears. Everything that tends towards the devaluation of happiness is what must be resisted. Not only the Alpine philosopher, fuming against the conformity of the valley-dweller from some rarefied peak of his own, but employers of sweated labour from the silver mines of South America to the garment workshops of East Asia no doubt subscribe to the view that too much happiness would spoil people. At all events, we should beware of wishing away what is a perishable commodity. As Bloch concludes, when we balance the attractions of the dangerous and the joyful, it is extremely difficult – though desirable – to get rid of danger, and all too easy – and catastrophic – to lose sight of joy.

Notwithstanding all this, there is still something slightly troubling about the happy life, and not just when, out of *Schadenfreude*, we resent the evidence of it in others to the extent of being reassured by their misfortunes. 'Happy the man,' say the Chinese, 'whose friend has fallen off the roof.' That intimation of unease has something to do with the faint air of brainlessness that very cheery people have, as though they were ill-equipped to appreciate the solemn side of life, understand the sublime, or feel their skin prickle at the phantasmal quality of a misty valley at twilight. The beauty of a ravishing landscape is immediately compromised when somebody says, 'How lovely!' If there is value in living dangerously, concedes Bloch, it consists in the extent to which the experiences gained thereby can guide us through what he calls 'the shallows of happiness' and into the true depths of joy. A prerequisite of shallow happiness is that it is absolutely essential to keep laughing. 'You have to laugh,' runs the old bit of folk wisdom, 'or else you'd cry,' although it is never satisfactorily explained what's wrong with crying. Thus are the television and radio schedules filled with stand-up comedy, situation comedy, comedy chat shows, comedy cooking, comedy history. I have myself participated in a comedy wine-tasting. This proliferation of hilarity, in which audiences have been trained to hoot uproariously regardless of whether the spectacle is at all amusing, has steadily devalued the spontaneity of genuine mirth. Such laughter, which can be at once vacuous and cruelly derisive, was once the proper preserve of mental infirmity, as one of Darwin's respondents reports: 'Dr Crichton Browne ... informs me that with idiots laughter is the most prevalent and frequent of all the emotional expressions.' Another reports that among the Wedda ethnic group of what is now Sri Lanka, there is no physiological or cultural tradition of laughter, and it could not be encouraged, not even despite the strenuous comic efforts of

Victorian researchers. When asked why they didn't laugh, the succinct response was, 'What is there to laugh at?' The interesting point about this reply, unanswerable as it is both practically and philosophically, is that it suggests the Wedda knew perfectly well what laughter was; they just rather felt it was beneath them. To them, it perhaps implied a lack of seriousness or reverence for life. The anecdote recalls the line that Marshall McLuhan used to be fond of quoting, in which, when asked by western ethnologists where their tradition of decorative arts was, a Balinese tribesman had declared, 'We have no art – we do everything well.' Again, the response was not puzzlement as to the concept, merely disinclination to engage in it.

'There is another large class of idiots,' continues Darwin, 'who are persistently joyous or benign, and who are constantly laughing or smiling.' Just as laughter is the most commonly expressed emotion among the mentally handicapped, it seems, so there are those who do nothing but laugh. To imagine that they are convulsively happy, however, would be to misread the situation, just as the tittering jollity of cheerful persons too often masks an inward despair. If laughter is about avoiding tears, we shouldn't be surprised to learn that the two emotional states are considered quite contiguous by Darwin. There is the curious fact that in the immediate aftermath of excessive laughter, people bear a striking resemblance to the state that follows crying. Both reactions involve the crumpling of the face, with the orbicular muscles contracted and the lachrymal glands producing their secretions, and there is disruption of the normal respiratory rhythm. We say of people in paroxysms of grief that they are 'choked with sobs', while hysterical laughter produces a state of spasmodic expiration, in which the laugher seems to have expelled all the breath from the body, and is still trying to force out more. Under the duress of extreme emotion, it is possible to go from one state to the other, and this sequence is by no means confined to those suffering from mental disturbance.

The proximity of helpless laughter and helpless grief has become more evident in modern times, so that they are the twin emotions that the film industry seeks to evoke in us. If we can be provoked to merriment and sympathetic weeping by the same movie, we tend to assume it must have been an uncommonly powerful and truthful work, overlooking the manipulative means by which these emotional responses are achieved. Similarly, our hope of finding a reconciliation to life in the happiness of others is undermined by the grinning rictus into which all public depictions of the human face have resolved. The woman on the side of the bus inviting you to come to a brand-new nightclub, and the man on the poster inside it who reminds you in smiling tones that you will be prosecuted if you haven't paid the correct fare, both grin as they address us, though their frozen expressions already look more like the faces of detainees under torture. An American president who launched two major wars within a single term of office appears to be speaking through a fixed, indelible smirk, perhaps intended to reassure the watching world that America's intentions are benign, but more likely an unconscious emblem of his contempt for an audience that would believe such a thing.

It is from the American world of letters, however, that the most accurately nuanced appreciations of the delicacy and frangibility of happiness in the modern world have come. The early output of Saul Bellow, in particular his masterwork *The Adventures of Augie March* (1953), a magisterial piece of post-war picaresque, offers a sustained take on how humble individuals attempt, and improbably succeed in, self-invention. There is true hope in this writing, which appeared at a time when Europe was doing profound despair rather well. It is present too in the poetry of the New Yorker John Ashbery, whose prolific output has often been thought of as difficult, and yet whose best work sparkles like quartz with philosophical depth. Ashbery's poetry guides us towards a celebration of the oddity, and the miraculous fragility, of our occasional joys. One of his major long poems, the title poem of a 1984 collection, *A Wave*, is richly articulate of the pain and partial recuperation that follow the ending of a relationship. The tone is nostalgic, but also speaks of the bereft person's determination to recover for himself the delight that once inhabited the world around him – the trees, fruits, waterfalls, car journeys, flowers –

                                    everything, in short,
That makes this explicit earth what it appears to be in our
Glassiest moments when a canoe shoots out from under some foliage
Into the river and finds it calm, not all that exciting but above all
Nothing to be afraid of, celebrates us
And what we have made of it.

Not something so very strange, but then seeming ordinary
Is strange too. Only the way we feel about the everything
And not the feeling itself is strange, strange to us, who live
And want to go on living under the same myopic stars we have known
Since childhood, when, looking out a window, we saw them
And immediately liked them.

What Ashbery's poetry teaches us is that perhaps the most restorative quality of human happiness is that it can be regained.

29

I CAN MAKE YOU HAPPY

Meditations on the best ways of ensuring happiness or contentment in one's personal life are all very well, but what if society could be so organised that the happiness of all was guaranteed? If some sublime overarching design were realised, that would bring an ideal state into being, a state whose citizens would be governed by an eternal compact between the people and those who devised it for them in their own best interests, then the eternal problem of human happiness would be solved. Each individual would be liberated from want, but also from the dilemma of how to get the best from life. The best would be daily delivered to him as his birthright.

From the moment Neolithic peoples began constructing dwellings that incorporated a modicum of comfort, as distinct from mere functionality, the human race began to dream of Utopia. As early as five thousand years ago in Britain, we find evidence of stone houses that provide not just for warmth and shelter, but a certain level of commodious amenity too: beds furnished with 'mattresses' of feathers and straw, and laid with coverlets of animal skins and fur. There is stone shelving, on which artefacts such as bone jewellery and decorated earthenware were displayed. This is a true culture, advanced to a level above simple subsistence: fishing, hunting, tending livestock, living in settled, seemingly durable communities, sufficiently removed from the imperative of sheer survival to allow itself the luxury of interior design. What the archaeological evidence of these dwellings speaks of is the desire to augment and consolidate a peaceable existence. In the great urban cultures of the classical era that was to follow, that impulse to give providence a secure grounding in the life of the community would be elevated from the incidental adornments of the Neolithic era to systematic theory. There were not just scarcity and the elements to guard against, but social malfunction too.

Plato's was the first promulgation of a secular utopia to make a significant impression on western thought. Composed in about 375 BC, *The Republic* is an extended visualisation, expressed always by the great mentor Socrates, of what a well-ordered, rationally regulated society would look like. Throughout the dialogue, Socrates' interlocutor Glaucon presses the sage to give concrete details of this state, as opposed to retailing airy fantasies. The text thus preoccupies itself with the practical arrangements by which such a state might be brought into being, and the political principles on which it would be run once established. Fearful of anarchy, it is a rigidly stratified society, in which a class of Rulers – 'Philosopher-Kings' in the standard translation – would oversee the activities of an Auxiliary class, whose functions would be variously administrative, combining executive, military and policing roles. Slaves, whose existence was taken to be axiomatic in the classical era, would not constitute their own class, but would simply be present as appendages of the other classes. The Rulers would live lives of exemplary austerity, forgoing family life and forsaking possessions. Women would play a full role in society, taking on exactly the same jobs as men, even where their physical aptitude may be less, on the grounds that society would want to draw the full potential from all. To the same end, a programme of eugenics would be administered, in which sickly or disabled infants would be disposed of by means of exposure (that is, abandoning them on hillsides for either predators or starvation to take their merciful tolls), and mass mating sessions, overseen by the Rulers, would regularly take place, during which suitable couples would be paired off and encouraged to breed. Not just defective infants, but those born to over-age parents, and those conceived outside the prescribed parameters of the mating festivals, were to be killed, or else demoted down a class. Medicine should concentrate on helping only those who have already looked after themselves, and if curing a person of an injury will still only leave him at partial capacity to carry out his job, it should be withheld from him as a waste of resources. Better no carpenter at all than a poor one. A symbiotic perfecting of both the body and the mind would be aimed at, to avoid the unseemly divisions of contemporary Athenian society, in which young men who relished the compulsory military training turned into super-fit blockheads, while those who derived greater pleasure from their literary education repined into softness and sensuality. Furthermore, there would be a ban on tragic drama as a morale-sapping diversion from the ideal of serving the community. If poetry were at all useful, it had best take the form of the heroic encomium. A ruling class couldn't just spring fully formed into existence, and so it would be necessary to train up the current Rulers in the ways of philosophy. After a while, they could relinquish such matters as the direction of martial campaigns to the Auxiliaries, while they themselves slipped into the shaded groves of contemplation, only occasionally emerging to draw up the mating schedule for the next collective love-in, or order another batch of executions and infanticides.

Few visions of the ideal *polis* dreamed up in the philosophical tradition are more hideous than Plato's, and yet this obscene farrago has been celebrated for centuries as the founding statement of western rational thought. Despite its equitable view of the politics of gender, and the enlightened stance it takes on the conduct of war and the treatment of captives, its insistence that intellect itself – as opposed to the ways in which it is applied – can rule humanity is what fatally undermines it. In the aftermath of the twentieth century, eugenics can no longer be tolerated, while the ethical manipulation of medicine, a trait that is still recognisable today when a doctor questions whether an individual who has wrecked his liver through over-use of alcohol really deserves a transplant is its scarcely less malevolent sibling. The Republic, in short, feels like a singular hybrid of the mindless communities created by cult religions.

Christian thought is the more recent focus for visions of the utopian state, perhaps the first and most glorious of which is St Augustine's fifth-century conception in *De Civilitate Dei* (*The City of God*). There are two cities, the earthly and the heavenly, which are at perpetual war with each other. The *locus classicus* of sin and temptation is the one in which we presently languish, founded not by Adam and Eve, but by their eldest son, the rebellious Cain. The other is that celestial abode upon which we must keep our sin-shrouded eyes fixed if we are to have any chance of being spiritually at peace. After a brisk, selective tour through human history up to the birth of Christ, Augustine goes on, in the closing sections of the work, to describe not the physical topography or administrative arrangements of this utopia, but the state of being that will flood through the souls of those who manage to attain it. The Platonic urge to resolve the ancient dualism of the physical and spiritual self is evident in Augustine's thinking. He announces that in paradise, complete harmony will be achieved between those two ancient antagonists, the body and the soul: 'the body shall forthwith be wherever the spirit wills, and the spirit shall will nothing which is unbecoming either to the spirit or to the body.' All heavenly beauty will appeal to reason, as opposed to the gullible senses, and all desire will be only for the contemplation of God, who will offer himself to be contemplated for all eternity. We shall retain free will, because there will be henceforth no risk of its abuse. Truly liberated once and for all, the self will find delight in the absence of sin. We shan't be able to sin. Indeed, sin will be forgotten, except in the eternal consciousness that we have been delivered from it, which will prompt our eternal gratitude to the deliverer. We shall dimly remember that we once suffered with illness and travails, but the precise feeling of such calamities will have been lost to us for ever, in a gorgeous sensory amnesia. History will cease its turmoil, and the ages of humanity will end not with a foreshadowed evening, but with eternal day, in which we shall have unlimited time to 'rest and see, see and love, love and praise'.

St Augustine wrote this, his major work, against the background of distant invasion. An incursion into the imperial city of Rome was mounted in AD 410 by an army of Visigoths under the leadership of Alaric. Although the attack was by no means one of the great catastrophes of the Empire's late history, many fled into exile in Augustine's native North Africa, where he was bishop of the city of Hippo. The exiles blamed the conversion of Rome to Christianity, and consequent displeasure of the ancestral Roman gods, for the Visigothic vengeance. Where once shrines to the deities of the marriage bed had been revered, there were now stinking barbarians taking the serving girls by force. In this context, Augustine was moved to write *The City of God* as a work of propaganda for the Church. You are justly yearning to return to a golden city, he told the exiles, but you have your eyes fixed on the wrong city. The yearning of the émigré for his homeland is recognised with delicate psychological acuity, and as a treatise upon what heaven might concretely consist in – a topic upon which the biblical sources are silent – it remains one of the great works of imaginative theology. Compared to Plato's nightmare of child murder and compulsory physical jerks, who wouldn't settle for a life in which all desire would have achieved its triumphant resolution, and all fear and memory of pain be sponged away?

A thousand years later, Utopia was given its name by the English parliamentarian Thomas More. Precociously enough in 1515, More's Utopians already lived according to the Marxian principle of 'From each according to his abilities, to each according to his needs', working for a minimum six hours a day at whatever they are best at, and making regular forays into the countryside to till the land and grow crops. Should they not wish to work, then they won't be fed. Their clothing is Maoist-plain and uniform, since the crucial human failing to be abolished is pride. Citizens will be required to move house once a decade, to guard against any unnecessary feathering of the nest, and eat in vast communal dining halls. As with the Platonic Republic, children become free agents of exchange, swapped around from one household to another, according to whichever trade or craft they appear to be skilled in. Because all are provided for, in a society free from economic strata and displays of conspicuous consumption, Utopia's citizens are free to enjoy the honest pleasures of life. There is music and dancing, fine food, and the tending of luscious gardens, and although the absence of intoxicating drink might seem occasion for disappointment (not to say a dreary prefiguration of English Puritanism), still, at least there are no inebriated indiscretions. In their place, philosophical contemplation is raised, a faculty distributed more fairly than it is in Plato's intellectual autocracy, and there is religion too. In fact, all citizens are required to believe in the immortality of the soul, and the existence of a hereafter in which rewards and punishments will be meted out. More's Utopia allows for an administrative magistracy to oversee things, cracking the whip at any outbreak of indolence among the citizenry, and for a people's assembly, at which public affairs will be subjected to duly solemn debate. Any magistrate or senator taking it upon himself to discuss these matters outside the proper forum will be killed.

Lord Chancellor under Henry VIII, More himself was killed by the state in 1535, having been convicted of treason for his refusal to swear the Oath of Supremacy, by which the English king was recognised as Head of the Church in place of the Pope. After languishing for fifteen months in the Tower of London, he was dispatched on the orders of a mildly regretful Henry. He was, as he insisted on the scaffold, 'the King's good servant, but God's first', an ordering of priorities for which, moments later, he lost his head. More was formally canonised by Pius XI in 1935, on the four-hundredth anniversary of his execution. His utopia, a punning coinage that announces its status as both no-place (u-topia) and a good place (eu-topia), has often been claimed as a precursor of the socialist vision of a classless society, and certainly made a profound influence on the young Marx. We would more accurately see it, however, as a specific reaction against the venality of its own time. The luxury of the Tudor court sickened More when he considered the general social deprivation that paid for it, and the threat of execution the text holds out for those who try to manipulate the mechanism of the state reflects his frustrations at serving his career in a court permanently abuzz with intrigue and conspiracy.

Parable paintings of the late Middle Ages evoke the imaginary life of ease envisioned in the Land of Cockaigne. Pieter Brueghel the Elder's *The Land of Cockaigne* (1567) depicts such an ideal state, in which a group of corpulent yokels loll like sloths amid an abundance of culinary delicacies. A cooked pig sports a carving knife in its back as it wanders by. A boiled egg comes scurrying up on little legs, its top already obligingly cracked. Laden tabletops literally grow on trees, since what seemed most attractive about any fantasy of the perfect life is that it be supplied with images of plenty. Visions of paradise in the century following this tended to depict a less fanciful version of pastoral tranquillity, as if in recognition that the world as it was had perfection to offer for those with the eyes and the spiritual disposition to see it. The luminous landscapes of seventeenth-century masters like Claude invite the eye to travel through dappled groves and across sparkling streams towards an infinitude of sunlit distance. It was a manner that endured through the fairytale tableaux of Watteau and into Corot's misty woodlands, and is given an English twist by Constable's rivers and cornfields, where small boys idle on the banks while carts are heaped with hay, but where, gloriously, work has been abolished, it's one long Sunday, and absolutely nothing ever happens.

On the other side of the Atlantic, Constable's contemporary, Nathaniel Hawthorne, took it upon himself to rid the western imagination of the utopian daydream. *The Blithedale Romance* (1852) is a parable of delusion. It tells the story of a group of American idealists who have wearied of the moral turpitude of their country, which has lost all its revolutionary purity, and decided to head off into the open country to found their own community. Their lofty intellectual pretensions doom the enterprise from the start, and they soon find that they aren't really interested in agricultural labour after all. Jealousies and possessiveness flourish among the fruit orchards, emotional entanglements abound, and tragedies supervene. The honest toil under the sun, noble self-sufficiency and co-operation have failed to vanquish the old competitive rivalries among the companions. And yet the narrator, looking back after his departure, cannot help but feel a twinge of nostalgia for a life never lived:

in these years that are darkening around me, I remember our beautiful scheme of a noble and unselfish life; and how fair, in that first summer, appeared the prospect that it might endure for generations, and be perfected, as the ages rolled away, into the system of a people and a world!

In Europe, the first of many attempts to realise the conditions of a workable socialist polity took place in Paris in the aftermath of France's defeat by Prussia in the war of 1870–71. The Commune was as much a spontaneous uprising as the events of 1789 had been, with government forces hopelessly outnumbered by members of the rebellious National Guard. Taking over the Hôtel de Ville in the centre of the city, and barricading themselves in, the Communards managed, rather impressively, to organise city-wide elections in which nearly a quarter of a million votes were cast. On 28 March 1871, the Commune was installed as the legitimate government of the French capital, its members resplendent in red on the steps of the Hôtel, from the top of which flew the red standard of the international workers' brigade. It was the first and last democratically elected revolutionary government of nineteenth-century Europe.

With virtually no administrative experience, the Communards' legislative assembly rapidly became a bitter parody of the kind of parliament they had sought to replace. Members were expected to see themselves as delegates of a sovereign people, rather than independent representatives, to which end they had to consult the small, local workers' clubs in which policies were often formulated in more practical detail than in the Assembly. Meanwhile, as the national leader Adolphe Thiers continued to procrastinate at Versailles over what should be done about the Commune, voices outside – most notably that of the German Chancellor Otto von Bismarck – threatened that if the national government failed to crush the socialist upstarts, they would not scruple to do the job for them.

After two months, government forces retook the city, but not without some of the fiercest resistance fighting ever seen on the streets of Paris. Towering barricades were constructed, and the hand-to-hand fighting took place amid a surreal miasma of blackened fragments of paper, the floating remnants of the bonfire of documents that had been made at the old Ministry of Finance. The Commune's strongholds were taken one by one, until its last stand was mounted at the Père Lachaise cemetery. For once, the cliché about fighting to the last man was true; the final barricade was manned by just one resistance fighter, who held out under attack for fifteen minutes until he had fired his last round, whereupon he laid down his rifle and, with admirable composure, walked away from his place in history. Martial law was declared in Paris in the aftermath of the Commune, and lasted for five years, in which period a brutal repression was instituted. Much as with the liberal revolution of 1848 in Paris, the

Commune had failed because it lacked central direction. Its most inspirational strategist, Louis-Auguste Blanqui, spent its entire short existence – as indeed half of his life – in prison, unable to direct events on the streets, and attempts by the Communards to secure his release for an exchange of hostages were firmly rebuffed. He was the model of what the twentieth century would come to recognise as the professional revolutionary, who viewed imprisonment and persecution as occupational hazards, but who couldn't steer clear of either long enough to influence events when the crunch moment arrived. It was not a mistake his greatest foreign admirer, Vladimir Ilyich Lenin, was to repeat.

If one aspect links all utopias, it may be the intimation that in the faultless world to come, what will be delivered to us will simply be all that we presently lack. Indeed, it seems positively dangerous to imagine the coming life in more concrete detail than this, if one is not to repel those who might subscribe to it. Utopias don't have to be our only glimpse of heaven on earth. In a sense, the more detailed they are, the less utopian they appear. On the other hand, the absence of a fully realised political structure is what has doomed many attempts at creating a revolutionary society to chaos and repression. What is clear is that the attempt to create a better world has to begin, not as the eighteenth-century voyages of discovery led some to think, on a far-flung tropical isle untouched by the ravages of civilisation (Utopia as a return to Eden), but in the here and now, as the revolutionary movements in the nineteenth and twentieth centuries realised. To say that utopias have so often failed is not to claim that the moment for great popular upheavals should not be seized. It is simply to remind ourselves that humanity is not best suited to social arrangements drawn up for it like the blueprints of a civil engineering project. There may have been administrative muddle, confusion and economic instability in the former Yugoslavia, but that does not mean it was wrong to overthrow Milošević.

30

I AM LEFT HAPPY

Once, on the Piazza San Marco in Venice, as the late afternoon sun began to lose its ferocity and turn to mellow apricot, a traveller and his companion sat drinking gin fizz and listening to a little orchestra. A violinist and clarinettist were accompanied by upright bass and piano, playing the well-worn famous bits from forgotten operettas, interspersed with show tunes and pop standards. Nobody was paying them much attention, except that the close of each item prompted a raggy smatter of applause, during which the pianist might catch somebody's eye, twinkling appreciatively back. The ambient cooing of the pigeons that carpet St Mark's during the day was declining, cut through with the occasional 'sssst' of white-jacketed waiters summoning each other's attention. The lights had come on in Florian's opposite, and a very large lady in a herd's-worth of fur was setting about something like a cream cake, while her pinched-looking escort gazed reflectively out on to the square.

The thought came over the traveller that to die here, like this, not now perhaps, but sometime, would be the very best way to go, surrounded not by discreetly sorrowing relatives, but by agitated waiters bringing him brandy in the midst of death's ineffable sweetness. The band wouldn't have noticed anything was amiss, and would proceed through its repertoire, perhaps essaying a burst of something classier – Verdi, *signori*? – as the outlines of the perceptual world dissolved from photo-realism, through late impressionism, to final Rothko.

One's innate sense that an ending ought to be happy stands confounded before an almighty paradox. It is that, if the period it marked were truly happy, it wouldn't be right that it should end. The satisfactory resolution of a difficult episode is natural cause for celebration, on the time-hallowed principle that all's well that ends well. To wish to find ourselves in a state of muted ecstasy, when the moment comes to quit the scene, is another matter entirely. It isn't at all surprising that Venice at the close of day should inspire these elated intimations of mortality, especially to one over-familiar with the image of the expiring Dirk Bogarde in Visconti's diaphanous *Death in Venice*, choking with cholera, his mascara streaming under the broiling sun on the Lido. Endings come upon us at every turn, though. Affairs end, eras end, and all end with that sense of finality first experienced in infancy, when the fairground ride that had thrilled for three minutes just perceptibly began to decelerate.

To this day, though we bridle to admit it, we still yearn for the reassurance of the happy ending. In classic fairy tales, such as those of the brothers Grimm, the ending requires not only that the good emerge from their tribulations intact, but that the evil are suitably punished. The Wicked Queen in *Snow White* must put on a pair of red-hot shoes and dance herself to death, while L Frank Baum, writing a more tender-hearted and sentimental children's narrative in *The Wonderful Wizard of Oz* (1900), still dissolves his bad witches to slurry as if with hydrochloric acid. It appears that a happy ending needs some element of vindictiveness if it is fully to satisfy. Something of the same questionable impulse is present in the injunction to bear one's troubles lightly, on the grounds that there are always others less fortunate than oneself (a homily that has always struck me as uncomfortably close to gloating). If all narrative has something to teach us, then the happy outcome is the moment when the lesson is driven home. Where a story is left hanging, as it is in Hitchcock's *The Birds*, we feel a sense of unease that evil might have been allowed to continue unchecked, or at least to live on in some only slightly modified form, a presentiment that was of course the precise intention of the filmmaker. The depraved cannibal serial killer Dr Lecter (Anthony Hopkins) of *The Silence of the Lambs* (1991), having escaped Houdini-like from his secure prison at the film's climax, leaves the police detective (Jodie Foster), who has been interviewing him throughout, in a state of ambiguous reassurance, when he declares that he harbours no final ill will against her, because the world is a far more interesting place with her in it. Is this a happy ending? Or is it more likely an ending for grown-ups? Evil is never finally defeated. We are simply called on to renew our vigilance in its presence.

Then again, it isn't necessarily childish to want a tale to end happily. It is no more infantile to hope that the estranged lovers are reunited with each other, or that the prodigal son returns to his parents, than it is to have wanted to hear a tale in the first place. It is only when we start to expect real-life crises to end well that we store up cognitive distress. If they do, we can be thankful, but where they don't, the desolation felt is compounded by the fact that we could have been better prepared. More than ever before, after a century of violent conflict unimaginable to the generations that preceded it, in which the evils of totalitarianism were vanquished by demonstrably more enlightened forces, modern warfare enables us in the west to believe that conflicts can be prosecuted to a safe and lasting conclusion, with few or no casualties being sustained on the side we support. This is the case as never before with the current global war on terrorism, which, by its unwinnable nature, comes increasingly to seem like a quest for one last great political utopia in the era that put an end to utopias. If we could only address the injustices that sustain terrorist fanaticism, it is postulated, we might stand a chance of reaching a happiness that has been denied to humanity at least since the decline of the Sumerians: the happiness of living without the threat of war.

The desire for a resolution of the world's conflicts is of course no more ignoble than the desire to see the characters in a story receive the dignity of a happy ending, and if achieved would certainly make us all feel we had stepped, like Alice, into an imaginary magical world. Until that happens, the reconciliation for which we yearn can only be accomplished in the realms of pure imagination. To curl the lip, then – as many modernist literary and artistic works did through most of the twentieth century – at the longing for happy endings and just resolutions, to find hope itself a polluting contaminant, is to expropriate from the wretched of the earth any glint of a vision that things could be better. Confronted with such desperation, it is quite easy, and probably right, to believe that they never will be. We don't have to turn to antique religion to discover hope, although many do, but only to rescue its notion of a final recompense, at which both the sufferings and the blindness of humanity will be washed away. This is finally what is wrong with the idea of making do by means of some pragmatic engagement with the way things are, for fear of being branded a hopeless romantic. It inscribes 'the way things are' in tablets of stone. The irritating verdict of his elders, on hearing of a boy's first enthusiastic encounter with Marxism, that it was all very well in theory but could never work in practice ('Look at Russia!'), did nothing to convince one casting about in search of redemption that 'the way things are' worked any better. And so one finds oneself too easily longing for a happiness that is highly unlikely to arrive.

Nothing else can explain the enduring, pervasive appeal of John Lennon's sugar-coated threnody 'Imagine', one of the very worst songs ever written. Despite its having a melody only a true simpleton could write, coupled with an excruciating freight of personal hypocrisy in the lyric, its impossibilist yearning for a unified world, free of all the detritus that currently divides it, is a sentiment to which millions subscribe. Much more radical, though, was a slightly earlier – now almost forgotten – recording of the Plastic Ono Band, in which, over a percussive background centred on Yoko rhythmically banging a cupboard door, an Indian-influenced choral mantra that demanded 'Give peace a chance', was intoned, less in the spirit of votive meditation than in the manner of the lobotomy ward. It was one of the most improbable of all improbable 1960s hits, and gained its power from the fact that the perfectly reasonable request contained in it became, by virtue of there being no other line in the refrain, an illustration of the terrible damage done to those who had no power to put it into effect.

At some point, though, there has to be more than just the desire for change, if hope itself is not to wither away. There is neither dignity nor dynamism in that state of impotent wishfulness that an obscure bit of Latinism – velleity – describes. Crooning vacantly along to a pop tune that invokes a world of peace and understanding, while secretly believing the Israelis and the Palestinians deserve each other, would be one contemporary version of it. At the other extreme is terrorism, of which Leon Trotsky remarked that, quite apart from the moral bankruptcy of indiscriminate murder, it constitutes the false appropriation of the insurrectionary urge, which should belong to all the dispossessed, by one self-appointed cabal. To sit in a field getting stoned does nothing to disturb the world around you. Detonating a bomb in a crowded railway station, by contrast, only adds to human misery. Somewhere between these two extremes is a place where the impulse for a changed world can be realised. It inevitably involves not just empathic contact with 'the way things are', but with the intention of making them different, not in order simply to tear off the big black cloud that comes wrapped around every silver lining, in a desire to show that there is good in everyone, that an unpresumptuous happiness can be had from the ordinary little moments of the darkest days, and that life, after all, is what you make it – bare-faced lies, every one.

If one manages to escape being labelled an unrealistic dreamer, the other charge likely to be levelled at you is that of the prophet of doom. Nobody likes a naysayer, in a culture where the enjoinder to 'lighten up!' is heard every time a critical voice is raised. And indeed, constant cynicism is a profoundly unattractive quality. Not much of value is advanced by the kind of self-torturing attitude that sees conspiracies everywhere, or that condemns everything as meaningless. The trick, as Marx announced in the 1840s, was to criticise everything, not condemn it out of hand. If it is a happy outcome that we seek, then we must look for the traces of it in the current impasse, constructing hope out of the least promising fragments of our reality. To those who protest that engaging with a benighted world risks diluting the purity of one's own chosen refusal of it, one can only plead guilty, before inviting them, if they have indeed managed to find a way of not being part of the same faulty reality, short of personal extinction, to let the rest of us in on the secret. To accept that our world is the only material we have to work with is not to acquiesce in 'the way things are'; it is to revile them sufficiently to grasp hold of and alter them. In childhood, one is encouraged to stand up to bullies, rather than try to evade them. Almost nobody took the advice, suspecting with good cause that it was more likely to ensure further victimisation. And when we confront them in adulthood, whether they be media moguls or supermarket chains, they still turn out to be bigger than us, and we find ourselves slinking away again.

The effect of the happy ending to a serious novel or film is twofold: it compensates the characters for the trials they have undergone, and it reassures the audience that there is some hope for the future. If the resolution is convincing, the example can be a powerful one. Another form of ending offers closure without defining the outcome as happy or tragic. The sense of a respite from further travails is most pronounced in a novel like *Jane Eyre* (1847) – 'Reader, I married him!' – whereas *Wuthering Heights* (1847) closes only with a resigned diminuendo, inviting us to share the wish that its deceased heroes are not, as is rumoured, still haunting the moors, but are slumbering quietly in the undisturbed earth.

Anthony Patch, in F Scott Fitzgerald's *The Beautiful and Damned* (1922), has fallen from inherited opulence and a glamorous, hedonistic marriage into alcoholic squalor and poverty, when, at the end, a court decision to restore his inheritance rescues him from final destitution. Seated in a wheelchair on the deck of an ocean liner bound for Europe, he finds himself the object of attention of a pair of gossips. They have read his story in the papers and mistakenly assume that he is gloating over his good fortune. Far from it:

– he was concerned with a series of reminiscences, much as a general might look back upon a successful campaign and analyse his victories. He was thinking of the hardships, the insufferable tribulations he had gone through. They had tried to penalise him for the mistakes of his youth. He had been exposed to ruthless misery, his very craving for romance had been punished, his friends had deserted him – even Gloria had turned against him. He had been alone, alone – facing it all.

Unlikeable as he has become, these self-pitying observations are accurate, and anybody who has ever won a pyrrhic victory will recognise the tone of embittered congratulation in Anthony's soliloquy. Essential to the relief at winning back his inheritance is the contiguous feeling of having been proved right, whether the rest of the world judges it a moral victory or not.

Only a few months before people had been urging him to give in, to submit to mediocrity, to go to work. But he had known that he was justified in his way of life – and he had stuck it out staunchly. Why, the very friends who had been most unkind had come to respect him, to know he had been right all along. Had not the Lacys and the Merediths and the Cartwright-Smiths called on Gloria and him at the Ritz-Carlton just a week before they sailed?

A sycophants' chorus of Cartwright-Smiths has become for the hero the living proof of his own integrity, since there is no other in sight. At the beginning of the narrative, we have seen him luxuriating in the opulence of his 52nd Street apartment, where the thick pile of the bathroom carpet envelops his bare feet, the sofas yield to his trim, athletic frame, and the wardrobe bulges with 'sufficient linen for three men'. Now, after service in the Great War and a subsequent fall into whisky-sodden delirium tremens, we find him restored to luxury, breathing an odious sigh of relief at the prospect of having escaped that ultimate humiliation, having to work – the preserve of the little people. The turmoil of the latter years, though, has not left him bereft of emotion:

Great tears stood in his eyes, and his voice was tremulous as he whispered to himself. 'I showed them,' he was saying. 'It was a hard fight, but I didn't give up and I came through!'

Pity and pride remain to him, but only for himself. He has indeed survived, but whether he deserved to is hard to say. This is the quintessential modern finale, a conclusion deeply ambiguous and undecidable in its moral status. The man got his money back, didn't die, defeated his rival, presumably prevailed in his battle with the bottle, and hasn't lost his radiant wife. But, like the pair of gossips in the final scene, however, we are inclined to think there is something a little 'unclean' about the charmed couple, and something distasteful in their clinging to an affected decadence, the famous 'way of life' of the *beau monde* in the era following the First World War, when tragedy has been swilling all around them. It is this 'way of life' that Ernst Bloch referred to as 'the shallows of happiness'.

We want our own endings, naturally, to be happier than this.

More to the point, we would like that elusive commodity now, but the principle of deferred gratification, which all the major religions peddle and which has been the graceful philosophical attitude ever since Plato, has bred into us the reflex that such a desire is unworthy. When true happiness does come, the sense of powerless yearning that constitutes so much of the rest of life is momentarily vanquished, and the notion that happiness itself should be a final state is rightly lost to us. We might also stop to note, *pace* the efforts of the utopianists, that the gladdened state in no way resembles their meticulously detailed blueprints, but is instead varicoloured, rich and surprising. The problem with the happy ending is not that it reflects a naïve wish for reconciliation in a world unlikely to deliver it, but that it is simply that – an ending. If joy only arrives at the end of the story, what of all the living that has to lead up to it?

Living in this state of anticipation of a joyful future is characterised for most people by a feeling of helplessness. Like passengers standing on a cold, dark platform, awaiting an indefinitely delayed train, we try to divert ourselves by rereading the morning paper or chattering idly on our phones, in the hope that the time will pass more quickly. But, as is observed by the Chorus in T S Eliot's *Murder in the Cathedral* (1935), it never does: 'Time is short, but waiting is long.' Haunted by the question to which we don't really want to hear the answer – 'Is this it?' – it might seem as though the hardest test of virtue is not of courage, but of patience. What might once have compensated for this strained patience, and still does for many, is the proposition that someone else is watching. It animates Kierkegaard's analysis, in *Fear and Trembling* (1843), of the story of Abraham, who has been led to the brink of killing his own son for God, simply as a test of his faith. Abraham's supreme achievement is his fidelity to the God he loves:

[A]nyone who loves God needs no tears, no admiration; he forgets the suffering in the love. Indeed, so completely has he forgotten it that there would not be the slightest trace of his suffering left if God himself did not remember it, for he sees in secret and recognises distress and counts the tears and forgets nothing.

If we can learn to love a God who demands tests of loyalty such as that commissioned of Abraham, we may after all be free. After 1945, this suggestion could be said to amount to heresy. If God made the earth and everything in it, he made the tears too, so well might he count and remember.

Of all our emotions, happiness is perhaps the strangest, subject to a far greater range of stimuli than those we conventionally associate with the negative feelings, but it is also the most fragile. It is the only one that doesn't gain a sense of purpose in its evanescence. When anger subsides, we recall our powers of forgiveness. When fear is conquered, we regain our sense of self. But when happiness abates, all there is to return to is more of that idle waiting. Its passing often seems to make a mockery of the circumstances that had produced it, and it has this at least in common with the negative emotions – that its vanishing makes its cause seem unreal. What should help us to continue is the thought that, however unrealistic the desire for happiness might appear, there remains its anticipation, that gathering intimation that accompanies the first faltering ascent of the rollercoaster. A better day will come, or might come, while the bad ones steal by in the interim. In these spaces, we feel time's elasticity as acutely as one who, alone in the house in the late evening, awaits the return of his beloved, in a state in which all other spiritual activity has ceased. He is, as the Chinese say, 'looking at the door', trusting that soon the key will grate in the lock, the handle turn, and the waiting, which can now be forgotten, be at an end. The power that radiates from this moment illuminates for a time the whole perceptual world. It recompenses the one who waited with the news that the waiting wasn't in vain, and it exercises its own untriumphal victory over the other emotions. A world glistening with joy is a world that can easily do without fear, without anger, disgust and jealousy, and a world that can do without these is a world worth living in.

BIBLIOGRAPHICAL NOTES

INTRODUCTION

The Smiths' case appears in chapter 16 of Tobias Smollett's work, *The History of England, from the Revolution in 1688, to the Death of George the Second* (Oxford, 1827), pp. 455–6. To the author, their actions remain 'very uncommon' and 'remarkable' because he accepts the prevailing medical orthodoxy of the eighteenth century (he is writing only twenty-five years after the event) that a suicide is indicative, by its nature, of insanity. The Smiths' case, and the ample publicity it received in the literature of the period, helped to give the lie to this view. Charles Dédéyan's *L'Angleterre dans la pensée de Diderot* (Gallimard, Paris, 1958) details the impression it made on the French Enlightenment philosopher.

Hannah Arendt's reflections on the nature of the public and private realms in society – *The Human Condition* (University of Chicago Press, Chicago, [1958] 1998) – are somewhat ahistorical but, although the argument appears largely directed towards the American society of the 1950s in which she was writing, its impact is interestingly far more illuminating if projected back a couple of hundred years. She is even able to propose, improbably enough in the post-war era, that love, for example – as distinct from friendship – is best kept hidden, for it risks extinction as soon as it becomes public. That her citation in support of the point is the already one-hundred-and-fifty-year-old sentiment of William Blake ('Never seek to tell thy love/ Love that never told can be;/ For the gentle wind does move/ Silently, invisibly') seems not entirely beside the point.

It was in 1966 that Paul Ekman and others began putting the central theory in Charles Darwin's *The Expression of the Emotions in Man and*

Animals (Fontana Press, London, [1872] 1998) to experimental validation, by comparing North American findings with those gleaned from
trips to South America and Japan. His and his colleagues' early papers on
the topic, such as P Ekman, E R Sorenson and W V Friesen, 'Pan-Cultural
Elements in Facial Displays of Emotions', *Science,* 164 (1969), pp. 86–88,
are majestic in their thoroughness. The fieldwork of Ekman in particular
was a latter-day HMS *Beagle* tour through the natural world of human
emotion, verifying and elaborating Darwin's century-old postulates.
Ekman's own *summa theologica* appeared as a slightly late centenary tribute, *Darwin and Facial Expression: A Century of Research in Review*
(Academic Press, New York, 1973). His third edition of *The Expression of
the Emotions in Man and Animals* itself is now the indispensable version
of Darwin's text.

The French works that Darwin himself principally drew on were
Guillaume-Benjamin Duchenne's cutting-edge *Mécanisme de la Physionomie Humaine* (Paris, 1862) and Pierre Gratiolet's posthumously
published *De La Physionomie et des Mouvements d'Expression* (Paris,
1865), the latter a collation of a lecture course given at the Sorbonne.

An important recent populariser of work in this field has been Antonio
Damasio, whose *The Feeling of What Happens: Body, Emotion and the
Making of Consciousness* (Heinemann, London, 2000) offers much
insight into the cerebro-cortical constitution of our emotional lives,
which in itself serves to buttress the idea that emotional aptitude is a universal language. William M Reddy, in *The Navigation of Feeling: A
Framework for the History of Emotions* (Cambridge University Press,
Cambridge, 2001), attempts something akin to what I do here, linking the
development of emotional articulacy to key historical configurations, in
his case Revolutionary France.

1: TO FEAR

Johannes Maringer's work on the archaeological evidence of early
spiritual beliefs unearthed by cave finds, *The Gods of Prehistoric Man,*
trans. Mary Ilford (Weidenfeld and Nicolson, London, [1956] 1960),
remains an elegant elucidation of the issues. A handful of its theories have

since been superseded, but its explanation of the central case, that a belief in one monolithic god probably predated the polytheistic system, is still persuasive.

Sigmund Freud's career-long propensity for airy speculation had not deserted him even as late as *Civilisation and its Discontents*, collected in *The Penguin Freud Library*, Vol. 12, trans. James Strachey and Angela Richards (Penguin, London, 1985), pp. 251–340. Somehow the notion that the control of fire originated through homoerotic pissing games could not have issued from any other thinker in the western canon.

Theodor Adorno and Max Horkheimer's *Dialectic of Enlightenment*, trans. John Cumming (Verso, London, [1944] 1979) was an early salvo in the Frankfurt School's ongoing dispute with western rationalism, which, far from illuminating the world with the healthy glow of enlightenment, had only completed the project of domination over humanity threatened by the god or gods of prehistoric times. From being at the mercy of an unfathomable nature, we were now subject to that advanced control over our own inner natures wrought by the sterility of a technological world, in which all social relations were subject to minute manipulation from above, and any capacity for independent thought had been willingly surrendered by the mass of society.

2: TO FRIGHTEN

It has become fashionable to propose, in a spirit of counter-suggestibility, that Machiavelli's *The Prince*, trans. Stephen J Milner (Everyman, London, [1516] 1995) is not the enabling text of malevolent political chicanery that posterity has it to be, but is either a dispassionate study in human psychology or an essay in wise pragmatism. Neither of these readings can honestly be borne out by the text itself, which to modern ears reads as alarmingly as it should, in its cool exhortations to murder and its axiomatic assumption of the chimerical nature of public morality.

George Orwell's most quoted novel, *Nineteen Eighty-four* (Penguin, London, [1949] 2003) was, almost from the moment of its publication, a gift to the reactionary right, who chose to read in it only an excoriation of Stalinism. While the lineaments of life in a totalitarian Britain certainly

BIBLIOGRAPHICAL NOTES

bear more resemblance to the bureaucratic degradation of the Soviet Union than to the then recently defeated Nazi Germany, there is nonetheless an indictment of all invasive authoritarianism at its heart.

Adorno's late masterwork, *Negative Dialectics*, trans. E B Ashton (Routledge, London, [1966] 1973), is probably the most richly nuanced, idiosyncratic and fearless philosophical text of the twentieth century.

3: I AM AFRAID

Giles MacDonogh's finely detailed, three-dimensional study, *Frederick the Great* (Weidenfeld and Nicolson, London, 1999), is a splendid recent biography of one of Europe's most fascinating rulers. While respecting his vast clinical experience, I find many of the conclusions Isaac M Marks draws with regard to irrational fear in *Living with Fear: Understanding and Coping with Anxiety* (McGraw-Hill, Maidenhead, second edition, 2001) raise quite as many questions as they appear to answer.

4: TO BE ANGRY

Carol Tavris has thought deeply and productively about anger at both the interpersonal and social levels, and the fruits of her labours are apparent in *Anger: The Misunderstood Emotion* (Touchstone, New York, revised edition, 1989).

G M Young's *Portrait of an Age* (Phoenix Press, London, [1936] 2002) is a fine document, both of the period it describes (Victorian England), and that in which it was written, when a historian could be less self-conscious than today about applying his craft to the widest of canvases. The writing is penetrating and beautiful, and the tautness of control of its extravagant theme an object-lesson.

Stephanie Griest's account of the Watts riot, which can be found on www.ustrek.org, is written with a keenly honed sense of both the drama and the injustices of the events it relates.

5: I ENRAGE

Given the proliferation of interest in the literature of the Great War, and the many poetry collections available, Arthur Graeme West's work is not anthologised enough. An exception, now published as a widely used school edition, which includes his 'God! How I Hate You . . .', is *Men Who March Away: Poems of the First World War*, ed. Ian Parsons (Chatto and Windus, London, [1965] 1978).

There is practically as much interest in Dada and surrealism these days as there is in the war poets. Two of the finest accounts of the twentieth century's premier art movements appear as volumes in Thames and Hudson's World of Art series. Hans Richter's *Dada* (Thames and Hudson, London, 1966) remains unsurpassed for its meticulous insider's view, while Sarane Alexandrian's *Surrealist Art*, trans. Gordon Clough (Thames and Hudson, London, [1969] 1970), which opens with Dada, is a nice blend of reportage and philosophical reflection.

An extraordinary piece of fevered prose by e-critic James Reich, 'The Case of Arthur Cravan Solved' at www.jamesreich.com, has Cravan expiring in the Gulf of Mexico, with sharks feeding on his entrails until he is put out of his agonies by a gunshot through the spine, fired from a rocky promontory by Isidore Ducasse. Also known as the Comte de Lautréamont, Ducasse was a nineteenth-century proto-Cravan, born in Uruguay, dead at twenty-four, author of a ranting poetic epic full of blasphemous outrages, *Les Chants de Maldoror* (1869), and another of Dada and surrealism's household gods. Had Ducasse not died in 1870 (Cravan disappeared in 1918), this might have seemed as likely as any other theory to account for Cravan's disappearance. Antonia Logue's outstanding debut novel, *Shadow-Box* (Bloomsbury, London, 1999), is an imaginative interweaving of the lives of Cravan, Mina Loy and Jack Johnson, which captures much of what must have been the torrid atmosphere of their briefly overlapping lives and times.

Greil Marcus's *Lipstick Traces: A Secret History of the Twentieth Century* (Secker and Warburg, London, 1989) rehearses the much-argued case for the continuities of punk rock with Zürich Dada (and much else besides, including the Parisian situationist movement founded by Guy

Debord). Eschewing overheated intellectualism but teeming with diligent research, Jon Savage's *England's Dreaming: Sex Pistols and Punk Rock* (Faber and Faber, London, 1991) is the definitive history of the upheaval of 1976–77.

6: I AM ANGERED

An impressive case against the presumptions of catharsis therapy was mounted in a number of papers by Jack E Hokanson and Michael Burgess, particularly 'The Effects of Three Types of Aggression on Vascular Processes', *Journal of Abnormal and Social Psychology*, Vol. 64 (1962), pp. 446–9; and 'The Effects of Status, Type of Frustration and Aggression on Vascular Processes', *Journal of Abnormal and Social Psychology*, Vol. 65 (1962), pp. 232–7. *Bioenergetics* by Alexander Lowen (Penguin, New York, [1979] 1994) gives as full a picture as one could wish of the counter-argument.

7: TO DISGUST

William Ian Miller's *The Anatomy of Disgust* (Harvard University Press, Cambridge, Mass., 1997) is full of suggestive exempla, and attempts as systematic an exploration of the subject as does Robert Burton's treatment of melancholy, the title of which it consciously echoes. I find it slightly spoiled by an excess of personal morality, of the kind that sits less easily in relativist Europe than it probably does in the University of Michigan, where he teaches.

An important early contribution to the anthropology of disgust was marked by Andras Angyal's paper, 'Disgust and Related Aversions', *Journal of Abnormal and Social Psychology*, Vol. 36 (1941), pp. 393–412. The work of Paul Rozin *et al* in the 1980s is also highly enlightening; see especially P Rozin and A E Fallon, 'A Perspective on Disgust', *Psychological Review,* Vol. 94 (1987), pp. 23–41.

Another anatomy, Erich Fromm's *The Anatomy of Human Destructiveness* (Pimlico, London, [1974] 1997), is hobbled by unquestioning reliance on Freudian analysis, but its handling of the biographical data on

Hitler is thought-provoking, and as objective as the subject-matter permits. Gitta Sereny's *Albert Speer: His Battle with Truth* (Picador, London, 1995) is a justly acclaimed account of the life of one of the Nazi Party's more complex figures.

8: I DISGUST

Michel Foucault's *The Birth of the Clinic: An Archaeology of Medical Perception*, trans. A M Sheridan (Routledge, London, [1963] 1997) is instructive on the transformation of clinical practice that took place in the late seventeenth and early eighteenth centuries. This was a period in which definitions of health and sickness were comprehensively reformulated, but in which also a new ethical consciousness of what patients had a right to expect from medicine came about.

In *Death, Dissection and the Destitute* (Phoenix Press, London, second edition, 2001), Ruth Richardson explains in compassionate detail the moral dilemmas occasioned by the experimental, sometimes public, dissection of the bodies of the poor facilitated by the 1832 Anatomy Act. Her discussion leads to a consideration of present-day concerns about organ transplant and the procurement of human tissue for the purposes of research.

9: I AM DISGUSTED

Jessica Warner offers a dispassionate account of the gin epidemic in *Craze: Gin and Debauchery in an Age of Reason* (Profile Books, London, 2002). Patrick Dillon tells the story with rather more affectation, and considerably less impact, in *The Much-Lamented Death of Madam Geneva: The Eighteenth-Century Gin Craze* (Justin, Charles and Co., London, 2002).

10: TO BE SAD

The notion that sadness has its invariable roots in some sense of loss, as opposed to sheer lack, is forcefully argued by Freud in *Group Psychology and the Analysis of the Ego* (The Penguin Freud Library, Vol. 12, op. cit., pp. 95–178). It is given a prolonged airing in Andrew Solomon's widely acclaimed *The Noonday Demon: An Anatomy of Depression* (Chatto and Windus, London, 2001), perhaps the best of a slew of general-interest books on the subject of clinical depression to be published in recent years.

St Augustine ties himself up in theological knots as he attempts to reconcile the sensual life of his early adulthood, with all its spiritually ruinous topography of self-abuse, with his devout maturity. The *Confessions*, trans. John K Ryan (Doubleday, New York, 1960) add up to an extraordinary document of personal revelation, one of the most stirring the medieval Christian tradition produced.

Without David Hume, the enterprise of European scepticism would have been substantially deferred. The *Dialogues Concerning Natural Religion* (Penguin, London, [1779] 1990), which recruit the Platonic dialogue form in the service of the eighteenth-century Enlightenment, are a meticulous, merciless inquiry into the nature of belief, and the conclusions it forces us to draw about a deeply faulty world. His natural successor is Arthur Schopenhauer, whose magisterial *The World as Will and Representation*, best read in the full dignity of E F J Payne's translation (Dover, New York, [1859] 1966), strove, hubristically enough, to be the last word on the whole grisly matter. Not so Søren Kierkegaard, who makes a valiant, countervailing attempt to invest the sceptical temperament with the responsibilities of Christian theology, wedding religion and existentialism together for the first and last time. *The Sickness Unto Death*, trans. Alastair Hannay (Penguin, London, [1849] 1989) is one of the touchstone texts.

The most famous set of notes in nineteenth-century philosophy, the *Theses on Feuerbach*, collected in C J Arthur, ed., *The German Ideology* (Lawrence and Wishart, London, second edition, 1974), discovered posthumously among Karl Marx's papers by Friedrich Engels and first published in 1888, represented the first attempt of the modern era to pass beyond the sterile scholasticism of the western speculative tradition and into the arena where the lives of real men and women were lived.

11: I MAKE YOU SAD

Despite its occasional solecism, George Steiner's early study of the tragic theatre, *The Death of Tragedy* (Faber and Faber, London, 1961), remains an impressive accomplishment. It engages with the central tenets of Aristotelian catharsis theory, asking whether they can still be held to apply to the events of the tragic theatre of the nineteenth and twentieth centuries. With one or two exceptional moments, in such works as Bertolt Brecht's *Mother Courage and her Children* (1941), his answer is a resounding 'No'. Tragedy has been richly re-theorised in a major recent work, *Sweet Violence: The Idea of the Tragic* (Blackwell, Oxford, 2003) by Terry Eagleton.

The Republic, trans. Desmond Lee (Penguin, London, second revised edition, 1987) is Plato's central text, a work of such overweening significance to the development of western philosophy as makes its suppositions, conclusions and prescriptions even now so difficult to challenge. But challenged, undoubtedly, they must be. The antidote to its hideous authoritarianism is to be found in the works of the Greek dramatists Plato drily scorns. The *Electra* of Euripides, trans. Emily Townsend Vermeule, collected in *Euripides*, Vol. v, (University of Chicago Press, London, [1959] 1968) is, conversely, among the brightest ornaments of Athenian culture.

12: I AM MELANCHOLY

Two great contrasting – and nearly contemporaneous – bodies of work that encompass much of the material of the present study are to be found in the forms of Michel de Montaigne's *Complete Essays*, trans. M A Screech (Penguin, London, [1580] 1991) and Robert Burton's *The Anatomy of Melancholy* (Kessinger, Whitefish, Montana, [1628] 2002), the one all Gallic phlegmatism, the other the product of a peculiarly English preoccupation with the ills and afflictions that flesh (and the mind) are heir to. For Montaigne, removing himself from human congress more fastidiously than any thinker until Nietzsche, the world is nonetheless a sounding-board for the human soul, something upon which, even tested to extremity, the individual can leave his mark, whereas for Burton, what is interesting is precisely what happens to us when the traffic is all in the contrary direction. If there be world enough and time, the two texts are worth immersing oneself in concurrently.

13: TO BE JEALOUS

The Bible Guide by Andrew Knowles (Lion Publishing, Oxford, 2001) does its best with the Cain story for a general readership, but imputes far too much in the way of impious disrespect to the luckless brother, which isn't borne out by the biblical text. George Steiner's Introduction to the Everyman Library edition of *The Old Testament: King James Version* (Everyman, New York, 1996) at least asks more searching questions of the Creator's motives.

John Armstrong's *Conditions of Love: The Philosophy of Intimacy* (Penguin, London, 2002) addresses nearly two dozen of the fundamental themes involved in sexual and romantic love, including jealousy, in an apparently methodical fashion, but without the passion or the intensity that the subject seems to mandate.

14: I MAKE HIM JEALOUS

In *Shakespeare's Language* (Allen Lane, London, 2001), Frank Kermode offers a tantalisingly brief hint at the moral dubiety of Desdemona's character in relation to Othello, but the point is left unexplored, as though to do so would overemphasise it. As will be clear from my own argument, I find it very much worth exploring. Stanley Cavell, in *The Claim of Reason: Wittgenstein, Skepticism, Morality and Tragedy* (Oxford University Press, New York, 1979), shows no such scruple in recording his own notice of the infernal and demonic natures of the troubled couple that appear thinly concealed in their names. He states that he cannot be the first to have remarked the point, and I for one can assure him he wasn't. While studying the play at A-level in the north of England, three years before his book was published, one of my classmates made the same observation.

Robin Norwood's *Women Who Love Too Much* (Arrow, London, 1986) is the celebrated definitive text on jealous possessiveness and how to survive it, a work that almost seems to pull the rug from under its own feet with the morale-sapping subtitle *When You Keep Wishing and Hoping He'll Change.*

Ian McEwan's *Enduring Love* (Jonathan Cape, London, 1997) is a brilliantly realised excursion into much the same territory as *Fatal Attraction* had covered, but with the variation that the stalker is a gay male with whom his straight victim has not had any sexual encounter.

David Smail's corpus of anti-therapy writing, collected in *The Nature of Unhappiness* (Robinson, London, 2001), is highly provocative, and contains much valuable insight into the ways in which we unnecessarily pathologise emotion.

15: I AM JEALOUS

Goethe's novella, *The Sorrows of Young Werther*, trans. Michael Hulse, (Penguin, London, [1774] 1989) may seem overloaded with incontinent sentimentality to a present-day readership, and yet the antagonistic emotional triangle of its three principal characters is a theme that has served television soap opera very durably. The theory of sympathetic suicide is aired in David P Phillips, 'The Influence of Suggestion on Suicide: Substantive and Theoretical Implications of the Werther Effect', *American Sociological Review*, Vol. 39, (1974), pp. 340–54.

16: TO BE CONTEMPTUOUS

Richard Webster's point about world-weary contempt being sanctioned by Christian teaching is a suggestive one. In fact, his entire book, *Why Freud Was Wrong: Sin, Science and Psychoanalysis* (Fontana, London, revised edition, 1996), is an object-lesson in how lightly academic contempt can be worn. It is the best comprehensive deconstruction of Freud's theories available.

In *The Road to Wigan Pier* (Penguin, London, [1937] 1989), George Orwell's quest is to discover exactly what the contempt of privileged society towards those who lived on its margins actually felt like, but the picture is rapidly complicated by other manifestations of the same emotion.

It is hard to decide finally which of these is the greater – the author's contempt for the hapless Brooker family on whom he billets himself, or his contempt at himself for so despising them.

17: I HOLD YOU IN CONTEMPT

The dilatations on the shifts in social status cited in the text are from the following sources: Caroline Norton, in Henry E Carlisle, ed., *A Selection from the Correspondence of Abraham Hayward Q.C. from 1834 to 1884*, 2 Vols (London, 1886); Henry Addington, in Devon Record Office, Sidmouth MSS, 38/7; Francis Jeffrey, in *Edinburgh Review*, Vol. 37 (1822); Hester Lynch Piozzi, *Observations and Reflections made in the Course of a Journey through France, Italy and Germany*, 2 vols, (London, 1789). All are cited in a fine, comprehensively detailed study of British social manners by Paul Langford, *Englishness Identified: Manners and Character 1650–1850* (Oxford University Press, Oxford, 2000).

Jean-Paul Sartre's *Huis Clos*, in *Huis Clos and Other Plays*, trans. Stuart Gilbert (Penguin, London, 2000), is the dreariest of all classics of the twentieth-century theatre. I sense the tide of intellectual fashion similarly turning against Samuel Beckett's dramatic works, but *Endgame* (Faber and Faber, London, 1964) at least has better jokes.

Sartre's *Being and Nothingness: An Essay on Phenomenological Ontology*, trans. Hazel E Barnes (Routledge, London, [1943] 2000) is existentialism's finest hour, a monstrous, dense hulk of a work that seems to lead one precisely into – nothingness.

18: I AM TREATED WITH CONTEMPT

The standard edition of Aesop's *Fables* was for many years Volume 17 of the Harvard Classics series, trans. Joseph Jacobs (Harvard University Press, Cambridge, Mass., 1914).

Wittgenstein's attempt to put a stop to philosophy, the *Tractatus Logico-Philosophicus*, trans. D F Pears and B F McGuinness (Routledge, London, [1921] 2001), may be seen in itself as a statement of radical boredom with speculative pretension.

The nineteenth century is an almost inexhaustible source of literary and dramatic exempla of the anomie that dragged like a sinker on the lives of the sensitive of soul. Required reading would have to encompass: Gustave Flaubert's *Madame Bovary*, trans. Geoffrey Wall (Penguin, London, [1857] 2003); Leo Tolstoy's *Anna Karenina*, trans. Richard Pevear and Larissa Volokhonsky (Penguin, London, [1877] 2003); Henrik Ibsen's *A Doll's House*, in *A Doll's House and Other Plays*, trans. Peter Watts (Penguin, London, 1973); and, at the century's end, the plays of Anton Chekhov, collected in *Plays*, trans. Peter Carson (Penguin, London, 2002).

In the twentieth century, the baton is taken up by William Gerhardie in his profoundly Chekhovian debut novel, *Futility* (W W Norton, New York, [1922] 1991), and by George Bernard Shaw's best play, *Heartbreak House: A Fantasia in the Russian Manner on English Themes* (Penguin, London, [1919] 2000). Sartre's autobiography, *Words*, trans. Irène Cléphane (Penguin, London, [1964] 2000), tells of the catastrophic boredom that the writer feels has dogged large tracts of his life.

The characters of the aged Smallweeds in Charles Dickens's *Bleak House* (Penguin, London, [1853] 1996) have always seemed to me to anticipate Beckett's decrepits by a century. Eugène Ionesco's works represent the high-water mark of post-war absurdism. *The Bald Prima Donna*, trans. Donald Watson (Samuel French, London, [1950] 1958) was his opening gambit, a satire on English conformity inspired by a simple-minded language primer, while the more fully realised works are collected in *Rhinoceros, The Chairs, The Lesson*, trans. Derek Prouse and Donald Watson (Penguin, London, 2000).

Friedrich Nietzsche's by turns exhilarating and infuriating body of work ushers in the philosophising of the twentieth century in all its conceptual violence and disruptive force. I have cited *The Gay Science*, trans. Josefine Nauckhoff and Adrian del Caro (Cambridge University Press, Cambridge, [1882] 2001); *Twilight of the Idols and The Antichrist*, trans. R J Hollingdale (Penguin, London, [1895] 1990); and *The Will to Power*, trans. Walter Kaufmann (Random House, New York, [1888] 1968).

19: TO BE ASHAMED

In *Totem and Taboo*, collected in The Penguin Freud Library, Vol. 13, op. cit., pp. 49–224, Freud attempts nothing less than to link the origins of religious customs in ancient taboos with the development of everything from social mores to dysfunctional mental conditions.

The story of the Rothschild family's encounter with nude bathers in Scarborough is retailed in Lucy Cohen, *Lady de Rothschild and her Daughters, 1821–1931* (John Murray, London, 1935); cited in Peter Gay, *The Bourgeois Experience: Victoria to Freud* (W W Norton, New York, 1984), Vol. 1, *Education of the Senses*, pp. 338-9. Gay notes that Cohen fails to state which of the daughters, Constance or Annie, is being quoted.

Giorgio Vasari's *The Lives of the Artists*, trans. Julia Conway Bondanella and Peter Bondanella (Oxford World's Classics, Oxford, [1550] 1998) can only tantalise us, as can the many surviving copies, with a mere suggestion of how magnificent Michelangelo's work, executed in a room of the Dyers' Hospital in San Onofrio, must have looked.

F T Prince's 'Soldiers Bathing', one of the most anthologised poems of the Second World War, can be found in his *Collected Poems 1935–1992* (Carcanet, Manchester, 1993).

20: I SHAME YOU

The uses to which public humiliation was put in the seventeenth and eighteenth centuries were especially lurid in regard to sexual acts committed between men, as is revealed in Colin Spencer's wide-ranging *Homosexuality: A History* (Fourth Estate, London, 1995).

A minutely detailed psychological portrait of the mechanics of shaming is Nathaniel Hawthorne's *The Scarlet Letter* (Oxford World's Classics, Oxford, [1850] 1990), a novel of extraordinarily simple construction that remains resonant with relevance in our own era.

V A C Gatrell's *The Hanging Tree: Execution and the English People 1770–1868* (Oxford University Press, Oxford, 1994) is a superb piece of social documentation, full of surprises in its descriptions of how public executions were received by those who attended them.

21: I AM SHAMED

The sacred text of nineteenth-century masochism, *Venus in Furs* by Leopold von Sacher-Masoch, trans. H J Stenning (Luxor, Marietta, Georgia, [1870] 1997), is a very turgid read, scarcely containing anything likely to persuade the sceptic. Richard von Krafft-Ebing's *Psychopathia Sexualis*, trans. Jack Hunter (Creation Books, London, [1886] 1997) remains, despite the supercession of many of its theories, a remarkable achievement for its time. By contrast, Freud's efforts in this area – in the *Three Essays on the Theory of Sexuality*, The Penguin Freud Library, Vol. 7, op. cit., pp. 139–69, and 'The Economic Problem of Masochism', The Penguin Freud Library, Vol. 11, op. cit., pp. 413–26 – seem positively crude.

Walter Kaufmann's *Tragedy and Philosophy* (Princeton University Press, Princeton, NJ, [1968] 1992) squares up quite well to the question that troubles many writers on the tragic theatre – namely, why it should provide us with such emotional satisfaction.

As will be clear from my argument, I found my doubts about masochistic sexuality raised to an even greater pitch by the arguments in Anita Phillips's *A Defence of Masochism* (Faber and Faber, London, 1998). Some of them are put with greater persuasive force in Jonathan Dollimore's *Sexual Dissidence: Augustine to Wilde, Freud to Foucault* (Clarendon Press, Oxford, 1991).

22: TO BE EMBARRASSED

James Crichton Browne's observations on the inducement of facial flushing by administration of amyl nitrite, and its possible links with the causes of blushing, are contained in the *West Riding Lunatic Asylum Medical Report*, 1871. Wilhelm Filehne's related findings are noted in a paper published in *Pflüger's Archiv für die Gesammte Physiologie des Menschen und der Tiere*, Vol. 9, 1874, in which the writer suggests that 'It is perhaps not too rash to assume that the amyl-nitrite and the psychical cause [of facial flushing] attack the same point in the nervous system and produce the same effects.' Both references are given in *The Expression of the Emotions in Man and Animals*, third edition, op. cit.

23: I CAUSE YOU EMBARRASSMENT

Valerie Grosvenor Myer's *Harriette Wilson: Lady of Pleasure* (Fern House, Ely, 1999) and Frances Wilson's *The Courtesan's Revenge: The Life of Harriette Wilson, the Woman Who Blackmailed the King* (Faber and Faber, London, 2003) are alike riveting accounts of Harriette's promenade through the sexual morals of late Georgian society. A more general portrait of the period is furnished by Donald A Low, *The Regency Underworld* (Sutton, Stroud, 1999).

George Eells offers an entertaining oversight of the careers of the two greatest Hollywood scandal-mongers in *Hedda and Louella: Hedda Hopper and Louella Parsons* (W H Allen, New York, 1972). Kenneth Anger's series of *Hollywood Babylon* books explores the limits of the reader's prurience to the extent that much of the content does not concern the stars' private foibles, but simply such matters as their battles against spectacular weight gain (Elizabeth Taylor) or the sickening manner of their deaths (James Dean, Jayne Mansfield). The first volume (Doubleday, New York, [1958] 1983) is undoubtedly the best.

24: I AM EMBARRASSED

Margaret Visser's *The Rituals of Dinner: The Origins, Evolution, Eccentricities and Meaning of Table Manners* (Viking, London, 1991) contains much to fascinate, and throws a valuable perspective on what remains of our own sense of obligation in this area. Of consuming historical interest are Erasmus's *De Civilitate Morum Puerilium*, collected in Vol. 25 of the *Collected Works of Erasmus*, trans. B McGregor (University of Toronto Press, Toronto, 1985) and John Trusler's *The Honours of the Table* (Cork, 1804) and *A System of Etiquette* (Bath, 1804).

Anna Eliza Bray's *Letters written during a Tour through Normandy, Brittany, and Other Parts of France, in 1818* (London, 1820), Harriet Pigott's *Records of Real Life in the Palace and the Cottage*, 3 vols, (London, 1839) and the quotations from Joseph Blanco White given in Martin Murphy's *Blanco White: Self-Banished Spaniard* (Yale University

Press, New Haven, Conn., 1989) are all cited in Langford, *Englishness Identified*, op. cit.

The opening volume, *The Limits of the Possible*, of Fernand Braudel's masterwork, *The Structures of Everyday Life: Civilisation and Capitalism 15th–18th Century*, trans. Siân Reynolds (Phoenix Press, London, [1979] 2002) is an indispensable source on the minutiae of how early modern lives were lived, from diet to habitation, clothing to transport.

25: TO BE SURPRISED

The Lisle Letters: An Abridgement, Muriel St Clare Byrne and Bridget Boland, eds (University of Chicago Press, Chicago, 1983) offers a portrait of the precarious social life of the nobility amid the rapacities of Henry VIII's court, indicating that the era's extravagant gift-giving was no mere frivolity, but could often guarantee one's advancement.

The Christmas Books (Penguin, London, 1994) contains three of Charles Dickens's most celebrated seasonal stories. *The Chimes* and *The Cricket on the Hearth* join the imperishable favourite, *A Christmas Carol*.

Adorno's *Minima Moralia: Reflections from Damaged Life*, trans. E F N Jephcott (Verso, London, [1951] 1978) is one of his most singular works, a set of small aphoristic essays on various aspects of the modern life he encountered while in wartime exile in the United States. The essay on gifts is No. 21, 'Articles may not be exchanged', pp. 42–3.

The Complete Short Stories of Saki (Penguin, London, 2000) is a useful reminder of the vanished allure of this slight, but enormously entertaining writer.

26: I SHOCK YOU

Frank Wedekind's *Spring Awakening*, trans. Tom Osborn (Calder and Boyars, London, [1891] 1969) fully deserves the copious recent theatrical attention it has received. Far more than any of the naturalistic works with which it was contemporaneous, it is a courageous work of mordant social criticism.

Adorno's *Aesthetic Theory*, trans. Christian Lenhardt (Routledge,

London, [1970] 1984) is his strangely unsatisfying (and unfinished) final work, but one that contains much to ponder on the ways art achieves its effects. For the Freud of *Beyond the Pleasure Principle* (The Penguin Freud Library, Vol. 11. op. cit., pp 275–338), the idea that the state of shock should be deliberately induced in others, even through art, could only seem a gratuitous form of cruelty.

27: YOU SURPRISE ME

Aristotle's *Poetics*, trans. Malcolm Heath (Penguin, London, 1996) remains the foundation work on the theory of tragedy, on which all succeeding eras have erected their own constructions. Its discussion of the question of recognition applies equally fittingly to the comic theatre. In Ben Jonson's sublime, and defiantly dark, comedy *Epicoene, or The Silent Woman* (A & C Black, London, [1609] 2002), the mechanisms of surprise and recognition are put to work with lethal moral force.

28: TO BE HAPPY

Ernst Bloch's *The Principle of Hope*, trans. Neville Plaice, Stephen Plaice and Paul Knight, 3 vols (MIT Press, Cambridge, Mass., [1959] 1995) is one of the enduring works of the Frankfurt School. Its idiosyncrasies are legion, but from within its complex reticulations emerge some of the most strikingly beautiful philosophising of the twentieth century.

The brothers Eugene Field and Roswell Martin Field brought a Victorian sententiousness to their translations from Horace, *Echoes from the Sabine Farm* (New York, 1892), which, to my mind, suits the blandly pastoral mood of the poetry perfectly.

Saul Bellow's *The Adventures of Augie March* (Penguin, London, [1953] 1984) is the great American post-war novel, a vibrantly coloured snapshot of a particular moment in American letters when the dour, neo-European tone of its 1930s predecessor had been joyously thrown off. Its sheer exhilaration in both language and narrative command enraptured attention. John Ashbery has achieved much the same effect throughout a prodigious career in poetry. His long, philosophical works are his most satisfying, among which I count the title poem of *A Wave* (Carcanet, Manchester, 1984) a major accomplishment.

29: I CAN MAKE YOU HAPPY

Herman Pleij's *Dreaming of Cockaigne: Medieval Fantasies of the Perfect Life*, trans. Diane Webb (Columbia University Press, New York, [1997] 2001) is a highly readable summary of what utopia was comprised of for the late medieval imagination.

Utopian visions that have inspired, or conversely, haunted western sensibility since Plato include St Augustine's *City of God*, trans. Henry Bettenson (Penguin, London, 2003), Thomas More's *Utopia*, trans. Paul Turner (Penguin, London, [1516] 2003) and Nathaniel Hawthorne's proto-syndicalist vision in *The Blithedale Romance* (Oxford World's Classics, Oxford, [1852] 1998).

30: I AM LEFT HAPPY

The absorbing stories of Wilhelm and Jacob Grimm, collected in *The Complete Fairy Tales of the Brothers Grimm*, trans. Jack Zipes (Doubleday, New York, 1992), repeatedly demonstrate that a happy ending requires a judicious apportionment to those twin sisters, felicity and calamity. L Frank Baum's *The Wonderful Wizard of Oz* (Penguin, London, [1900] 1995) is interesting for its revelation that the goal of its heroine's efforts turns out to be delusive. There is no Wizard, only a charlatan with a neat line in pyrotechnics, and her restitution, the return to Kansas, can only be effected from within.

F Scott Fitzgerald's small corpus of novels is the defining portrait, for me, of the hopes and disappointments of the American 1920s. *The Beautiful and Damned* (Penguin, London, [1922] 2001) stands out, but each has its particular appeal.

Kierkegaard's *Fear and Trembling*, trans. Alastair Hannay (Penguin, London, [1843] 1985) attempts to reassure us that the Almighty hasn't, despite appearances, forgotten us, and that the happiest ending of all will lie in his eventual rescue of suffering humanity.

INDEX

Cromwell, Oliver 24, 25
Crowe, Russell 111
Crucifixion 252–3
Cruise, Tom xvii
crystals 15
cubism 100
Cummings, Alexander 92
cutting, the art of 217–18
Cynicism 130

Dada 60, 63–5, 67–72, 331
Daily Telegraph 329
Dakota tribe 208
Dali, Salvador
  Autumn Cannibalism 69
  The Great Masturbator 68
  The Lugubrious Game 68
  Soft Construction with Boiled Beans 61,
    68
Damasio, Antonio xviii
Darwin, Charles 158, 247
  and contempt 220, 221
  discovery that all have the same registers
    of emotional awareness xxii
  discovery that all share one common
    humanity xxii
  disgust and the sense of taste 87–8
  and embarrassment 283–6, 288–90
  and happiness 348, 355, 356
  and jealousy 171, 172, 173
  list of basic emotions xiv
  and music 155–6
  physical indicators of anger 43
  physical indicators of contempt 205, 207,
    208
  physical indicators of disgust 85, 125
  physical indicators of embarrassment
    279
  physical indicators of fear 1
  physical indicators of happiness 345
  physical indicators of sadness 129
  physical indicators of shame 241
  physical indicators of surprise 315
  and surprise 317, 336, 337
  three principles about the way emotional
    expression works xviii
  *The Expression of the Emotions in Man
    and Animals* xii–xvi, xxi, 283
  The Origin of Species 9
Darwin, Erasmus 105
Darwinism xvii
Davies, Marion 299

Day, Doris 158
de Clérambault's syndrome 195, 196
de la Salle, Jean-Baptiste: *Les Règles de la
    Bienséance et de la Civilité Chrétienne*
  307
de Quincey, Thomas 220
death
  fear of 7, 9
  inevitability 8
death instinct 271
Death in Venice (film) 157, 370
Defoe, Daniel: *The Shortest Way with the
  Dissenters* 258
Degenerate Art exhiition 100
democracy 22, 23
Descartes, René 224
despair 137
Devoto, Howard 46
Dickens, Charles 56, 273, 295
  Bleak House 234
  A Christmas Carol 321–2
  David Copperfield 219
  Great Expectations 219
dictatorship 22
Diderot, Denis xi
Dillon, Patrick 122
Dionysian tradition 10
Dionysius 212
disgust
  Darwin's physical indicators 85
  defined 85
  I am disgusted 116–25
  I disgust 103–115
  one of Darwin's basic emotions xvi
  and the sense of taste 87–8
  to disgust 87–102
Disney xxi
Disraeli, Benjamin 305
dissection 103–8
Dollimore, Jonathan 276
Don't Look Back (film) 331
dos Passos, John 235
Dostoevsky, Fyodor 273
Douglas, Michael 81, 178, 193, 203
Dryden, John 345
Duchamp, Marcel 64
  'L.H.O.O.Q.' 64–5
Dufour, Judith 116–17, 119, 125
Dunaway, Faye 79
Dürer, Albrecht 167
  Melencolia I 165
Dworkin, Andrea 52

Fukuyama, Francis 140, 277
Futurism 68

music 142–3, 152–9
Muslims 246
Myer, Valerie Grosvenor 296

nakedness 243–7, 249–54
Napoleon Bonaparte 202
National Guard (US) 58
National Theatre, London 329
nationalism 35
Nazis, Nazism 28, 100, 101, 214, 222, 276, 350
Neolithic peoples 359
Network (film) 79–80, 81, 84
neurosis 248, 272
New Age
  beliefs 15
  complementary therapies 130
  cosmologies 130
  occultism 4
New Statesman 331
New Year's Eve 320
New York 69
New York Globe 113
Newgate prison 258
Newton, Sir Isaac 14
Nico 159
Nietzsche, Friedrich 226, 235–7, 350–51, 352
  The Antichrist 236
  The Gay Science 235–6
  The Birth of Tragedy 143, 150
Nitsch, Hermann 62
Noah 246–7
Northern Ireland: Protestants and Catholics 77
Norton, Caroline 215–16, 219
Norwood, Robin 193
nuclear arms race 60
NWA (Niggas With Attitude) 71

Octavian 351
Odd Couple, The (film) 281–2
Olivier, Laurence, Lord 329
Ono, Yoko 373
opium 122
Orbach, Jerry 341
Orco, Remirro de 20
Orgy Mystery Theatre performances 62
Orphic tradition 9–10
Orwell, George 28, 213–14
  Nineteen Eighty-four 27
  The Road to Wigan Pier 214

Osborne, John: *Look Back In Anger* 331
Ovid 47–8
  Metamorphoses 162, 348
Oxford English Dictionary (OED) 3, 90, 173, 312
Oxford University 304, 308

pain 136, 138, 267, 274
Palace of Knossos, Crete 95
Palestinians 77, 373
Paley, William 14
  Natural Theology 12
Papua New Guinea 88
Paradise 246, 253
Paris 64, 66, 67, 68, 204, 222
  liberal revolution (1848) 367
Paris Commune 366–8
Parker, Dorothy 68
Parsons, Louella 299, 300
Parton, Dolly 77
Pascal, Blaise 13
Paul, St 176
  epistle to the Hebrews 174
Peninsular War 61
Pennebaker, D A 331
People's Courts (Soviet Union) 26
Père Lachaise cemetery, Paris 367
Peter and Paul Fortress, St Petersburg 26
Peter, St 267
Phaedrus 231
Philip the Handsome 192–3
Phillips, Anita: *A Defence of Masochism* 274–8
Phillips, David P 204
Philocles 143
phobias 36–40
Picabia, Francis 67–8, 70, 71
Pigott, Harriet 310–311
pillory 256, 257–9
Pink Floyd 71–2
Pinochet, General Augusto 24
Piozzi, Hester Lynch 218
pity 273
Pius XI, Pope 365
Plastic Ono Band 373
Plato 46–7, 99, 100, 145–6, 159, 236, 377
  The Republic 47, 145, 146, 360–62, 363
  Timaeus 47
Plautus 211
Poliziano, Angelo 231
polytheism 6
Ponsonby, Lord John 295

Shakespeare, William 21, 135
   Hamlet 148, 201
   Henry V 340
   Henry VI, Part II 172
   Julius Caesar 172
   King Lear 61, 134, 209, 252, 274, 339
   Othello xxi, 172, 183–96, 209
   Romeo and Juliet 208, 288–9
   Timon of Athens 209, 340
   Titus Andronicus 189, 190, 209
shame
   added to Darwin's list of basic emotions
     xiv
   Darwin's physical indicators 241
   defined 241
   I am shamed 266–78
   I shame you 255–65
   to be ashamed 243–54
Shangqiu county, Henan province, China 95
Shaw, George Bernard: *Heartbreak House*
   234
shell-shock 334
Shem 246
Shikibu, Murasaki: *The Tale of Genji* 54
shocking artworks 327–44
Shorter Oxford Dictionary, The 282, 283
Silence of the Lambs, The (film) 371
Sim, Alastair 322
Simpsons, The (TV animation series) 74, 75
Sinatra, Frank 158
singers 158–9
singing duels 53
Smail, David 195–6
Smith, Patti 91
Smith family suicide ix–xii
Smollett, Tobias: *History of England* ix–xi
snobbery 219–20
socialism 178
Socrates 161, 239, 240
Soderini, Piero 19
Solomon, Andrew 132, 137
Sophia Dorothea, Queen of Prussia 31–4
Sophocles 139, 143, 145, 148
   Oedipus Tyrannos 143, 151, 339
Sorrows of Young Werther, The (Goethe)
   xix
South Fore tribes people, Papua New
   Guinea 88
Soviet Union 24, 26
Spalding, Methuselah 264
Spanish Civil War 61
Speer, Albert 101

Speucippus 47
spirits 14, 15, 16
spiritualism 14
Sri Lanka 355
stalking 195
Star Trek TV series xvi
Steiner, George 150, 177
   The Death of Tragedy 143–4
Stephen, St 267
Stewart, James 332
Stockdale, Joseph 293, 296
stocks 256–7
Stoddard, Elizabeth 166–7
   '"Me and My Son"' 166
   'Waiting at the Station' 166
Stoicism 130
Stone, Oliver 178
storms 5, 6
Streete, Horton 300–301
Strindberg, August 330
Sturm und Drang 201
Styne, Jule 158
Styrene, Poly 278
suffering 131, 138, 139–40, 266
suffragette movement 51
suicide, Smith family ix–xii
suicide bombers 28
Summer of Hate (1977) 69
Summer of Love 59
Sunday Theatre Club, London 329
superego 271
surgery 108–110
surprise
   Darwin's physical indicators 315
   defined 315
   I shock you 327–35
   one of Darwin's basic emotions xvi
   you surprise me 336–44
surrealism 68, 69
Susanna and the Elders 250–51
Swaggart, Jimmy 263
Swift, Jonathan 90

table manners 303–314
taboos 247, 248–9
tactilism 68
talking 348–9
tantric sex rituals 15
Tate, Nahum 334
Tavris, Carol 46, 74–5, 82
terror 273
Tertullian: *Ad Martyres* 267